Equal Democracies?
Gender and Politics in the Nordic Countries

Equal Democracies?
Gender and Politics in the
Nordic Countries

Editorial board:

> **Christina Bergqvist (Editor in Chief)**
> **Anette Borchorst**
> **Ann-Dorte Christensen**
> **Viveca Ramstedt-Silén**
> **Nina C. Raaum**
> **Auður Styrkársdóttir**

Scandinavian University Press

Oslo

Published by
Scandinavian University Press (Universitetsforlaget AS)
P.O.Box 2959 Tøyen
N-0608 Oslo, Norway
www.scup.no

Chapters 1, 2, 3, 4, 5, 9, 10, 11, Appendices, parts of Chapter 12, and parts of Conclusion translated by Chris Saunders.
Introduction, chapters 6, 7, 8, 13, 14, and parts of Chapter 12 translated by Mike McDaid.
Parts of Conclusion translated by Chris Mathieu.

Cover Design: Valiant, Stavanger, Norway
Cover Photo: MPS/Gary Buss
Typeset: BokVerket, Sande i Vestfold/Jan Olav Hauge
Printed in Norway by PowerPrint AS, Steinkjer

Published in co-operation with the Nordic Council of Ministers.

The Nordic Council of Ministers was established in 1971. It submits proposals on co-operation between the governments of the five Nordic countries to the Nordic Council, implements the Council's recommendations and reports on results, while directing the work carried out in the targeted areas. The Prime Ministers of the five Nordic countries assume overall responsibility for the co-operation measures, which are co-ordinated by the ministers for co-operation and the Nordic Co-operation committee. The composition of the Council of Ministers varies, depending on the nature of the issue to be treated.

Nordic Council of Ministers
Store Strandstræde 18
DK- 1255 Copenhagen K
www.norden.org

Acknowledgements

Equal democracies? Gender and politics in the Nordic countries is the result of a joint effort between several Nordic scholars specialising in the study of gender and politics. We greatly appreciate the generous financial support granted by the Nordic Council of Ministers without which the project would never have materialised. We would especially like to thank Marianne Laxén at the Council for ensuring that our collaboration with the Council proceeded as smoothly and pleasantly as it did.

Under the general leadership of Viveca Ramstedt-Silén the co-ordination and administration of the project has been carried out at the Swedish School of Social Science, University of Helsinki. Christina Bergqvist has been in charge of the editorial work together with Anette Borchorst, Ann-Dorte Christensen, Nina Raaum, Viveca Ramstedt-Silén and Auður Styrkársdóttir. The book is thus the outcome of a relatively intense teamwork between the members of the editorial board and the remaining authors. But others have also assisted in the creation of the book in various roles. Susanne Jungersam-Mulders has been with us from the start. We warmly thank her for being such an able research assistant and project secretary. We would also like to thank Tina Andtbacka of the Swedish School of Social Science and Patrik Olofsson of the Department of Government at Uppsala University for their assistance in editing the book. Last, but not least, Viveca Ramstedt-Silén, together with Susanne-Jungerstam Mulders and Aard Mulders at Swedish School of Social Science, has prepared the statistical appendix.

The Scandinavian edition of this book was originally written and published in three of the Nordic languages, Danish, Norwegian, and Swedish. It has therefore been a comparatively exacting task translating the various texts into English. We would like to express our sincere gratitude to Mike McDaid and Chris Saunders who went about the job with such application and patience.

Uppsala, Aarhus, Aalborg, Helsinki, Bergen, and Reykjavik, November 1999

Christina Bergqvist   Viveca Ramstedt-Silén
Anette Borchorst   Nina C. Raaum
Ann-Dorte Christensen   Auður Styrkársdóttir

TABLE OF CONTENTS

PART III

Institutionalised gender equality

Theme editor: Anette Borchorst

Conclusions

Appendices

Appendix II
Overview of the political parties in the Nordic countries

Appendix III
Gender equality, bodies and legislation

TABLES AND FIGURES

Tables

Figures

Contributors

Solveig Bergman, Researcher and Lecturer, Department of Sociology, Åbo Akademi University, Finland.

Christina Bergqvist, Ph. D., Researcher at National Institute for Working Life, Stockholm, and Lecturer at Department of Government, Uppsala University, Sweden.

Anette Borchorst, Ph. D., Researcher at Department of Political Science, University of Aarhus, Denmark.

Ann-Dorte Christensen, Ph. D., Researcher at Department of Development and Planning, Aalborg University, Denmark.

Anne Maria Holli, Researcher at Department of Political Science, University of Helsinki, Finland.

Susanne Jungerstam-Mulders, Doctoral Student at Swedish School of Social Science, University of Helsinki, Finland.

Jaana Kuusipalo, Senior Researcher at Department of Political Science and International Relations, University of Tampere, Finland.

Ingrid Pincus, Doctoral Student at Department of Political Science, University of Göteborg and Center for Women's Studies, University of Örebro, Sweden.

Nina C. Raaum, Ph. D., Researcher at Department of Comparative Politics, University of Bergen, Norway.

Viveca Ramstedt-Silén, Lecturer and Researcher in Political Science at Swedish School of Social Science, University of Helsinki, Finland.

Janneke van der Ros, Senior Lecturer and Programme Director of the Gender and Politics Programme, Lillehammer College, Norway.

Auður Styrkársdóttir, Ph. D., Project manager and Research Director at Step by Step Consulting and Research Company, Reykjavik, Iceland.

Stefania Traustadóttir, Senior Adviser, Office for Gender Equality, Reykjavik, Iceland.

Introduction

The Nordic Countries – One Model or Several?

Christina Bergqvist

This book sets out to analyse aspects of the relations between gender, politics and democracy in the Nordic countries.[1] A unitary Nordic area, inhabited by politically successful women who work for peace, welfare and gender equality is both a well known and a common image in international discussions. A large proportion of women in politics, a high rate of labour market participation and a well-developed public welfare sector, especially in respect of caring and service provision, are also part of this image. Many examples exist to show that the presence of women in the most senior political posts is no longer exceptional. Two famous examples are Gro Harlem Brundtland, who was Prime Minister of Norway for many years, and Vigdis Finnbogadóttir, who held the office of President of Iceland for sixteen years. From a European and an international perspective, Nordic women have an unusually prominent place amongst cabinet ministers, party leaders and elected representatives at all levels. One of the ambitions of this book is to offer a better understanding of this image and explore its many nuances.

In comparative studies of the Nordic countries, emphasis has often been laid on homogeneity. This is hardly surprising since, from the outside, the Nordic countries appear as a unified region, not only geographically, but also politically, socially and culturally. In terms of their populations, the Nordic countries are small, relatively homogenous and, as a consequence, they exhibit a limited number of politically relevant lines of cleavage. Studies that try to explain the uniqueness of the Nordic area often emphasise the central value attached to equal-

---

1. The five Nordic countries are Denmark (including the Faeroe Islands and Greenland), Finland (including Åland), Iceland, Norway and Sweden. Sometimes the term Scandinavia is, somewhat inaccurately, used as a synonym for the Nordic countries. According to the Swedish National Encyclopaedia, Scandinavia is partly a name for the Scandinavian peninsula and partly a collective noun for Denmark, Norway and Sweden, and sometimes Finland as well. In this book "the Nordic countries" will be used for all five countries and "Scandinavia" for Denmark, Norway and Sweden.

ity in the region. "The Nordic states, in one way or other, demonstrating a high regard for efficiency and equality, perhaps also in Tocqueville's words, showing a 'true passion for equality', have managed to institutionalize state procedures that guarantee the basic physical needs of their citizens, young and old" (Graubard 1986:8). The idea of a unified Nordic region is both appealing and commonly expressed. The *Nordic* or *Scandinavian model* has become a familiar concept in international research. What is put into this concept and what is emphasised can vary depending on whether the focus of attention is the welfare state, economic policies or the democratic system.

The Nordic welfare policy model is characterised by an extensive social policy directed more or less to all sections of the population. Citizens and people who are legally residents in a Nordic country have basic rights of access to a broad range of services and entitlements, and social legislation is founded on principles of solidarity and universality. According to Esping-Andersen, the Scandinavian countries form a type of welfare regime, the *social democratic regime*, that differs from the *liberal regime* found, for example, in the USA, Canada and Australia and the *conservative* or *corporatist regime* found, for example, in Austria and Germany (Esping-Andersen 1990; see also Kuhnle 1994).[2]

The Nordic democratic model is usually described by words such as openness, spirit of consensus and pragmatism. The ideal of equality has been borne by strong social democratic parties, which have played a central political role throughout the past century and which have characterised the development of the Nordic welfare states (Karvonen and Sundberg, eds. 1991). This picture of the Nordic Model requires modification to take account of circumstances in individual Nordic countries. It squares best with Norway and Sweden, somewhat worse with Denmark, and worst with Finland and Iceland. Many similarities also exist in respect of the political institutions in the Nordic area. Amongst other things, all countries are multiparty democracies in which elections are conducted on the basis of proportional representation.[3] An integral part of this picture of the Nordic Model concerns the potential that large interest organisations, especially on the labour market, have to influence the policy-making process. The interaction between the state and these organisations, corporatism, has been most prominent in Norway and Sweden.

The Nordic countries have also appeared as special cases in matters of gender equality, both with regard to their women-friendly welfare policies and women's participation and integration in politics and the public sphere. For example, as feminist welfare research indicates, good opportunities for combining parent-

---

2. The liberal regime is characterised by means-tested benefits, few universal transfers and few forms of social insurance. The conservative regime is characterised by social stratification: entitlement to social insurance transfers is related to labour market contributions, and the church and the family play a major role in the generation of welfare on a "voluntary basis".

3. As several comparative studies have shown, there is a positive connection between elections based upon proportional representation and women's share of popularly elected assemblies (see, e.g. Lovenduski and Norris 1993).

hood with paid employment exist through the provision of an extensive system of public daycare. This situation has contributed to the weakening or abandoning of the male breadwinner-model. Individual and universal entitlements have included women and men in the welfare state on a more equal basis than has been the case in many other societies. The view of the state is in general positive. This has resulted in the idea of the women-friendly state and some kind of partnership or alliance between women and the welfare state (Hernes 1987; Siim 1988). Furthermore, there has been an institutionalisation of the equality principle through legislation on gender equality, the setting up of public boards and councils, the establishment of ombudsmen for gender equality etc. The importance of changed gender relations for the Nordic model is nowadays also reflected within so-called mainstream research.

Without doubt, the last twenty-five to thirty years have seen major changes in Nordic women's *social* and *political citizenship*. There has been a marked equalisation of the gender composition of political posts within the democratic institutions. The inclusion of women within the political processes of decision making has been especially clear in the parliamentary field. In 1995, four out of the five Nordic parliaments were among the five national parliaments in the world where women constituted more than 30 per cent of elected representatives.[4] The average figure for all parliaments across the world was 11 per cent, while the figure for European parliaments was 13 per cent. Thus, social and gender equality has developed in parallel with the increasing proportion of women in politics. One of the aims of this book is to throw light on the connection between participation in, and the contents of, politics. In order to do this, we first need to question the image of the Nordic countries as a unity. Specifically, the generally positive picture of women's successes in this area masks large variations both within and between the Nordic countries. In those fields that are studied in this book such variations relate, for example, to the differences in the design of public childcare and gender equality policies. In the political arena there are also major variations that place a question mark over the image of the Nordic countries as an oasis of equality. Even in such a narrow area as the composition of parliamentary assemblies, the percentage of seats held by women in Nordic countries has varied a lot. In 1998, women held more than 40 per cent of the parliamentary seats in Sweden, while the corresponding figure was only 25 per cent in Iceland. In Denmark, Finland and Norway, women made up around 35 per cent of parliamentary representatives. The differences between Nordic countries were even bigger in respect of the gender composition of their governments, ranging from only 10 per cent of government posts being held by women in Iceland to around half of government posts going to women in Sweden (Appendix 1, Tables 3 and 4).[5]

---

4. The fifth country was the Netherlands.

5. In the parliamentary elections held in Iceland in the spring of 1999, women's share of the seats rose from 25 per cent to 35 per cent. In the present Icelandic government, 25 per cent of the posts are held by women.

It is important to emphasise that this book analyses some of the fields where women have been unusually successful. In other fields, which fall outside the focus of the book, the differences between the countries and the sexes are greater. For example, on the labour market and in the home relatively strong traditional gender patterns prevail, where women have the main responsibility for both unpaid and paid reproductive work. Moreover, there are relatively few women in top positions within the trade union organisations, even though a large proportion of their members are women. Men overwhelmingly predominate when it comes to the highest positions of power within business life. This naturally implies that the influence and the degree of equality, which is possible within the democratically governed sphere, is restricted by the prevailing male dominance within the very influential market-oriented sphere (Tema Nord 1996:586).

Gender and Democracy

Today, increasing attention is paid to the connection between a developed and well-functioning democracy and the provision of equal opportunities to enable all groups of citizens to participate in the political process of decision making. Interest has been growing, in both feminist inspired research and more traditional scholarship within the political sciences, in the failure of democratic institutions with respect to the integration of groups that earlier were excluded for reasons of gender, class, ethnicity etc. Because one of the major characteristics of the political process has been the marginalisation and exclusion of women from the institutions of liberal democracy, feminist research has long been very critical of the possibilities available under democracy for women to participate in, and influence this process. Anne Phillips has commented on this problem in the following way:

> In more academic circles the literature on "women in politics" (more accurately women not in politics) operated perilously close to the threshold of boredom. For those who knew that women were oppressed, the dreary statistics lacked the element of surprise. The common sense explanations for women's low profile held little appeal for minds still buzzing with the latest theoretical fashions (1991:61 f.).

One result of this lack of interest is that both the theoretical and the empirical literature on gender, democracy and politics are relatively limited.

Many feminist researchers have argued in favour of an extended notion of democracy. In doing so, their gaze has been directed to political arenas beyond that of the political establishment. The women's movement of the 1960s and 1970s has inspired much research in this area. Activists within the movement were often wary of working within the traditional political institutions. Instead, they favoured more direct forms of democracy and activity-based participation. It is interesting to note that in *Engendering Democracy* Anne Phillips says that the experience of the Nordic countries has been one factor encouraging her belief in the possibility of increased political equality within political institutions (1991:83).

Nordic Women's Studies – Explanatory Models

During the 1970s and the 1980s, the marginalisation and lack of influence of women within politics have also provided the starting point for most theories and explanatory models used in women's studies within the Nordic countries. In part, this may be seen as a consequence of the conditions prevailing at the time and how women experienced them, but it may also be seen as a consequence of the then predominant developments within feminist research. The first comparative study on gender and politics in the Nordic countries, *Unfinished Democracy: Women in Nordic Politics*, is a valuable empirical compilation of women's political mobilisation and their position in the corporatist organisations and elected assemblies. The book emphasises that Nordic women have increasingly become active and are holding representative positions within the political system. Nevertheless, its main conclusion is that "politics is still a man's world" and that "the higher up one moves in the power hierarchy, the fewer women there are to be found" (Dahlerup and Haavio-Mannila 1985:160, 164).

Another picture of the Nordic countries has begun to emerge more than a decade after the publication of *Unfinished Democracy*. Lise Togeby concludes her studies on women's political mobilisation with the words: "During the 1970s and the 1980s women in the Nordic countries began to be integrated into political life as self-evident and self-conscious participants in the struggle for power and influence" (1994a:57). Moreover, in the most recent Nordic comparative study, *Women in Nordic Politics: Closing the Gap,* the main conclusions are that the increased integration of women is extremely important, and that this has produced big changes in the political culture of the Nordic countries (Karvonen and Selle 1995). The spread of this more optimistic view can be understood partly as a new interpretation of the importance of gender in political history, and partly as an expression of the real changes that have taken place.

During the 1980s, both international and Nordic women's studies grew in scope and this led to an enriching of theoretical perspectives. As indicated above, two main streams can be said to characterise the way in which changes in women's relationship to the state and to politics have been understood by feminist thinkers. To simplify matters somewhat, these approaches may be referred to as the pessimistic and optimistic perspectives. The theoretical emphasis in the pessimistic perspective, which was also the first approach to be developed, was on structural explanations of the continuous predominance of male power and of women's marginalisation within society. The notion of a decline in the power and significance of political institutions was used to explain the increase in the proportion of women within these bodies. This thesis, which was originally formulated and long promoted by Harriet Holter (1981, 1996), achieved widespread acceptance in a number of societal fields. According to this theoretical approach, power shifts take place between various institutions in ways that disadvantage women. Yvonne Hirdman also expresses similar ideas in her theory of the "gender system" set out in the main report of the Power and Democracy Investigation in Sweden. These theories operate on an overarching macro level and may, for example, be difficult to employ in analyses of political institutions and political actors. Hirdman does, however, attempt such an analysis in her writing on women's marginalisation within different institutions. According to Hirdman, the importance of the increased proportion of women in politics has been limited because women have entered low status fields:"Women are more and more located within the so-called "reproductive" or "soft" fields of politics: social welfare, education etc." This is said to lead to an internal segregation that limits women's chances to act under the same conditions as men (SOU 1990: 44:113).

Helga Hernes has presented an alternative understanding of the development of the Nordic countries, in which the welfare states in this area are seen as "*women-friendly*". Instead of viewing the above changes as an expression of a transition from one kind of subordination to another, Hernes stressed the significance of change in terms of new opportunities for women to take part in the formation of a women-friendly welfare state. She argued that new welfare policy developments could be seen as the outcome of a positive interaction between women's organising and mobilising from below and women-friendly politicians and policies from above (Hernes 1987). Furthermore, several researchers have directly criticised the theses of the decline of the importance of institutions and of women's marginalisation in politics. Amongst other things, they claim that an excessive emphasis on the conditions structuring power relations tends to devalue the role of the actors involved. Power structures in the Nordic countries differ. Thus it is also important to analyse how women's participation and representation are both limited and enabled by different institutional arrangements. Many people have also strongly questioned the idea of the social sector as "soft" and having a low status, given the huge investments made by the Nordic welfare state in the public sector, social policy and social services (Skjeie 1992; Bergqvist 1994; Raaum 1995a, b; Wängnerud 1998).

The starting point for the optimistic line is that politics and political institutions have a certain degree of autonomy, which has made positive changes in the power relations between the sexes possible. The question here is one of analyses within a certain historical and institutional context. The proponents of this line of argument do not seek to encapsulate the whole social system (nor the gender system) within their theoretical framework. Ann-Dorte Christensen (1997) describes the changes in thinking about gender and politics within women's studies as follows: "The first analyses of developments were basically pessimistic. Thereafter there was a period where the pessimistic and the optimistic views were in open competition. Today the optimistic way of looking at the situation is predominant." However, the differences and conflicts between the two perspectives should not be exaggerated. Both perspectives share the view that the unequal power relation between the sexes must be taken seriously and should form the starting point for analysis. Certain differences between the perspectives are evident, of course. A stronger emphasis on structures is evident in the pessimistic perspective, whereas the optimistic perspective places greater emphasis on actors. However, it would be simplistic to claim that this is the basic difference, since both perspectives contain analyses of both structures and actors.

Following the tendency within international feminist research, many feminist scholars in the Nordic countries turned their attention to studies of non-traditional forms of politics. The split between a private and a public sphere was seen as an important factor explaining gender differences in relationship to political power. By giving support to a more extensive notion of politics it became possible to include more forms for political participation and provide a broader and more accurate picture of women's engagement as citizens (Halsaa Albrektsen 1977). Thereby, this research has helped illuminate many important issues regarding women's participation in non-traditional political activities.

At the ideological level, as well as in practical politics, there is a certain degree of conflict between those feminists who argue that the best way for women to look after their interests is to organise separately in independent women's groups and organisations, and those who argue that women ought to strive for integration in order to change the presently male-dominated organisations and institutions. This division can also be traced within the research literature. The starting point for the authors of a recent Swedish book on democracy is that women's demands and interests cannot be integrated into the present male-dominated political institutions without being distorted and changed. The book, *Towards a new Democratic Order?* (Gustafsson, Eduards and Rönnblom 1997), claims that "women-specific demands, or disputes about gender and power, cannot be integrated into existing governmental institutions and parties. In order to develop a form of politics which serves women's interests, women must therefore find new ways of organizing". Furthermore, they argue that "the political order in Sweden is an expression of a comprehensive gendered power order, or more precisely a male or patriarchal order" (Eduards 1997:21). The authors do, however, accept that there is a connection between women's political mobilisation and political representation, but they are critical of research that emphasises women's integration into the formal political system.

The starting point for this book is that it is not fruitful to counterpose women's mobilisation and participation, alongside men, within established politics to women's organising within independent women's organisations, networks, groups etc. From a research-centred perspective, the importance of studying all the different forms of political participation and ways of organising politically is self-evident, and nowadays most political scientists agree that politics is not only that which takes place within government and parliamentary circles. The expansion of the notion of politics and the growth of interest in studying political participation from a broad perspective is partially the result of women's studies, but this need not mean that research on gender within the established political institutions has declined in importance.

The Rich Diversity of the Nordic Countries

An emphasis on common Nordic features has been a striking aspect of research in the Nordic countries. Often, generalised conclusions have been drawn from single country studies. Lise Togeby refers to this phenomenon as "the longing for the general". She claims: "It seems to be a widespread phenomenon that social scientists seek to interpret circumstances in their own countries within the more general context of tendencies described in the international literature. As a result, the countries in question appear more homogenous than they are in reality" (Togeby 1989:164). Even if many features are common to the Nordic countries, such as cultural homogeneity, egalitarian social structures, a parallel development of economic and welfare policy, and these features play an important role in explaining the shared sense of "the Nordic", a risk remains that these similarities may be exaggerated. When it comes to analysing the differences between the countries, historical and structural explanations are often too deterministic and "tend to do away with concrete *actors*, their aspirations and strategies" (Karvonen and Sundberg 1991:2 f.).

This book seeks to shift the focus from a view of the Nordic countries as essentially homogenous towards a view of these countries as being rich in diversity. A fundamental question here is whether differences between the Nordic countries are so great as to invalidate all talk of a Nordic gender policy model. As outlined in more detail below, this book consists of four parts. Part I analyses the historical lines of development of women's integration within public politics and women's political mobilisation and citizenship in today's Nordic countries. Thus, the first part deals with the *participatory side of politics*. Parts II and III deal with different aspects relating to the *content of politics*. The analysis here begins with childcare policy, which has been one of the classic women's issues ever since the early days of industrialisation, when women started to work outside the home to a greater degree than before. In Part III, gender equality policies in the Nordic countries are compared with respect to the content of these policies, the actors involved and the extent of institutionalisation. Finally, in Part IV, the gaze turns to a lesser known part of the Nordic area, namely the autonomous territories of the Faeroe Islands, Greenland and Åland.

The above-mentioned fields have been chosen partly in order to follow up on some of the results published in *Unfinished Democracy*, and partly because of the lack of systematic comparisons of developments between the Nordic countries. The last fifteen to twenty years of dramatic development of women's political participation and representation and the relatively radical nature of gender equality policies in the Nordic area has aroused much interest beyond Nordic borders. By contrast, a relative lack of research-based comparative analyses of these changes is evident. As far as possible, it has been our ambition to include all the Nordic countries in this study. Due to gaps in earlier research and deficiencies in comparative data it has not always been possible to achieve this aim. The starting point for our analyses has been primarily one of building upon and synthesising research from the different countries. But, in practice, the lack of relevant research has meant that we have had to gather quite a lot of new material, the findings of which are presented here for the first time. The analyses in this book lay much stress upon the role of the political actors as well as on the various strategies and political solutions that have been adopted in different country contexts. These comparative analyses seek to contribute to our understanding of the similarities and differences both between women and men and between the Nordic countries themselves.

On the one hand, the different parts of the book stand on their own. Each describes and explains differences and similarities between the Nordic countries with respect to gender and politics. On the other hand, the parts are not totally independent of each other. Clearly, there is a link between the increased mobilisation of women and their greater representation within politics, and the changing content of that politics, with public care and gender equality becoming increasingly politicised. The issue that lies behind all this is whether an equalisation between women and men in respect of political posts has "only" led to increased numerical equality, or whether it also has led to more women-friendly politics. Thus, what are the implications of more women entering the political decision-making process? Today, a growing empirical body of research gives support to the thesis that increasing the proportion of women within political institutions helps to change both the *contents* of politics and the *conditions* for decision-making. Studies of individual Nordic countries support this conclusion (see, e.g. Skjeie 1992; Bergqvist 1994; Wängnerud 1998). In respect of the Nordic countries, we can only hint at the answer to this question here as, in general, we have not been able to gather sufficient comparable data. This means that in many cases we have been forced to rely on the use of existing research material and data. Instead, the results provide us with an opportunity to reflect upon this question.

The Structure and Contents of the Book

In the first part of the book, *The Mobilisation of Women in the Nordic Countries*, the authors analyse different aspects of the question of women's mobilisation, political values and participation in both the established political institutions and in voluntary organisations (chapters 1–6). In chapter 2, Nina Raaum shows how women have overcome a number of barriers since the formation of the first women's organisations and women's suffrage associations. In the spirit of Stein Rokkan, she describes how women have passed four institutional thresholds. The first threshold concerns *legitimation*, or the creation of an acceptance of women as political actors. The second threshold concerns *incorporation,* and refers to the introduction of universal and equal suffrage for women and men. The third threshold relates to parliamentary *representation* and the fourth to the *exercise of power*. The chapter analyses how variations in this development are connected to the specific state- and nation-building processes in the Nordic countries.

The increased mobilisation and presence of women in the political and institutional spheres also evoke questions about gender differences. What does women's newly increased participation in politics mean for the political values held by citizens? Do women and men differ with respect to their political participation and political values? In chapter 3, Nina Raaum looks at the question of whether certain gender differences still persist in respect of women's and men's political activities and values. The basis for the analysis consists primarily of the surveys on citizenship that were carried out in Denmark, Norway and Sweden around 1990.

Traditionally, the political parties have been the backbone of the Nordic model of democracy and it is from these parties that decision-makers in politics are recruited. In chapter 4, Ann-Dorte Christensen examines women's relationship to the established political parties of today. Amongst other things, she discusses questions about differences in party membership (between the Nordic countries as well as between the sexes), the significance of women's federations within the political parties, and how the Nordic parties differ with respect to the recruitment of women. Christensen differentiates between a classical model of integrating women into the political system through the women's federations and the adoption of a modern strategy centred around the use of quotas. She explores the extent to which these models have been employed in the different countries. In chapter 5, Auður Styrkarsdóttir describes Icelandic Women's "response to political lethargy" through the formation of women's lists at both the local and national levels. The question is whether women's lists have proven to be a successful strategy to increase the number of women within the political assemblies. Since the 1970s, the new social movements have also had an important role beyond the arena of party politics. In chapter 6, Solveig Bergman reflects upon this development and analyses, amongst other things, the question of whether there is a conflict between engagement in social movements and more institutionally orientated forms of participation.

In Part II, *Family Policies in the Nordic Welfare States*, policies regarding the care of small children are analysed. Since the 1970s, this "classic" women's issue has occupied a central place in the debate on gender equality. In chapter 7, Christina Bergqvist describes parental leave and public childcare models in the Nordic countries. She explores the ways in which the different models affect the opportunities available to women and men for combining working life and parenthood. In chapter 8, Christina Bergqvist, Jaana Kuusipalo and Auður Styrkarsdóttir describe differences and similarities in parliamentary debates on the public reform of childcare and parental leave in Sweden, Finland and Iceland. The three countries represent three different lines of development. Amongst other things, the authors examine the extent to which female politicians have been able to influence political support for greater public responsibility for childcare.

Research within the areas discussed in Parts I and II of this book are currently both rather extensive and growing. However, gender equality policies and political bodies in the Nordic countries have less often been objects of comparative study. In Part III, *Institutionalised Gender Equality,* the analysis of public gender equality policies at the central and local levels is the first to employ a comparative Nordic perspective since *Unfinished democracy* (Eduards *et al.* 1985). In chapter 9, Anette Borchorst provides an introduction to this field before going on (in chapter 10) to describe and explain the differences and similarities in the growth of the Nordic gender equality institutions. Finally, in chapter 11, Borchorst's focus shifts to gender equality legislation. Her analysis includes, amongst other things, an assessment of the possibilities that exist for the use of quotas and the introduction of policies of positive action.

In chapter 12, Ingrid Pincus and Janneke van der Ros explore the local level as an arena for promoting gender equality policy. Municipal autonomy is a part of Nordic political culture and therefore the municipalities are in some respects, independent political-administrative units, although in other respects they are subject to central government control. The authors discuss the implications of this situation for local gender equality work. Pincus and van der Ros have also looked at the difficulties and obstacles that confront gender equality officers ("femocrats") during the course of their work.

Everybody who is involved, in one way or another, in discussion and research on gender-related questions, knows that equality is not a very easy or unambiguous concept. Therefore, a more deep-going analysis of the notion of gender equality and different ideologies of gender equality is undertaken in chapter 13. By taking the Finnish discussion of gender equality within the national defence forces as her point of departure, Anne Maria Holli throws light on the ambiguities and problematic nature of the concept of gender equality.

The Nordic area also includes the island communities of the Faeroe Islands, Greenland and Åland. These communities are often ignored in comparative studies. We have tried to redress the balance somewhat, although we freely admit that a lack of earlier research and empirical data has restricted our ability to provide more extensive analyses. In Part IV, *Women on the Self-governing Islands,* Susanne Jungerstam-Mulders presents an overview of the development of women's representation and gender equality on these islands. Changes in these areas, she shows, are connected to similar developments in their respective "mother countries". The book concludes with the chapter *Equal Democracies? Summary and Perspectives,* in which some of the main results are presented. A major aim of this presentation is to outline the gender profiles of the different countries. Finally, the conclusion also contains a discussion of the need for future research and perspectives for such research.

PART I

The mobilisation of women in the Nordic countries

Theme editors: Ann-Dorte Christensen and Nina C. Raaum

1

Models of political mobilisation

Ann-Dorte Christensen and Nina C. Raaum

Democratic citizenship concerns the citizens' relationship to political institutions; but it is also about the relationships that prevail between the citizens themselves. In the former case we refer to the *vertical* aspect of citizenship. The relationship between the citizens and the political institutions (nationally and locally) is structured in part by the rights enjoyed by citizens in the community, for which the authorities stand as guarantor, and in part by the duties of the citizens *vis-à-vis* the state and society. In the latter case we refer to the *horizontal* aspect of citizenship, that is to say, the relationship that prevails between citizens when they come together (directly or indirectly) to discuss and form an opinion on matters of common interest. Through these types of more or less formalised associations we take on political identities which reflect our place in the world and our beliefs (Andersen *et al.* 1993:18 ff.).

There is no ready-made definition or formulation of the concept of mobilisation. It is more the case that political mobilisation is used interchangeably with terms such as political recruitment, political integration, and political participation, i.e., chiefly as a descriptive term associated with various forms of political activity. Research on social movements has shown that processes of mobilisation are characterised by an interplay *between, on the one hand, a high level of political activity, and, on the other, the formulation of (distinct) political values* (Svensson and Togeby 1986; Christensen 1997).

Mainstream political sociology has traditionally distinguished between two basically different forms of mobilisation processes, the one individual and the other collective (for example Verba, Nie and Kim 1978). *Individual mobilisation* is an extension of the classical resource approach in which the extent of mobilisation depends on the amount of political and social resources available to the individual. In contrast to this, theories of *collective mobilisation* focus more on the aspects of interests and organisation, and have been used, *inter alia*, to explain how certain social groups – despite limited resources – succeed in organising themselves and taking an active part in political life, as depicted, for example, by Piven and Cloward in their well-known analysis of the Poor People's Movement in the USA (Piven and Cloward 1977). In line with this, an understanding of the development of collective awareness and the formulation of common values have been *essential prerequisites* underlying the mobilisation of the great movements of the 1800s such as the labour movement, the civil rights movement in the USA, and the early women's liberation movement. As regards the new social movements dating from the end of the 1960s in the USA and Europe, there has been less mobilisation among groups with scant resources; mobilisation has tended rather to take place among the more advantaged groups, first and foremost the well-educated. Several researchers have pointed out that the combination of ample resources on the individual as well as the collective level results in widespread mobilisation characterised by a high level of activity and the articulation of new values (Verba, Nie and Kim 1978; Togeby and Svensson 1986; Inglehart 1990; Andersen *et al.* 1993).

What, in our estimation, is important to understand is that processes of mobilisation *concern activities as well as values*. It goes without saying that political actions derive from political opinions and values, just as new interests, values, and identities are formed and shaped through the processes of mobilisation. And of course, people's motives to get involved in politics vary. Such motives might be *instrumental*, that is, aimed at influencing which issues become the objects of which decisions. Participation here is primarily a means to promote political views, interests, and values. But the participation of the citizenry in politics may also be expressively motivated, fuelled by a desire to belong to one or more groups, thus leading to a more or less long-lasting sense of community with others. In this case, participation may be an objective in itself, but political views and values will, whatever the circumstances, play a role in defining the type of association a person seeks out. Last, but not least, people may participate simply because they want to learn more about politics and become more politically competent. In this case, participation has a *consciousness-raising and educational function* which, in turn, may facilitate political mobilisation by enhancing both the person's motivation and their capacity to take part. In the literature, these processes are referred to as *empowerment*, and writers stress that political institutions and bodies which have no express political objective in themselves – such as the family, school, friendships, place of work, and associations – also exert an effect on the abilities and interests of the citizens to become involved in political activities (Verba, Scholzman and Brady 1995).

In the chapters which follow in the first part of the book, more attention will be paid to political activities than to changing values. Our main aim is to give the lie to the myth of a single model of women's mobilisation which should be appropriate for all the Nordic countries, as well as to the belief that the rise in the level of women's participation in paid work is in itself the most important driving force behind the mobilisation of women. We anticipate that, behind the apparent similarities in the processes of political mobilisation among Nordic women, some significant and meaningful differences will be found. On the one hand, these might contribute to refining our understanding of women's political mobilisation in the whole Nordic region, while, on the other, putting into perspective our understanding of women's mobilisation in each of the individual countries.

Even though, ideally speaking, we ought to maintain a perspective in which activities and changes in values in the Nordic countries are analysed in terms of their interplay with one another, we have chosen to examine actions rather than values. The reason for this lies mainly in considerations to do with comparisons between countries, since there is a greater amount of comparative data on political activities than there is on attitudes and values. We have focused on variety in the forms of political organisation, and on the general nature of citizenship. This means that we have examined political mobilisation within more or less institutionalised arenas, open, in principle, to all citizens,[6] and as it is manifested in élite politics as much as in mass politics.

The lack of comparative data has left its mark on the analysis. As far as has been feasible we have tried to maintain an inclusive perspective through which to compare all five countries. However, in several areas this has proved impossible, and we give an account of the relevant methodological problems as they appear. Another weakness is that, due to the scope of the analysis, "women" tend to emerge as a homogeneous mass. A more finely-tuned perspective, which allowed for greater generational and social differentiation, would have benefited the analysis, but that again would have been incompatible with the comparative perspective. It is therefore important to stress that our ambition has *not* been to present an overall analysis of the mobilisation processes of Nordic women, but rather to lay bare some of the differences, sharpen some of the distinctions, and, not least, raise some pertinent and fresh questions regarding both the developments and their explanations.

In what follows we shall specify the framework of our analysis. We take our point of departure in concept of mobilisation and firstly discuss Lise Togeby's theory on the mobilisation of women. After this we briefly look at perceptions of mobilisation that have been dominant in research into the new social movements. Finally, we present Stein Rokkan's threshold model, a model which has played a key role in studies on mobilisation within institutionalised parliamentary politics. This model is a suitable tool with which to analyse the thresholds and barriers encountered by new mobilised groups. In extending the model, we also define our approach to our analysis as well as its concrete structure.

---

6. This limitation means that the type of mobilisation that is associated with the affiliation of citizens to special groups or special interests (for instance, user participation in the welfare state at the local level, and union activities) will not be addressed. This limitation is due firstly to the lack of sufficient data to illuminate this form of participation in a genderised perspective; and secondly, because the institutionalisation of the sectional interests of the citizens vary considerably between the countries, thus rendering comparison difficult.

A common Nordic model of women's mobilisation?

The Danish researcher Lise Togeby has conducted the most wide-ranging empirical study on the political mobilisation of women in the Nordic countries – mostly with reference to Denmark, but also extending, in some of her contributions, to the other Nordic countries. Against this background she argues that any theory of women's political integration in highly industrialised and pluralistic societies should contain at least four elements, namely (Togeby 1994a:18):

- the high level of women's participation in paid work
- that paid work increases women's resources
- that the political opportunity structures are sensitive to new political demands
- that women in fact define the goals, and organise and mobilise themselves

Togeby emphasises that it is women's participation in working life (and, more indirectly, their involvement in the educational system) that constitutes the main factor behind mobilisation. A stable connection with educational institutions and the labour market has contributed to end women's social isolation and the creation of a social homogeneity consistent with a common identity (Togeby 1994a:56). The strength of Togeby's conception of mobilisation is that it serves as a general framework around women's mobilisation in so-called highly industrialised and pluralistic societies. By focusing on employment, the level of education, and the welfare state, it says something both about the social framework around mobilisation and about the conditions underlying individual and collective action (Christensen 1997).

But there is a problem inherent in Togeby's theory, namely its implicit assumption that mobilisation among women results in itself in equality between the sexes. Other studies show that in some cases mobilisation can widen the gap between the sexes – that, for instance, the rising educational level can exert at least as great an effect on men as it does on women (Andersen et al. 1993; Raaum 1995a). Another and more pressing shortcoming in the theory, is that it focuses only on structural factors, primarily the labour market. While there is no doubt that the broad mobilisation of women largely emerged in the wake of an increased involvement in the labour market, that does not necessarily mean that such involvement brings about mobilisation of itself. Many non-Nordic countries have witnessed an equally powerful growth in women's paid employment without this making any noticeable difference to their degree of political mobilisation, and certainly not in the area of institutionalised politics. The Norwegian case shows that, even though Norway in many respects was the most successful of the Nordic countries in the seventies and eighties in reducing gender inequality in political life, the growth in women's participation in the labour market happened relatively late in a Nordic and European context. At the present time, 50 per cent of employed women in Norway still work part-time; this is a very high proportion indeed in comparison with other countries (Nordisk statistisk år-bok).

This shows that the political mobilisation of women is not only affected by their participation in the labour market; it is possible to imagine other factors that håve played a major role in women's simultaneous movement into the labour market and into politics. This is, indeed, what Togeby herself implies in the third and fourth entries on her list, which highlight the political opportunity structure as well as the processes of mobilisation. It is these latter preconditions which in our opinion are the most interesting and important ones.

We want to argue for a more sensitive approach to women's mobilisation in the Nordic countries, an approach which takes into account structural as well as cultural factors, and – not least – political circumstances. We agree with Birte Siim when she argues that structural explanations should be toned down. She suggests instead that a gendered and pluralistic citizenship must focus more on the relative autonomy of politics and the dynamics inherent in the political institutions (Siim 1997b:204). Just as a single explanation cannot encompass the complexity of women's political integration in the Nordic countries, neither can a single theory of women's mobilisation suffice for the Nordic countries – or other countries of Western Europe. Processes of mobilisation are complex and diverse. Firstly, they are closely bound up with contexts – for example, the capacity of the political system to interact with new forms of political participation and involvement, and second, to the identity of the political actors and their values. Rather than seeking out the general and the universal in mobilisation processes, the perspective should give scope for differentiation and diversity.

Analyses of women's involvement in the new peace movement in Denmark and Sweden in the eighties have indicated the way in which the diversity of women's experiences, identities, and values developed in the actual processes of mobilisation. In both countries, there were large differences not only between the basis on which the mobilisation of members took place, but also in the values around which the movement was organised. Where some women were mobilised on the basis of an identification with an earlier woman's role which was rooted in the family and motherhood, another group was mobilised from the perspective of gender equality, and a third was mobilised on a radical feminist platform (Christensen 1991; Peterson 1985; Peterson 1987).

This accentuation of the differences in these channels of mobilisation is very similar to Iris Young's *politics of difference*. Young does not write expressly about mobilisation, but about communities. Young is critical of the community ideal, and she claims that the feminist conception of community has often been counter-productive because the need for uniformity and a common ground of identification has given rise to dichotomies, divisions and exclusion. For this reason, the community ideal may oppose the formulation of alternative models of political organisation. Instead of creating a false sense of unity, such communities, and analyses of them, must be oriented towards diversity and heterogeneity (Young 1990).

Mobilisation in the social movements

Following the rise of the new social movements, different approaches have emerged in social movement studies over the past two decades. Drude Dahlerup identifies three such schools: the resource mobilisation school; the new social movement school; and the social constructionist school. While the resource mobilisation school concentrates on the meso level, with a particular focus on actors and the social movements' organisations, the new social movement school studies macro level phenomena and lays greater weight on the movements as agents of fundamental social change or on the (national) conditions behind the rise and development of the movements.[7]

The third and most recent school focuses on the movements in relation to the construction of ideas, meanings, and new identities. In extension of this latter approach it is Drude Dahlerup's opinion that the social movements – and in her case, the Danish Red Stocking movement – have been key producers of alternative interpretations and alternative visions. These aspects are contained in her concept of innovative thinking which embraces both new ideas and new praxis (Dahlerup 1998:54 ff.).

All three approaches are central to analyses of mobilisation processes. However, because our point of departure is the concept of citizenship and the various forms of political participation, we focus primarily on the actor and the grass-roots approach. In the seventies and eighties, when involvement at the grass-roots level proved a new and extremely popular form of participation in the Nordic countries, several Nordic researchers stressed the importance of the movements for the mobilisation of new groups (particularly the well-educated middle class and women) (see, for example, Olsen and Sætren 1980; Svensson and Togeby 1986). In a subsequent analysis of grass-roots participation in the Nordic countries, Togeby distinguishes between mobilisation theory and supplementation theory. Here she brings mobilisation theory to bear on the political mobilisation of the well-educated, new middle classes and women, while supplementation theory is grounded on the expectation that existing forms of political conduct are enhanced by grass-roots activities (Togeby 1989:17).

McAdam *et al.* (1996) argue that new ideas in social movement studies ought to be developed by incorporating elements from all the schools. This inclusive approach is echoed by Rucht too. Among other things he writes that

> As a rule, political opportunity approaches have neglected the structural basis for resource mobilization, whereas resource mobilization approaches have largely

---

7.   Peter Gundelach has stressed the connection between the social movements and social changes. Using a wide-ranging historical perspective he shows how movements spring up in the transition from one type of society to an other. Gundelach distinguishes between three types of society: traditional society; modern society; and programmed society. It was in the transition from traditional to modern society that the old social movements emerged, of which some were based on class relations. For Gundelach, the most important movements in Denmark were the labour movement and the women's movement. It is in the transition from the modern to programmed society, that we see the emergence of the new social movements (Gundelach 1988).

ignored the broader political environments in which social movement organizations are embedded. In linking both research strands, we can achieve fuller understanding of factors that directly or indirectly influence social movement mobilization. (Rucht 1996:185)

Rucht prescribes a more flexible approach to the movements, and especially to their interaction with other forms of political organisations. He identifies three agents of mobilisation: (1) social movements; (2) interest groups; and (3) political parties. Analytically one can distinguish between the three agents with regard to, for instance, strategies of political action, the utilisation of resources, and organisational structure. Rucht's idea, however, is that, in spite of this analytical distinction, it may yet prove extremely difficult to demarcate precisely where the one ends and the other begins. Interest groups and political parties often make use of action-oriented strategies, to mention one instance, without being social movements, or they develop organisational structures which are less hierarchic than organisations in general. Likewise, social movements and action groups can give a relatively formal and well-organised impression, at the same time as a considerable proportion of their demands are narrowly aimed at the official political system. For example, interest groups and parties can form organisations which are less formalised and hierarchic than normal, just as social movements can encompass a relatively broad-ranging organisational apparatus.[8]

Rucht contends that there ought to be greater awareness of the co-existence of these forms, and he identifies three types of social movement (1996:188):

(1) a *grass-roots-oriented model*, which has a comparatively loose organisational structure, focuses on radical protests, and is based on active participants;

(2) an *interest-group model*, which emphasises the production of influential policies and has a formalised organisational apparatus;

(3) a *party-oriented model*, which stresses elections and representation, party politics, and a formalised organisational apparatus.

According to Rucht, all these models of social movements share the objectives of promoting collective interests, influencing political decision-making processes, as well as, in the last instance, bringing about social change. Viewed in relation to our present concern, one could say that they have formed a continuous framework around the mobilisation of Nordic women over the past thirty years – a mobilisation process characterised by a fundamental interplay between political organisations institutionalised in the political system, and political organ-

---

8. This has been the case in the peace movement, for instance. Large segments of this movement fought in the fifties against atomic energy and in the eighties for the removal of intermediate-range ballistic missiles from Europe (Hoadley 1989; Krasner and Petersen 1986), while other parts of the peace movement were engaged in a broader political peace stance. As we shall see, the Icelandic Women's Alliance is an example of an organisation that is something in between a political party and a social movement.

isations associated primarily with civil society. Our starting point in the political parties and the new social movements involves at the same time focusing on the first and third models, while the second model – the interest-group model – will be hardly touched on at all.

Mobilisation in the parliamentary political system

The work of the Norwegian political scientist Stein Rokkan occupies a unique place in the field of comparative studies of political mobilisation processes in systems of parliamentary and party politics (Rokkan and Lipset 1967; Rokkan 1970). Rokkan has compared elections with the locks of a canal: "They allow rising socio-cultural currents to continue to flow through the canal system, but they also make it possible to stem the tide, and to keep flood waters at bay." The next analogy may serve as an even better description of the sequences typically found in democratisation processes and the mobilisation of the masses: "All emerging political movements have to negotiate a number of locks on their way towards the core of the political system, and upwards towards the central arena of executive authority: decision-making" (Rokkan 1970, 1987:274 ff.). After conducting historical analyses of processes of political mobilisation in seventeen West-European countries, Rokkan identified *four crucial barriers* or *institutional thresholds*.

The first threshold is *legitimisation*. When, in the history of state formation and nation-building, have citizens been granted a right to express themselves in public through the establishment of universal rights such as the rights of assembly, free speech and freedom of expression? The challenge of this phase is to strengthen the collective identity of the mobilising group, as well as to influence public opinion and political élites to facilitate entry into the political arena.

The next threshold is that of *incorporation*, or inclusion into political life. How much time passed before supporters of a growing political movement were granted formal rights to participate in elections in accordance with established and prevailing criteria in the community? It is during this phase that equal rights are introduced, but it is also about encouraging potential participants to make use of new rights.

The third threshold is political *representation*. How high were the original barriers to political representation for a new political movement? When and how were the barriers lowered, thus easing the admission of the mobilising groups to the legislative assemblies? Compared with the previous threshold, this one implies a more qualified presence, namely in the form of direct participation in decision-making processes.

The fourth and final threshold is the step to *executive power*. How resistant were the executive bodies to pressures from the new lawgivers? How much time did it take before parliamentary strength was transformed into influence at the level of government, and what were the factors which helped forge a passage across the threshold to government?

If one threshold changes, new pressures will be generated to change the others as well. But Rokkan underlines at the same time that the actual point in time at which such changes occurred varied considerably from system to system: between nation-states and also between sub-national entities in the individual countries. The crux of the matter is that processes of democratisation are contextually determined: structural, cultural, and political conditions, combined with different types of strategies on the part of the political élite as well as the mobilising groups themselves, contribute to diversify the processes of mobilisation. There has been a debate among Nordic researchers in the field of women's studies concerning the extent to which Rokkan's threshold model (also called the lag hypothesis) can be used to explain women's political mobilisation in the post-war era (Nagel 1995; Karvonen and Selle 1995; Raaum 1995b, c). Critics have particularly highlighted the model's deterministic nature, claiming that it is ill-adapted to explain the ambiguities and complexities in the evolution of that mobilisation (Siim 1997b:212; Christensen 1997:228). These controversies may be due the fact that the premises underlying the threshold model have not been inadequately clarified. Firstly, the threshold model only refers to the institutionalised political system, and thus only to a limited aspect of women's mobilisation. Secondly, the deterministic element means simply that the crossing of a barrier will *sooner or later* result in pressure being exerted on the next threshold. Indeed, Rokkan points out unequivocally that the time needed to break through the barriers will vary from system to system. Different types of mobilisation are generated by variations in existing opportunity structures – that is, different combinations of structural, cultural, and political factors.

The strength of Rokkan's threshold model lies in the close links to the various institutionalised levels in modern, representative democracies. As we shall see in Chapter 2, the model is well suited to detect the incorporation of new mobilised groups into the parliamentary political system – in this case women's progress towards formal democratic citizenship. On the other hand, the model is unable to register mobilisation processes which do not target the institutionalised system. It is therefore not particularly applicable in an analysis of mobilisation processes which lie beyond, or on the fringes of, the formal political system, such as, for instance, the new social movements.

The structure of the analysis

In accordance with the above description of social movement research and Stein Rokkan's threshold model we analyse in this section of the book the mobilisation of Nordic women in an interplay with institutionalised and non-institutionalised forms of political organisation in a perspective in which we retain both the horizontal and the vertical aspects of citizenship. This means that what we are interested in is firstly women's relationship to the political institutions and the rights and duties that followed from this relationship, and secondly, the political communities which act as a framework around women's collective political acts (both in collaboration with other women and with men). We anticipate that, given this approach, a pattern will emerge which will allow us to unravel and differentiate the notion of a single model of women's mobilisation in the Nordic countries and which will give rise to fresh questions concerning both what is common to the Nordic countries as a whole and developments in each of the countries individually.

Chapter 2, *Women in parliamentary politics: Historical lines of development* by Nina C. Raaum analyses the integration of women in the broader processes of democratisation in the Nordic countries. Here we focus on vertical citizenship. The chapter takes as its starting point Rokkan's threshold model and analyses the differences and similarities in the ways in which Nordic women have surmounted the four institutional thresholds in parliamentary politics.

The four chapters which follow focus particularly on the mobilisation of modern women over the past three decades – partly on mass participation and partly on the relationship between political parties and social movements as central and contiguous channels of mobilisation. There are similarities as well as dissimilarities in the political parties' and the social movements' relationship to feminism, but plainly also in women's relationship to them and in their choice of organisational framework for the processes of mobilisation.

Chapter 3, *Political citizenship: New participants, new values?* by Nina C. Raaum is based on a comparison of data collected from surveys on citizenship in Denmark, Norway, and Sweden. Here, horizontal citizenship is addressed with the focus on gender differences in patterns of political participation in the three countries. In extension of this, a brief presentation is provided of the main gender differences in values and attitudes.

Chapter 4, *Women in the political parties* by Ann-Dorte Christensen discusses the growth of the political parties in the Nordic countries in relation to the development of traditional as well as modern strategies for the integration of women. In addition, the analysis examines critically the theory of women's integration into shrinking institutions, that is, in institutions that are in the process of losing their former significance.

Chapter 5, *Women's lists in Iceland* – A response to political lethargy by Auður Styrkársdóttir is a case study. Against the historical background of the women-only candidate list and its association with a radical feminist movement, the analysis sheds light on principal strengths and weaknesses which the status of the Women's Alliance as partly political party and partly social movement has engendered.

Chapter 6, *Women in the new social movements* by Solveig Bergman analyses the feminist movements in the Nordic countries and especially the developmental phases of the new women's movements. In addition, comparative differences in the involvement of Nordic women in grass-roots activities are noted, as is their mobilisation in the peace movement and the crisis centre movement respectively.

2

Women in parliamentary politics: Historical lines of development

Nina C. Raaum

The Nordic countries are renowned for their state-dominated democracy and welfare model in which the state assumes wide-ranging responsibility for welfare of the citizens and the citizens in turn enjoy relatively extensive and universal rights in social and economic matters. The central role of the state does not mean that the private sector has had little say in Nordic politics. On the contrary, since the end of the 1800s close collaborative ties have endured between public and private enterprise and society at large. This integration of the public and the private has given Nordic society a "state-friendly" character (Klausen and Selle 1996), but it also means that participation in politics has been channelled not only through the political parties of the parliamentary system of government, but equally through business sector and civic organisations.

We shall start by addressing processes of political mobilisation which relate to citizens' roles as voters and elected representatives. The aim here is to elucidate, by applying Rokkan's threshold model, the broad-brushed historical lines of development in the parliamentary sphere. Through his historical and sociological analyses of the Nordic countries, and a number of other West-European countries as well, Rokkan (1970) concluded that, on their upward path through the parliamentary system, mobilising groups must surmount four institutional thresholds. These four thresholds are (1) legitimisation; (2) incorporation; (3) representation; and (4) executive power (see Chapter 1). The processes of democratisation, including the crossing of thresholds and a steadily more open and competitive grass-roots mobilisation, have varied from country to country in the Nordic region. Different social and political frameworks have meant that people have been faced with a variety of options, a consequence, among other things, of the different processes of state formation and nation-building the countries have undergone, and their geographical position in a wider European context, i.e., politically, economically, and culturally. We shall map out similar and contrasting patterns in the political mobilisation of Nordic women in respect of the four thresholds, and discuss what it is that might explain the similarities and differences between them. The question is whether structural, cultural, and political factors, which underlay the variations in the mobilisation of men, have had a similar impact on the mobilisation of women, and also whether other factors have played a particularly important role for women's mobilisation.

The interlocking of the public and private spheres, which is a characteristic of Nordic politics, means that participation in the decision-making processes that take place in the relations between the state and civil organisations has been an important aspect of political citizenship in the Nordic countries. For this reason we shall also discuss women's involvement in such organisations. Until the end of the eighties, social studies – including women's and gender studies – generally concentrated on exploring the relationship between the state and the non-government organisations through the lens of corporatism theory. The customary view is that – apart from government itself – it is the economic interest groups in the labour and commodity markets which have played the leading roles in the so-called corporatist institutions, and that women's organisations have had little access to the state apparatus. We shall not perform any in-depth analysis of the historical relationship between the state and the non-government organisations. Our primary objective is to discuss whether alternative approaches – which turn the spotlight from the market to the voluntary organisations of civil society – can shed new light on the political impact of women's voluntary organisations, that is, whether we, up to the present, have underplayed significant aspects of women's political history.

We shall first outline some general characteristics of the processes of democratisation found in the Nordic countries. This will clarify how the prevailing social and political conditions have influenced the political mobilisation of women historically, as they have that of men, just as it may reveal differences between women and men in each of the countries.

The growth and structuring of mass politics [9]

When mobilisation among ordinary citizens evolved in the latter part of the 1800s, only Denmark and Sweden enjoyed independent status and had any experience of successful state-building. While absolutism in Denmark persisted right up until 1849, absolutist rule in Sweden lasted only for a brief period (1680–1718); the latter country had also retained a tradition of class assemblies reaching back to the 1400s. The three remaining areas in the Nordic region were dependent socially, culturally, and politically. Finland, which had been under Swedish dominion for many years, was conquered by Russia in 1809 and made

---

9.   This section is based mainly on Rokkan (1981).

an autonomous grand duchy under the Russian tsar. Independence came to Finland only with the Russian Revolution of 1917. Norway, which from the end of the fourteenth century had been under Danish rule, declared independence in 1814, but only a few months later was forced into a union with Sweden, a situation which prevailed until 1905. Norway and Finland were self-governing with regard to domestic matters, and had their own legislative and executive institutions, but their sovereignty was nonetheless quite restricted due to the lack of control over foreign policy. Iceland was subject to Denmark for a long time, and it was only after 1870 that it was awarded limited powers of self-determination, powers which were widened somewhat in 1904. In 1918 Iceland was recognised as a sovereign state, although it remained in the union with Denmark until 1944, at which point it declared itself an independent republic.

Rokkan (1981:62) summarises the way in which the countries' social and political frameworks affected the political incorporation of Nordic men in the following two statements:

(1) A strong tradition of representative rule makes for *slow and stepwise* extensions of political rights, while protracted absolutism is more likely to lead on to sudden extensions to most adult men.

(2) This regularity, however, is modified in peripheral territories: the broader the range of mobilizing issues, the more sudden the transition to universal suffrage.

Three of the Nordic countries – Denmark, Norway, and Finland – are notable for their early and sudden extension of the right to vote. In Sweden and Iceland, on the other hand, political rights were introduced more as piecemeal reforms. Norway was the first of the Nordic (and European) countries to come anywhere near a democracy of and for the people. With the adoption of its Constitution in 1814, when Norway declared its independence from Denmark, political rights were extended to all male farmers. This gave 45 per cent of all men aged twenty-five years and over the right to vote. Throughout the remainder of the nineteenth century, reforms were introduced at a more moderate pace. An effective wave of mobilisation was not seen until the 1860s, partly because a first wave around 1830 had been effectively doused by the Local Authorities Act of 1837. The Act introduced the municipal system of local government along with the principle of municipal self-government, thus bestowing on the farmers a "guarantee of autonomy" which placed restrictions on the (Swedish) state's chance to interfere in local affairs. The Norwegians' nation-wide mobilisation for independence was linked to cultural and political issues. The prime target was the Danish written language – a legacy of four hundred years of Danish rule and practised in all official contexts. Later the spread of secularisation from the towns to the country became the object of popular mobilisation. The growing opposition – which consisted of radicals and farmers – forced a settlement with the Swedish king, resulting in the introduction of parliamentarianism as far back as 1884. In 1898 Norway was the first of the Nordic countries to introduce universal suffrage for men. The final showdown with the Swedish overlords in the matter of foreign affairs, and the dissolution of the union with Sweden following a referendum in 1905, was a continuation of the broader counter-cultural (i.e. Danish culture) protest.

Denmark, being closest to the continental network of trade and commerce, became urbanised at an early date, a development which lay the foundations of a strong tradition of bourgeois commercial capitalism. Entering into an alliance with the middle classes, the Danish king succeeded in prolonging absolutist rule for quite some time, and the transition to popular democracy took a more dramatic turn than was the case in Norway. In its break with absolutism in 1849 Denmark acquired a bicameral parliamentary system and a sudden extension of the right to vote to all male householders though barring servants and recipients of poor relief. Denmark was the first country to see the formation of party political organisations by men – which took place in the early 1870s (Petersson 1995) – but the introduction of universal male suffrage did not come to pass until 1901, two years after Norway.

Had Finland, which shared the Swedish tradition of class assemblies, attained independence after the Napoleonic Wars, a process of gradual extensions of suffrage might have started in the country. Instead, the nation was trapped in a threefold mobilisation process: culturally against the old Swedish élites; politically against Russia; and socio-economically against the large landowners. Finland suffered from an unyielding policy of Russification from 1890. The powers of the Lantdag (the legislative assembly) were curtailed in 1899; Russian became the main official language in 1900; and the Russian governor-general was given dictatorial powers in 1903. After the defeat of Russia in the war with Japan in 1905, the revolution in Russia the same year, and internal dissent in Finland accompanied by general strikes, the tsar was prevailed upon to grant Finland internal self-government. The revolutionary situation in Russia created an opening to transform the old four-estate Lantdag into a unicameral legislature, and, in 1906, the right to vote was extended to *all men and women* twenty-five years of age and older. In his depiction of this early and radical electoral reform in Finland, Rokkan points out that the calls for national independence were being made at a time of social, cultural, and political conflicts, but the reform is also seen as tactical move on the part of the Russian governor-general to appease the masses (Pryser 1997). The next election in 1907 unleashed an extraordinary process of radicalisation and mobilisation which made the fight for independence quite different from that in Norway. The final round in the fight for national independence exploded into civil war with class pitted against class, making Finland's transition to popular democracy the most violent and painful of all the Nordic countries.

Sweden and Iceland were the last countries to adopt universal suffrage for the male part of the population, but their more faltering and spasmodic processes of reform have different explanations. In Sweden the strong Vasa state had been based on alliances between the aristocracy, the free farmers, and the royal house, and the tradition of class assemblies had been endorsed in the Constitution of

1809. This gave the farmers their own channel of representation, which quelled the pressure for further extensions of suffrage. In 1866 a bicameral parliament or Riksdag was substituted for the old class-based assembly. Men of a certain financial standing were awarded the right to vote in elections to the lower chamber, but the reform also strengthened the position of the wealthiest farmers in the upper house of the Riksdag. Contrary to Norway and Denmark, where the mobilisation of male farmers and workers was organised through alliances already represented in the Norwegian parliament, the Swedish "masses" had be mobilised through groups which stood *outside* the established system of representation (Lindström 1989:93). A decisive shift took place in 1907 with voting rights being granted to all men, scaled according to the amount of taxes levied, and it was not until 1919, with the introduction of universal suffrage, that the system was finally abandoned.

The gradual pace of development in Iceland must be viewed in light of the large geographical distance to Denmark, and Iceland's weak, agriculturally based economy. Both factors meant that Denmark would profit little from increasing the level of centralised control. Contrary to Finland and Norway, outside governance did not represent a sufficiently potent firebrand to trigger a comprehensive mobilisation of the Icelandic population. As was the case with Sweden and Finland, Iceland had a strong – though broken – tradition of democratic governance, and, unlike Norway and Finland, the Icelanders had avoided having the written language of their overlords forced upon them. They had managed since the Middle Ages to preserve a strong cultural identity which allayed the need to concentrate mobilisation efforts on the cultural front. The relatively late industrialisation and the narrower scope of the issues which mobilised the people of Iceland behind demands for political independence represent important reasons why Iceland's steps towards full civil rights were slow and considered, and coincidental with their gradual liberation from Denmark. The political mobilisation of women would come to reflect many of the general features of the processes of democratisation in the Nordic countries. The countries' particular structural, cultural and political situation played a role in determining the time at which women crossed the thresholds on their way up the ladder of the parliamentary system, a ladder which men had ascended before them.

The parliamentary arena

Table 2.1 shows women's negotiation of the four institutional thresholds in national, parliamentary politics. The first threshold, *legitimisation*, was about getting women's emerging demands for political equality onto the agenda. It was about achieving a place in the public arena: legitimising women's issues and paving the way for an acceptance of women as political actors. To accomplish this the women's movement adopted various strategies, from collective organisation to influencing opinion and entering into alliances with progressively-minded men among the political and cultural élites (Björkhem, Engström and

Table 2.1 The four institutional thresholds in parliamentary politics - legitimis-ation, incorporation, representation, and executive power - and the time at which women crossed them:

THRESHOLDS	Denmark	Finland	Iceland	Norway	Sweden
1. *LEGITIMISATION* - Founding of:					
- feminist organisations	1871	1884	1894	1884	1884
- suffrage societies	1889	a	1907	1885	1903
2. INCORPORATION:					
Universal suffrage, enacted	1915	1906	1920	1913	1919
3. REPRESENTATION (Parliamentary):					
1. election, ordinary representatives	1918	1907	1922	1921	1921
1. election, over 10 % of representatives	1966	1907	1983	1973	1953
1. election, over 20 % of representatives	1979	1970	1987	1977	1973
1. election, over 30 % of representatives	1990	1983	never	1985	1986
Proportion of women 1998	37 %	34 %[b]	25 %	36 %[b]	40 %[b]
Highest proportion of women	37 %	38 %	25 %	39 %	40 %
4. EXECUTIVE POWER (Government)					
First ordinary minister	1924[c]	1926[c]	1970	1945	1947
1. Cabinet, at least 10 % of ministers	1953	1953	1983	1965	1966
1. Cabinet, at least 20 % of ministers	1981	1987	never	1973	1976
1. Cabinet, at least 30 % of ministers	1994	1991	never	1986	1991
1. Cabinet, at least 40 % of ministers	never	1991	never	1986	d
1. Cabinet, at least 50 % of ministers	never	never	never	never	1994
Proportion of women 1998	35 %	28 %	10 %	47 %	50 %
1. Prime Minister	never	never	never	1981	never
1. President (Iceland, Finland)	–	never	1980	–	–

a. In Finland no societies were founded with the express purpose of campaigning for the right to vote.
b. There has been one national or local election in Sweden, Norway and Finland during the 1990s (in 1991, 1997, and 1995 respectively) at which the proportion of women returned underwent a decline (Appendix 1, Table 8).
c. The world's first female minister was the Dane Nina Bang (Christensen and Damkjær 1998), but her period of incumbency lasted only for a short while (1924–26). Finland's first female minister, Miina Sillanpää, maintained a place on the Government for twenty years.
d. When a social-democratic government replaced a non-socialist government in 1994, the proportion of women increased from 38 to 50 per cent.
Sources: Bergman 1998; Bergqvist 1998; Haavio-Mannila *et al.* 1983; Raaum 1995c; Christensen and Damkjær 1998.

Wängnerud 1994; Haavio-Mannila *et al.* 1983; Hagemann and Krogstad 1994; Nagel 1995).

The actual establishment of organisations centred on the women's movement – an event which marks the crossing of the legitimacy threshold – did not take place until the 1870s with the formation of the first women's suffragette society, (Nagel 1995).[10]

Just as the first Nordic party political organisations had been started by Danish men, so it was the Danish women were the first to found a dedicated feminist organisation in an effort to legitimise the fight for women's rights. This organisation was established in 1871, concurrently with the formation of the first political parties. The formation of a Danish society for women's suffrage did not take place until 1889, nearly twenty years later. In Sweden, Norway, and Finland, feminist organisations were founded in 1884, more than ten years after Denmark, but also in these countries more or less concurrently with men's founding of the political parties. Norway is an exception in that, as early as the following year, 1885, Norwegian women founded the Nordic countries' first society for women's suffrage. The simultaneous emergence of organisations for women's liberation and suffrage must be seen in light of the special politicisation of Norwegian society at the time, characterised by the nation-wide mobilisation for independence from Sweden and the introduction of parliamentarianism as early as in 1884.

As in Denmark, the formation of a Swedish society for women's suffrage came nearly twenty years after the foundation of the first feminist organisation. Finnish women worked for the right to vote in women's organisations and the labour movement, but contrary to the rest of the Nordic countries, they never founded a society specifically for the purpose of campaigning for women's suffrage. The reason for this most likely lies in the extremely broad cultural, economic, and political mobilisation that took place in favour of independence, and the radical reform which introduced in the same period universal suffrage for both women and men in 1906.

In Iceland, the first women's organisation was also founded prior to the first society for women's suffrage, but in other respects the course of developments in Iceland deviate from the rest of the Nordic countries. The establishment of organisations dedicated to women's liberation not only occurred later here than elsewhere, it also took place before men started to organise political parties. The emergence of political parties in Iceland belongs to the post-1916 period, but as early as in 1908, Icelandic women were running for office on a separate women's list in a local election in Reykjavik. Women's lists were put up in three municipalities in local elections up to 1921 as well as in the general elections of 1922 and 1926. After this, however, class antagonism fuelled the establishment of parties in Iceland (Rafnsdóttir 1995; Styrkársdóttir 1994). The causes behind this belated development in Iceland lie in structural factors such as the relatively late industrialisation of the country, but also the narrow scope of the political conflicts of the day played an important part (Rokkan 1981).

With the radical Finnish reform of the voting system in 1906, Finnish women became the first to cross the second institutional threshold, that of *incorporation*, which not only entailed the introduction of universal suffrage but also the exercise of the right to vote through participation in elections. Finland's particular political situation, with extensive mobilisation around deep-seated conflicts of a social, cultural and political nature, was, as mentioned, decisive for the abrupt

---

10. In several of the countries more than one organisation were being established. The table shows the date of the establishment of the first organisation.

transition. In Norway and Denmark women gained the right to vote more or less simultaneously: 1913 in Norway and 1915 in Denmark. Viewed in light of the establishment of the first feminist organisations, the legitimisation phase was shorter in Norway than in Denmark. The reason might be that the broader sweep of the counter-cultural protest in Norway, including the Union controversy with Sweden, contributed to the mobilisation of Norwegian women. In 1905, women were protesting their lack of voting rights in the referendum on the dissolution of the union with Sweden, and organised a petition on the issue. Lists from "the women's referendum", which were handed to the Government on the day of the referendum, comprised the addresses of 565 societies and as many as 278,298 signatures. "300,000 women and 600 associations" became an effective argument for women's right to vote (Nagel 1995:65), not least because the number of signatures added up at the time to about half of the female population of Norway at the time between twenty and seventy (NOS 1995).

Sweden and Iceland, the last countries to grant voting rights to all men, were also the last to introduce suffrage for women, in 1919 and 1920 respectively. While Sweden's past history of class governance tended to stem the tide of radical reforms, the measured development in Iceland was a consequence of the relatively narrow range of issues mobilising the people behind national sovereignty (Rokkan 1981). It is an interesting point, moreover, that foreign policy issues contributed to the introduction of women's right to vote – as had been the case in the two other dependent countries, Finland and Norway. In Iceland, however, it was external rather than domestic pressure that tipped the balance. The Icelandic Cabinet had originally committed itself to the introduction of universal suffrage in 1930, and it was only after pressure from the Danish authorities that this date was brought forward to 1920.[11]

A common feature of all the Nordic countries is that women, compared to men, encountered particularly resilient barriers in their attempts to cross the next two thresholds, *representation* and *executive power*. In addition, fresh patterns were crystallising in the mobilisation processes, especially in the post-Second World War years (Appendix 1, Table 3). As early as in the first election after the introduction of universal suffrage in Finland in 1907, women gained 10 per cent of the seats in the parliament. In the rest of the Nordic countries, women did not

---

11. International statistics put the date of the introduction of universal female suffrage in Iceland as 1915. (IPU 1995). This is not correct. In 1915 the right to vote was extended to include all women over forty years of age, while the age limit for men was twenty-five. There was considerable opposition to the prospect of women gaining the right to vote in Iceland, especially in the years following 1911. The popular Women's List had given the political establishment something to think about. To forestall the women's party, an age limit of forty years was adopted in 1915, with a proviso that it would be reduced stepwise at each election, which meant that women would not be on an equal footing with men until 1930. It is generally assumed that the Danes stood in the way of women's suffrage, but in fact the opposite is the case. In 1918 the Danish and the Icelandic Government decided that Iceland should be an independent realm under the Danish king, and that citizenship should be dual. The Icelandic parliament was obliged to give women and men equal rights because the Danes balked at the prospect of Danish women as second-rate citizens in Iceland.

pass the "ten-per-cent limit" until after the Second World War. With the exception of the elections held during the depression in the thirties, Finnish women retained about 10 per cent of the seats throughout the period up to the Second World War. It is assumed that the radical reform of voting rights in 1906 in itself contributed to the special situation in Finland, but a relatively high participation in paid work and early party political organising among women may also have had an effect (Bergman 1998; Kuusipalo 1993). At the level of government Finland also distinguished itself prior to the Second World War. A female minister, Miina Sillanpää, attained office as early as 1926, and, in contrast to the relatively short incumbency of Denmark's first female minister in 1924, Nina Bang, Sillanpää held sway in the Cabinet for a very long time indeed – twenty years all told.

After the Second World War and until the 1970s, what is particularly striking is the increasing speed with which mobilisation among Swedish women took place. Women gained 10 per cent of parliamentary seats in 1953. In doing this they surpassed their Norwegian and Danish sisters, and, on the threshold of the sixties, they were on a par with Finnish women. Further developments must be viewed in light of the position of the Nordic social democrats. The Swedish SAP was at that time the Nordic countries' most powerful social-democratic party, and the Swedish public sector was growing strongly. Added to this, the Second World War had changed the social and political landscape in which the Nordic social democrats were operating. While Sweden had remained neutral during the war, in the years immediately following the other countries faced debilitating tasks of reconstruction, as well as foreign policy worries. The Swedish social democrats were not only in a better position to protect the labour movement as a separate culture (Lindström 1989:98), they were also in a better position to address at an early date the situation of women in society, inspired, among others, by the social democratic women's federation and key political actors such as Alva Myrdal and Gustav Möller. The favourable social and political context, and the politicisation of issues relevant to Swedish women, contributed to the upswing in Swedish women's representation. This supports Siim's argument that politics in itself is important for women's political integration (Hirdman 1989; Rothstein 1994; Siim 1997b).

While Swedish women gained 10 per cent of the Riksdag seats in the general election of 1953, Danish women did not pass this threshold until 1966, when they won 11 per cent of the seats. Norway, and especially Iceland, lagged even further behind during the first four decades of the post-war period. In Iceland the women's proportion of parliamentary representatives remained very low throughout the whole of the seventies. It was only after the election in 1983 that Icelandic women could celebrate a record-breaking gain, from 5 per cent in the 1979 election to 15 per cent in 1983. This landslide performance was a result of women's exasperation and the ensuing mobilisation behind the Icelandic Women's List in 1982. In the shape of the Women's Alliance, the list won 6 per cent of the votes in 1983, and 10 per cent in 1987, and, in addition, brought considerable pressure to bear on the other parties to recruit more women (see chapters

4 and 5). Today, the main cause of the low representation of Icelandic women –
in a Nordic context – is to be found in the electoral procedures. Although all the
Nordic countries employ a system of proportional representation which, compared with majority-vote representation, contributes very positively to the recruitment of women, in Iceland it is combined with a system of direct primaries
(as in the USA), a circumstance which, without doubt, impedes the integration
of women (Rule and Zimmerman 1994; Matland 1998). The proportion of wom-
en that run for office is far higher than the proportion of women among the elected representatives: In 1995 the figures were 50 and 25 per cent respectively. In
the rest of the Nordic countries today only small differences exist between the
proportion of women among the candidates and the numbers elected to office in
general elections.

   With the exception of Iceland, all the Nordic countries witnessed a fresh mobilisation of women in the wake of the new women's movement from the end of
the sixties, but after 1970 and until the mid-eighties, the parliamentary mobilisation of Norwegian women was without doubt the most far-reaching in the
whole of the Nordic region. In the course of two elections in the seventies, wom-
en broke first through the ten-per-cent and then the twenty-per-cent barrier. The
proportion of women in the Norwegian national assembly, the Storting, increased from 9 per cent prior to 1973, to 24 per cent in 1977. With this, Norwegian women's parliamentary representation came abreast of that of Finnish,
Danish and Swedish women. Surmounting the fourth threshold, gaining entry to
executive power, happened very quickly indeed: after the general election of
1973 women secured 20 per cent of the seats in the Cabinet, and, in 1981, the
first – and so far only – Nordic female prime minister, Gro Harlem Brundtland
– was appointed. A few years later in 1986, Brundtland's "women's Government" made the headlines world-wide with eight women in the eighteen-minis-
ter Cabinet. Since then the proportion of women in the Government has never
sunk below 42 per cent (Appendix 1, Table 3–5). This is due to a provision in
the Gender Equality Act, which, since 1988, has required the authorities to ensure a representation of at least 40 per cent of both sexes on non-elected public
boards, councils, and committees – including the Cabinet.

   The reasons behind the relatively belated mobilisation in Norway before
1970 and the ensuing, but much faster developments thereafter, may lie in structural and political factors. In the post-war period Norway was one of Europe's
leading "housewife countries", and it was not until the seventies that women's
participation in the labour market increased to any significant extent (Nagel
1995). In 1970, only 23 per cent of Norwegian women worked outside the home.
In contrast, 53 per cent of Swedish women had paid jobs (Frønes 1996). The low
level of employment among Norwegian women may initially have contributed
to delaying their political mobilisation. In similar fashion, the powerful growth
in employment throughout the seventies, together with a political factor, the
Gender Equality Act's quota requirements, may have contributed to the subsequent rapid upswing. The political parties in Norway are not formally bound by
the Act, but many of them have adopted rules to ensure a 40-per-cent represen-

tation of women on their electoral lists and in their governing bodies. Indeed, some parties had made this move prior to the enactment of the law (Heidar and Raaum 1995, see Chapter 4, too). This indicates once more that political actors and political choices are decisive: the reason why Norwegian women were able in such a short time to reach the level of women in Finland, Sweden and Denmark was, *inter alia*, the determination of the politicians to formulate and enforce within the political system a policy of positive discrimination. The significance of political strategies and actors was later demonstrated in Sweden. What is referred to as the "backlash election" of 1991, when the proportion of women in the Riksdag fell from 38 to 33 per cent, provoked strong reactions and wide public debate and further mobilisation among women. Political parties and public authorities were met with insistent demands to incorporate more women. The result at the following election in 1994 eclipsed all previous records in the Nordic countries, with 40 per cent of all seats in the parliament going to women, and half of the places in the Cabinet (Bergqvist 1998).

Since 1970, Sweden and Norway have led the field with regard to women's parliamentary representation. The proportion of women in Norway sank slightly after the general election in 1997 due to the large measure of support accorded to the extreme right-wing Progress Party, which has very few women among its nominated candidates. Among Danish women who, in the last century, were the first to establish formal associations dedicated to women's liberation, the proportion of women in parliament has stagnated at around 34 per cent since the mid-eighties. This reflects, among other things, the relatively low level of party political organisation among women, probably the absence of specifically feminist organisations, and the lack of equal status measures, such as quota requirements, within the Danish political parties (see chapters 3, 4, and 6). After the last election in 1997, however, the proportion of female representatives increased to 37 per cent, which means that Denmark and Norway are now level. The situation in Finland, where women won the right to vote and achieved parliamentary representation at an early date, has been more akin to that in Denmark than in Norway and Sweden. After the election in 1991, Finnish women gained 39 per cent of the seats in the Finnish parliament, but throughout the remainder of the eighties and nineties the percentage of women has been closer to 30 than 40. At the level of government too, Finnish women have succeeded less well than women in Norway and Sweden (Appendix 1, Table 5). The representation of Icelandic women is still much lower than in the rest of the Nordic countries. Historically, a number of structural, cultural, and political factors have contributed to this predicament, but today, it seems as if the Icelandic electoral and party system is the most weighty explanation.

The national versus the local – a rejoinder

Up to now we have concentrated on politics at the national level, and we shall not enter into any detailed discussion of local government level. There is, however, one factor of interest which deserves mention, and that is that women in the Nordic countries are represented just as well locally as they are nationally. In most countries women are better represented in local rather than national politics, a fact that accords with the "iron law" or "the law of increasing inequality" (Haavio-Mannila *et al.* 1983) which states that the number of women (and other groups lacking élite status) declines the closer one comes to the power centres of the political hierarchies. The Nordic countries represent a remarkable exception to this "basic sociological principle". In Sweden and Iceland, the representation of women locally and nationally has largely been evenly balanced, and – more intriguingly – in Denmark, Finland, and especially in Norway, the pyramid has even been turned on its head: in general women have fared better at the national level than locally (Appendix 1, Table 8).

The recruitment of women depends on factors both on the *demand side*, that is, on the parties' and voters' readiness to nominate and vote for women, and on factors on the *supply side*, that is, on women's resources and inclination to participate (Lovenduski and Norris 1995:14 ff.). The Danish, Norwegian, and Finnish cases illustrate this in an interesting manner: In Norway and Finland, the weaker presence of women in local politics is related to voter and party behaviour, and to the manner in which the electoral procedures work, in other words, to factors on the demand side. In Denmark, on the other hand, it appears that women's self-selection, which is a supply side factor, plays a greater role. In Norway the parties put up so-called "closed" lists for general elections. The candidates are ranked by the parties, and voters are not allowed to indicate their preferences for particular candidates. In relative terms, the parties nominate as many women in local elections as in general elections, but in the local elections the voters have the right to alter the parties' lists by striking out the names of certain candidates on the ballot papers and/or giving certain candidates extra votes (i.e., cumulating votes). This seldom affects the parties' predetermined order of cumulated candidates to be elected by transfers, who are often listed twice, but in relation to the first-choice candidates, the voters wield considerable leverage over who is elected. Nationally, about every fourth voter uses his or her right to change the ballot paper, but this right is made use of far more often in the peripheral municipalities (whose populations are small and whose economy is largely dependent on the primary sector) than in the central and more populous municipalities (Raaum 1995c). In the years following 1970, a few "ballot-paper-changing campaigns" were organised in the form of "women's coups", which gave women a higher proportion of the representatives than their share of the candidates would indicate. A small number of "women's coups" thus created the impression that changing ballot papers benefits women's representation. In practice, the reverse is the case. At all local elections since 1970, the proportion of votes cast for women has fallen by between 5 and 10 percentage points compared to what the results would have been given a gender-neutral alteration of ballot papers. Data on attitudes do not indicate, however, that voters consciously deselect women, rather that there are other factors at work which indirectly favour men (Hellevik and Bjørklund 1995).

In Finland, the proportional electoral system allows for a significant degree of individual voting preference. The parties put up "open" lists enabling the voters to determine the ranking of the candidates. One reason why the proportion of women has been smaller in local than in national-level politics may be that the parties have entered a slightly smaller proportion of women on the local candidate lists than the national lists. In all of the local elections since 1960, however, the voters have given more votes to women than their share of the candidates would predict, but, paradoxically, women have nonetheless ended up with a smaller proportion of the seats than would have been commensurate with their share of the votes. Pikkala suggests that the situation is related to two aspects of the local electoral procedure:

> Firstly, a strong concentration of votes for individual female "vote-magnets" can spoil the chances of other women candidates. On the other hand, a wide distribution of the votes to many equally strong female candidates can lead to a situation in which none or only a few of them are able to cross the electoral threshold. This happens when many female candidates share the same potential group of voters. (Pikkala 1997: 353).

In Denmark, where political parties have suffered considerable losses during recent decades, there is little to indicate that women are being "locked out". It is true that some of the smaller political parties have consigned women to places so far down the electoral lists that they have hardly any chance of being elected, but this is largely balanced by the preferences of the voters, who move the women candidates a bit further up the lists (Elklit and Jensen 1997). The reason seems rather to be that Danish women think twice about becoming involved with political parties at all, opting for other and less institutionalised forms of participation (Dahlerup 1998; see also chapters 3 and 4).

We will return, in chapters 3, 4, and 5, to voter and party behaviour, and there we will elaborate more, *inter alia*, on the way in which the situation in élite politics reflects circumstances at the political grass-roots level and internally in party politics. However, before we get that far we shall look at women's accession to positions of public authority through organisations other than political parties.

The state and organised interest groups

It is usual to draw a sharp line between the categories of "pluralism" and "corporatism" when depicting the relationship between the state and non-government organisations. Essentially, *pluralism* means that organised interest groups compete in political arenas beyond the confines of formal political institutions, while *corporatism* involves a close and formal linkage between interest groups and the public authorities by means of, among other things, regular negotiations and party representation on state committees, boards and councils. In spite of the disparate definitions and operationalisations of "corporatism", researchers have arrived at similar results with regard to its proliferation at the *national* level. The economic interest groups of the labour and commodity markets have occupied a position of no little power in the corporatist system. Together with Austria, Norway and Sweden have figured among the most corporatist countries. Corporatism in Denmark and Finland has been less prevalent, but far stronger than in the least corporatist countries such as Great Britain, France, USA, and Canada (Gallagher, Laver and Mair 1995:359 ff.; Hermansson 1993:39).

The integration of women into corporatist politics is generally analysed on the basis of their share of seats and chairs on state committees, boards and councils. The representation of women in the corporatist domain has always been much smaller than in the parliamentary sphere, but as early as in the seventies there were already marked differences between the Nordic countries in this respect. Women's corporatist presence in Norway in particular was higher than in other countries: throughout the seventies, together with the surge in women's mobilisation in the parliamentary domain, considerable advances were made through the corporatist channel as well. Norwegian women increased their share of seats on state committees from 7 per cent in 1965 to 27 per cent in 1981. In the other Nordic countries, the picture was less heartening: at the beginning of the eighties, the proportion of female board members was 16 per cent in Sweden, 10 per cent in Finland, 9 per cent in Denmark, and 7 per cent in Iceland.

In the eighties, and especially the nineties, the figures have grown in all of the Nordic countries. This development reflects the increasing level of women's employment and education which not only signifies that women have been integrated into the organisations of the market, but also that the authorities in several of the Nordic countries have tightened the rules relating to a more equal representation of women and men. In Norway, where the Gender Equality Act has stipulated since 1988 that each sex shall have at least 40 per cent of the seats on publicly appointed committees, from the beginning of the 1990s women have indeed had about 40 per cent of the seats. At the chairperson level the ratio is substantially lower, around 20 per cent (Raaum 1995a). There was an upswing in Sweden following the publication of the report entitled *Varannan damernas*,[12] when the Swedish state threatened to apply a system of gender quotas if organisations refused to do anything to achieve a more equitable distribution of the sexes. In the course of the past decade, the proportion of women has more than doubled in Sweden, and is today between 35 and 40 per cent. As in Norway, the proportion of women chairing committees is much lower, around 20 per cent. In Finland the Act on Equality was amended in 1995. It now stipulates that each sex must be represented on state committees (and corresponding municipal bodies) by at least 40 per cent. In 1994, Finnish and Icelandic women had 28 and 24 per cent respectively of committee seats. In Finnish committees set up during

12. The expression *Varannan damernas* refers in fact to a Swedish dance tradition in which women are permitted to engage the male partner of their choice every second dance or so rather than the usual convention of waiting for the men to ask them. This corresponds to the "ladies' dance" phenomenon in Anglo-Saxon countries. The intended meaning is "every other council or parliamentary seat to a woman". For want of anything better, we translate this "every other seat a woman's seat".

1996 the ratio was 42 per cent (Vähäsaari 1995; Kaasinen 1996; Bergqvist 1997). Denmark and Iceland have no regulations on gender quotas, but throughout the past decade in Denmark women have generally held 38 per cent of the seats on councils, boards and committees.

The reasons given to explain the traditionally weak position of women in the corporatist domain are twofold: (1) the perceived political irrelevancy of women's organisations; and (2) the low number of women, especially in positions of leadership in organisations and institutions, that have played a leading role the corporatist sphere. There is no doubt that the situation has reflected women's weak position in the market. The Nordic countries distinguish themselves internationally for their many women in political life, but in working life they are no more advanced than other Western countries. Up to the nineties, women had a minority of the top positions in the trade union movement and even fewer in the management of private and public companies (Hernes and Hänninen-Salmelin 1983:157 ff.; Raaum 1996; Tema Nord 1996:586). On the other hand, however, there is reason to question whether women's organisations in fact have lacked political relevance in the form of political legitimacy and influence.

Recent research has stressed two intriguing factors which touch on the relations between the state and civil organisations. Firstly, there are indications that Nordic politics are in a process of de-corporatisation. There is evidence for this in contemporary developments in the form of fewer committees and reports, a growing amount of lobbying, and an increasing number of financial enterprises which communicate with the authorities directly, bypassing the intermediary channel of organisations outside the government. Contemporary developments in society, including decentralisation and internationalisation, make it difficult to sustain centralised governance (Nordby 1994; Petersson 1996; Rothstein 1994). The parallel de-corporatisation of politics and the appointment of more and more women on state committees may be viewed as an instance of the integration of women into shrinking institutions, that is, institutions that are in the process of losing their influence and significance (Holter 1996). In our opinion, this interpretation would be too emphatic. Firstly, men are in the majority in these institutions, so we are not dealing with a process that only affects women. Secondly, more research is needed to assess the degree and consequences of the changes. The extent of corporatism remains unclear not only with regard to the present and the future, but also with regard to the past.

This brings us to the second factor highlighted by recent research: previous research has been criticised for having focused too narrowly on economic pressure groups in the market to the detriment of voluntary organisations in civil society. It has understated the extent of the voluntary or third sector as well as the extent of the connections between the public authorities and the voluntary sector. *In other words, there has been too much focus on the market and corporatism, and much too little on civil society.* Thus, not only is our picture of civil society skewed, but our picture of democracy itself:

The state and the market have been regarded as the most important sectors in the development of society, and third-sector organisations are often only referred to as interesting in relation to developments in these two sectors, that is, as an addition or an afterthought – but not as having any intrinsic interest (Klausen and Selle 1995:15; see also Putnam 1993).

International third-sector research, which previously accentuated the universal, today focuses on the contextual. While the American voluntary sector has been characterised by market ideas and distance from the state, the voluntary sector in "state-dominated" societies has played a far from minimal role, contrary to previous assumptions. In contrast to the situation on the Continent, and in the USA and Great Britain, the Nordic countries' voluntary organisations have been member-based and democratic institutions (Gidron, Kramer and Salamon 1992; Kuhnle and Selle 1992). They have functioned as community and identity-building institutions, and have contributed to ushering new groups into political life. The voluntary organisations were particularly important for women, whose presence in other areas of the public sector was weak: *From the middle of the 1800s, men were simultaneously mobilised through political parties (the state), the trade union movement (the market), and voluntary organisations (civil society). For women, however, the voluntary organisations represented their most important public and political arena right up until the seventies.*

A distinctive feature of such highly organised societies as the Nordic ones is that voluntary work – in the sense of "an autonomous way of life", or independence from the state – have played a less important part. The collaboration between public authorities and the voluntary sector has followed an established *modus operandi* since the last century. The ambits and influence of various types of organisations, from religious associations to broad-based welfare organisations and the co-operative movement, have differed from country to country. A common feature is nonetheless that all these organisations have urged the development of the welfare state, and have endeavoured to establish close collaborative contact with the public authorities. Rather than carrying out tasks independently of the authorities, they have worked to have those tasks taken over by the state, and/or to acquire state funding for their organisational work (Klausen and Selle 1995, 1996; Lorentzen 1994; Lundström and Wijkström 1997; Selle and Øymyr 1992a, 1995a, 1995b).

Organisations dominated by women were making themselves heard as early as in the last years of the nineteenth century. Unfortunately, little social research has been done to shed light on intra-regional variations in the voluntary organisation of Nordic women. Relevant *social studies* primarily concern Norway. Norwegian studies show that women's organisations have played a key role in defining welfare policy from the end of the last century right up to the present day, if mostly at the grass-roots level rather than as leaders – even though some important organisations have indeed had women as their leaders (Selle 1996: ff.). The pre-eminent example is the *Norske Kvinners Sanitetsforening* (Norwegian Women's Public Health Association), a broad-brush welfare organisation which has appealed to an impressively large number of women, and which very early on emerged as a very professional organisation. Support for this organisation reached a peak in 1962, at which time more than 246,000 persons could be counted as members, that is, every fourth woman between the ages of twenty and seventy in Norway was a member (NOS 1995, Table 3.4). During the development of the welfare state, and especially during the first thirty years after the Second World War, the Association worked actively together with the public authorities at the national, regional and local levels (Bjarnar 1995:65; Wærness 1995).

Women's organisations uncovered fresh needs, pioneered new interventions, and carried out extensive voluntary work. In short, they filled the roles of *pioneers, service providers, welfare workers, and guardians of values* (Grindheim 1991; Kramer 1981). At the local level, too, the voluntary organisations, together with the municipal authorities, were innovative in the area of welfare policy. Seip emphasises that the Norwegian welfare state is the product of a triangular interaction between voluntary organisations, the municipalities, and the state: "Without welfare organisations and welfare municipalities, no welfare state." She says that the earliest and most interesting socio-political groupings in Norway emerged prior to 1890, as a result of the collaboration between the voluntary organisations and local authorities. The ensuing breakthrough for a municipal welfare policy, between 1890 and 1920, was a purely *political* product. The welfare municipalities "arose at the same time as the right to vote [was granted] and the emergence of the [political] parties. This is no accidental correlation" (Seip 1991:26 ff.). Throughout the 1900s, women's involvement in health-care and social services and especially in preventative work had a decisive influence on the formation of the welfare state. Particularly in the 1950s and 1960s, while Norway was still an archetypal "land of housewives", women's organisations were active participants in the extended political environment in which public policies for many areas were hammered out. They gave more and more women the opportunity to unite behind political programmes, and not least of their achievements was to forge a channel to the political authorities (Bjarnar 1995:198).

In Sweden, too, from the latter half of the 1800s, the women's welfare organisations played an important part in the development of social work together with the state:

> The women of the middle and upper classes who performed welfare work did so in close collaboration and with an open channel to the local authorities who administered poor relief. In fact, the divisions between the welfare organisations and the state sector were not considered to be problematic. One could say that the drawing of lines of demarcation is a question which belongs to our time (Lundström 1995).

Women researchers were quick to point out that the state, in many ways, "exploited" women's voluntary and unpaid work: women's marginal position in the labour market was a precondition for their extensive voluntary commitment (Wærness 1995). But Nordic women's studies have also focused on the positive relations between women and the state, and contributed early on to weakening previous theories on the patriarchal nature of the state. As early as in 1987, Hernes was arguing that the Nordic countries had a "state-feminist" nature which could be attributed to a "woman-friendly" policy from above, in combination with women's mobilisation from below (Hernes 1987:11): "Woman-friendliness refers here both to the new bargaining situations in which women find themselves, and to the aspects of equality which have created the normative foundations of the Nordic state (Skjeie and Hernes 1997:370). In a similar vein, the historian Blom (1998) says that Nordic history shows that a state apparatus dominated by men can still implement a feminist policy, even though she does question the actual strength of the alliances between the state and women. Siim (1988) has stressed similar points in her analyses of the "complex partnership" between the state and women. In subsequent contributions she argues, moreover, that the actor's perspectives should play a more central role in assessments of women's political leverage: "The development of the welfare state, the ideal of active citizenship, and the relatively open political institutions, have been crucial to women's empowerment" (Siim 1997b:198).

It is precisely the roles played by the women's organisations as political actors that we wish to underline. The state, no doubt, had reasons of its own to conduct a "women-friendly" policy, even when women had no positions of public authority. *That public institutions, which were dominated by men, in many areas enacted a "woman-friendly" policy, must be linked to the extensive involvement of women themselves.* So as to achieve a closer understanding of this state of affairs, it is essential that analyses of the relationship of the state to the organisations distinguish between different types of organisations. This is because the interaction between the state and the voluntary organisations of civil society assumed forms that differed from the interaction between the state and the profit-oriented organisations of the market.

A great deal of the collaboration between the state and the voluntary sector has taken place outside of state committees in the corporatist system, and has therefore been less visible than the state's consultations with corporatist organisations. It is therefore not sufficient to measure the leverage of the organisations by counting seats on state committees; nor will public documents give us an adequate picture. In Norway, for instance, the interplay between the state and the Norwegian Women's Public Health Association was "so close that none of the parties really had any need to formulate it in steering documents or long-term plans" (Bjarnar 1995:198). The collaboration between the state and the voluntary organisations emerged as a consequence of *common* objectives aimed at extending the state's sphere of responsibility. In contrast to the market, the voluntary sector has worked to get the state to *take on board* tasks carried out in the private sphere, tasks which traditionally have belonged to the family and other segments of civil society. It is true that the state needed to delegate tasks, but it relied in particular on the non-government organisations to strengthen the knowledge base on which public policy was built. Women's organisations communicated their experiences culled from their own areas of work and knowledge of existing social needs. They were thus able to give a feminine angle to the needs defined by the welfare state (Bjarnar 1995). In contrast to the type of interaction that prevailed between the state and the market, many of the decisions to transfer responsibility from the private sphere to the public were made by majority decisions in popularly elected bodies. This meant that there was less need to institutionalise permanent corporatist bodies to deal with perpetual conflicts and negotiations.

The interaction between the state and the parties in the labour and commodity market has been based implicitly on a completely different *division* between the state and the private sphere. In addition, the state had different motives for working with market-based organisations than with those of civil society. There was a particular need to bring the tensions surrounding wage negotiations and settlements in the fishery and agricultural sectors under control, and even though the state had made efforts to regulate many aspects of the activities of the free market, taking on its functions directly has seldom been an issue. The collaboration between the state and the market has involved both potentially and in practice far more and severer conflicts than the co-operation between the state and the voluntary sector. A smaller number of common goals, in combination, it must be said, with a desire to preserve the mutual trust and understanding that existed between the two parties, had an effect on the organisational side of the collaboration. To underline the *autonomy* of the market, any interaction had to be clearly demarcated as separate from the parliamentary system. Corporatist institutions, where decisions are made through bargaining rather than majority decision, therefore became an important arena for this interaction.

Because previous research has mostly focused on participation in formal corporatist institutions, we have probably partly overlooked the less formalised – and therefore less visible – collaboration between the state and the voluntary sector. If this is the case, then we have accorded the voluntary organisations in general and women's organisations in particular a more marginal political past than they deserve (Selle 1996). The interplay between the state and the voluntary sector is the least researched aspect of the Nordic welfare states, and probably the most important field remaining in Nordic welfare state research. It is an exacting challenge because in many ways it concerns an "invisible" decision-making power that is only partially formalised, but which is also a normative and defining power.

In the Nordic countries today, not only is there an ongoing process of de-corporatisation which will alter the balance between the state and the market organisations, but the landscape in which the voluntary organisations operate is also undergoing profound changes. Organisational life is less gender segregated than previously, but, at the same time, women constitute a minority in the types of organisations which are experiencing the most powerful growth. This includes organisations which are related to the interests of the individual and to leisure time in a wider sense. The wide-ranging idea- and welfare-based organisations – which have primarily done work for others and not so much for themselves, and in which women have played key roles – are confronting a process of steady decline. This frailty means that the potential of the idea-based organisations for socialisation and empowerment is also being weakened. Never before have mass social movements, organised through outward-looking, change-oriented, and intensely socialising associations, played such a limited role in organisational life and democracy as today. At present, these organisations are less concerned with attracting members, and individual and voluntary activity (especially service work) is set on a downhill trajectory. The voluntary sector is being professionalised: the work is being carried out more and more by paid employees; the power structure is being centralised; and contracts are increasingly being entered into with the public authorities for the performance of paid work (Klausen and Selle 1995; Selle 1996; Lundström and Wijkström 1997).

Ironically enough, the increasing pressures on the welfare state have contributed to the re-discovery of the voluntary sector. Decentralisation and autonomy, privatisation and voluntary work are projected as the "new" measures to ensure welfare and quality of life. The issue now centres on transferring tasks in the opposite direction, from the public sphere and over to the private. Since contemporary women, as men, are active in the labour market, the state can no longer rely on women filling their traditional roles in the organisations of civil society. The interpenetration of the public sphere and the private will not necessarily be less than it has been, but the forms it takes will be different. The state's need of assistance from the voluntary sector could mean that the relationship between the state and the voluntary sector becomes more formalised than it once was. Similarly, the ongoing de-corporatisation may augur a less formalised and visible collaboration between the state and the market than has been customary. Both developments could mean that men's, and particularly women's, status as working people and consumers of services will have a greater and greater effect on the realisation of political citizenship. It is crucial, if we are to gain a greater understanding of these processes – those of the past as well as the future – to distinguish between different sorts of organisation and to be receptive to models which allow for the fact that collaboration between the state and the organisations may take on very different forms.

Summary

From an international point of view, women in the Nordic countries have occupied a strong position in the political system, but behind this apparent conformity can be found many dissimilarities between the countries. The processes of mobilisation of Nordic women have varied considerably from country to country, due, among other things, to their special structural, cultural, and political contexts. The legitimisation and formal establishment of feminist organisations, which occurred simultaneously with the formation of the first all-male political parties, began in Denmark with the creation of the first feminist organisation in 1871. In all of the three independent countries at the end of the 1800s – that is, Norway, Iceland, and Finland – political discord on the issue of national independence contributed to hastening the enfranchisement of women; most dramatically in Finland with the granting of the right to vote for women and men simultaneously in 1906. Sweden and Iceland were the last to introduce the right to vote for women, in about 1920, after reform processes of a more piecemeal nature than had been the case in Finland, Denmark, and Norway. The time-lag in Sweden may be accounted for by the country's long tradition of class assemblies, which generally imply a gradual extension of civic rights, while the late developments in Iceland were primarily a consequence of the relatively late industrialisation of the country and – in Nordic terms – the narrow scope of the issues mobilising the citizens behind national independence.

In the period leading up to the Second World War, only Finnish women were represented to any substantial degree, with about 10 per cent of the seats in the parliament, the Eduskunta. In the other Nordic countries, women only started to gain a similar degree of representation after the war. As the seventies approached, things happened very quickly indeed in Sweden, because, among other things, the country's neutral stance during the war meant that it was in a better position to give priority to welfare policy and equal status issues. Until 1970, Denmark held an intermediate position, with a slow, but steadily improving level in women's representation. In Norway and Iceland, on the other hand, progress was lagging behind. In Iceland, there was no significant change until after the election of 1983; in Norway, after 1970, a strong mobilisation of women was seen across the country. Since 1970, women in Sweden and Norway have generally enjoyed the highest level of representation in parliamentary politics, while Finland and Denmark have lagged a little behind. Women in Iceland are represented to a far lesser degree now than they were. Historically, a number of structural and political factors have contributed to this, but the chief explanation behind the persistence of this state of affairs is that Iceland's electoral system includes primary elections, which obstruct the integration of women.

A special characteristic of Nordic politics has been the comprehensive responsibility of the state in the field of welfare policy, but political work has also been characterised by a close contact between the state and the organised interests of the market as well as civil society's. Earlier research, which was specially taken up with the study of women's admission into corporatist institutions, has concluded that women have been in a weak position in the interaction between the state and the organisations. This picture gives a relatively accurate description of women's situation in the relations between the state and the market, but we have argued that women's voluntary organisations in civil society have played a much more decisive role in the building of the Nordic welfare states than has previously been assumed. While men from the end of the 1800s were being mobilised through political parties (the state), the trade union movement (the market), and voluntary organisations (civil society), the voluntary organisations represented the most important public and political arena for women until the seventies. They gave women the opportunity to unite behind political programmes, and they exerted a crucial influence on the formation of public policy. Closer studies of these connections represent one of the most important remaining challenges in research on the Nordic welfare states. Such studies could shed light on important aspects of women's political history, as well as on the similar and dissimilar aspects of the Nordic democracies.

3

Political citizenship: New participants, new values?

Nina C. Raaum

The political mobilisation of women has been affected not only by contextual limitations within the various countries, the electoral and party systems together with the attitude of the élites towards the participation of women have also been of significance. In addition to this, women have played a decisive role themselves, of course. We shall therefore examine in this chapter the political commitment of ordinary citizens – the political rank-and-file. We will be focusing for the most part on degrees of involvement but we will also discuss the extent to which a gender gap can be traced between men and women's political preferences. This question revolves around the strength of persisting gender differences and the degree to which we find analogous or disparate tendencies in the three Scandinavian countries of Norway, Denmark, and Sweden. Finland and Iceland have not been included for practical reasons; we have not had access to comparable data for these two countries.

We examine two main types of activities (Andersen *et al.* 1993:36 ff.). First, participation which in some way is linked to specific institutions and organisations, is repeated from time to time and is fairly regular. This *institutionalised* participation comprises activities such as voting in elections, involvement in political parties and other organisations, and the holding of public offices (positions of trust). The other type of participation concerns working for specific, isolated issues, and is more irregular and occasional: this is *situational* participation such as making political contacts and taking part in political discussions, as well as any activity that could be termed grass-roots participation. This type of participation emerged towards the end of the sixties and was linked especially to new issues confronting the welfare state; it embraces such undertakings as petitions and demonstrations (Togeby 1989:10).

To begin with we present some of the main conclusions found in existing research, conclusions which shed light on the way in which gender-related differences in political participation have changed from the seventies to the present day. Following this we elaborate on variations among the countries by analysing data from three comparable studies carried out in Denmark, Norway and Sweden. Finally we briefly consider political values, with a particular focus on important differences in the political opinions and party preferences of the two sexes.

From onlooker to participant?

Twenty years ago gender-related differences in political participation were considerable. In Norway, gender was the most significant factor behind variations in the level of public involvement. Overall, men's participation was at least twice that of women, and women's interest in politics – as well as their self-confidence – was considerably lower than men's. In the other Nordic countries the situation was more or less the same (Halsaa Albrektsen 1977; Lafferty 1978:1981; Dahlerup 1979b; Eduards 1977; Goul Andersen 1984; Togeby 1984).

With regard to situational participation, a different pattern emerged as early as in the seventies. Compared with other types of activity, Danish researchers found insignificant gender-related differences in activist-type participation, and in the younger age-groups (16–28 years old), women's participation was on a par with that of men's (Togeby 1984). Nor were gender differences of any magnitude being reported in Norway (Olsen and Sætren 1980). A comparative study on grass-roots participation in the Nordic countries shows that this sort of participation remained gender-neutral throughout the eighties, but it also reveals some interesting disparities between the countries. In Denmark, Norway and Iceland, the activist type of participant had a particularly mobilising effect on young, well-educated women, women who were more active than their otherwise comparable male counterparts. In Sweden this pattern has been less noticeable, and in Finland there are no differences between the age-groups. What is more, Finland departs from the other Nordic countries in its very low level of grass-roots participation (Togeby 1989; see Chapter 6 as well). Apart from Togeby's work there are no comparative studies on gender differences in the mass politics of the Nordic countries. For this reason, to shed light on gender differences which have persisted through the nineties, we must resort to research from each of the countries separately.

The 1987 *Swedish* survey on citizenship showed that people were generally far more active at the beginning of the nineties than twenty years earlier. The exception was the political parties, which had entered a period of apparent stagnation. The differences between the sexes had lessened quite considerably, but only one dimension of participation – turnout at elections – was gender-neutral. Of the four other dimensions, two were dominated by men and two by women. The male-dominated areas consisted of the most traditional channels of political influence. Swedish men were most frequently in contact with the civil service and politicians, they utilised the media more aggressively, and they were more often members of parties; they held official positions more often, and they were the most active in decision-making processes at the workplace. The areas dominated by women involved situational activities such as political demonstrations and protests. Moreover, women were most often to be found working with issues at the local democratic level as parents, patients, and relatives (Petersson *et al.* 1989; SOU 1990: 44).

A Swedish survey from 1994 shows that gender differences have continued to shrink since 1987, but that party support has waned considerably during the nineties. Party membership reached its peak around 1983–84 at which time 15–16 per cent of the adult population were members of some party or other. In 1994 the rate had sunk to 9 per cent; 10 per cent of men and 8 per cent of women. A new situation in the nineties is that the trade union movement is recording slightly more support from women than men, 87 and 82 per cent respectively, and, compared with many other organisations, the level of activity among women more or less equals that of men. Gender differences in Swedish organisations in general are insignificant as far as membership is concerned, but measured on the basis of positions such as union officers and attendance at meetings, men are generally (slightly) more active than women. Organisational life is still marked by strong gender segregation: men comprise the majority of members of sports clubs, leisure interest groups, share-holders' associations, temperance or abstinence organisations, co-operatives (apart from consumer organisations), car clubs / automobile associations, as well as civil defence organisations. Swedish women make up a majority in cultural interest groups, groups dealing with the concerns of parenthood, associations within the Swedish Church and the non-conformist denominations, consumer co-operatives, organisations campaigning for the rights of patients and the disabled, humanitarian aid organisations and peace campaigning organisations, including organisations such as Amnesty International, the United Nations Association of Sweden and various types of solidarity organisations (Levnadsförhållanden 1996:66 ff.).

The 1990 *Danish* survey on citizenship failed to reveal any areas of participation with a female bias; all were either male-dominated or gender-neutral. The gender-neutral areas in Denmark are more or less the same as the female-dominated areas in Sweden, that is (1) activist-type activities and (2) participation in local service institutions such as schools and daycare establishments. The gender-neutral pattern in Danish local consumer organisations, which was a female-dominated area in Sweden, is not due to women being less active in Denmark than in Sweden, but because men are more so. This may indicate that the traditional division of labour between the sexes has undergone greater changes in Denmark than in Sweden. Also with regard to organisations in Denmark women and men are committed to different types of organisations, but the gender differences in the level of activity are smaller in Denmark than in Sweden. The differences are most easily detectable among the older generation, that is, those over sixty years old. Danes are currently members of more organisations than used to be the case, but in comparison with other Nordic countries the membership is relatively passive (Andersen *et al.* 1993:169 ff.). In Norway and Sweden, well over half of all members of organisations are active in one or more organisations, while in Denmark the figure is under the 40-per-cent mark (Goul Andersen 1996:57).[13]

. In other areas, and especially in the area of conventional politics, "men continue to dominate the political arena. The political mobilisation of women in Denmark, of which much has been spoken, has not resulted in equal participation by the sexes" (Andersen *et al.* 1993:133 ff.). In 1990 Danish men were involved in an average of 6.6 activities out of a total of 27 investigated. The corresponding figure for women was 5.6. It is an open question whether this constitutes a significant difference because, translated into relative figures, it means that men on average have been involved in 24 per cent of the activities, while women have participated in 21 per cent (Raaum 1995b:230). Which of the possible interpretations we opt for depends on the context we want to emphasise: the current situation or the course of developments after 1970. The Danish researcher Lise Togeby lays less weight on the remaining differences, preferring to highlight the process of change. She characterises the collective mobilisation of Danish women as a success story, but adds that "This does not mean that the difference between the sexes has been abolished once and for all, or that men's oppression of women is now confined to the history books. What it means is that women, over the course of the past twenty-five years, have been mobilised and have attained majority status, and today are natural participants in the political life of the community" (Togeby 1994a:9, 1995).

The *Norwegian* survey of 1990 on citizenship did not include questions on democratic participation in local consumer organisations because this is a much less evolved area in Norway than in Denmark and Sweden (Larsen and Offerdal 1994:101). In general the Norwegian data showed smaller differences between the sexes' political involvement: of a total of 17 general activities, men on average had been involved in 6.3 and women in 6.0. Further, the least politically active were no longer the women, but men with no connection to the labour market. An important remaining gender difference is that more men than women – 14 as against 10 per cent – have held some sort of public office as elected representatives in local, regional, and national bodies (Raaum 1995b).

Norwegian women's involvement in voluntary organisations is not quite as high as men's, but the difference is negligible. At the end of the eighties, about 61 per cent of adult men, as against 57 per cent of women, were members of one or more voluntary organisations, excluding trade unions and other labour organisations. As in Sweden and Denmark, Norwegian organisations are extremely segregated sexually. At the end of the eighties women comprised a large majority of the membership of humanitarian and social organisations as well as religious and ethical organisations. On the other hand, men made up a large majority

---

13. These figures are based on information on attendance at meetings and official positions in organisations.

Table 3.1.Institutional participation by sex and age. In per cent.

	Denmark		Norway		Sweden	
	M	W	M	W	M	W
- *Turnout, national elections*						
- *18–44 years old*	91	92	84	87	n.a.	n.a.
- *45–70 years old*	96	94	91	93	n.a.	n.a.
- *Turnout, local elections*						
- *18–44 years old*	84	83	n.a.	n.a.	79	80
- *45–70 years old*	94	89[b]	n.a.	n.a.	94	90
- *Member of political party*						
- *18–44 years old*	9	6[b]	9	10	14	9[a]
- *45–70 years old*	18	7[a]	20	15	23	15[a]
- *Held public office*						
- *18–44 years old*	n.a.	n.a.	9	9	3	4
- *45–70 years old*	n.a.	n.a.	22	13[a]	14	6[a]

Denmark N=1812, Sweden N=1782, Norway N=1622

a: significant at the .01 level
b: significant at the .01 level
n.a.: not available in the surveys on citizenship

of the membership of sports organisations, residents' associations and leisure activity associations (Raaum 1995c; Selle and Øymyr 1995c; Wikborg 1988).

Both Danish and Norwegian studies reveal that the higher educational level among women does not automatically lead to a narrowing of the gender gap in political participation. Education generally increases political activity among both women and men, and the well-educated and employed men are still more active than the women in the same category (Andersen *et al.* 1993; Andersen and Torpe 1994; Raaum 1995b). This may be connected with the difference in the political interests of women and men, an area in which surprisingly large gender-related dissimilarities are still to be found (Siim 1997b). We will return in the next section to this seemingly paradoxical situation, i.e., that gender differences in political activity have narrowed far more than gender differences in political interests. What can account for the fact that women participate more actively than gender differences in political interests would lead us to expect?

All in all there is much to indicate that the greatest reduction in gender differences in political participation around 1990 had occurred in Norway. However, one should not be too categorical about this on the basis of research emanating from each of the countries. Variations between the Nordic countries can be attributed to differing activity profiles among women, but there may also be a connection to differences among the men. To explore this in greater detail we shall now take a closer look at the surveys on citizenship to which we have already referred.

Homogeneous or differing patterns in the Nordic countries?

The Nordic surveys on citizenship carried out in Denmark, Norway, and Sweden – all of which were conducted around 1990[14] – include some identically formulated questions. This gives a more reliable basis from which to compare the countries. Unfortunately, the number of such comparative questions is relatively small, but at least they can serve as a pointer as to whether the participation profiles among women and men are characterised by patterns of homogeneity or disparity. We study how gender differences in political participation vary among older and younger citizens. With regard to gender differences among other social groups, we refer to studies from each of the countries for details. Here, we refer to two generations, the older and the younger, even though we are employing data from a single point in time, and strictly speaking are not in a position to ascertain whether the differences between age-groups reflect generational or life-cycle effects. The elder generation was forty-five years old or older at the time of the citizens surveys, which means that their year of birth was 1945 (1942 in Sweden) or before. The younger generation was under forty-five years old, that is, born in 1946 (1943 in Sweden) or later. It is not easy, of course, to paint a standardized picture of the two generations, but very roughly, we find in the elder generation the traditional division of labour between the two sexes. In this generation, far fewer women acquired an education relative to men, and when children arrived in the family, it was expected that the woman should bear the main responsibility for their care. For women belonging to the younger generation, gaining an education on a par with men has increasingly become the norm, and most such women work full-time while their children are small. What is more, women and men of this generation attained adulthood during a period in which gender equality figured more prominently on the political agenda.

Table 3.1 shows participation related to formal political institutions, participation in elections, party membership and public office.[15]

There is no gender bias in participation in elections in Norway, Sweden, or Denmark. A distinctive feature with regard to Denmark, however, is the weak-

---

14. The Nordic surveys on citizenship were carried out between 1987 and 1990 (Hoff 1995); the Swedish in 1987, and the Danish and Norwegian in 1990. Here we analyse data on persons aged between 18 and 70 years of age at the time of the survey. Thanks are due to Jørgen Goul Andersen who helped prepare the Danish and Swedish data, and to Paal Zanstra Nielsen who performed the statistical analysis. Responsibility for the interpretation of the results is ours.

15. The surveys also include questions about membership and activities in organisations other than political parties. .....(Continued on next page)

Table 3.2. Situational participation by sex and age. In per cent.

	Denmark		Norway		Sweden	
	M	W	M	W	M	W
- Political discussions, family (regularly)						
- 18–44 years old	36	34	27	23		i.t.
- 45–70 years old	32	29	24	23		i.t.
- Political discussions, friends (regularly						
- 18–44 years old	41	29[a]	30	20[a]		i.t.
- 45–70 years old	40	22[a]	25	16[a]		i.t.
- Petitions:						
- 18–44 years old	47	51	37	36	38	51[a]
- 45–70 years old	34	29	28	24	25	33[b]
- Donated money:						
- 18–44 years old	23	25	21	22	38	45[a]
- 45–70 years old	28	20[b]	20	17	37	38
- Meetings and demonstrations:						
- 18–44 years old	21	21	21	23	28	35[a]
- 45–70 years old	17	9[a]	18	15	26	27

Denmark N=1812, Sweden N=1782, Norway N=1622

a: significant at the .01 level
b: significant at the .05 level
n.a.: not available in the surveys on citizenship

ness of women's ties to the political parties: only 6–7 per cent are members of political parties – and this holds true both for the older as well as the younger women. Among women and men in the other two countries, as well as among Danish men, attachment to a party is much more widespread among the elder generation than the younger. This is partly due to life-cycle effects: the young have always been less politically organised than their seniors, but it would not

(Footnote 15, continued from previous page)

Several factors, among them the type of organisations sampled, vary considerably from country to country (for instance, "voluntary organisation" is defined much more widely in the Swedish and Danish surveys than in the Norwegian one). In our opinion, the data set is not very well suited to comparative analyses of participation in organisations. This is particularly the case with respect to economic interest or pressure groups, the non-response rate among men in the Norwegian study being extremely high.

Table 3.3 Affiliation to social movements by sex and age. Degree of affiliati-on measured on a scale from 0 - 10[c]

	Denmark		Norway		Sweden	
	M	W	M	W	M	W
- Labour movement						
- 18–44 years old	4.1	4.4	2.7	2.8	3.3	3.1
- 45–70 years old	4.2	4.0	3.2	3.1	4.7	4.3
- Environmental movement						
- 18–44 years old	5.2	5.9[a]	4.2	5.0[a]	5.1	5.6
- 45–70 years old	4.6	4.9	3.8	4.8[b]	6.1	6.1
- Peace movement						
- 18–44 years old	3.8	4.9[a]	3.0	4.3[a]	5.0	6.0[a]
- 45–70 years old	2.9	3.7[a]	3.3	4.3[a]	5.7	6.6[a]
- Feminist movement						
- 18–44 years old	2.1	3.5[a]	1.1	3.2[a]	2.5	3.9[a]
- 45–70 years old	2.2	2.6[a]	1.8	2.8[a]	4.1	5.0[a]

Denmark N=1812, Sweden N=1782, Norway N=1622

a: significant at the .01 level
b: significant at the .05 level
c: In the original surveys the scale for Denmark was 1–11, 1–10 for Sweden, and 1–4 for Norway. For the present analysis the ranges have been standardised to a 1–10 scale. The effect of this conversion on recorded gender differences in each of the countries is slight but caution should nevertheless be shown when comparing figures across countries – especially with regard to the Norwegian figures, since the original scale deviated quite considerably from those applied for the other countries.

be beyond the realms of possibility to assume that what we are seeing here are traces of generational effects, that is, that the majority of those actually turning their backs on the parties are the younger citizens. The declining support for the political parties, which up to now has been most apparent in Denmark (Togeby 1989; Sundberg 1995), reflects, among other things, the lack of success of Danish parties in attracting women.

Compared with Norway and Sweden, the political mobilisation of Danish women has tended to take place more on the outside of the party system (see Chapter 4). According to the Norwegian survey, there are no significant differences in the support given by men and women to the political parties. In Sweden, as in Denmark, support for the parties at the beginning of the nineties continued to be higher among men than women. The table shows, moreover, that affiliation to political parties among Norwegian and Swedish women, as well as among

Table 3.4 Political interest by sex and age. In per cent

	Denmark		Norway		Sweden	
Very or moderately interested in politics	*M*	*W*	*M*	*W*	*M*	*W*
< 45 years old	70	56[a]	63	57[a]	59	44[a]
45 years and older	68	60[a]	65	53[a]	64	46[a]

Denmark N=1812, Sweden N=1782, Norway N=1622

a: significant at the .01 level

Danish men, was relatively similar around 1990. But while the support of Danish women has languished, Swedish men in particular have set themselves apart with their relatively high level of party support.

With respect to positions of public office, data is available only from Norway and Sweden. In both countries the differences between women and men are only significant for the older generation. This is a reflection of the fact that political mobilisation among younger women has been particularly strong. It is striking, moreover, that a substantially larger proportion of the population in Norway than in Sweden has held office. The explanation may be that the ratio between the number of eligible voters and the elected representatives is far higher in Norway than in Sweden. Calculated on the basis of local community politics (where a very large proportion of the holders of public office are to be found), at the last election there were a little over 260 eligible voters behind each representative in Norway, while the corresponding figure for Sweden was about 480. Relatively speaking, then, there are more public jobs to share among Norwegian citizens, and in addition to this, the high replacement rate of public officers at local elections in Norway contributes to increasing the turnover of elected representatives. In Norway only about one out of every three representatives is re-elected, while in the other Nordic countries as many as two out of three are returned to office for a new period (Larsen and Offerdal 1994).

With regard to situational types of activity, the gender differences are smaller, as expected (table 3.2). But even concerning an activity as undemanding as political discussions, it turns out that men more often than their female counterparts discuss political matters with their friends. The intergenerational differences are minimal, but in both Denmark and Norway there is a slight tendency for the younger to participate in such discussions more frequently than members of the elder generation. The Swedish survey on citizenship does not contain any information on participation in political discussions, but the living conditions survey of 1994 shows that, in Sweden as well, the tendency is for men, especially those belonging to the older generation, to discuss political affairs more often than women do (Levnadsförhållanden 1996:189). Otherwise it appears that the Danes, and especially Danish men, discuss politics more often than the Norwegians seem to do. Danish women have family discussions more frequently than

Norwegian men do; and among friends, Danish women and Norwegian men appear to be more or less equally active.

When it comes to activist-type participation, we find both differences and similarities between the countries. An acknowledged tendency is for younger pårticipants, with few exceptions, to be more active than their older counterparts. This propensity is particularly evident among women. However, the gender differences do vary from country to country. In Denmark there are still differences between women and men of the older generation. We must remember though that we are only considering a small sample of activities here, and that no differences have been registered between Danish women and men when their participation has been measured on the basis of a number of indicators (Andersen *et al.* 1993: 41:135). In Norway there are no discernible differences in the levels of activity between men and women. For all that, Norwegian women are no more active than Danish and Swedish women, rather the contrary, but Norwegian men are generally less active than men in Denmark and Sweden. Sweden stands out from Norway and Denmark, and not only because Swedish women are much more involved than Swedish men in activist-type participation. Swedish women, young and old, are generally also more active than both women and men in the other countries.

The Swedish government research project on "Democracy and Power" stresses that characterising the involvement of citizens simply on the basis of outwardly visible activities is insufficient. Observable participation on its own undervalues that aspect of people's political engagement which finds expression through psychological means, for instance through an interest in political concerns in general and a sense of affiliation to political movements. Organisations and movements are supposed to protect and promote interests, but they also have an ideological implication. This applies in particular to movements based on an ideal, i.e., the popular movements, whose goal, more or less clearly iterated, is to change society. They function as "opinion formers. They create a system of co-ordinates of sorts, or social signposts. For the general public, not necessarily just for their own members, the organisations become symbols of ideology and struggle" (SOU 1990: 44:74).

Swedish data on the membership of organisations is very different from data showing the sense of belonging to more informal movements among the population. Organisations whose membership is small – such as the peace movement, the environmental movement, the feminist movement – find echoed in the population at large a strong "sense of solidarity". As we can see from Table 3.3 the same phenomenon is apparent in Norway and Denmark. Women have in general a stronger sense of solidarity with the new political movements than do men, and with regard to the old labour movement, there are – perhaps equally surprising – no significant gender differences.

In addition to the feminist movement, which naturally appeals more strongly to women than to men, there is a particularly distinct difference in the support granted to the peace movement by women and men. In all three countries, both the younger and the older women have a stronger commitment than men. In the green movement the differences related to gender are smaller, but younger as well as older Norwegian women, and younger women in Denmark, seem to feel a stronger sense of solidarity than equivalent groupings among men.

In spite of a considerable narrowing of the gap with regard to the level of activity of women and men respectively, and women's strong sense of commitment to the social movements, there are still marked differences in political interest between women and men in the Nordic countries. Political interest is often measured in surveys by means of a generalised question such as: "How interested would you say you are in politics: a lot, a little, hardly at all, or not at all?" Table 3.4 shows that, for the most part, women express less interest in politics than men. It would be natural to assume that this tendency would be more strongly represented among the older than the younger respondents, but we find no definite pattern to corroborate this. In Denmark, Norway and Sweden alike, women – irrespective of age – manifest less interest than men. The difference is especially noticeable in Sweden where less than half of the women state that they are very or only slightly interested in politics. In Norway and Denmark, about 55–60 per cent of the women say that they share an interest in politics. The countries part ways, however, when the interest factor is viewed together with age. In Norway, the gender difference is smaller among the younger than it is among the elder generation. In Sweden, a comparable pattern is less discernible, and in Denmark the greatest difference is that found between women and men under the age of forty-five.

It seems paradoxical that women participate nearly as much as men at the grass roots level in politics, but state, nonetheless, that they are less interested in politics. Especially among Swedish women there is a strikingly large gap between levels of activity and stated interest. This must be viewed in light of the men's continued dominance of the public arena. Political parties and public bodies still consist mostly of men: most government and especially private-sector executives are men; it is men who figure most often in the newspapers, etc. If a general question regarding political interest sparks associations in the direction of this state of affairs, it is not at all to be wondered at that men express a greater interest than women. The reasons could just as well be substantive as methodological. Perhaps women in general identify less with the political establishment, but it is also conceivable that gender-stereotypical norms – especially in abstract questions such as the one on interest in politics – exert an influence on the responses given by men and women.

Gender differences in political interest may also indicate that women and men react differently to questions relating to politics. We know that women are more reserved than men and more frequently give a "don't know" response to scaled questions. Studies of political knowledge have also revealed that more women than men respond with a "don't know". Men most often give correct answers to questions concerning politics, especially matter-of-fact questions about names and numbers, but they also make up the majority of those who give the wrong answer. Men seem more confident than women; they would rather take the chance (or risk) of giving a response (right or wrong), than declaring that they don't know. That could mean that men have a tendency to over-report while women are more restrained and possibly under-report. If that is the case, then many men may be giving an impression of being more interested than they in fact are, while a number of women estimate their own interest too lowly. Last, but not least, the gender differences in political interest may mirror a difference in the political concerns which stimulate the interest of women and men, a matter which is not easy to pick up by means of a question on general political interests (Oskarson and Wängnerud 1995; Strømsnes 1995; Siim 1997b). In the next section we shall look at the ways in which women and men relate to political content. Do the differences in the political involvement of the sexes leave a mark in the form of varying political opinions and party preferences?

New participants, new values?

The traditional differences found in women and men's political involvement did not just concern the lower level of political activity found in women. Women's opinions and party preferences have also stood out from those of men. They were more pacifist-oriented, but also more moralistic in the sense that they expressed a lower political tolerance than men. Women and men have also identified themselves with different parties: women have been more inclined to vote for non-socialist parties. The gender differences have rarely been extreme, and psephologists (election experts) stress that the attitudes of the two sexes and their party preferences are mostly characterised by similarities rather than differences (see for example Bratterud 1994; Aardal and Valen 1994; Bjørklund 1986; Goul Andersen 1984; Oskarson and Wängnerud 1995; Listhaug et al. 1995; Togeby 1994a).

However, there are some important differences between women and men in a number of areas both with regard to political opinions and party preferences. Election studies show as a rule that gender only indirectly impacts on the political priorities of the voters, that is, it is other factors such as social background and party identification which are the cause of differences in opinion in political matters between men and women. Gender differences are "controlled out", so to speak, as if no systematic correlations existed between gender, social background, and political preferences. Oskarson and Wängnerud challenge this perception using data obtained from Swedish election studies. Many political areas are given an equally high priority by women and men, but in all surveys since 1982 there is a greater proportion of women who state that family policy, together with social and health care policy, are for them the issues of greatest importance in determining their choice of party. On the other hand, the economy and taxation issues are the areas most frequently reported by men. The interesting point is that this relationship not only shows that the party preferences of women and men differ, because the gender differences are replicated among voters in all the political parties (Oskarson and Wängnerud 1995:68).

A corresponding pattern has also been documented among Norwegian political party members. Within all parties, apart from the small Socialist Left Party, women largely give higher priority to public welfare issues and the empowerment of local communities than their male counterparts, who are more interested in economic issues (Heidar and Raaum 1995). Skjeie stresses likewise that fresh issues have emerged on the parties' agendas in parallel with the integration of female members of parliament, and she documents that male as well as female parliamentarians in Norway confirm that the mobilisation of women *vis-à-vis* the political parties has contributed to a change in the parties' programmes on issues such as disarmament, the environment, gender equality, and welfare and family policies (Skjeie 1993). Similar differences have been found among Norwegian voters. Bratterud (1994) points out that gender differences in general are relatively moderate, but she also shows that women, irrespective of party preference, are more supportive of the welfare state than are men. More women than men prioritise health and care of the elderly, housing benefit and social security, and especially among the younger voters there are far more women than men who oppose the privatisation of public enterprises.

Danish studies also show that women belonging to more exclusive groups such as high-ranking white-collar workers and civil servants are more left-leaning than men. Considering the population as a whole, the differences are not dramatic, but they are pervasive. Especially among the well-educated section of the population, Danish women are more in favour of retaining social reforms and public welfare. In one of the most profound political controversies in the Nordic countries in recent decades – the question of membership of the European Union – the gender differences are very clear indeed. Women in Denmark as well as in Sweden and Norway have been more wary of EU membership than have men. Opposition is particularly strong among women working in the public sector, but sector affiliation can not explain all of the gender difference since the same differences are evident in the private sector too. Many women justify their "No" standpoint by pointing to the negative repercussions of membership on gender equality, welfare policy, and regional and agricultural policy (Goul Andersen 1984; Borre and Goul Andersen 1997; Jenssen and Bratterud 1997; Oskarson 1996; Siim 1997b; Jenssen, Pesonen and Gilljam 1998).

Perceptions of political issues figure among the factors determining the voters' party preferences. In a comparative study of Nordic general elections around 1990, Oskarson found that the differences in the party preferences of men and women in the population as a whole were insignificant, but that there were more marked gender differences among younger than older voters. In Norway, Denmark, and, to a certain extent, Sweden, among younger voters (under forty-five years of age) there were slightly more women who voted for socialist parties. Among older voters, on the other hand, there were relatively fewer men who voted for a socialist party. In Finland, however, the gender relations were reversed: the left-wing parties won more votes from men than women. Overall, Oskarson concludes that

> From this analysis it is hardly possible to conclude that there is a general gender
> gap in voting behavior in the Nordic countries – the gender differences are quite

modest and also do not follow the same pattern in the five countries. (Oskarson 1995: 79)

Oskarson has only analysed data from one election, around 1990. For our purpose, which is to shed light on changes in women's political preferences, developments need to be studied diachronically, i.e. over a substantial period of time. In a multi-party system as operates in the Nordic lands, the picture we gain simply from studying differences between the socialist and the non-socialist bloc is not particularly detailed. We lose information on individual parties within each of the blocs. The varying size of the parties, measured in number of votes, means that analysing differences between the percentages of women and men voting for the various parties is far from adequate. A difference of 4 percentage points may be considered to be small for a party enjoying wide support, but the same span will comprise a considerable gap for a party with less relative backing (Listhaug et al. 1995). To illustrate this let us look at a party whose share of the votes amounts to 4 per cent of the male vote and 8 per cent of the female vote. The difference in percentage points is quite small, just 4, but the ratio between women and men is 2:1 (8/4), which means that the party has twice as many female as male voters. If we analyse the differences in female and male party preferences, then the figures in brackets showing the support for the parties in percentage points by the two sexes need to be supplemented with ratios showing the distribution between female and male voters.

In Norway, the support for the socialist parties at the beginning of the 1950s was about 8 percentage points higher among men than among women (Bjørklund 1986). During the fifties and sixties the gap narrowed to about 5 percentage points; in the seventies and eighties there were no perceptible gender differences; but starting with the election in 1985 women have voted for socialist parties more frequently than men (Listhaug et al. 1995). The difference between the sexes has been quite small in many of the individual elections, but viewed in the long term, the changes become quite significant. Moreover, as we penetrate beyond the rough and ready division into blocs, we discover several more interesting dissimilarities.

The traditional predominance of women on the non-socialist side of the Norwegian political landscape is primarily due to the support women have lent to the Christian Democratic Party. This party has generally enjoyed twice as much support among women as among men. The former predominance of women on the non-socialist side is not therefore due to women's support for the values of a liberal market economy, but because they have been more religiously minded than men. The growing proportion of women on the socialist side after 1980 is especially due to the success of the Socialist Left Party in attracting female voters. In 1965 the party had only half as many women as men among its voters, but during the eighties it gained a large predominance of women voters. At the same time as women have moved leftwards, men have moved rightwards. The right-wing Conservative Party has, with the exception of two elections (1973 and 1989), found far more support among men than women, and particularly from the seventies, the preponderance of male voters has been palpable. The Progress Party, on the extreme right, which contested an election for the first time in 1973, has at all subsequent elections found nearly twice as much support among men, and especially younger men, as it has among women (Listhaug *et al.* 1995). The widening gender gap is thus the result of a swing to the left by women which has been taking place simultaneously as a swing to the right by men.

Until 1979 men in Sweden were in the majority among socialist voters, though the margin was small, and women comprised a small majority on the non-socialist side. Since then the relationship has been reversed, but only in two elections, those of 1985 and 1988, in which a considerable preponderance of women could be found among the socialist bloc voters. The 1994 election revealed gender differences that had little to do with the traditional blocs: both the socialist and the non-socialist blocs had a majority of male voters, but the Christian Democratic Party and the Green Party – which are difficult to fit into any of the blocs – had a clear majority of women (Oskarson and Wängnerud 1995:76 ff.). In Sweden as well the party preferences of the two sexes vary with age. Among the youngest voters (under twenty-five years of age), both the left-wing socialist Left Party and the Green Party enjoy twice as much support among women as among men, while among the voters of the Conservative Party there were three times as many young men as young women. A corresponding tendency, but weaker, is apparent among voters under forty-five years of age. There exists, then, a gender gap in Sweden in the sense that "women do not vote for the conservative side to the same extent as men, and that younger women are more inclined to vote to the left than the younger men" (Oskarson and Wängnerud 1995: 79).

In Denmark it was difficult to discern any particular trend in the balance between female and male voters in the socialist bloc up until the 1981 election. At all elections subsequent to 1980 the parties making up the socialist bloc have enjoyed greater support from women than men, fluctuating between 3 and 6 per cent. As in Norway and Sweden, the differences are most conspicuous among younger voters. On the other hand, Danish men, especially of the younger generations, have rallied in greater numbers behind the right-wing liberal and conservative parties (Borre and Goul Andersen 1997:186 ff.). Borre and Goul Andersen show in addition that the changes reflect generational effects. The gender gap in Danish politics widened from 1971 to 1994 not only because fresh generations of voters arrived on the scene. The swing to the right among men and the move towards the left among women are equally responsible.

In Denmark too the gender differences with regard to party preferences are particularly evident among the parties at either extreme of the political spectrum. Developments in the Socialist People's Party have replicated those of the Norwegian Socialist Left Party: in 1964 57 per cent of the party's voters were men; by 1994 almost two-thirds were women. The two small parties, the Christian People's Party and the middle-of-the-road party, the Centre Democrats, also have a clear female bias. Among the other non-socialist parties, the Conservative Party had a female majority in 1964, but a male majority in 1994. The Progress

Party, on the extreme right wing, has enjoyed a constant male majority since its foundation in 1972; in 1994 as many as two-thirds of its voters were men (Borre and Goul Andersen 1997:183).

It would not be correct to say that there is a marked gender gap in Nordic politics, but the differences are greater than we are often led to believe. Over the years a significant change has come about, and the tendency has persisted in Denmark, Norway and Sweden: women have shifted towards the left, men to the right. This polarisation is currently especially noticeable among the younger voters. In future studies one of the challenges will be to illuminate what it is that draws so many young women and men to the extremes of the left–right axis, and it will be particularly interesting to see whether we are witnessing a strengthening and permanent polarisation of the younger generation of women and men, or whether this present polarisation is a reflection of temporary and transient factors.

Conclusion

A feature common to all the Nordic countries is that clear differences can still be found between men and women as regards political activity. This applies particularly to types of activities which are linked to institutions, but also in this area the gender differences are much smaller than they once were. Significant differences are only detectable among citizens born prior to 1945. The gender differences vary in magnitude from country to country, but this is not just a consequence of variations in levels of activity amongst women. The activity levels of men vary from land to land as well. Norwegian men are distinguished by a relatively high level of participation in elections and as holders of public office. Swedish men have thus far been most active in party politics, but, like Danish men, they turn more often than Norwegian men to activist forms of participation. And with regard to the women, Norwegian women are also most active in elections and in public offices. What is more, Norwegian women – and Swedish women too – tend to support the political parties much more than women in Denmark. In situational activities, on the other hand, Norwegian women (and Norwegian men) are less active than their Danish and Swedish counterparts. Swedish women reap the highest score – among women and men in the Nordic countries – with regard to participation in petitions, demonstrations and fund-raising campaigns.

There is a gender gap in Nordic politics: reviewing the changes that have taken place over the years, it is apparent that a shift to the left has occurred among women together with a shift to the right among men. These changes are not immense, but in a few areas they are nonetheless quite noticeable. They apply to opinions on concrete political issues, such as welfare policy and the EU, and they also apply to party preferences. The differences in the party preferences of the two sexes are easier to discern when we look beyond the bipartite division into socialist and non-socialist blocs. In many of the smaller parties the gender gap is pronounced; the gender distribution of the parties' voters is extremely biased.

There is a great deal to indicate that the mobilisation of women has occurred in response to particular political issues. At all political levels – among voters, party members and representatives – women give a higher priority to public welfare than men. If we are to be able to say anything more with any degree of certainty about gender differences in political values and opinions, and thus about the consequences of the political presence of women, then we need above all studies which shed light on developments over time. The absence of gender differences at one point in time, between women and men whose sympathies lie with the same parties – or other types of organisations or movements – does not necessarily imply that women are adopting the same opinions as men; it could just as well imply that men are moving in the direction of the women.

4

Women in the political parties

Ann-Dorte Christensen

The political parties have played a critical role in the modern Nordic democracies. As a link between electors and elected they have formed one of the cornerstones of the system of parliamentary representation. Political parties in the Nordic countries have generally been mass parties that have enjoyed both wide public support and a footing in various parts of the population. The parties have thus helped promote equality as well as – particularly through the social democratic parties – the institutionalisation of the egalitarian ideal that we have witnessed in the welfare state. Since the sixties, however, political parties have undergone sweeping changes – changes which are intimately connected with other changes in the political arena such as, for example, the emergence of the new social movements, and which therefore have great implications for the future of democracy. There is little doubt that one of the most important developments in relation to the political parties has been the manifest decline in membership and the deteriorating level of activity. The parties have thereby lost their role as mass parties with a relatively stable underpinning in their electorate.

As we shall see in this section, declining membership is characteristic not only of the Nordic countries but of western Europe as a whole. Nonetheless, the situation in Denmark is seen as unique in this respect because membership in political parties dropped in the space of a couple of decades from a place at the top of the league (together with Sweden) to a relatively low level (Bille 1995). But in a recent comparative study on citizenship in Scandinavia, Jørgen Goul Andersen and Jens Hoff contest the notion that the weakening of the Nordic political parties is limited to Denmark. On the contrary, they say, Denmark has merely functioned as a "model country" in so far as the weakening of the political parties started earlier here and developed more rapidly than in the other Nordic countries (Goul Andersen and Hoff 1998).

Recent analyses of the political parties have chosen to highlight different aspects of the changes affecting the parties. When the participatory aspect is emphasised the ensuing discussion centres on the dissolution of (old) bonds and associations and of the organisational structure enabling democratic dialogue based on common interests and an overall perspective (Andersen *et al.* 1993). Other researchers focus on the opposite trends and the need for differentiated analyses of the parties. For instance, Strøm and Svåsand (1997) argue on the basis of Norwegian developments that even though the parties have suffered a decline in membership, they are coping better than ever as regards resources, professionalisation, and flexibility in their handling of fresh issues (gender equality, the environment, etc.). These trends, which are evident in other areas of society, too, are also noted by Lars Bille in his book about changes in the Danish political parties, in which he contends that it is not the parties as such, but a particular type of party that is undergoing change – namely the mass party. Both Bille, on the one hand, and Strøm and Svåsand on the other, maintain that the position of political parties in civil society (the partyness of society) has weakened, but that their capacity to control and carry out executive functions at the level of government has strengthened (the partyness of gòvernment) (Bille 1997:236; Strøm and Svåsand 1997:355).

Political parties and the mobilisation of women

The aim of this chapter is to address the connections between developments within the political parties and the mobilisation of women. We know that there are large disparities both between countries and between parties with regard to the extent to which women and the gender issue have been taken on board by the political parties. But what we know too little about is how these differences have interlocked with the specific form taken by women's mobilisation in the individual Nordic countries. For there is no doubt that, even though the parties were dominated by men until about the seventies, they have also represented central arenas for the mobilisation of women. A concurrent trend is also suggested in which central components of this process of mobilisation have taken place outside of the political parties. On the one hand, there is little doubt that the political parties have represented focal points for women to attain full citizenship and political equality. On the other hand, we are also dealing – at least in some of the Nordic countries – with political organisations which both historically and contemporarily have demonstrated considerable ambivalence *vis-à-vis* the integration of women and the issue of gender equality in political parties.

There is a limited amount of research on gender in the political parties. *Classical party theory* has largely ignored the gender aspect with research efforts concentrating instead on the formulation of class interests and class affiliations. The same could be said in general of the recent and contemporary analyses of political parties which, for example, pinpoint the dissolution of class affiliation as the reason behind the parties' decline. How such tendencies relate to the mobilisation of women (which itself is closely linked to the mobilisation of the well-educated, middle strata of society) has rarely been addressed. Interest in the political parties on the part of women's and gender studies has been slim. Even though the parties have been invoked as underlying factors in relation to, among other things, analyses of the development in women's representation, the prime focus of women's and gender studies has rarely been the political parties themselves, but rather women's mobilisation in the social movements.

In two early joint Nordic book projects on gender and politics in the Nordic countries, the parties are, however, brought into the picture as well. In *Det uferdige demokrati* (*Unfinished Democracy*) (Haavio-Mannila *et al.* 1985) the Nordic countries' historical development is addressed with an eye to the role it has played in the development of independent women's organisations within the political parties, among other things. The main focus, though, is on women's lack of power, also within the parties. One of the book's conclusions is that the iron law of power also prevailed in the political parties since there was still (at that point in time) a noticeable absence of women in the party organisations and of female nominees in the election of representatives (Haavio-Mannila *et al.* 1983).

In *Women in Nordic Politics – Closing the Gap* (Karvonen and Selle 1995), Jan Sundberg addresses the issue of women and the political parties. The crux of his argument is that gender has always played a significant role in the political parties in the Nordic countries, from the suffrage movements down to the present day. Sundberg holds that women in the Nordic countries really started to become integrated into the political parties from the seventies, which is evident in the growing number of female members as well as their enhanced opportunity to exert influence within the democratic party organisation. It is praiseworthy of Sundberg to highlight the strengths and advantages that women's mobilisation has brought to the political parties both in a historical and a contemporary perspective, and he is correct in saying that the mobilisation of women in the seventies and eighties also made headway within the political parties. But in his attempt to reveal women's strength in the parties, Jan Sundberg commits the error of overstating women's power and, in particular, of exaggerating the similarities between developments in the countries. Finally, a general weakness running through Sundberg's analysis is that he fails to compare the development of women's (growing) share of party membership with the parallel decline in party membership overall.

There is a great need for comparative studies of the relationship between gender and the political parties in the Nordic region, both in historical and in contemporary terms. There is no space here for any such comprehensive analysis, merely a limited contribution which concentrates on the following three points:

(1) The relationship between developments in party membership and the integration of women. We compare Sundberg's thesis on women's integration with the declining membership of the political parties. In light of this we discuss the thesis on women's integration in shrinking institutions.

(2) On the basis of the issue of *women's organisation* in the parties, we address the degree to which the parties, historically speaking, have had strategies to integrate women.

(3) Using *gender quotas* as an example we ask whether the parties of today have developed integration strategies for women.

Against the background of these three areas, we conclude by putting into perspective the differences and similarities between the countries in relation to the development of classical and modern strategies to integrate women.[16]

Developments in party membership

Jan Sundberg contends that the traditional gender differences in the political parties have been underrated over the past 25–30 years – first at the level of the ordinary member and then at the level of the leadership. By comparing survey data from Denmark, Finland, Norway and Sweden, he is able to show that the pro-

Table 4.1. Membership of political parties in the Nordic countries

Country	Percentage of those eligible to vote		
Denmark	1960	1979	1992
	22	8	6
Finland	1962	1979	1992
	19	15	12
Norway	1961	1979	1993
	16	15	11[a]
Sweden	1960	1979	1992
	22	24	9

a: The figure for membership of political parties in Norway for the year 1993 is probably slightly overestimated since only people over 25 years of age were included.

Source: Goul Andersen and Hoff 1998; Listhaug 1998.

16. The main focus of the analysis is on Norway, Sweden, Finland, and Denmark. Iceland is only touched on incidentally, primarily in connection with the discussion on gender quotas. The reason for this is not only because Iceland, unfortunately, has not figured in the comparative Nordic studies but also because the relationship between gender, political party, and social movement in Iceland – which come together in the Women's Alliance – has its own particular significance which will be analysed in Chapter 5. The term *integration strategy* originates in Heidar and Raaum (1995). The term is applied here to strategies whose aim has been to promote the integration of women into the political parties as manifested by the parties' women's sections (the classic strategies of women's integration) and through regulations on positive discrimination (the modern strategy of women's integration).

Table 4.2. Membership of political parties and reasons for not joining a party in Denmark and Norway. In per cent

Membership of political parties	Denmark		Norway	
	Men	Women	Men	Women
All	13	6[b]	13	12
18-44 years old	9	6[a]	9	10
45-70 years old	18	7[b]	20	15
Reason given for not joining a party				
1. No spare time				
- < 45 years old	58	58	64	55[b]
- 45 years old and older	34	34	58	45[b]
2. Uninteresting and boring				
- < 45 years old	43	36[b]	32	40[a]
- 45 years old and older	38	34[a]	34	40
3. Members do not wield enough influence				
- < 45 years old	36	31[b]	50	44[a]
- 45 years old and older	37	31[b]	53	48
4. Prefer to take a stand on an issue-to-issue basis				
- < 45 years old	67	59[b]	79	76
- 45 years old and older	60	55	76	72
5. My interests are better served by other organisations				
- < 45 years old	27	22[b]	27	22[b]
- 45 years old and older	25	19[b]	25	19[b]

a: significant at the 0.1 level
b: significant at the 0.5 level

Source: Danish and Norwegian citizenship surveys

portion of women members of the political parties in the sample has shifted from about 35 per cent on average at the start of the seventies, to a level almost equal to that of men at the end of the 1980s in Denmark and Norway, while remaining at around a third in the Finnish and Swedish parties (Sundberg 1995:93 ff.).

These figures, as Sundberg is at pains to point out, are far from totally reliable. For instance, the figures for the 1990s both from the Danish and the Swedish surveys indicate that the political parties are precisely one of those (gradually diminishing) forms of participation which may be spoken of as "male-dominated". The explanation in both of the surveys is that significant aspects of women's mobilisation have occurred outside the political parties (Andersen *et al.* 1993, Petersson *et al.* 1989). As Sundberg indicates *with regard to Norway in particular*, it is in that country where one could say that an equal balance in the distribution of men and women in party membership is on the way to becoming an established fact.

However, the integration of women in the parties should not be judged only on the basis of percentage changes in the gender distribution of the members. Such changes must also be viewed in connection with the fundamental changes that have affected the party organisations throughout the post-war period, of which the most apparent factor in the Nordic countries is the declining party membership. One may well ask what difference it makes if women happen to account for about half the membership in a party if there are hardly any members left to count anyway?

Table 4.1 shows the steep drop in membership of the political parties seen more or less across the board in the Nordic countries. At the beginning of the sixties about 20 per cent of the Nordic population were members of a political party, while early in the nineties the figure had fallen to about 10 per cent. While this process has taken hold with varying degrees of swiftness in the separate countries, the overall trend is nevertheless the same everywhere. The membership crisis began in Denmark as early as at the end of the sixties, and it is here that it appears to be most acute. In Sweden and Norway it was not until the end of the eighties that the crisis became apparent; in Sweden there is a close link between the decline and the gradual phasing out of the practice of collective union membership in the Social Democratic Party (Goul Andersen and Hoff 1998). Strøm and Svåsand (1997) stress that the fall in membership in Norway came very late in the day compared to the other countries, but that no parties are unscathed. Nonetheless, Norway and Finland still have the most members in their party organisations. The Nordic surveys give us the opportunity to include the gender aspect and, in the case of Norway and Denmark, analyse reasons respondents have given for not being a member of a political party.

As mentioned in the previous chapter, the surveys reveal that most *party members* belong to the age-group consisting of people over forty-five years old. The surveys also show that men are more likely to be members of a party than are women, and more so in Denmark than in Norway. On the other hand, Danish and Norwegian men are party members in more or less equal measures. Among women of the older generation, (forty-five years and older), there are twice as many members in Norway as in Denmark, relatively speaking (15 and 7 per cent respectively). And as far as the young women are concerned there are far more of them in Norway who are party members than in Denmark (15 and 7 per cent respectively).

Turning to the *reasons people give for not being a member of a political party*, the most frequent relate to insufficient time and especially the wish to make up one's mind on an issue-to-issue basis (Table 4.2). However, there does not seem to be any correlation between not being a member and the reasons given for avoiding membership. On the contrary. In fact, it is the group boasting the largest proportion of members – Norwegian men over forty-five – which is most likely to formulate reasons in support of non-membership, while the justifications proffered by Danish women – who are also the least active – are the most vague. Thus these responses cannot tell us why, for example, the mobilisation of Danish women has apparently progressed beyond the confines of the political parties. Both Danish men and Norwegian men and women, for instance, score more than Danish women on the two exit questions, this is, on the choice of alternatives to party membership (4 and 5). In this context it is striking that over 70 per cent of the Norwegian respondents so clearly formulate a desire to consider issues on an individual basis as their justification for non-membership.

For these reasons, then, the table is not a reliable basis on which to analyse women's critique of the political parties or their search for alternative ways to participate. Instead it looks as if the norm stating that one "should" belong to a party also entails a greater degree of reflection over why one in fact is not.

If we return to the general fall-off in party membership and link this phenomenon to Sundberg's contention that the integration of women into the parties did not occur until the seventies and eighties, then the question concerning whether women have been integrated into shrinking institutions cannot be avoided.[17]

Rather than attempting to verify this thesis, in what follows we will argue that the inter-country differences in this area can contribute to its refutation.

The thesis on women's integration into shrinking institutions was originally formulated by Harriet Holter in 1976. According to the argument, as women attain positions of power in society, then they often do so within shrinking institutions, i.e., institutions that are in the process becoming less and less important. Holter's not only includes the political institutions in her argument, but also a number of other areas of society. She mentions, for instance, the egalitarian but functionally empty family, and the opportunity women now enjoy to become ordained as ministers of the Church in an age in which the powers of the Church have declined considerably. In extension of this, Holter believes that a development has taken place from limited but real rights for women – to equal but empty rights (Holter 1981). The thesis of women's integration into shrinking institutions has sparked off a great deal of debate in the Nordic countries, and many have responded critically to it (see, for example, Bergqvist 1994; Raaum 1995a; Skjeie 1992; Christensen 1997; Karvonen and Selle 1995). The chief objections have been that the thesis is based on the structural approach of patriarchy theories which obstruct a more dynamic and actor-oriented view of, for instance, the

---

17. The term *shrinking institution* is much too rough and ready. Despite the fact that membership of the parties has declined considerably, we are not in a position to say that the parties are in the process of "shrinking" in all areas. As we mentioned above, several researchers have noted that a strengthening of the parties' executive and control possibilities at government level has indeed taken place. So when we discuss the theory of the shrinking institutions here, it is because of the impact it has had in the Nordic countries and because the interpretation is not inappropriate given Sundberg's line of argument

mobilisation of women. For this reason it perpetuates a pessimistic view of women's ability to gain power and wield influence in society.

In 1996 Harriet Holter returned to the debate on women's empowerment and shrinking institutions twenty years after she had started it. She still supported her basic premise, but added that it should not be understood as a universal explanation, rather as one of the "relatively invisible cornerstones of male power". At the same time she raised the question of whether the theory today could have become "a sort of standard version of the way in which democracies achieve the semi-integration of partially undesired groups, such as immigrants for example" (Holter 1996:34). As far as we are concerned, the problem is not so much the object of inquiry (women and immigrants) or new considerations regarding the location of real power, but rather the determinism that Holter continued to ascribe to institutions and which appeared to deny any role to individual and collective actors.

If we return to women's relations to the political parties and explore the correlation between the development of the parties' membership in general and the female proportion of the membership in the Nordic countries, it is difficult to find a connection between the parties' "signs of weakness" and the rising proportion of women members. On the contrary, it is in Denmark and Sweden that the decline in membership rates has been most apparent. In the case of Sweden the proportion of women in the parties has not really changed, fluctuating between 33–37 per cent between 1964–1988 (Sundberg 1995:94). In Denmark, where the decline in membership has been greatest and where it started first, there is nothing to indicate that women have been integrated into shrinking parties; it is rather the case that women have consciously rejected the political parties and chosen alternative forms of participation. As we shall see in Chapter 6, the mobilisation of women in Denmark has been oriented precisely towards the grass-roots movements (Togeby 1992; Andersen *et al.* 1993). In Finland, women's share of party membership has remained more or less constant throughout the whole of the period. It is primarily in relation to Norway that it is feasible to speak of a growing female membership, but it is also here that the decline in overall party membership started last and has been less extensive than in Denmark and Sweden.

There is nothing to indicate then that women have been integrated into shrinking institutions; but there has been some sort of interplay between the mobilisation of women on the one hand and the changes in the gender profile of the political parties on the other. In other words, Norwegian women have helped to strengthen the political parties – or at least have helped to reduce the extent and possibly even delay the onset of the crisis. Nor is there any evidence to indicate that women have been integrated into shrinking party organisations either – that a place has been "carved out" for women at the same time as the parties' influence has drained away. What does seem to be the case is rather that women can be – and, especially in Norway, were – involved in strengthening and influencing the parties. As we have seen, the differences in the party membership of Danish and Norwegian men are not that large, while it is quite apparent that Danish women have chosen to turn their backs on the parties, a phenomenon which in all likelihood has contributed to the decline of the parties at such an early date in the wider Nordic context. This bears out the assumption that the choices made by women in connection with processes of mobilisation are interconnected with the developments in the political institutions.

Women's organisations in the political parties

One significant feature of the political history of the Nordic countries is that we are dealing with highly organised societies. This has been evident in the many and diverse ways in which women have come together and organised themselves down through the ages – creating organisations in relation to the political system, to the labour market, and society at large. In a number of areas, women followed similar paths in setting up their organisations in the Nordic lands; but there are, nonetheless, some significant differences.[18]

The fact that all of the Nordic countries have hosted *national councils* which have functioned as umbrella organisations for a wide range of women's organisations gives a measure of the scope of these organisations which extend from housewives' associations and women's liberation groups to women's sections in professional and political organisations. Apart from in Iceland, the national councils of the Nordic countries were founded around the turn of the century, and their main purpose has been to influence public authorities by representing "women" across the range of organisations dedicated to women's interests. There has been a blend of equal value and equal status feminism. Where the Norwegian national council has been strongly oriented towards the achievement of equal value, the Danish has been more concerned with the fight for equal status. Generally speaking, the impact of the national councils has been most profound in Denmark and Iceland, less so in Finland and Norway, due, among other things, to the fact that the Social Democrats and the left-wing parties have not played a role here, i.e., the organisations have had more of a non-socialist character. The Swedish national council was dissolved in 1981. The connections to the women's liberation groups and to the women's liberation movement have also varied among the countries. For example, the Danish, the Norwegian, and the Finnish women's liberation associations withdrew their membership of the national councils during the 1980s. And the new women's movements have vot-

---

18. In *Unfinished Democracy* a distinction is drawn between, on the one hand, the organising of women based on the classic woman's role (housewives' associations, for example) and, on the other, feminist organisations whose aim has been to combat male dominance (Haavio-Mannila *et al.* 1985). From the vantage point of the nineties this categorisation no longer fits the bill. Firstly it is based on a complementary division of labour between the sexes, which, not least in the Nordic countries, has been subject to considerable modifications. Secondly, it is problematic to limit the discussion purely to the organising of women and feminism in an age also known for the organising of men, for example men's movements, fatherhood associations, and men's studies. Compare in addition the growing interest in male equality which we review in Part III.

ed down membership of the national councils. In Finland, NYTKIS (*Kvinnoorganisationernas samarbetsorgan* – The Coalition of Finnish Women's Associations for Joint Action), which was established in 1988, is generally considered to be the most important women's organisation of a political nature. At present its membership numbers 600,000 and it has thirteen member organisations. Besides the national council this amounts to all of the political women's associations, the women's studies' associations, as well as the new women's movement (www.nytkis.org).

As far as trade union activity is concerned, it is worth mentioning that Denmark and Iceland are the only places in world with women-only trade unions. The Women Workers' Union in Denmark (*Kvindelige Arbejderforbund* – KAD) has been in existence since 1885. The union represents unskilled female workers and its present membership is about 90,000 members (Jørgensen *et al.* 1992:28). In Iceland there are now three trade unions for women with a membership in the range of about 5,300 members. These unions do not pool their efforts in a separate federation of women's unions; instead they have chosen to work within the framework of ASI (the Icelandic confederation of trade unions). The most likely future outcome is that the specialised women's unions will eventually merge with ASI. Several of the women's unions have begun to accept male members, and according to Rafnsdóttir (1995), what characterises these unions at present is their lack of a pro-active policy.

There is also a well-established tradition of separate women's sections within the political parties – though the variations between countries are large. Most of these women's sections originated at the same time as women became enfranchised. Considered from a narrow party point of view, the purpose of the women's sections was to recruit new members and inspire voters; the idea was that women should be persuaded to vote for a particular party and thereafter be enrolled as members. Considered from the point of view of feminist politics, the independent women's organisations in the parties have functioned as a framework for sisterhood and a forum for the formulation of women's concerns. The degree of autonomy and influence has varied considerably – from women's sections which throughout the greater part of this century have formulated their own political manifestoes, to women's societies which for a limited period gathered women together to attend embroidery courses, run bazaars and take part in keep-fit classes.[19]

---

19. However, during the past 25–30 years the parties' women's organisations have related to public gender equality policies by setting out resolutions and action plans. In this fashion the parties' policies in relation to women have generally progressed from a focus on equal value and the complementary role of women to a focus on the gender equality aspects of the respective parties and society as a whole.

Women's sections in the political parties

Jan Sundberg (1995) highlights the political strengths inherent in the electoral mobilisation of women by the Social Democrats of the Nordic countries. He particularly emphasises the power once held by the separate sections in Sweden, Finland and, to some extent, Norway. In contrast to this, no independent women's organisation ever saw the light of day in Denmark. Instead of the women's sections, women's committees were formed in the Danish Social Democratic Party in the years 1929–1969. These committees lacked most of the powers of their sister organisations in the other Nordic countries, however. In what follows we shall address the development of the independent women's organisations. Since the lack of empirical data means that a general comparative perspective is out of the question, we have opted to focus on the differences between the Danish and the Swedish social democratic parties. In this province the differences in the way in which feminist issues became organised are considerable, even though there are certain developmental similarities between the parties of course

Agreement has existed between the Social Democrats of Denmark and Sweden that the critical thing is not gender but class. At the turn of the century both parties set great store by the organising of women, but they wanted in addition to retain a single and united party organisation, and were far from eager to countenance an independent women's organisation of any standing. What actually lay behind the successful creation of an extremely influential social democratic women's section in Sweden, while nothing resembling that initiative took place in Denmark, requires more comparative research to answer. Nevertheless, the pros and cons aired in the debate on independent women's organisations in the two countries are very much the same, and this is intriguing because they embody the same essential elements of a classic gender–class debate as it has unfolded in the political parties. Let us take a look at a couple of examples.

The first is from the year of the national congress of the Danish Social Democratic Party in 1908; women had just been granted the right to vote in municipal elections and the Women Worker's Union in Denmark – KAD – had been in existence for almost twenty-five years:

> In consideration of the recent enactment of the Municipal Election Act by which Women are called to participation in public life, the question of Women's affiliation to political organisations requires urgent attention.

> The Party Congress may only recognise a single Labour Movement, the socialist movement, and finds it therefore necessary to state that, as regards working women, there is no room for a special women's movement or a separate women's party.

> In the economic field women have found their place in trade unions which attend no less to the concerns of men than to those of women. Only in certain trades or groups where men do not participate, can separate trade unions for women be justified, and these have, moreover, as is entirely befitting, affiliated themselves to

the executive organisation [Centralorganisation]. (Resolution passed at the Congress of the Danish Social Democratic Party 1908, quoted in Dahlerup, 1979a)

As the quotations make clear, the Danish Social Democratic Party was totally averse to independent women's organisations, and it would only accept such organisations within the framework of the labour movement where their presence could be justified with reference to the "natural" division of labour between the sexes. Instead of a women's union, in Denmark women's committees were established. These committees were primarily local-level affairs with no independent programmes of their own. In 1969 they were abolished in the name of gender equality (Dahlerup 1979a).

The National Federation of Social Democratic Women in Sweden (SSKF) was founded in 1920. Gunnel Karlsson uses three key concepts to characterise the SSKF: opposition, loyalty, and clarity of vision. With the term *opposition* she focuses on the reluctance of the male Social Democrats to respect the existence of the women's section, and especially their reluctance to accept that views emanating from the women's section did not always tally with those of the main party (Karlsson 1996:13). By *loyalty* she means the different perceptions of the woman's role held by male and female party members. Was loyalty associated with a tacit (tea-brewing) support in the party and a consensus that women should renounce wage work for the sake of unemployed men, as was an issue in the thirties, Karlsson wonders. Or was loyalty to the party in effect tantamount to the development of a forceful feminist policy, for which the women's section was fighting (Karlsson 1996:13)? In other words, specific demands by women were often construed as a threat to the party and thus perceived as manifestations of disloyalty. Lastly, with *clarity of vision* Karlsson emphasises the ability to analyse the potentialities of the women's section in a very male-dominated party. She refers in this connection to, among others, Disa Västberg who in 1949 proclaimed that

> No longer will we women rest content with a friendly pat on the shoulder from our male party comrades during and after an election campaign. We want to do our bit by lending a helping hand, but we also want to have a hand in making the decisions. (Karlsson 1996:11)

What the Swedish Social Democrats expected of its women's section was that it should act as a support group and organise those (female) members which the party otherwise had great difficulties in reaching through the customary recruitment channels in the workplace and the trade unions. But this expectation, according to Gunnel Karlsson, was incompatible with the women's tendency to formulate independent political demands (for instance, increased child allowances in the 1930s, defence without nuclear energy in the 1950s, and a mandatory paternity leave for fathers in the 1970s).[20]

---

20. For a good presentation of the independent formulation of policies by the women's section, see Anna-Grete Nilsson Hoadley's analysis of the section's nuclear weapons policy 1955–1960 (Hoadley 1989).

One of Gunnel Karlsson's conclusions is that there has been a gradual transition from brotherhood (in the twenties and thirties) to sisterhood (in the seventies and eighties). But the relationship between the party and the women's section remains tense, even though the situation has changed in that the membership of the women's section has dropped as the number of women in the party proper has increased.[21]

Despite the ability of the autonomous social democratic women's organisations to create an impact is very different in Denmark and Sweden, it appears that the debate, and particularly the resistance to such organisations, have basically been of a feather in each of the countries. But if we look at the women's sections in more general terms, in Finland as in Sweden the role they have played has been very significant indeed. The Working Women's Federation (*Arbetarkvinnornas Förbund*) was founded as early as 1900. The organisation splintered in the sixties, only to reform in 1979 as a single organisation designated quite simply Finnish Social Democratic Women (*Sosialidemokraattiset Naiset*). Today the section enjoys a membership of about 20,000. The liberal parties' women's sections were formed at a later date, but their authority has not been any the less. To cite an example, the Women's Organisation of the Finnish Centre Party (*Centerpartiets Kvinnor*) now boasts about 60,000 members (Ramstedt-Silén 1998a). That the women's sections are apparently an integrated component of Finnish political culture is evident, among other things, from the fact that new women's sections have been established along with the creation of new political parties in the nineties. But Ramstedt-Silén also points out that the explanation behind this is not only to be found in political traditions, but also in the fact that 7 per cent of the financial support allotted by the state to the party since 1975 has gone directly to the independent women's organisations in the political parties.

The impact of the women's sections in the Nordic countries has been very considerable – not only in relation to the tasks which are often the focus of attention (the mobilisation of women at elections, the recruitment of women for party-related work, the organisation of activities associated with leisure pursuits), but also in relation to the formulation of women's interests. As far as the social democratic women's sections are concerned, matters of gender and class have been put on the political agenda. Broadly speaking it appears that the independent women's sections have enjoyed, and still enjoy, the greatest degree of autonomy and influence in the political parties of Sweden and Finland. As mentioned, there is no tradition in Denmark of independent women's sections. Norway's position is somewhere in between (cf. in addition Haavio-Mannila et al. 1985).

---

21. The membership of the SSKF fell from 63,491 in 1965 to 25,610 in 1995. This decline is associated with difficulties in recruiting young women to the women's section (Karlsson 1996).

Table 4.3 Gender quotas in the political parties in the Nordic countries 1974--1997

Country	Party	Party quotas	Candidate quotas
Denmark[a]	Socialist People's Party	1977-1996	1988-1990
	Social Democratic Party	1983-1996	1988-1996
	Left Socialist Party	1985-	-
Finland	Social Democratic Party	1996-	-
	Left Wing Alliance	1990-	-
	Green League	1993-	-
Iceland	People's Alliance	1983-	-
	Social Democratic Party	1983-	-
	Progressive Party	1984-	-
	National Party[b]	1984-	-
Norway	Liberal Party	1974-	-
	Socialist Left Party	1975-	1975-
	Labour Party[c]	1983-	1983-
	Workers' Communist Party (Marxist-Leni-	1984-	-
	nists)	1989-	1989-
	Centre Party	1993-	1993-
	Christian Democratic Party		
Sweden	Green Party	1983-	-
	Social Democratic Party	1993-	1993-
	Left Party	1990-	-

a: In elections to the European Parliament the Socialist People's Party used gender quotas from 1983 to 1990. In the Social Democratic Party the candidate quotas did not extend to general (Folketing) elections; they were only applied at elections to municipal and county councils. The statutes of the Social Democratic Party from 1996 contain a proposal requesting an equal gender distribution, for example on the executive committee. As from 1990 the Left Socialist Party has competed in elections as part of the Red-Green Alliance. The Alliance does not use gender quotas.

b: The four National Party members of parliament are now integrated into the Social Democratic Party.

c: In the Norwegian Labour Party the use of gender quotas at elections is restricted to the nomination process.

Sources: Dahlerup 1988a, 1997; Heidar and Raaum 1995; Christensen and Damkjær 1998; Bergman 1998; Bergqvist 1998; Ramstedt-Silén 1998a; in addition extensive information from the individual political parties in the various countries.

Gender quotas in the political parties

Anne Phillips, who from the perspective of democracy theory has previously stressed the importance of women's political presence, has emphasised in the same connection the impact the Nordic countries' system of gender quotas has had (see for instance Phillips 1991:83 ff., and 1995:59). In conformance with Skjeie (1992), Phillips contends that it is not only the actual gender quota regulations in themselves but the symbolic impact of the gender dimension on élite politics that has wrought dramatic changes in political culture in general and in women's political presence in the Nordic countries in particular.

We agree that it is this broader significance of positive discrimination which has had the widest impact and is of greatest interest. But when we nevertheless choose to address positive discrimination in a relatively concrete fashion, the reasons reflect our general concern to uncover concealed details in the Nordic model. In relation to the parties' rules on gender quotas, the Nordic countries are often referred to as a compact entity even though there are, as we shall see, considerable differences in the application of such quotas. This disparity is obviously due first and foremost to the political parties themselves, but need also to be understood in light of the general debate in the Nordic countries on positive discrimination. The debates and the practice that is now an institutionalised part of the state's gender equality policy (cf. Part III of this book) have without doubt shaped attitudes to gender quotas within the political parties themselves. The aim here is not to address this debate in any greater detail, nor to discuss the general effects of quotas. For example, the analysis does not allow us to assess the correlation between the internationally high level of women's representation and the use of gender quotas. We want to retain our original point of departure, i.e. the party organisations, and to investigate *the degree to which the political parties, by applying gender quotas, have developed strategies to integrate women.*[22]

The system of gender quotas in the form with which we are familiar today was devised at the start of the seventies as a means to enhance women's share of political power. The system of quotas, as it was referred to then, must not be confused with the old quota rules on the parties' statutes which typically ensured a couple of seats in the party leadership for representatives of women's organisations in the parties, thus creating a channel of communication to the top. The newer practice of gender quotas was developed hand in hand with the mobilisation of women and is more radical in that its immediate goal was to secure improved access to power and influence in élite politics for women / the underrepresented sex (Dahlerup 1988a).

The idea of quotas either of women or of men is founded on the assumption that an approximately equal representation of women and men is important. There is also an implicit assumption here to the effect that people have an interest in being represented in their capacity as gendered subjects. That this argument has enjoyed a relatively fruitful environment in Norway (and partly in the other Nordic countries) is linked, according to Hege Skjeie, to the traditional Norwegian practice of group representation (with respect to class and geographical location for example) (Skjeie 1992:32). Opponents of gender quotas have

---

22. It is essential to stress that the system of gender quotas is not regarded as an example of such an integrational strategy. Other strategies to enhance the representation of women in party organisations are not hereby excluded. The term integration strategy has its origin in Heidar and Raaum (1995).

generally rested their case on two main arguments: the irreconcilability of the principle with a system of representative democracy in which decisions concerning who a citizen wants as his or her elected representative are made by means of free ballot; and its incompatibility with a system of selection based on qualifications and political views.

In what follows we discuss gender quotas only insofar as the parties have adopted statutes for the purpose. This means that general gender equality programmes and declarations of aims and goals are not dealt with here. Thus, our approach to gender quotas is more limited than the broader alternative of analysing party strategies to enhance the women's representation, as proposed by Lovendutski and Norris. These authors define three such strategies: (1) rhetorical strategies, i.e., upbeat statements are made on the importance of increasing women's influence in the parties; (2) "affirmative action" – the development of programmes to support and encourage women to assume power; and (3) positive discrimination whereby quotas are allocated (Lovenduski and Norris 1993). What we are about to address then is the most radical strategy of all – namely gender quotas.

When we speak of gender quotas in the political parties, two different forms of quotas must be kept in mind:

- Gender quotas designed for *elections and the system of representative democracy*. These are quotas for popular elections in which the concrete quota arrangements are adapted to the electoral system of the country in question. This form of quotas will be referred to as *candidate quotas* in what follows.
- Gender quotas designed for *party democracies*. These are "internal" quotas within the party organisations; typically a statute is adopted to secure a 40–60 per cent gender ratio. This form we will term *party quotas*.

Even though the two methods differ in principle, in practice the points of contact are very close indeed: Where the first aims to further the political representation of women, the second is concerned with the integration of women into the party apparatus.

Table 4.3 shows that the use of statutes to regulate gender quotas in the political parties in the Nordic countries varies widely, as does the frequency with which the rules are applied in any given instance. In *Denmark* the gender-quota device has primarily been exercised by the Socialist People's Party and by the Social Democratic Party. However, candidate quotas have only been used to a limited extent since the Social Democratic Party has only applied quotas at municipal and county-level elections, and the Socialist People's Party's regulations governing candidate quotas were only on the books for a period of two years. Viewed in a Nordic perspective, what is most intriguing as far as Denmark is concerned is that both the Social Democrats and the Socialist People's Party *abolished gender quotas* at their congresses in 1996. This means that no Danish political parties practise a form of quotas today.[23]

It gives pause for thought that, as the Swedish and the Finnish social democracies are in the process of introducing gender quotas for the first time, the practice is being voted out by their Danish sister party after having been in use for about fifteen years.

Despite the fact that a serious discussion has been going on in Finland on gender quotas throughout the eighties and nineties, only a limited application is oñ the cards. Until 1996, when the Social Democratic Party passed a resolution in favour of quotas, quota statutes had only been adopted for internal elections in the Left Wing Alliance and the Green League. The Finnish case is interesting because, on the one hand, women here can look back on a well-established tradition of using the parliamentary channel as well as of independent women's organisations within the political parties. On the other hand, however, the development of strategies which might promote further integration – for instance by means of gender quotas – has not figured on the agenda at all. One of the reasons is doubtless the Finnish electoral system, which is based on a personal ballot. This means that the application of quotas has less of an effect than when votes are cast for party lists. In Finland it has been of crucial importance to vote specifically for a woman, and the foremost strategy of the political women's organisations has been the "Vote for a Woman" campaigns. The number of women nominated on the lists is therefore quite critical, and the gender quota instrument is difficult to use and has less of an effect than list ballots (cf. in addition Sundberg 1995:102).

The electoral system in *Iceland* is often said to place special institutional impediments in the way of gender quotas (see for instance Dahlerup 1988a).[24]

As Table 4.3 makes clear, none of the Icelandic parties practise gender quotas in popular elections (candidate quotas) either. The Progressive Party (and formerly the National Party, too) has, however, emitted declarations of intent to boost the proportion of women. It might be pertinent to ask if the significance the electoral system may not have been overestimated, and therefore hindered the development of strategies to advance women's representation to an unnecessary degree. In Iceland, what has evolved instead is a rather strong tradition of party quotas: four parties have practised the system since the mid-eighties. The Women's Alliance, to which we shall return in the next chapter, was founded in 1983 mainly because the political parties were ignoring demands for increased

---

23. There has always been a large measure of opposition in the Danish Social Democratic Party to gender quotas and the congress refused to endorse a recommendation on the issue by the executive committee. What remain on the party statutes are relatively vaguely worded guidelines concerning, for instance, the equal representation of both sexes in the seats reserved for the county branches on the executive committee, and that gender may be taken into account in cases in which the one sex is totally absent from supplementary lists in counties and large constituencies. In the Socialist People's Party, opposition to quota rules was particularly vocal among the young women of the party, the reason no doubt being the general feeling of opposition in Denmark in the nineties towards any form of positive discrimination. Moreover, experience has shown that it can be very difficult to abide by the gender quota regulations because so few women are party members in Denmark anyway (Christensen and Knopp Damkjær 1998).

24. The Icelandic electoral system is based on primaries in which the nomination of the candidates and their ranking on the electoral lists takes place through decentralised test ballots both in municipal and elections to the national assembly (the Alþingi).

women's representation. According to the Alliance's statutes, men are permitted as members, but may not stand as representatives. What is noticeable is that the other parties introduced party quotas at the same time as the Women's Alliance was established. This indicates – as we shall discuss below – that there was an effect of the political mobilisation of women at this time which extended further than simply to the formation of the Women's Alliance.

The Nordic country to apply gender quotas to the greatest extent has without doubt been *Norway*, and the most consistent application has been in the party organisations and in political representation. The Socialist Left Party has employed both forms of gender quotas since the mid-seventies, the Labour Party following suit from the mid-eighties. The Centre Party and the Christian Democratic Party adopted gender quotas at a later date. Currently only the Conservative Party and the Progress Party have no form of gender quotas. Political parties without gender quotas are therefore more the exception than the rule in Norway today. Against this background, Heidar and Raaum (1995) have examined the effect of the quota mechanism on party democracy. One of their conclusions is that women's influence in the party hierarchies has increased significantly in what they designate as the "established quota parties" (The Liberal Party, the Socialist Left Party, and the Labour Party).

The Swedish situation with regard to party quotas contrasts strongly with that of the Norwegian. With the exception of the Green Party, it was not until the nineties that gender quotas were adopted by Swedish parties and the only party to actually apply quotas in public elections remains to this day the Social Democratic Party. This notwithstanding, the Swedish case illustrates the problems arising from concentrating solely on statutes and regulations, in that the principle of *Varannan Damernas* – Every Other Seat a Woman's Seat – has been in effect since the eighties.[25]

According to Christina Bergqvist opposition within the Swedish parties to the idea of formalising gender quotas has been considerable; instead, the principle of "mixed lists" – that is, lists in which every other candidate is either a women or a man – has been advocated. But the demand for gender-balanced lists was so intense prior to the general election in 1994 (not least due to the activities of the *Stödstrumporna* or "Support Stockings") that the Swedish Social Democratic Party the adopted the principle of "Every Other Seat a Woman's Seat" at its congress in 1993 (in 1997 it was institutionalised even further by inclusion in the party's statutes) (Bergqvist 1994:69, 1998).[26]

---

25. The principle known as *Varannan Damernas* or "Every Other Seat a Woman's Seat" originated in a government report (SOU 1987:19), on the representation of women in state bodies. The report had a great impact among other things on attitudes to elected bodies. (See footnote 12 on page 40 in Chapter 2 for a clarification of the origin of the term *Varannan Damernas*.)

26. There is a pun at work here. The term *Stödstrumporna* – *support stockings*, i.e., surgical or relief stockings used for venous conditions – alludes to the ageing of the once vigorous and radical first wave of red-stocking feminists of the first years of the century. The pun lies in the alliterative play on the Swedish words for *red* – röd, i.e., radical – and *support* – stöd, i.e. in need of propping up (trans. note).

As we have seen, there are significant differences in the ways in which the political parties in the Nordic countries apply gender quotas. We can therefore not agree with Anne Phillips that the Nordic countries as such represent a clear-cut alternative in this respect (Phillips 1995:59). Even though developments in the political parties and in the integration of women in élite politics share certain obvious developmental features, the foregoing shows that there have been, and still are, fundamental differences between the Nordic countries in this area.

In Norway the use of quotas in the political parties and in public elections stretches back twenty years. This can not be said of the other Nordic countries. In relation to Finland and Iceland, the combination of an electoral system with considerable institutional barriers coupled with resistance to gender quotas in some of the parties is evidently one explanation for the extremely weak position of candidate quotas. In contrast, about a half of the parties in these two countries apply gender quotas in their internal party nominations. In both Sweden and Denmark there has been considerable opposition to gender quotas within the parties, but the outcomes have varied. In the nineties in Denmark gender quotas have been rejected as a suitable mechanism at the same time as the Swedish Social Democratic Party, for instance, has adopted the method, thanks among other things to the great popularity of the principle of *Varannan Damernas* or "Every Other Seat a Woman's Seat".

In addition to national differences it appears that party-political differences also play a part. Pippa Norris (1997b), in an analysis of quota use in the EU countries, shows that the left-wing socialist parties are more inclined to say yes to gender quotas than centrist and right-wing parties. The explanation being, according to Norris, that the left-wing parties in general are more equality oriented and have a greater faith in the power of quotas to bring about change. Our analysis of the Nordic countries seems to sustain this point, since it is the social democratic parties and the non-dogmatic left-wing parties that have especially practised gender quotas.[27]

Heidar and Raaum's analysis of attitudes to gender quotas in Norway corroborate this pattern. At the same time, their investigation reveals that gender means less than party affiliation. For example, the greatest difference in attitudes to gender quotas is between the women of the Socialist Left Party and the women of the Progress Party.[28]

---

27. Nonetheless, Hege Skjeie stresses that it is difficult – based on the Norwegian data – to find such "consistent differences" between the parties. If one considers the representation of women over a period of time, both at the local and the national level, the similarity in the patterns of integration stands out (Skjeie 1992:30). It is indicative, however, that as far as the other Nordic countries are concerned – where the use of gender quotas is less common – the practice has mainly been adopted by the left-wing parties, just as in Norway today the only parties to have seen fit not to adopt gender quotas are the extreme right-wing parties (the Conservative Party and the Progress Party).

28. In addition, Heidar and Raaum's (1995) study shows that the attitudes of the men in parties that had not adopted gender quotas before 1990.... (Continued on next page)

And like Hege Skjeie, Heidar and Raaum show that the higher one climbs up the ladder in the party apparatus, the more conformist and loyal both the women and men become (Heidar and Raaum 1995; Skjeie 1992).

It is far from easy to say how the gender quota issue will develop in the future. There is a great deal to indicate that, in Norway at least, the mechanism is here to stay. Future developments in the other countries are considerably more uncertain. There are two factors which could be conceived as potential future barriers standing in the way of the gender quota mechanism. First there is the question of the declining membership of the parties. Even though the women's share of the membership has grown, as we have seen in the last chapter, there are far fewer female party members than there were twenty years ago. This could represent a barrier to the adoption of rules on gender quotas for which a prerequisite is the presence of a pool of female party members willing to be nominated. Secondly, the pressure to adopt gender quotas appears to be ebbing, not least because the younger generations of female politicians have no desire for such regulations.

In a situation in which the parties' membership basis is probably their greatest challenge, it does not seem as if the demand for gender quotas can persist in isolation. It may be the case that the system no longer conjures up associations of a positive symbolic nature for Nordic women, and we may have entered upon a phase in which additional forms of integrational strategies need to be developed, strategies whose aim is to recruit fresh female party members, for example, not merely to integrate existing members.

As we mentioned initially, by restricting ourselves to the gender quota issue, we have also bridled our the assessment of women's integration into the political parties. This notwithstanding, there is little doubt that the political significance of the gender issue extends beyond the matter of regulations on gender quotas. We agree with Hege Skjeie when she says that the political relevance of the gender dimension (for instance through a focus on differences between women's and men's political interests as well as the desire among women voters to be represented by one of "their own") is an experience common to all the Nordic countries (Skjeie 1992). That means that the male-only and strongly male-dominated assemblages within political parties and the political élite have lost their legitimacy. Women and gender differences are now integrated into mainstream political culture. Gender quotas have been a stepping-stone in this process of integration, and have at the same time functioned as a positive signal expressing a conscious desire to take gender issues seriously.

(Footnote 28, continued from previous page)

.....(the Conservative Party, the Progress Party, the Christian Democratic Party, and the Centre Party), are more negative to gender quotas the higher up in the party hierarchy one goes. In the so-called "established gender quota parties" (The Socialist Left Party, the Left Party, and the Labour Party), the trend is the reverse, namely that the men's attitudes become more positive to gender quotas the higher the men are in the party apparatus.

Conclusion

Even though women's share of the membership of the political parties has been growing at the same time as the parties' overall membership has been going through a steep decline, our analysis finds no evidence to support the thesis that women are being integrated into shrinking institutions. On the contrary, it appears that there has been an interplay between, on the one side, the degree to which the mobilisation of women has focused on the political parties and, on the other, the present strength of the parties. Rather than clinging to a conception of women as passive actors in the process of being integrated into empty and insignificant institutions, it is necessary to stress that women, throughout the past thirty years, have represented *an active potential for mobilisation*. Thus, the ability of the political institutions to attract this female potential has also rebounded on the institutions' potency and vitality.

But the issue is not restricted to the differing degrees of women's integration in the political parties. The analysis has also shown that, over a period of time, different models of women's integration have been developed, which, in a Nordic perspective contain some interesting variations. These concern firstly the degree to which there exists a tradition of autonomous organisations for women within the parties (the classic model of women's integration). Secondly they concern the degree to which – with gender quotas as the example – integration strategies have been elaborated in the Nordic countries (the modern model of women's integration). We view these features as differences and similarities which – without going so far as to claim them as the only parameters – are central to a more clearly defined conception of a single Nordic model of women's mobilisation, which in summary looks like this:

Sweden/Finland – The classic strategy for integrating women
- A strong historic tradition of independent women's sections in the political parties
- Limited use of modern strategies for integrating women by means of gender quotas, primarily in the 1990s
- The new mobilisation of women has penetrated the parties in Finland
- The new mobilisation of women has partly penetrated the parties in Sweden

Norway – The modern strategy for integrating women
- "Sporadic" historical tradition of independent women's sections within the political parties
- Well-developed strategies for integrating women by means of quotas
- The new mobilisation of women has strengthened the parties

Denmark – No women's integration strategy
- No historic tradition of independent women's sections within the political parties
- Decline in membership of the political parties began, and was most extensive here
- Limited use of modern strategies to integrate women primarily in the eighties
- No modern strategies to integrate women in the nineties
- The new mobilisation of women has largely taken place beyond the confines of the political parties.

This chapter has raised a number of questions of relevance for future research. We have registered and discussed differences of central importance among the countries, but we have been unable to provide explanations of any weight. More knowledge and comparative research will be required to answer *why*, for example, in spite of a number of similarities, the Nordic differences are so great both the in classic and the modern strategies to achieve the integration of women. Similarly we need more studies which focus on the *effects* of the integration of women into the parties and élite politics. Up to now there have been relatively few such studies (see for example Heidar and Raaum 1995; Skjeie 1992; Wängnerud 1998). Their results emphasise the great impact on developments in political culture towards the end of the eighties resulting from the integration of women. Concerning matters of actual policy, it is emphasised that female politicians represent a "mandate of difference" and that they "bear" a feminist responsibility – a so-called "politics of care". This is why it is not unreasonable, according to Skjeie, to speak of "a female dimension" and "a male dimension" in élite politics, but in a way which breaks substantially with the traditional split into "the political" and "the non-political", contributing instead to legitimatise the presence of women and of the gender dimension in politics (Skjeie 1992:33). It is an open question whether coming generations of female politicians will continue to represent such a mandate of difference, and, if they do, whether they will use the political parties within the system of representative democracy as a channel for its expression.

Figure 4.1. Classical and modern strategies to integrate women in the Nordic countries[a]

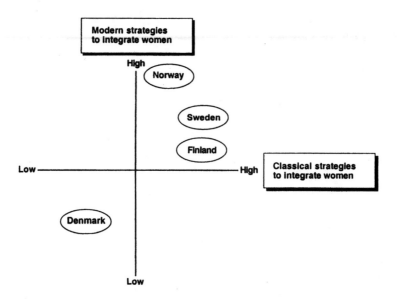

a: It is important to note that the model only depicts the general time-lags between what we have designated the modern and the classical strategies to integrate women. It does not therefore render the time-lags within the two categories. For instance, it is impossible to see the time-lag between Denmark on the one hand and Sweden and Finland on the other with respect to the use of gender quotas. Due to the special conditions prevailing on Iceland associated with the Women's Alliance, Iceland has not been included.

5

Women's lists in Iceland – A response to political lethargy

Auður Styrkársdóttir

The history of the Icelandic women's lists started in 1908 when Reykjavik women's associations campaigned in local elections on a separate electoral list. Women's lists contested local elections in Reykjavik and in two other towns right up until 1921, and in 1922 the first female member of the Icelandic parliament (the Alþingi) was elected from a women's list (Styrkársdóttir 1998). In those days it was relatively common for women to seek political representation through women's lists; indeed, such lists were being put up in all of the Nordic countries, with the exception of Finland, as well as in a good number of other countries in Europe (Dahlerup 1977; Haavio-Mannila *et al.* 1983:71 ff.; Fosshaug 1989). They were particularly popular in Norway, Denmark and Iceland, but were seen mostly in local elections. What distinguishes the Icelandic case is the re-emergence of these women's lists in the eighties and their subsequent success both in local politics and nationally; in other countries women's lists have seldom enjoyed much success in recent times (however, see Part IV on the Faeroes). In the present chapter we will address the particular conditions in Iceland which led to the re-emergence of the women's lists in the eighties, and explain how they managed to be as successful as they were. We will also examine in some detail the campaigning methods of the parliamentary Women's Alliance, its organisation and its impact on Icelandic society.

The emergence of the women's lists

The women's movement in Iceland has managed to catch the eye of the public on several occasions by its use of fairly original methods in the struggle for women's rights (Styrkársdóttir 1986; Helgadóttir 1996). For instance, the women's strike of 1975 paralysed the entire Icelandic community for a whole day, while in 1980 Vigdís Finnbogadóttir was elected as the world's first popularly elected female president. The Icelandic women's movement was extremely active in the seventies. The Red Stocking Movement (*Rauðsokkahreyfingin*) was founded in 1970 and took the lead in highlighting women's social status by means of relatively unconventional methods. Among the movement's demands were the right to abortion on demand, equal representation, equal pay, and equal opportunities. The enactment of the Equal Pay Act of 1973 together with the Equal Opportunities Act and the establishment of the Equal Opportunities Council of 1976 are advances partly attributable to this new Icelandic women's movement in the 1970s. One of the most important demands during this decade was for a substantial increase in the representation of women. In the other Nordic countries women's representation was growing rapidly, but efforts to integrate women into the political system in Iceland was not meeting with comparable success. Icelandic women remained cut off from the political decision-making process; for example, the representation of women at the local level only rose from 2 per cent in 1970 to 6 per cent in 1978, and the representation of women in parliament remained at a mere 5 per cent throughout the seventies (Appendix 1, Tables 3 and 8). Thus the emergence of the women's lists should be seen primarily as a reaction against, but also an attempt to gain a foothold in, a political system which for some time had been doing little but tread water.

The women's lists also represented a protest against prevailing social conditions in Iceland. For instance, the municipality of Reykjavik had for a long time pursued a policy the result of which was that only a few children had access to full-time daycare because children of married women were only allowed to attend daycare centres for four to five hours a day, even though many women had full-time jobs (see also Part II). There were not enough daycare centres in the city, and the need for places far exceeded the supply. The situation was the same in other municipalities. In the spring of 1981 a few women belonging to the Red Stocking Movement in Reykjavik decided to start an open discussion group on women's social and political situation in the city, and in the autumn the group resolved to put up a women's list at the next local election in Reykjavik. The Red Stocking Movement was formally dissolved at the turn of 1981–82 because most of the members had left it by then to join the group behind the women's list. In addition, for some years the Red Stockings had been riven by internal strife between various groups of left-leaning women, and was no longer able to recruit younger members.

Women's lists and representation

Women's lists were put up at the 1982 local elections in the capital, Reykjavik, as well as in the largest city on the northern coast, Akureyri. The lists were well received by the electorate. In Reykjavik the women's list won 11 per cent of the ballot resulting in two women on a city council of twenty-one representatives. In the municipality of Akureyri the women's list achieved 17 per cent of the

Table 5.1 Women MPs in the Alþingi 1971–1999, and proportion of votes and seats for the Women's Alliance, 1983–1995. In per cent

Year	Women MPs in the Alþingi	Women's Alliance proportion of votes	Women's Alliance proportion of seats
1971	5.0		
1974	5.0		
1978	5.0		
1979	5.0		
1983	15.0	5.5	3 (60)
1987	20.6	10.1	6 (63)
1991	23.8	8.3	5 (63)
1995	25.4	4.9	3 (63)
1999	34.9		

Source: Auður Styrkársdóttir 1997

votes and two women on a city council of eleven members. From 1982 to 1994, women's lists have been put up in seven municipalities (in 1982 the total number of municipalities in Iceland was 202, in 1994 171). These lists have enjoyed varying degrees of electoral success. For instance, the women's list in Reykjavik won 11 per cent of the poll in 1982, but only 8 per cent and 6 per cent in 1986 and 1990 respectively, 1990 being the last election at which a women's list competed in Reykjavik. The lists have obviously been a contributive factor behind the considerable increase in the representation of women on local councils in general, from 6 per cent in 1978 to 28 per cent at the last election in 1998. One of the reasons is that the established parties felt the mere existence of women's lists to be a threat, a fear to which the women of these parties are more than willing to admit (Dahlerup 1988a:112).

At the local Reykjavik election in 1994 the party system underwent a significant change. Four parties – the Social Democrats, the People's Alliance, the Progressive Party, and the Women's List of Reykjavik – joined forces to form a single party, the Reykjavik List. The creation of this party was a response to the success of the Independence Party in holding on to power in the city council almost without a break since 1930; and there was therefore little hope that reforms would be implemented in the area of children's daycare, for instance, unless forces were pooled under a single banner. Another motivational factor lay in the shrinking popularity of all four parties. The new party won a majority: eight out of fifteen council members in Reykjavik. A woman from the Women's List is presently mayor of Reykjavik. One could say that in 1994 the Reykjavik Women's List achieved its original goal: that women comprise half (53 per cent in the period 1994–98) of the city council, and that the mayor be a woman. Policies in Reykjavik have changed considerably since then: married women as well as single parents now have access to full-time daycare for their children, and there is considerable determination to meet the total need for daycare places by the year 2000.

The success of the women's lists in Reykjavik and Akureyri in 1982 led to the founding of the parliamentary Women's Alliance (*Kvennalistinn*) at the general election of 1983. There was a great deal of contention within the Alliance's Reykjavik branch as to whether to put up a special women's list at the election. At a meeting arranged to debate the issue, three alternative definitions were discussed (Sigurbjarnardóttir 1992): (1) the Women's Alliance is a broad-based grass-roots movement; (2) the Women's Alliance is an election movement whose main objective is to achieve representation; (3) the Women's Alliance is both 1 and 2. A considerable number maintained that work on the council would lay claim to all of their available resources, and that such work might well require answers to questions which the women might not be able to agree on, such as in the economic area for instance, or the position they should take with regard to the American military base in Iceland, which at the time was the source of considerable dissension between the parties. The institutionalisation of the movement was also questioned. Many women feared that entering the "big" political arena would lead to co-optation and that they would be obliged to jettison some of their feminist demands. This dispute about the very foundations of the Women's Alliance left its mark on discussions concerning the organising of the party and its strategies: conflicts arose between those who wanted to maintain "grass-roots principles" and those who wanted to strengthen the electoral aspect and practical politics.

Parliamentary women's lists were declared in three of Iceland's eight constituencies in 1983. They won 5.5 per cent of the poll and three of the sixty seats in the parliament. In the elections of 1987, 1991, and 1995, the Women's Alliance put up candidates in every constituency. The proportion of the votes won is given in Table 5.1. The table also shows the percentage of women members of parliament for the period 1971–99. As can be seen, the percentage of women MPs rose markedly from the period prior to the 1983 election, from 5 per cent to 25.4 per cent in 1995. The Women's Alliance's own representatives have accounted for a considerable share of the increase, but the established parties have been compelled to nominate more female candidates, even though difficulties have strewn the way since they no longer have a system of centralised nominations. In 1983 and 1984, three of the four big parties adopted a system of gender quotas for internal purposes (see Chapter 4). Up to now they have refused to use quotas in nominations to party lists, but the internal quotas should be viewed as a response to the pressures that were brought to bear on the parties by the formation of the Women's Alliance.

The Women's Alliance also contributed to a distinct gender difference in the party preferences of the Icelandic electorate. At the general election of 1983 the Alliance gained 11 per cent of the women's vote in Iceland; it peaked at 22 per cent in 1987 but fell back to 17 per cent in 1991 and 11 per cent in 1995 (Harðarson). Only 2–3 per cent of Icelandic men voted for the Women's Alliance in the parliamentary elections (men were allowed to join the Alliance as members, but could not represent the party). With respect to the more established parties, the most marked gender differences in electoral behaviour are to be found among voters of the Independence Party. (The Independence Party is the only party to have rejected quotas out of hand.)

Obstacles in the Icelandic electoral and party system

There are two reasons why the established parties have taken such a long time to respond to the demands of women for increased representation. One is the absence of commitments on the part of the party leaderships. The other is the Icelandic nomination system. There are a number of mechanisms available to party managers to increase the representation of women. Norris (1997a:218 ff.) points out that the most efficient way would be for parties to adopt some form of "affirmative action"; quotas for instance. The four established parties in Iceland have thus far rejected proposals to adopt quotas in nominations to party lists (though as mentioned in Chapter 4, the Progressive Party is planning to do so). The party leaders have not seen fit to put the problem of women's representation high up on the agenda, nor do they appear to consider it a problematic issue. The only party (apart from the Women's Alliance) to have made any attempt to deal with the issue is the National Party *(Þjóðvaki)* which first contested an election in 1995, and which adopted the Swedish social democratic model called "*Varannan damernas*" or "every other seat a woman's seat" (see Chapter 2). Although 75 per cent of the National Party's representation in parliament was female – the percentage for the other parties lay between 14 and 20 per cent – the number of its representatives totalled only four persons in all.

Norris also points out that many studies have shown that parties may increase their representation of women by centralising the nomination of party candidates. Svanur Kristjánsson's (1998) study of the Icelandic party system corroborates this finding. In the years 1970–78 the established parties generally relinquished central responsibility for who should represent them. The nomination of candidates has subsequently often taken place through decentralised trial ballots (primaries) both at local and general elections. The decision to mount trial ballots is taken locally by the party branches prior to each election. If the local party branch decides that it wants to hold trial ballots, which is generally the case, they are carried out a few months before the election proper. People with an interest in being nominated as a party candidate approach the party. The person receiving the largest number of votes at the trial ballot tops the candidate list at the election; the person with the next largest poll secures second place, and so on. Since 1970 it has happened on several occasions that the turnout at the parties' trial ballots has surpassed that at the ensuing local or general election.

The trial ballots in Iceland can influence the representation of women in two ways. Firstly, the parties do not extend financial support to the trial ballot candidates. It follows from this that the candidates themselves have to lay their hands on the means to campaign for a seat. Buying advertisement space is the main expense (in large constituencies such as Reykjavik, standing for an election can cost a candidate anything between DKK 40,000 and 90,000). Being well-known figure is an advantage, as is the ability to gain access to influential party members or large organisations which might be willing to support one's candidature (Rule and Zimmerman 1994). As a rule, women have less access to such resources than do men so it should not come as a surprise that relatively fewer women put themselves forward for the trial ballot. In addition, it has been shown that men experience difficulty recollecting women's names (SOU 1993: 21:69). This may be an obstacle to women's attempts to unite behind a woman candidate, especially if more men than women turn out at the trial ballots, which is generally the case. According to an election study conducted in 1995, 23 per cent of Icelandic men participated in a trial ballot prior to the general election; the turnout of the women did not exceed 17 per cent (Harðarson).

The controversial manner in which the Women's Alliance was organised

The Women's Alliance views itself a grass-roots movement even though it was established as a party organisation. The women believe that the traditional party structures and methods suited women badly; and that it could represented a hindrance in itself to women's involvement in politics. In addition, they feel that achieving representation in the national assembly or gaining seats on a council is insufficient unless they do so as feminists with an unambiguous political profile (Sigurbjarnardóttir 1993:7). Inspired by the theory launched by Berit Ås on women's culture (Ås 1975, 1981) the women decided to make use of the notion as a basis for a political strategy because they felt that the focus of the women's movement's on legislative changes and women's integration into the labour market had failed. The starting point was the existence of a suppressed and invisible women's culture which primarily belonged to the private sphere. The culture of men has the public sphere as its main arena, and it is also extremely visible. One of the Women's Alliance's chief objectives was to shed light on women's culture and make it as respected as the public culture (of men) (Jónsdóttir 1993:527).

The Women's Alliance had no real leader; the parliamentary group elected a spokeswoman for a year at a time. There was no central leadership, but the national congress, which in principle was open to all women, was authorised to formulate the political manifesto. The Alliance adhered to the principle of rotation which meant that no one could represent the party for more than four to six years at a time. The Alliance also turned down seats reserved for it on public boards and committees on which political parties are generally represented (for instance the board of the Bank of Iceland and the Broadcasting Council). By renouncing this opportunity to exert influence the Alliance wished to convey its unwillingness to take part in what it called the parties' system of "mutual back-slapping". Unfortunately, however, it also created an impression of a negative attitude to gender equality policy. Issues raised at Alliance meetings were supposed to be

settled by means of discussion rather than a show of hands. All in all, such organisational stratagems show that the Women's Alliance sought to live up to an
organisational ideal of a pure, ideal-type of grass-roots movement with a "non-
hierarchical structure" (Freeman 1975:103 ff.).

The Women's Alliance in Reykjavik was quick to discover that the system
of direct democracy it had attempted to practise turned out to be a great consumer of time, a commodity of which women generally have very little to spare
(Dominelli and Jónsdóttir 1988:44). This democratic grass-roots form of organisation can also stand in the way of rapid and effective decision-making – which
is often required in political work. In fact, it has been shown that it is the representatives who generally draw up the guidelines for the issues under consideration in the local councils or the national assembly (Jónsdóttir 1993:527).

The structure of the Women's Alliance underwent several major refurbish-
ments over the years. The principle of non-participation on public committees
was openly criticised, especially the uncooperative attitude of the Alliance to the
Equal Opportunities Council; this stance was abandoned in 1991. A decision
was made in 1989 to increase the rotation term from 4–6 years to 6–8 years. In
1993 one of the Alliance's parliamentary representatives refused to toe the party
line of unconditional opposition to the EU. This led the women to conclude that
what was needed was greater order and the possibility to set up a central leadership. In 1994 the structure was accordingly changed, and all members gained the
right to put any issue to the vote. The many disagreements related to the strategies of the Women's Alliance and its organisational form (participation on public boards and committees, how long members can represent the party, internal
decision-making processes, etc.) were debated and criticised in the media giving
rise to speculation that the Women's Alliance was neither particularly credible
nor reliable. This was one of the key factors behind the Alliance's decline in
popularity at the 1995 election.

The legacy of the Women's Lists

The Women's Alliance has consistently refused to define itself as leaning to the
right or the left, rejecting this sort of classification as anachronistic. However,
examining its voting record in parliament makes it clear that the Women's Alliance has tended to vote further to the left than the socialist People's Alliance
(Schneier 1992). The fact that a women's list was contributory to the formation
of a clearly leftist umbrella organisation at the 1994 local election in Reykjavik
confirmed even more the Alliance's public image as a leftist party. This led to a
call for the Alliance to take part in the formation of other alternatives in places
other than Reykjavik together with the other left-wing parties, and especially at
the parliamentary level. It was the young women in the Women's Alliance who
wanted to see changes made to the party system, and they also spoke of the need
for organisational changes in the Alliance. At the party congress in November
1997, the congress voted in favour of starting discussions about possible changes. Shortly after this one of the three Alliance MPs stated that she had withdrawn

her membership of the Alliance, but that she was not intending to resign her political posts. A few others also left the Alliance for similar reasons.

At the 1998 local elections no women's lists were put up anywhere, but in many of the larger municipalities former Women's List members formed umbrella parties in league with the Social Democratic Party and the People's Alliance. At the parliamentary election of 1999, the Women's Alliance joined forces with the Social Democratic Party and the People's Alliance to form a new party, the United Alliance, which won seventeen seats, nine of which went to women. After an innings lasting sixteen years, the women's lists have left a deep mark on the political environment in Iceland, not to speak of the impact on the women themselves. The most significant parts of this legacy may be summarised as follows: The women's lists have both directly and indirectly contributed to a marked increase in the proportion of women in the political institutions. The emergence of the women's lists also led indirectly to the appointment in 1983 of a woman government minister. The representatives of the Women's Alliance have made sure that the women's issue has had a place high up on the parliamentary agenda. Issues such as incest, sexual abuse, violence against women, and low pay for women's work have been debated, at times very heatedly, and resulted in new Bills and laws. To a certain extent the women's lists were successful in their attempts to gain a foothold within a number of key organisations wielding both power and authority. As already mentioned, at the local elections of 1998 many women's list members were nominated as candidates on the leftist umbrella party lists. The women's lists' most significant victory to date is without doubt the mayorship of Reykjavik. Childcare policy has changed radically thanks to the new city executive board.[29]

Last, but not least, the parliamentary Women's Alliance and the women's lists in the municipalities contributed to enhancing the mobilisation of many women.

The story of the Icelandic women's lists attests once again to the difficulties involved in trying to combine the "flat" structure of grass-roots movements with political influence (Freeman 1975; Phillips 1991). A flat structure requires a high level of activity on the part of the members. For instance, they must constantly keep abreast of developments and new information to take part in the decision-making process. Meetings where issues are decided upon through discussions have a tendency to go on and on – which puts demands on time and energy. The parliamentary Women's Alliance was not organised as a political party with a basic structure and an emphasis on rapid decision-making processes, political experience and competence. On the contrary, the Women's Alliance tried to avoid such paraphernalia. The outcome was a rather isolationist policy which held sway for many years. The leaders never managed to develop sufficient proficiency or to gain sufficient experience. Nor did the Women's Alliance establish political connections, such as to people involved in the area of equal

---

29. Like Oslo Reykjavik has a parliamentary system of government with an Executive Board or cabinet, which is responsible to the City Council (the "parliament").

opportunities in Iceland, or to women in other political parties by accepting seats on government councils and commissions. This ambivalence in relation to leadership and organisation resulted in declining popularity.

The final – and also the most important – legacy of the Women's Alliance is that, throughout the past couple of decades, the integration of Icelandic women into the political system has met with a large degree of success. The Women's Alliance has played both a direct and indirect role in this respect. This being the situation, one could say that there are few reasons today to put up separate women's lists in Iceland, and that the Alliance itself has thus contributed to eliminating a large part of its own *raison d'être*.

6

Women in New Social Movements

Solveig Bergman[30]

Since the end of the 1950s, the Western world has experienced a resurgence of collective participation in social movements as well as in *ad hoc* and grass roots-based initiatives. Political protest was stimulated by the growth of the anti-authoritarian student movement of the 1960s. This opened up a space for the *new social movements* that spread out during the following decades as, for example, environmental, anti-nuclear power, gay and lesbian, feminist, and peace movements. Extra-parliamentary and unconventional forms of activity also became an important part of the political repertoire of women, youth and significant sections of the new middle classes in the Nordic countries. Much of the political energy of Nordic women during the 1970s and 1980s was channelled into movement activity that was outside the established parties and political institutions.

The use of "new social movements" as a collective term to describe a variety of different forms of movement activity reflects the similarities in the conditions underlying the emergence of these movements, as well as in their bases of recruitment, organisational patterns and sets of values. The memberships of the movements partly overlapped and formed a coherent bloc for political activity, i.e. they were embedded in a "movement family" (della Porta and Rucht 1995). Even if the movements' mobilising power and political importance may have decreased since, they exercised a considerable impact on political and cultural life in many Western countries during the 1980s (see, e.g., Eyerman and Jamison 1991).

Non-institutionalised political activity is an interesting field of research from a gender perspective, because women have been at least as active in this arena as men (Svensson and Togeby 1986). Yet, for a long time, more substantial studies

30. I wish to thank the Nordic Academy for Advanced Study (NorFA) for a scholarship that enabled me to work with this chapter during a stay at the Nordic Institute for Women's Studies and Gender Research (NIKK) in Oslo in 1997.

of women's engagement in the new social movements, with the exception of the women's movement, were scarce. But movement activity is not a new phenomenon. It is evident from the discussion in chapter 2 that social movements and voluntary organisations have been strongly anchored in Nordic civil society since the last century. For women, social movements and idealistic and humanitarian organisations have long been an important field of political activity. While earlier we mainly focused on the political meaning of women's voluntary organisations, below the main emphasis is placed on forms of women's mobilisation that have taken place in the new social movements over the last few decades.

The new women's movement, the women's peace movement and the crisis centre movement[31] may be seen as cases exemplifying women's mobilisation within a new social movement context. We wish to emphasise, however, that women's mobilisation within these movements has assumed many different forms. The women's peace movement and the crisis centre movement are treated here as examples of the extension into other areas of the politics of the new women's movement that has taken place especially since the 1980s. Pragmatic reasons have played an important role in our choice of these particular movements. A lack of appropriate research data restricts our opportunities to study female mobilisation in other movements, such as the environmental and the anti-nuclear power movements or the anti-EU orientated citizens' movements. But before exploring why women mobilised within our chosen social movements, we discuss women and movement activity in the Nordic countries in more general terms.

Distinctive Features of Movement Activity in the Nordic Countries

Attempts are often made to link the upsurge in grass-roots and action-orientated political behaviour to presumed changes in the value patterns of the post-second world war generations. In some approaches the new movements are seen to express post-materialist values, such as an emphasis on the quality of life, community, self-realisation and the pursuit of individual satisfaction (Inglehart 1977). Other researchers have sought to locate the emergence of the movements in the citizens' assumed wish to defend and restore those traditional social values that are apparently threatened by the processes of modernisation as expressed, for example, in ecological, social and cultural crises. Mats Friberg (1984:363f.) advances the claim that the prominent position of women in the movements can be accounted for by the particular attraction that the above-mentioned value patterns might hold for them. According to him, this is the case not only for young, urban and educated women with post-materialist values, but also for women with traditional or anti-modernist orientations. Another theory advanced as to

---

31. The term "crisis centre" is used here specifically to refer to refuges for battered women.

why women prefer movement politics and grass-roots activity is that they are attracted to informal, spontaneous and non-hierarchical patterns of communication and expressively orientated strategies (Rubart 1987:15 f.). Helga Hernes and Kirsten Voje (1982) have also sought to explain why women seem to be especially attracted to movement activity. They argue that structural barriers prevent some women from participating in traditional politics. Such women are either excluded from institutionalised arenas of activity, face discrimination, or fail to have their interests prioritised. As a consequence, it is claimed that these women search for alternative political channels. Other women are thought to be attracted by the movements' focus on the sphere of caring, local community and everyday life. The gender-based division of labour in society may be seen here as contributing to the attractiveness to women of movement policy.

Danish and Norwegian studies have shown that grass-roots participation soon became a means for obtaining political influence, especially for citizens with the appropriate resources, and that it was particularly common within those new groups that were politicised (youth, women, and the new middle classes). Initially, *ad hoc* protest crystallised around issues pertaining to women's rights, peace and the environment, but such spontaneous actions were soon transformed into more structured temporary or permanent action groups that complemented other forms of political activity (cf. Gundelach 1993:341 ff.). Since the end of the 1980s, the engagement in collective political contexts has declined considerably, in terms of both conventional and unconventional forms of political participation. Recently, the new movements have been much less visible, while forms of democratic participation in the local community and within the institutions of the welfare state have become more common (Andersen *et al.* 1993; cf. chapters 3 and 4 above).

From a Nordic perspective, it is important to question the dominant thesis in research on new social movements, according to which movements primarily attract new urban middle classes with anti-modernist ways of thinking and with a preference for decentralised organisational structures as well as for unconventional and grass-root strategies. The problem with accepting such views uncritically is that the rich complexity of the movements is easily lost and, consequently, important aspects of movement activity might remain hidden. True, the traditional patterns of organisation have been challenged by the grass-roots type of organisation. Yet, the "association" has remained the dominant type of organisation in the Nordic countries (Klausen and Selle 1995: 22).

In most Western countries, the mobilisation of women during the 1970s and 1980s did not result in any decisive increase in their proportionate presence on political bodies. However, in the Nordic countries, women's activity was channelled into both the new social movements and the traditional political organisations (Siim 1991:175).[32] Rather than seeing these two channels of influence as mutually exclusive alternatives, they may be regarded as different ways of expressing the same collective organisational processes. The spectre of a broad

32. The exception was Iceland, where women's representation in political institutions did not increase during the 1970s. This was one reason why women engaged in the activities described in chapter 5.

mobilisation by women is thus extended in the form of a continuum, ranging from autonomous action groups to formal and quasi-state organisations.

Whereas researchers earlier emphasised the conflictual nature of the relationship between the movements and conventional forms of political participation, current interpretations are more complex (Diani and Eyerman 1992). The borderline between the state and civil society has become somewhat blurred. The Nordic "state-friendly" political culture is characterised by a close interaction between the political system and the movements (Morken and Selle 1995:177). On the one hand, the open political system and "opportunity structures" of the Nordic countries have resulted in a relatively sympathetic reception of movement demands among decision-makers. On the other hand, such openness may imply a tendency to co-opt movement activists and water down their demands. This interpretation is in line with the thesis advanced by Thomas Mathiesen (1982) that movements are met by a double strategy of inclusion and exclusion.[33] Debate within the movements on the question of co-option has been lively and the strategies they have adopted to resist such pressures vary across national borders and between different movements. These features are also characteristic of women's movement mobilisation in the Nordic countries.

Lise Togeby (1989) has shown that grass-roots orientated activity, as well as other non-conventional forms of political participation, developed in similar but non-identical ways and with varying degrees of success in the Nordic countries (cf. chapter 3 above). During the 1970s and the first part of the 1980s a relatively strong collective mobilisation took place in Denmark, Norway and Iceland. This was concentrated within the younger age groups, well-educated women and representatives of the new middle classes as well as the left-wing parties. Sweden diverged from this pattern. Participation in the Swedish grass-roots actions was quantitatively larger but more evenly distributed across different social and political groups. Age, educational level and gender were only weakly connected to the extent of mobilisation. Grass-roots participation in Sweden functioned rather as a complement to the general repertoire of politically active citizens (see also Gundelach 1993).

Political culture in Denmark has developed in constant interaction with counter-cultural influences. Conflict between the new social movements and the formal political system has not been marked. In general, however, the Danish movements have distanced themselves from the formal decision-making bodies and authorities to a greater extent than similar movements have done in the other Nordic countries. This may be due to the fact that historically civil society has been relatively well developed, a fact reflected in the ability of the antiauthoritarian movements to connect with popular concerns during the 1960s and 1970s.

---

33. According to Mathiesen (1982), inclusion may be adopted to detach the radical head of the movement from its broader body of support and thus to weaken or hobble it, while exclusion is used as part of a strategy to label the movement as "extreme" and "deviant". Thus, the movement has to choose between holding firm to its original demands and risk marginalisation or accept compromises and risk incorporation.

For a long time, the new movements maintained an oppositional and counter-cultural stance, although protest eventually became institutionalised in Denmark as well (Gundelach 1993). As chapter 4 showed, Danish women have been especially active in searching for alternative channels to political participation. Thus, to a large extent, the new women's movement mobilisation during the 1970s and 1980s took place outside of the political parties.

Finland differed markedly from the rest of the Nordic countries because movement activity there did not emerge until the end of the 1970s and grass-roots participation never became an established part of political life. Instead, traditional peace, environmental and women's rights organisations have provided the mainstay of collective activity in Finland. Both the country's political and historical traditions and its "special relationship" with the former Soviet Union have been used to account for its divergent patterns (Togeby 1989). The comparatively late modernisation of the country could provide another explanation. A consequence of this was that a dominant agrarian-conservative culture did not start to break down until the end of the 1960s. The politicisation of the youth and student organisations along party lines contributed to the delay in the emergence of the new movements. As the history of the New Left was short in Finland, there was no comparable anti-authoritarian tradition to draw upon. This may offer another explanation for the low level of activity, and the conventional forms of action, within the Finnish movements (Paastela 1987; Siisiäinen 1995:99 f.).

Furthermore, it is interesting to note that in contrast to other Nordic countries, there have been few signs of a high level of movement activity amongst women in Finland. This may be related to the fact that women's situation in working life did not change as explosively, and traditional gender patterns were not challenged in such a thorough way, as elsewhere in the Nordic region. The roots of women's labour market participation in Finland stretch back further than is the case in other Western countries, as does the tradition of political organising by women. Possibly for this reason, women's mobilisation has been directed primarily into the established political organisations rather than into social movements (Togeby 1989; Bergman 1998; cf. chapter 4).

There is, however, no clear-cut connection between participation in movement politics or in grass-roots activity and the role of the movements as cultural and social agents of change. The movements may be subject to wider changes in value patterns and consciousness, without such changes always being reflected at the organisational level. Gundelach points out that this could be particularly true for the Nordic countries, where the openness of the political system may mean that there is insufficient time for a movement to be formed before reform policies lead to an incorporation of protest. For this reason, it is interesting to look at the way in which the surveys on citizenship in Denmark, Norway and Sweden have analysed the affinity that inhabitants have for social movements (cf. Table 3.3. in chapter 3). According to these studies, women seem to show a higher affinity than men and the young tend to feel more attachment to movements than their older peers. Comparable data are lacking in Finland and Iceland. However, in a European study where the attitudes of the population to social movements were measured, a similar pattern was evident in all Nordic countries. Sympathy for the movements was generally high everywhere (cf. Gundelach 1993:358 f.). This study indicates that Finns were also attracted by the sorts of issues prioritised by the movements, a conclusion that seems to be confirmed by the relatively strong political support in Finland for the Green movement.

The New Women's Movement in the Nordic Countries

It is possible to differentiate between two periods during which Nordic women's movement activity has shown special diversity and strength: the period around the turn of the century, and again during the 1970s and the 1980s. The focus of this chapter is that part of women's political mobilisation that has been channelled through the new social movements over the last few decades. First, though, we discuss the central developmental features of the feminist orientated, "new" women's movement.

The term *feminist movement* has usually been reserved for forms of women's activity that explicitly aim to challenge the dominant power relations or division of labour between the sexes. However, the difficulty of providing a general definition of the rich diversity of feminisms has led many scholars to use the term simply as a synonym for *women's movement*.[34] Against this latter tendency, critical voices have warned that it is not possible to draw general conclusions from women's political history on the basis of an analysis that is restricted to feminist movements or women's rights organisations. Our gaze must also be turned to other citizens' movements and voluntary organisations where women have been active (Saarinen 1992). For example, narrow definitions of women's movements can easily obscure those political and social activities that emanate from female difference, irrespective of whether this is based upon motherhood, women's welfare, or women's caring orientation. Thus, despite the fact that the feminist movement has attracted fewer participants than several of the traditional women's organisations, it is nonetheless an interesting example of how large groups of women in the Western world were rapidly mobilised within a broad and diverse culture of protest. The political and cultural effects of the new feminism were thereby extended far beyond the actual ranks of movement activists.

Several scholars of women's movements have used an approach based upon "developmental phases" to periodise the history of the new women's movement. The discussion below is partly inspired by Drude Dahlerup's (1998) discussion of the phases of the new women's movement in Denmark. However, the move-

---

34. Yet, a broad definition may be problematic if it also includes organisations, networks and groups that do not strive for feminist reforms or that fail to confront the gender order. Some researchers have therefore sought to use "women's movement" as an umbrella term for different forms of women's organising and "feminist movement" as a more narrow concept (cf. Andreasen *et al.* 1991; Eduards 1992; Rönnblom 1993; Bergman 1995).

ment seems to have gone through similar developmental phases in other countries as well (cf. Björkander-Mannheimer 1984; Bergman 1995; Lønnå 1996). An exception here is Finland, where new feminist forms of mobilisation occurred later and were less extensive than was the case in the other Nordic countries. Because of the exceptional character of the Finnish case, extra space is devoted to this issue. The general picture given below should primarily be seen as a starting point for further comparative studies. Clearly, more research is needed to produce a fully adequate picture. An analysis of the differences between the Nordic countries is hindered by the general lack of empirical research on the women's movement in most of these countries. The majority of studies of the organisational and ideological development of the new women's movement in the Nordic countries have focused on the 1970s and the early 1980s, while later phases have only recently become central concerns for research (see, however, Kuusipalo 1994; Lønnå 1996; Gustafsson 1997; Dahlerup 1998).[35]

We distinguish between the sex-role debate of the 1960s; consciousness raising and feminist activity during the first half of the 1970s; women's projects and feminist counter-culture from the mid-1970s and the institutionalisation of the movement since the 1980s. In addition, we will deal with some of the central issues of feminist organisation during the 1990s in our concluding discussion.

The Sex-Role Debate

When we study the new women's movement in the Nordic countries, it is important to treat the sex-role movement as a separate phase rather than to reduce it to the "prehistory" of new feminism. The movement had an important impact on later debates on women's position and roles and, not least, on the formation of gender equality policy (Haavio-Mannila 1979:60; Lönnå 1996:192 ff.).[36] As early as the 1950s, Nordic social scientists emphasised the socially constructed and thus changeable nature of sex roles. The growing influence of sociology and new insights into the impact of socialisation and the social environment on human behaviour combined to undermine the basis for the traditional division of labour. In 1962, Swedish and Norwegian social scientists (Dahlström et al. 1962) published *Kvinnors liv och arbete* ("Women's Life and Work"). The publication of this "Bible of the sex-role movement" (Vestbro 1992:58) received considerable attention in all the Nordic countries and soon led to the establish-

---

35. Studies of the new women's movement in the Nordic countries in the 1980s include Haukaa 1982; Streijffert 1983; Jallinoja 1983; Dahlerup and Gulli 1983a; Styrkarsdóttir 1986; Dahlerup 1986. There are very few comparative Nordic studies on the women's movement. Instead, the recollections of Nordic movement activists have been documented in a Finnish-language publication based on the contributions to a workshop at the Nordic Forum in Turku/Åbo in 1994 (Mattila and Suorsa 1994).

36. The publications from this period are still worthy of attention today in order to avoid what one 1990s Swedish feminist warns against, namely that "young feminists may be enticed to believe that the latest wave of the women's struggle started with Group 8" (Hultman 1995, footnote 16, p. 204).

ment of a Nordic research network on sex-role issues (Baude 1992; Dahlerup 1998).

The debate spread beyond the academic community after the Swedish journalist Eva Moberg published *Kvinnans villkorliga frigivning* ("The Circumscribed Liberation of Woman"; reproduced in print in Baude 1992, app. 3). Moberg emphasised that women and men ought to have the same roles and that both sexes should be seen as individuals rather than gendered beings. These ideas received a positive response throughout the Nordic region and led to lively Nordic cooperation. Discussion of sex roles and equality issues was particularly associated with the social democrats, but the debate also spread to the women's organisations and youth sections of the liberal parties. The gender ideology that is still dominant in the Nordic countries grew out of this academic and political debate on sex roles (Jallinoja 1983:146 ff; Lønnå 1996:221 ff.).

In political terms, the impact of the sex-role debate was probably greatest in Sweden. Gender equality policies were not as important a part of party politics in either Denmark or Norway during the 1960s. The Swedish Social Democrats incorporated sex-role thinking into their ambitious reform policies (Kalleberg 1979:74). In Finland, the sex-role debate led, through the founding of Association 9 in 1966, to a series of nation-wide initiatives.[37] After the ideological-political atmosphere had become more state-orientated at the end of the 1960s, the sex-role activists decided to act "where the real decisions are made" (Jallinoja 1983:184). Association 9 was dissolved and the sex-role debate was integrated into the political parties and organisations (see also Holli 1990).

Consciousness Raising and Feminist Activity

The discussion of issues surrounding sex roles and gender equality occurred comparatively early on in the Nordic countries. However, the new feminist movement emerged first in the United States, and subsequently spread at the end of the 1960s to Western Europe. The roots of the new feminism in the Nordic countries are to be found in both the sex-role debate and the diffusion of international currents. The beginning of the 1970s saw a growing engagement in women's issues. The old women's rights organisations received ideological and organisational-strategic impulses, at the same time as new groupings grew in the wake of student movement and New Left radicalism. Initially these groupings espoused essentially socialist goals, although later these were combined with, or replaced by, more feminist orientated perspectives. The core of the new women's movement during the 1970s comprised party-politically non-aligned groups and organisations: in Denmark, the Redstockings (plus splinter groups); in Norway, the Women's Front, the New Feminists and Bread and Roses; in Finland,

---

37. See, however, Vestbro (1992:60) on corresponding activities at the local level in Sweden. In Denmark, a radical youth movement emerged within the Danish Women's Society at the end of the 1960s. This organisation later cooperated with the Redstockings (Dahlerup 1998). In Iceland, a youth group was also active within the Icelandic women's rights association in the 1960s (Styrkarsdóttir 1986).

the Feminists and the Women's Union;[38] in Sweden, Group 8 and the Lund Women's League; and in Iceland, the Redstockings. Lesbian groups were formed in the mid-1970s in Denmark, Norway and Sweden. In Finland, lesbian organising was not visible until the 1980s (Gråt inte, kämpa 1982; Dahlerup and Gulli 1983a; Saarinen 1990; Halsaa 1992; Lønnå 1996:221 f.).

Initially feminist activity was offensive in character and directed outwards to societal issues of crucial importance to women, but gradually it became more introverted in the form of *consciousness-raising groups*. Instead of working through official channels with the state as the focus, the primary strategy was to build up non-hierarchical, autonomous and decentralised groups. However, there were exceptions from this "flat" model of organising: the Women's Front in Norway and the Women's Union in Finland followed a more traditional structure than the New Feminists in Norway and the Feminists in Finland. Between these groups the conflicts were sometimes bitter (Haukaa 1992; Jallinoja 1983:201).

Internationally speaking, the Nordic countries are characterised by a relatively weak "new" women's movement, even if variations within the Nordic region are large. In its autonomous and radical form, the movement was most widely spread in Denmark and Iceland during the 1970s and weakest in Finland, with the movement in Norway and Sweden occupying a middle position. These differences have been accounted for by reference to the role of the New Left and the importance of the party-political women's organisations in acting as channels for women's protest (Dahlerup and Gulli 1983a). The antiauthoritarian influence of the New Left on political culture was especially strong in Denmark. The Redstockings emerged in part as an extension of the youth rebellion of the 1960s, and in part as a protest against its dominance by men (Christensen 1986). The party-political women's organisations have been relatively strong and independent in Finland and Sweden, while they were abolished in Denmark in the 1960s "in the name of equality". In Sweden, the gender role ideology was integrated in the 1960s by the hegemonic Social Democratic Party and its women's federation as well as the trade union movement. In Finland, the sex-role activists were also directed into the state apparatus and recruited as the builders of the welfare state (Rubart and Peterson 1985; Holli 1990).

Thus, gender issues were politicised early on in both Finland and Sweden. One consequence of this early politicisation of gender issues was that space for the development of the new movements and associated protest activity remained limited. Several other reasons may be advanced for this state of affairs including: the predominance of the consensus orientation of the Swedish and Finnish societies, the high level of trust placed in gender neutral reforms, and the strong emphasis placed upon the avoidance of confrontation between the sexes. The more

---

38. The Women's Union is treated here as a part of the feminism of the 1970s, because power within this old and venerable organisation passed to younger feminists following a coup in the mid-1970s. The years during which the shift in power occurred were very conflict-laden (Jallinoja 1983:200 f.).

limited spread of consciousness-raising groups in Sweden and Finland, compared to the rest of the Nordic countries, can also be regarded as an expression
of differences between the countries in these areas (cf. Jallinoja 1983:198 f.;
Gelb 1989:146; Elman 1996; Julkunen 1997).[39]

Thus, Denmark and Finland can be seen as opposite poles regarding the development and impact of the new women's movement. The Danish Redstocking
movement formed an offensive and highly visible political counter-force during
the 1970s. To a greater extent than in the other countries, the movement was
characterised by both a pronounced feminist counter-culture and a politics of
confrontation, including spectacular and anarchistic protest actions. The wom-
en's cultural festivals in Copenhagen and the summer camps on Femø attracted
the interest of broad groups of women (Dahlerup 1998).

In Finland, the new women's movement was established much later than in
the other Nordic countries and the role of radical feminism was especially modest. While the new feminism was mostly embedded in the student movement and
grew in protest against its sexism and male dominance, the Finnish movement
emerged on the periphery of the party-politically organised student movement
and amongst the politically non-aligned. One reason for this was that the New
Left was short-lived and weak in Finland, being succeeded by a rapid party-
politicisation of the student and youth movements. In particular, Soviet Union-
orientated "minority communism" was attractive to many student activists and
intellectuals; groups who otherwise might have been attracted to the new feminism.[40] Only after the stagnation of the student movement at the close of the
1970s, did feminism gain some wind under its sails. Mariella Lindén (1981:66)
has described this in the following way:

> The growth of the women's movement to a large extent has occurred simultane-
> ously with the diluted remains of Stalinism reaching such a level of passivity that
> the monolith finally started to disintegrate from the inside, thus opening up in-
> creasing space for new ideas.

During the greater part of the decade the new feminism was concentrated within
the Swedish-language parts of Finland (Haavio-Mannila 1979). As "minority
communism" was never very strong amongst Swedish-speaking intellectuals,
more space existed for radical and non-dogmatic currents independent of party
politics (Siisiäinen 1991:35 f.; Paastela 1987:34). Another reason was the position of the Finland-Swedes as gateways for cultural and social currents from
Scandinavia.[41]

The Finland-Swedish dominance of the discussion may have contributed to
the lack of interest in the new feminism on the part of Finnish speakers (Haavio-

---

39. However, the lack of comparative research makes it difficult for us to schematically classify
    Denmark and Norway as less consensus-orientated than Finland and Sweden.

40. While the more reform-minded faction of the People's Democratic League (cf. Appendix) was
    included in government, only the "minority communists" represented a "fundamental opposi-
    tion" that attracted radical students and intellectuals (Siisiäinen 1990:67).

Mannila 1979:60). This suspicion can be discerned in a contribution to the Left Wing newspaper *Kansan Uutiset* (19.4.1978):

> One has tried to deny the international nature of the Finnish feminist movement by reducing it to some kind of mental disorder that a small group of frustrated Finland-Swedes in Helsinki suffer from. The fact that most of us are Finland-Swedes is because we have been able to follow the rich theoretical and political literature that has been shaped by the new women's movement and which, unfortunately, despite our persistent efforts, has not been translated into Finnish.

Some years later the language wall was broken down and during the 1980s the new feminism spread to the majority population.

The ideologically new element in the feminism of the 1970s may be summed up by the slogan "the private is political". One of its most important demands concerned "free" abortion on demand. The struggle for abortion mobilised many feminists in the Nordic countries. Self-determined abortion became possible in 1973 in Denmark, in 1975 in Sweden, and in 1979 in Norway. In Finland, the abortion issue never became such a focus for a feminist struggle as was the case in many other countries. The amendment of the Finnish legislation on abortion in 1970 was motivated more by equality concerns in respect of social, regional and health policy than it was by a concern for women's sexual and reproductive integrity. In Iceland, abortion is not self-determined either, but the Abortion Act of 1975 gives medical doctors the right to decide. In practice, however, abortion legislation has been applied in a liberal way in both Finland and Iceland (Styrkársdóttir 1986; Parvikko 1991; Outshoorn 1996; also, see Julkunen 1997:54).[42]

The international similarities in core areas of the new feminism are striking. Economic rights, political influence, and the bodily and sexual integrity of women have been important themes everywhere. Women's social rights, which have engaged feminists in many countries, have been incorporated in legislation on social and family policies in the Nordic countries. The attitudes of the women's movement to pornography and prostitution have varied within the Nordic area. For example, in Norway campaigns against pornography have been carried out since the end of the 1970s, whereas this issue has not been so important in Denmark (Dahlerup and Gulli 1983b:8; Lønnå 1996:277 f.; Dahlerup 1998).

In the mid-1970s, women's experiences and values became a focus for debate amongst Nordic feminists. The emphasis on gender difference and wom-

---

41. We argue that these factors were more important for the generally stronger grass-roots mobilisation that occurred amongst the Swedish-language population of Finland than is given credit for by Togeby, who mistakes the small size of this group for a marginalised minority position that was "hard pressed by the predominant development"(1989:129).

42. A Nordic comparison of the decision-making processes and the dynamics behind the liberalisation of the legislation on abortion would be interesting. For example, Raija Julkunen (1997) points out that in both Finland and Sweden it was the principle of social justice rather than women's autonomy that was followed. However, women's rights were considered to be of even less importance in Finland.

en's specificity was concretely expressed by Berit Ås' notion (1975) of "women's culture". This trend had an impact on both the new women's movement and more traditional women's organisations. It contributed to the broadening of the movement with respect to its social and age composition. Frauke Rubart has pointed out that the "delayed start" of the new feminism in Finland resulted in the movement jumping over a phase of spectacular mass activism that was so characteristic of other countries. Instead, from the beginning, the movement had an orientation towards a women-centred culture. Herein lies one possible explanation as to why it was the women's peace movement that gained such strong support in Finland, whereas, for a long time, questions of the body, sexuality and violence against women remained taboo and were almost invisible in political debates on gender issues (Witt-Brattström 1981:45; Rubart 1993; Lønnå 1996:229 ff.).

The various women's movements also differed in respect to their attitudes to political institutions and authorities. For a long time the radical core of the international women's movement preferred to maintain organisational autonomy. The state was considered to act as the "long arm" of capital and/or patriarchy. Nordic feminist theoreticians treated the state as a form of public patriarchy and argued that women had exchanged a dependence on private patriarchy for a dependence on the state. Later, attitudes towards the state became more differentiated and many activists began to support the type of "state feminism" that had developed in the Nordic countries. The state was seen as having the potential to develop women-friendly features (Hernes 1987; Siim 1993; Leira 1993; Borchorst 1994; Rantalaiho 1994).

From the beginning, the new women's movement in Norway and Iceland argued in favour of integration within the system of party politics, something that feminists in Denmark and Sweden distanced themselves from. In the latter countries it was the mainstream party-political and other established women's organisations that sought to increase the proportion of women on political bodies (Kalleberg 1979:71; Dahlerup and Gulli 1983b:8; Hedlund-Ruth and van der Ros Schive 1983; Styrkarsdóttir 1986). One of the first feminist campaigns in Norway concerned promoting an increase in female representation in politics. Some municipalities even obtained a female majority on their municipal boards by effectively carrying out a "women's coup". Cooperation between movement and party activists with the aim of increasing women's representation was already common in the 1970s. The engagement of the women's movement in such campaigns contributed to the exceptionally high level, by international standards, of female representation in parliament and government. Thus, the mobilisation of the new women's movement in Norway was partially directed into the political parties (cf. chapter 4). Whereas the Norwegian integration strategy increased the opportunities for cooperation with the political organisations and gave feminism political legitimacy, the situation was markedly different in Iceland. The background to the Icelandic women's activities in the 1970s was the failure of women to increase their representation in both the national parliament and in municipal politics. Only the emergence of special women's lists in the

1980s forced the established parties to comply, at least to some extent, with feminist demands (cf. chapter 5).

From Women's Projects and Feminist Counter-Culture to Movement Institutionalisation

Since the latter half of the1970s, a number of important changes have taken place in the strategies adopted by the new women's movement. The consciousness-raising groups encouraged a willingness to work with self-organised or autonomous women's projects. These projects involved the dissemination of information (through the setting up of publishing houses, magazines, bulletins, newsletters and bookshops), a strengthening of social interaction and communication (using institutions such as pubs, cafés, camps, holiday houses), the provision of social services (in the form of advice, therapy, centres for battered women, rape lines, etc.) and the development of culture, education and research (based around theatre, film and music groups, museums, women's studies, documentation and information centres, libraries, and archives). The feminist counter-culture that resulted was, above all, characterised by the development of the movement's own networks of projects, alternative institutions and experimentation in life styles. This counter-culture was not explicitly or exclusively orientated towards the political system.

During the 1980s the women's movement developed from an essentially diffuse social movement into an organised political interest. A number of movement activists began to enter social institutions and established organisations. The orientation that started with a project focus was deepened by the increasing institutionalisation, specialisation and professionalisation of the women's movement. This explains why the new women's movement appeared to lose strength. Feminists increasingly began to campaign for gender equality policies, join political organisations, engage in women's studies, set up women's refuges, etc. Even if an acknowledged need for leadership and more formal structures resulted in the new women's movement gradually developing elements of interest organisation activity, the small group-centred structure was never fully abandoned. Indeed, it has influenced forms of organising and working methods far beyond the actual core of the feminist movement.

Activity within the women's movement at this time was not limited solely to organising within the new women's movement itself. It also extended to involvement in other movements and projects, which often could be regarded as extensions of the women's movement in terms of form and content. For example, many women were mobilised by environmental or anti-nuclear power movements or eco-feminist groups with roots in the new women's movement. In Sweden, the nuclear power issue led to a widespread participation of women before the referendum in 1980. The coverage of the new peace movement was extensive throughout the Nordic region and, for example, the Swedish women's movement was above all visible at the beginning of the 1980s as a peace movement. In Finland and Sweden the women's peace movement partially grew out of the opposition to nuclear power (Rantanen 1980:49; Peterson and Merchant 1985; Rubart and Peterson 1985; Peterson 1985; Christensen 1986; Rubart 1993). The popular movements and the campaigns against membership of the European Community engaged many feminists and, especially in Norway and Denmark, gave the women's movement a distinctive profile. The movement "Women in the Nordic countries against the EC" was founded in 1991 (Skjøns-berg et al. 1993; Dahlerup 1998).

Tensions between the gender equality orientated women's organisations and grass-roots orientated feminism gave way to more pragmatic cooperation. One consequence of this development was that long established women's rights organisations and women's political organisations, as well as new social movements, became platforms for feminist ideas. The remaining differences between these organisations lay primarily in questions of organisational structure, political strategy, forms of action and styles of activity. The contents of demands were similar, despite differences in rhetorical emphasis. However, ideological differences still persisted. Whereas the traditional women's organisations were essentially reform-minded, the new feminist movement was, for example, more critical of the public gender equality policy. Differences were also marked in respect of attitudes towards "male society". The new feminists sought confrontation and conflict, whereas the established women's organisations appealed for consensus and harmony (Jallinoja 1983:201; Dahlerup and Gulli 1983a; Streijffert 1983; Halsaa 1992:17; Lønnå 1996:225 ff.).[43]

In terms of ideology, the earlier tendency to divide feminism into radical, socialist and liberal branches was replaced in the 1980s by other categorisations, such as equality and difference feminism, constructivist and essentialist feminism, women-centred or "standpoint" feminism and deconstructivist diversity feminism. The move towards a feminism characterised by self-reflexive post-modernism meant that earlier "truths" were increasingly questioned. The divergences between women and different types of womanhood occupied the centre of debate. Today, feminist theorising and women's politics face challenges from lesbian activists, migrant and rural women, and post-colonial women (see, e.g., Saarinen 1992; Ravn 1995; Rönnblom 1997).

Women's Mobilisation through the Peace and Crisis Centre Movements

In this section the women's peace movement and the crisis centre movement will be used to exemplify the transformation of the new women's movement arising out of the growth of women's activity in other new social movements and specialised projects and organisations during the 1980s. Violent military con-

---

43. The fact that the lines of division between radical-autonomous feminism and more reformist feminism were scarcely sharp, even before this, is something that is sometimes played down in descriptions of the new women's movement (cf. Lønnå, footnote 656, p. 305).

flicts and violence against women were important factors encouraging the women's movement to seek out new institutional forms. The cross-party political women's peace movement appealed to broad groups of women in all Nordic countries. Yet, to a large extent, it may simultaneously be regarded as an extension of the new women's movement in an ideological and organisational sense. The movement's traditional concern with the issue of violence against women led to the setting up of crisis centres and refuges for women in all the Nordic countries, except Finland. The crisis centre movement is an example of a successful and stable institutionalisation of a grass-roots initiative. It is a broad-based movement that is supported from many directions, whilst simultaneously standing upon feminist principles.

The availability of empirical research material has influenced the perspectives used in our analysis of the movements. Although we were able to study and compare the political-ideological contents of the Nordic women's movements, their style of activities and working methods, participant structures and political effects, the existing research on women's peace movements or crisis centre movements was more limited in this respect. Here we primarily focus on the political contents of these movements. We also apply a participant perspective in respect of the women's peace movement, whereas we discuss instead the political and legislative impact of the crisis centre movement.

The Peace Issue is also a Women's Issue

The peace movement is not a "new" movement. The first peace organisations were established back in the nineteenth century. Independent organising by women around the peace issue also has long roots: the Women's International League for Peace and Freedom was founded in 1915. The Cold War contributed to an ideological split in the peace movement during the first few decades after the Second World War. This also had an impact on the Nordic peace movements. In Finland, in particular, the peace movement was sharply divided into two ideological camps.

The campaigns against nuclear weapons and the pacifist currents within the student and the New Left movements altered the political strategies and ideological orientation of the peace organisations. Opposition to the arms race and weapons of mass destruction provided a bridge to the new peace movement. NATO's decision in 1979 to deploy cruise missiles in Europe, the heightened conflicts between the Super Powers and the spiralling arms race represented a turning-point for the international peace movement. At the beginning of the 1980s the peace movement in Europe grew into a broad-based mass movement (Brock-Utne 1981; Paastela 1987; Christensen 1990, 1991).[44]

The emergence of the new peace movement in the Nordic countries led to reorganisation and renewed activity on the part of the traditional peace organisations alongside the formation of new peace groups. The peace movement itself has always contained both women who prefer to organise separately and women who choose to work within mixed-sex peace organisations. The new women's

peace movement in the Nordic countries comprised both traditional women's organisations who involved themselves in peace issues as well as women who mobilised within mixed-sex peace organisations. In addition, women organised
within the autonomous and cross-party political movement *Women for Peace*.
This movement was based upon feminist principles, with an emphasis on autonomous and non-hierarchical small groups. The movement initially organised a
petition against the stationing of cruise missiles in Europe. The campaign was
launched around a kitchen table in Denmark. A Nordic meeting followed in Oslo
and, in January 1980, a decision was made to initiate a common Nordic peace
campaign. Within four months of the launch of the petition more than 500,000
women's signatures (in Finland the petition was also extended to men) were collected. The petition was handed over to the Secretary General of the United Nations, Kurt Waldheim, during the UN Women's Year conference held in
Copenhagen in July 1980 and it was subsequently sent to the leaders of the USA
and the USSR (Naisten rauhanpamfletti 1981; Brock-Utne 1981; Christensen
1990:38).

Soon thereafter the first peace marches and peace seminars took place. These
were followed in 1981 by the Nordic Peace March from Copenhagen to Paris,
the central demand of which was "A Nuclear Free Norden". The following year
a peace march was organised from Stockholm to Moscow and Minsk and in
1983 a march was organised to Washington and Latin America. Peace marches
and other mass protests attracted large groups of people during the first part of
the 1980s. The establishment of special women's peace camps, such as that at
Greenham Common in Great Britain was a concrete expression of the connection between the new women's movement and the women's peace movement.
In Denmark, a peace camp for women similar to the Greenham Common camp
was set up during the years 1984–85 in Ravnstrup. The movement lost impetus
towards the end of the decade, but the peace issue continued to be raised within
the political parties and organisations (Naisten rauhanpamfletti 1981; Brock-
Utne 1981; Christensen 1990).

Danish and Swedish studies have revealed wide variations in women's motives for participating in the peace movements. We can differentiate between a
radical feminist orientated women's peace movement and a humanitarian-moral
inspired women's peace movement. As a result, the collective identity of activists can be categorised as either that of the "oppressed female citizen" or that of
the "mother". The first-mentioned group assumes that women are an oppressed

---

44. Since the second World War, the Finnish peace movement has consisted of the Moscow-friend-
ly Peace Fighters (who were led by the communists together with the Centre Party and parts of
Social Democracy) and the pacifist Peace Union, the main support for which came from
amongst Christian peace activists. These movements were challenged in the 1960s by the radical pacifist Committee of One Hundred, until its marginalisation during the fierce political in-
fighting of the 1970s. It was only towards the end of the decade, when the political fortunes of
the Peace Fighters had already begun to wane, that pacifist ideas started to take root. The Committee of One Hundred and the Peace Union expanded rapidly and, together with the women's
peace movement, they formed the core of the new peace movement (Paastela 1987).

group and it tends to see war and violence as a by-product of the destructive forms of power politics pursued by men. Often the background of this group of activists lay in the feminist movement and the political and organisational ideas they held were frequently formed through their contact with that milieu. The other group was dominated by women who previously had not been politically active or who had no direct experience of the feminist movement. A part of this second group regarded feminists as too radical or "hostile towards men". Many of the women cited their roles as mothers and their responsibility for the coming generations as reasons for their commitment to peace work. Their involvement was based on the existing gender-based division of labour in society (Peterson 1985; Christensen 1991; Lønnå 1996:264 f.).

Different points of emphasis were evident within the national "Women for Peace" campaigns, with the differences especially significant between Denmark and Sweden. The Danish movement had ideological and organisational ties to the broader women's movement, although not necessarily to the Redstockings. In the case of Denmark, participants were mobilised on the basis of the traditional values associated with the idea of a common female culture (Christensen 1990:42). In the case of Sweden, by contrast, the peace movement was tied to the feminist movement and had a partly overlapping membership and core of activists (Peterson 1985). In Finland, the peace movement grew alongside the new women's movement and adopted its cultural "women-specific" orientation. "Women for Peace" was founded in Finland on the initiative of the Women's Union (Jallinoja 1983:208). The women's peace movement was relatively strong in Finland, possibly because it was considered to be less provocative than radical feminism.

The new peace movement was probably the most important movement of the 1980s and it mobilised the greatest numbers of people. The Danish, Norwegian and Swedish surveys on citizenship indicate that empathy for the peace movement among women was greater than it was among men in all age groups. Similarly, in Finland, women participated in peace marches in greater numbers than men (cf. Paastela 1987). Women's organisations cooperated on peace issues across party-political boundaries. At the beginning of the 1980s, the peace issue could be regarded as the common denominator of the broad women's movement. For example, in 1983 all women's organisations in Sweden (altogether more than fifty) mentioned "peace" as the issue they gave the highest priority to (Peterson 1985:633). The women's peace movement reached younger and older women, women in cities as well as on the countryside, women from all social groupings and classes.

The Crisis Centre Movement

The struggle against violence against women has engaged women activists in the Nordic countries since the 1970s. The autonomous consciousness-raising groups, which formed the core of the new women's movement during the 1970s politicised areas of life, which earlier had been considered private and personal.

Issues taken up by these small groups gradually developed into demands for, among other things, crisis centres and battered women's refuges. Such centres and refuges were subsequently founded by activists within the new women's movement as alternative grass-roots initiatives. Although today they are usually supported, and in some cases even wholly run, by the public sector. The crisis centre movement is an excellent example of the close cooperation that exists between civil society and the state (Morken and Selle 1995; Dahlerup 1998). The movement redefined violence against women. Henceforth it was to be treated as a structural problem of social concern rather than as a private and invisible phenomenon. Nordic crisis centres are still partially run on a voluntary basis and follow feminist and non-hierarchical principles (cf. Gelb 1989:147; Halsaa 1992:13; Eduards 1997; Dahlerup 1998).

The first battered women's refuges were founded in 1978–79, in Denmark, Norway and Sweden, and in 1982, in Iceland. During the 1980s national movements for women's refuges quickly sprang up. At the beginning of the 1990s there were around thirty battered women's refuges in Denmark, more than fifty in Norway and more than 130 in Sweden. The questions of organisational structure and strategy towards the authorities have often generated conflicts within the movements (Halsaa 1992:13; Morken and Selle 1995:180; Eduards 1997; Dahlerup 1998). Interestingly, one feature that strongly distinguishes Finland from the rest of the Nordic countries is the almost total absence of battered women's refuges with origins in the feminist movement.[45] Instead, so-called "protection homes", for women and children suffering from what is generally referred to in Finland as "family violence", have been established by municipalities and other public associations. Today, there are approximately fifty "protection homes" in Finland. In contrast to the refuges in the other countries, these homes are mainly run by employed staff, not voluntary workers. The service they provide is based upon the principles of child protection and every effort is made to bring about a reconciliation between the parties in conflict. The battering of women is not conceived of as a consequence of the power relations between the sexes. Rather, it is primarily seen to result from problems of communication within the family. Men have access to the protected homes both as clients and as employees, and the addresses of the homes are not kept secret (Naisiin kohdistuva väkivalta 1991:36 ff.).

Similarly, Finnish legislation on violence against women and sexualised violence has lagged behind the other Nordic countries (Julkunen 1997). The same is also true for gay and lesbian rights. Hence, the association "Nordic Women Against Violence" has emphasised that with regard to sexual and bodily integrity, Finnish women live "under considerably worse conditions than women elsewhere in the Nordic region" (cf. Eduards 1997:144). This Finnish

---

45. Two exceptions to this general state of affairs are the Women's Refuge in the Finland-Swedish town of Jakobstad in Ostrobothnia and a newly initiated project in Turku/Åbo. Yet, feminists did discuss questions of violence against women as far back as the late 1970s, but this did not result in the setting up of any crisis centres (Naisiin kohdistuva väkivalta 1991:33 ff.).

exceptionalism may possibly be connected to the fact that radical-autonomous feminism has been relatively weak, and that the struggle for abortion rights never became a catalyst for reorientating the women's movement towards issues of sexual and bodily integrity as was the case in many other Western countries. More recently, however, the gender equality authorities in Finland have taken many initiatives to reform legislation, and the issue of violence against women has gained more political visibility during the 1990s.

The 1990s: "Post-feminism" and "Backlash"?

Since the 1980s both women's movements and other new social movements in the Nordic countries have focused on new types of political issues and arenas. The orientation towards loose coalitions, networks and action groups has been deepened. At the same time, the 1990s have been described in the mass media as a period characterised by "post-feminism" and political apathy. Both the feminist movement and other movements have been seen as paralysed, if not declared "dead". On the one hand, it is claimed that, to a large degree, movement demands have been realised. On the other hand, the political conservatism of the 1990s is regarded to have brought a reduced commitment to gender equality policies and feminism.

During the first half of the 1990s many women experienced a "backlash" against gender equality.[46] For this reason, opinion forming activity and lobbying was intensified and collective campaign activity by the women's movement became more visible once again. In Sweden, the cuts in welfare state provisions and in the public sector, as well as women's reduced representation in the parliament after the 1991 general election, prompted renewed feminist activity. Much publicity was given to the Supportstocking Movement, with its slogan "Half the Power and the Full Salary", and the strategic threat posed by the formation of a Women's Party (Eduards 1992; Gustafsson 1997). The events in Sweden show that women's movement activity can be regarded as a process characterised both by fluctuations between rising and falling levels of activity, and recurring periods during which movement activity remains "in abeyance" (cf. Rupp and Taylor 1991). At the same time the movement remains latent in the collective consciousness, as well as in a multitude of different social and political institutions and organisations. Once stimulated, a new mobilisation may therefore occur relatively rapidly and effectively.

Women have become increasingly well organised in their own networks, groupings and projects, as well as political and trade union organisations at a time when the established party political organisations have encountered growing difficulties in the recruitment and retention of members (Gustafsson 1997). Another trend points to an increased dialogue between party political organisa-

---

46. Susan Faludi's best-seller *Backlash* (1991), which describes the political reaction to the women's movement in the United States, created quite a stir in the Nordic countries (cf. Backlash i Sverige 1993; Backlash i Norge 1993; Julkunen 1994).

tions and independent women's movements. In addition, cooperation across party political boundaries has become more common.[47] Nordic cooperation between "grass-roots" and "established" women has been expressed, for example, in the major women's and gender equality event, Nordic Forum, which brought some 10,000 participants together in Oslo, the Norwegian capital, in 1988 and around 16,000 participants to the Finnish city of Turku/Åbo six years later.

Conclusion

Women's mobilisation and organisation in social movements reflect national political cultures and movement traditions. Therefore it is not strange to discover that autonomous feminism occurred in its most "pure" form in Denmark, and that grass-roots activity in general was remarkably active in that country, or that it was especially low in Finland. The extension of the women's movement into such forms of movement organising as the women's peace movement and the movement for battered women's refuges, reflected the nationally conditioned differences in new feminist mobilisation. At the same time, striking similarities between the movements have been apparent across the Western world. This is a consequence, among other things, of the diffusion of ideas and collective learning processes. In recent years, movement activity has gradually become more diverse and pluralistic everywhere. Hence it has become more difficult to talk about national characteristics in women's organising or indeed about the movement in a particular country being characterised by a single "feminism".

The new social movements in the Nordic countries have sought to influence the political system to a greater extent than similar movements have done elsewhere. The attitude of the movements to institutional politics has certainly varied according to country due to differences in political culture and movement traditions. Yet, the movements have also become integrated into political organisations and institutions in those countries where earlier the preference was to remain outside of the parliamentary sphere. Thus, a certain convergence in approach between the movements in the various Nordic countries is also evident in this respect. On the one hand, the movements have created new institutions everywhere, while, on the other hand, they have also influenced existing institutions. For example, the environmental movements in Finland and Sweden have formed formal organisations and new political parties at the same time as ecological and nuclear power concerns have been integrated into the political programmes of several of the old "established" parties. Certain new party formations (the environmental parties and left socialist parties) have been closely associated with the new movements and have functioned as channels linking

---

47. Examples of such cooperation include the women's network in the Finnish parliament and the Coalition of Finnish Women's Association for Joint Action (Nytkis) between women's party-political federations, the National Council for Women in Finland, the Women's Union and the Finnish Women's Studies Association (cf. Gustafsson 1997:47 for corresponding examples from Sweden).

them to the formal political system, but the traditional parties have also been influenced by these developments.

Similarly, some women's issues have been taken up by the political parties and included within gender equality policy at the same time that the new women's movement has developed specialised and professional projects and institutions. Critiques of male dominance and traditional power hierarchies do not necessarily require the movement to abstain from participating in the political exercise of power. An interesting case study in this respect concerns the rapid transformation of a social movement into a political interest organisation through the emergence of a women's party in Iceland (cf. chapter 5). At the same time, we can state that a heterogeneous movement such as the women's movement has simultaneously been subject to both inclusion and exclusion. Formal political organisations and the state have integrated those issues that suited them, while more radical ideas have been rejected. However, this selective institutionalisation need not necessarily be interpreted as a defeat for the movement. The redirection of movement demands towards the institutional level might also be regarded as something positive, even in cases where it leads to movement passivity or dissolution.

More recent women's movement research has argued that the movement has been in a state of "abeyance" since the 1980s. Despite the undoubted decline in many forms of grass-roots activity, the movement has continued to exercise influence within Nordic political institutions and organisations, the public equality apparatuses, women's culture, women's groups, projects and networks, as well as within women's studies and gender research in all its great variety. Above all, the movement continues to exist as a widespread collective identity. The more moderate equality oriented feminism may have achieved the most visible political successes, but radical-autonomous feminism has left deep impressions in the collective consciousness. Other movements of the 1970s and the 1980s have witnessed a similar decline into fragmented action groups, often orientated to single-issue campaigns within the local community. Thus, social movements can also exist in the form of changed norms, values and identities as well as political action, even if they do not necessarily trigger a response from the political and organisational system.

The new social movements in the Nordic countries have stimulated new groups of women into becoming politically active. At the same time they have contributed to a discursive extension of the concept of politics. The content of politics has been redefined as questions relating to abortion, sexuality, violence against women, policies on gender equality and caring, as well as the environment and peace, have been integrated into mainstream political agendas. The movements have had a decisive impact by revealing the political potential of women. On the one hand, they have expressly attracted women. On the other hand, they have related to a sphere of life and experience that many women have valued highly. Women's mobilisation into new social movements and collective action in civil society has thereby given the concept of political citizenship a novel and deeper meaning.

PART II

Family policy in the Nordic welfare states

Theme editor: Christina Bergqvist

7

Childcare and Parental Leave Models

Christina Bergqvist[48]

As the previous chapters showed, the last twenty to thirty years have seen major changes, not only in way in which women have mobilised politically, but also in the ways in which they have participated and been represented at all levels within politics. In addition, the attachment of women to the labour market has generally strengthened, even if large differences remain between countries and between women and men. Furthermore, the Nordic countries are characterised by a strong public sector that provides social services of various kinds. Family policies make up an important part of the welfare system in all the Nordic countries. The bulk of childcare is financed by public means.[49] Each country has legislation on parental leave, which provides for either the mother or the father to take time away from work with compensation for loss of income in order to take care of the youngest children. Public responsibilities with respect to childcare and parental leave exist in other countries as well, but what is distinctive about the Nordic countries is the scope of such policies, their high level, and the public commitment to facilitate the combination of parenthood and paid employment for both women and men. Helga Hernes, who launched the notion of the women-friendly state, understood by this term that the Nordic welfare state has the potential to develop in such a way that greater justice and equality between women and men can be achieved. Other Nordic feminist scholars argue that women-friendliness is also connected to the idea that women should be treated as individuals within social legislation, not as the dependents of men (Hernes 1987; Borchorst 1994; Julkunen 1994; Sainsbury 1996). Family and welfare policies have become part of gender

---

48. The author wishes to thank Solveig Bergman, Jaana Kuusipalo, Minna Salmi and Auður Styrkarsdóttir for valuable information and comments.

49. This also applies to care of the elderly and other forms of publicly provided care, which are not dealt with here.

equality policy but, as this chapter will show, this has also taken different forms within the Nordic area.

The aim of this chapter is to provide an understanding of how the Nordic countries have organised the relationship between the state, the market and the family. By analysing reforms at the intersection of production and reproduction, such as *parental leave* and *childcare*, images of women as mothers and employees and, just as importantly, of men as fathers and employees are illustrated. The chapter gives an overview of the present situation regarding arrangements for childcare and parental leave in the five Nordic countries. Our findings point to a number of differences between the countries, especially in respect of the details of political development and the formation of policies. If, however, we look at the broad outlines and orientation of policies during the most recent years, we notice a growing convergence between the countries, amongst other things, as a consequence of Norway and Iceland "catching up" with the other Nordic countries through the expansion of their public responsibilities in these areas.

Care and Breadwinner Models

Feminist researchers have highlighted the lack of clarity in earlier research on the ways in which different welfare states vary in respect of their breadwinner models. Welfare policies which primarily build upon a model where the husband is the main breadwinner within the family, lead to gender related consequences that differ from those found in models based upon the individual/citizen. Diane Sainsbury has described two ideal-typical models, which she refers to as the *male breadwinner model* and the *individual model*. According to the male breadwinner model, social and taxation policies are constructed in such a way as to favour a family model based upon a primary breadwinner-husband and his primarily homemaker-spouse. Thus, wives and children are assumed to be economically dependent upon their respective husbands/fathers. By contrast, the individual model is based on the notion of the adult citizen as an autonomous individual. The individual model does not presuppose different policy models for the sexes; both women and men can, in turn, be either breadwinners or carers. Social and taxation policies are tied to the individual, not the family unit (1996:40 ff.).[50] The different ways in which care is structured affects both breadwinner models and helps to shape the broader discussion about the establishment of the welfare state and gender equality.

As several researchers have shown, the development of the Nordic countries has, in general, been associated with a transition from the idea of the male breadwinner model to the idea of a dual breadwinner family, that is to say the individual model (Julkunen 1994). Birte Siim claims that one of the biggest changes in Denmark during the last thirty years has been "the move from a male-breadwin-

---

50. Sainsbury's empirical comparison between the Netherlands, Great Britain, Sweden and the United States shows that Sweden comes closest to the individual model. See also Borchorst 1998a on the discussion of different breadwinner models.

ner to a dual-breadwinner norm, that is the public and the cultural expectation that both women and men are wage workers" (Siim 1997a:140). Today, women's share of the labour force is almost as large as men's. Norway is an exception in this respect due to the fact that women's rate of labour market activity there is somewhat lower than in the other countries. Yet in Norway, as in the other countries, the labour force participation rate for mothers with small children is higher than the rate for all women. In 1996, on average, 73.5 per cent of women and 79.8 per cent of the men were part of the labour force. The differences between women and men are no longer about who is engaged in waged work and who is not, rather they are about the kind of work women and men do, and the extent to which they are employed. In general, the labour market is both vertically and horizontally segregated: men are over represented at the higher levels of working life and most professional fields have a large majority either of women or of men (Nordic Statistical Yearbook 1997; see also Borchorst 1998a:133 ff.).

Unequal and gendered patterns in working life have their counterpart in the home, where the main responsibility for unpaid labour and the care of children falls to women/mothers. A gap exists between what is theoretically possible in terms of equality in the Nordic welfare states and what has been realised in practice. In many respects, gender specific patterns in the Nordic countries, as elsewhere, are being recast. At the same time, international comparisons show that married/cohabiting women in the Nordic countries are considerably less economically dependent on their partners than, for example, women elsewhere in Europe or North America. Levels of poverty amongst Nordic lone mothers are also very low in relative terms (Hobson and Takahashi 1997:122). Lone parents constitute a fairly large group in Nordic societies. According to statistics, women make up 80–90 per cent of this group (NOSOSKO 8:1998). Divorce is frequent, but as new partnerships are common after divorce, the total number of people registered as lone parents is larger than the number of individual adults who actually live alone with children. In addition, many parents share responsibility for the care of their children after divorce, which may also lead to a statistical exaggeration of lone motherhood. Furthermore, being a lone mother no longer carries the same stigma as earlier. Children born both within wedlock and outside of it have the same legal status, and lone parents are compensated economically through various welfare programmes.

The Vision of Equal Parenthood

Carole Pateman argues that Western feminists are now, for the first time, outlining a theory of social practice that equally includes women and men. This practice is based upon "the interrelationship of the individual to collective life, or personal to political life, instead of their separation and opposition" (Pateman 1989:135). According to Pateman, at an immediate practical level, the goal of gender quality requires that women and men share the household chores and the care of children. Thus, Pateman stresses that the possibility of achieving an equal partnership between the sexes is related to the way in which working life and the public sector is organised. Nordic legislation concerning opportunities for parents to share in the care of infants corresponds rather well to what Pateman describes as practical feminist policies. Different forms of maternity policies have existed since the start of industrialism, but it was only in the 1970s and 1980s that the idea gained widespread acceptance that fathers could participate in the care of their children. Sweden became the first country to introduce a reform of parental leave that included fathers in 1974. This policy innovation was explicitly meant to contribute to equality between women and men. It was based on the idea of the dual breadwinner family. Thereby parents were seen as economically independent individuals, both with obligations and rights in respect of their children as well as the labour market.

The introduction of the parental leave scheme institutionalised a new view of gender relations. The feminist idea that fathers as well as mothers can and should be responsible for the care of infants was legitimised through state regulation. This is an idea that breaks with millennia of tradition and praxis, but which has received relatively little attention in research on the welfare state. Ann-Sofie Ohlander is an exception in this respect. She writes:

Historically this is an extraordinarily important change. The conflict between reproduction and production is made visible here, not only as a problem and a responsibility for women, but also as a conflict and a responsibility for men. It is too early to say whether this way of making visible the fundamental conflict that emerges in a society that does not recognise the central role of reproduction will result in corresponding social changes (Ohlander 1989:186).

Legislation on parental leave was used in the Nordic countries to take a step away from the idea of the male breadwinner. As we will see, the countries differ in both their structure and practice. No country can be said to have achieved equality of parenting. But the most important thing is that this reform has opened up the *possibility* of more equal parenting, something that was difficult to achieve earlier due to the existence of gender specific legislation in this area. The fact is that the opportunities for women and men to combine parenting and paid employment have increased. Arnlaug Leira argues that rights to parental leave are important not only because of the practical support such rights imply for parents, but also "as evidence of an interesting shift in the conceptualisation of 'the worker', such that the demands of social reproduction take priority over those of production" (Leira 1993:333). This is reason enough to throw light on parental legislation. Another reason is that few other comparable countries have such extensive and universal legislation on parental leave as the Nordic countries (Haas 1992:13).[51]

Clearly, a policy of shared parental leave is likely to have a greater impact on the private sphere than a policy of institutional childcare. Policies on childcare

---

51. See also, Ds 1996:49 *Samhällets stöd till barnfamiljerna i Europa*, where the Nordic countries, with the exception of Iceland, are compared with France, the Netherlands, Great Britain and Germany.

and *maternity* leave can be regarded as measures that offer women opportunities for combining motherhood and paid employment without, as such, influencing private relations between the sexes and the dominant view of fatherhood. At a more overarching level, reforms which give support to children and women may håve certain emancipatory effects and increase the chances for women to achieve economic independence. But if the traditional gender-based division of labour in the home is not altered, it will also become more difficult to bring about changes in the public sphere. The basic notion behind the idea of shared parental leave may be seen as that of removing the consequences of unequal relations between the sexes, for example, in respect of the opportunities that women and men have for career advancement. If fathers of small children were to use their entitlement to parental leave to the same extent as mothers, this would have major consequences for the organisation of paid work and the way in which gender is conceptualised. Another important notion has been that an entitlement to parental leave offers opportunities for both men and women to develop closer relations with their children that could generate positive effects for children, the family and society.

It is, however, important to differentiate here between those gender equality goals and principles that have been agreed upon at a more general level – childcare and parental leave – and the actual outcome of policies based upon them. To give one example, even if the explicit political goals in respect of shared parental leave recognise the desirability of a greater participation on the part of fathers, and this has been institutionalised through legislation that grants both parents the possibility to stay at home, the outcome will most probably remain gender-specific. The mothers will, as a rule, continue to take up the major part of the parental leave because the outcome is determined by more factors than that of the legislation alone. However, this does not mean that regulation is unimportant. On the contrary, it is very important and, as the variations between the different countries indicate, the structure of parental leave can influence the division of labour between the sexes.

The Structure of Parental Leave

The parental leave scheme contains a number of different entitlements relating to the birth or adoption of a child.[52] These include *parental allowance*, which is a benefit paid for a certain, limited, period of time to the parent who stays at home to look after the child. Usually, the parental allowance constitutes a form of compensation for loss of income. In all countries except Denmark, parental allowance also contains a universal element, so that persons with no attachment to the labour market may enjoy a right to some compensation. Parental allowances in the Nordic countries have generally been set at relatively high levels of

---

52. If not otherwise indicated, factual information is taken from the Nordic Social-Statistical Committee reports *Social tryghed i de nordiske lande. Omfang, udgifter og finansiering*, NOSOSKO 1:1995 and NOSOSKO 8: 1998.

Table 7.1 Parental leave and fertility in the Nordic countries, 1998

	Denmark	*Finland*	*Iceland*	*Norway*	*Sweden*
Year of intro-duction of paren-tal leave for fathers	1984	1980	1981	1978	1974
Maximum num-ber of weeks	28	44	26	42/52^a	64
- of which, only for the mother	18	18	8	9	4
- of which, only for the father ("father's month")	2^b	-	-	4	4
- of which, for either the fat-her or the mother	8	26	18	29/39	56
Paternity leave alongside mater-nity leave	2 weeks	18 days	2 weeks	2 weeks	10 days
Compensation level as a % of salary	90	71^c	100 % for wo-men em-ployed in the public sector, otherwise a flat rate	100/80	80 % during 360 days + 60 SEK during 90 days
Fertility					
1992	1.8	1.8	2.2	1.9	2.1
1995	1.8	1.8	2.0	1.9^d	1.6^d

a: The shorter period is at 100 per cent compensation, the longer period is at 80 per cent
b: Since April 1998, a "father's quota" of 14 days has been introduced during the 24th to the 26th week of the leave
c: Average level of compensation in 1996
d: 1996

Sources: Women and Men in the Nordic Countries. Facts and figures 1994; Ds 1996:49; NOSO-SKO 1:1995 and 8:1998; oral information from the countries concerned.

compensation, and this has afforded good protection against loss of income. The structure and level of the compensation are on a par with sickness and unem-ployment benefits in the Nordic countries. Today, the length of time that paren-tal allowance may be claimed varies from more than half a year in Iceland and

Table 7.2 Share of parental allowance days taken up by men, 1990–1996

Year	Denmark	Finland	Iceland	Norway	Sweden
1990	4.1	2.4	-	-	8.8
1995	4.4	3.6	0.1	5.8	10.3
1996	4.3	3.6	0.1	6.3	11.7

Source: NOSOSKO 8: 1998.

Denmark to over a year in Norway and Sweden (see Table 7.1). Generally, the duration of parental leave entitlements has been successively lengthened. In Norway, for example, the number of weeks of entitlement was increased in 1993 from twenty-eight weeks to forty-two weeks with full compensation for loss of salary, or fifty-two weeks at 80 per cent of the salary.

The principal entitlement to leave following the birth of a child is reserved for the mother in all countries, except Sweden. There is also a special *paternity leave*, which, during the period immediately following labour, may be taken alongside the *mothers' leave*.[53] "The aim is to provide the mother with support during the first few weeks after the birth and to give the father an opportunity to establish an early bond with the child" (Ds 1996:49). As is clear from Table 7.1, the paternity leave was usually a question of a couple of weeks. It is interesting to note that Iceland introduced this measure in 1998. This gives some indication of the increased extent of convergence over time. Some degree of convergence between the countries is also evident in the introduction of "*quotas for fathers*", the aim of which is to persuade the father to stay at home with the child for a period of time. Norway was the first country to introduce a "father's quota", (of four weeks), in 1993. Similar arrangements were subsequently introduced in Sweden, in 1995, and Denmark, in 1998. In Sweden, the scheme includes a "father's month" and a "mother's month", the entitlements to which are not transferable between parents. In Denmark, nowadays two weeks of leave are reserved for the father. In addition, and as a complement to the parental insurance, allowances also exist in some Nordic countries to enable parents to take care of children at home. These provisions will be discussed in more detail in the next section.

After Ireland, the Nordic countries are at the top of the fertility league table for the combined Nordic-EU area. In 1992, the fertility rates for Iceland and Sweden were 2.2 and 2.1 respectively, while Italy and Germany had fertility rates of 1.3. In recent years, however, fertility has been falling in Sweden and

---

53. Since 1997, fathers in Finland have been able to take 6–12 days of paternity leave at any time during the 18 weeks of leave entitlement reserved for mothers following labour. As mothers' leave may not be taken by fathers, it is referred to as maternity leave in Finland. However, an additional five days of paternity leave may be taken during the maternity or parental leave period.

Table 7.3 Children 0–6 years in daycare centres and family daycare (child minder) as a percentage of the respective age group, 1990–1996

Year	Denmark	Finland	Iceland	Norway	Sweden
1990					
0–2 years	47	31	24	11	29
3–6 years	77	58	60	57	64
0–6 years, in total	64	44	43	36	48
1995					
0–2 years	46	18	37	21	37
3–6 years	81	55	64	61	74
0–6 years, in total	65	39	53	44	59
1996					
0–2 years	48	22	37	23	40
3–6 years	83	63	64	61	83
0–6 years, in total	67	46	53	45	66

Source: NOSOSKO 8: 1998.

has now reached a level that is comparable to the population crisis of the 1930s. In general, the Nordic countries devote a larger share of their total social expenditure to families and children than do most other countries in the EU. The relatively high fertility rates are often seen as an effect of the generous family policies.

Who Stays at Home?

Who should stay at home on parental leave is a decision for the parents themselves to make. In some cases, however, increased equality between the parents is made difficult by the way the system is structured. The outcome is still roughly in line with the traditional gender division within the family.The statistics show that the use of this possibility by fathers is modest, even if a weak upward trend may be discerned. Swedish fathers have a higher uptake of parental leave than do their Nordic brothers, but since the introduction of the "father's quota" in Norway, the uptake of parental leave by Norwegian men has increased strongly. If one looks at the proportion of the total number of parental allowance days that are taken up by fathers, the figure is relatively low. In Sweden, fathers account for almost 12 per cent of the parental allowance days. They are followed by fathers in Norway, who account for more than 6 per cent of such days. However, fathers in the other countries take up less than 5 per cent of the statutory parental allowance (see Table 7.2).

Although, as a rule, men do not take up long continuous periods of parental leave, the proportion who take any parental leave, and especially who take up their entitlement to fathers' days and use the possibility to stay at home with a

Table 7.4 Children in the Nordic countries in receipt of public childcare as a percentage of all children in the age group, 1981

	Denmark		Finland		Iceland		Norway		Sweden	
Age	0–2	3–6	0–2	3–6	0–2	3–6	0–2	3–6	0–2	3–6
Daycare centre										
- full time	15	31	6	15	5	18	4	12	13	26
- part time	–	8	–	10	4	30	1	23	–	24
Total in daycare centers	15	39	6	25	9	38	5	35	13	50
Child minders	22	8	11	12	9	3	–	–	11	15
Total	37	47	17	37	18	41	5	35	24	65

Source: Nordic Statistical Yearbook

Table 7.5 Children in the Nordic countries in receipt of public childcare as a percentage of all children in the age group, 1993

	Denmark		Finland		Iceland (1992)		Norway		Sweden	
Age	0–2	3–6	0–2	3–6	0–2	3–6	0–2	3–6	0–2	3–6
Daycare centre										
- full time	18	57	8	27	5	16	14	37	23	49
- part time	–	11	–	8	8	48	3	24	–	14
Total in daycare centers	18	68	8	35	13	64	17	61	23	63
Child minders	29	6	8	16	11	4	3	2	9	14
Total	47	74	16	51	24	68	20	63	32	77

Source: Nordic Statistical Yearbook

Table 7.6 Different Types of Support for Families with Children

	Denmark	*Finland*	*Iceland*	*Norway*	*Sweden*
Child allowance	Yes	Yes	Yes	Yes	Yes
Child maintenance allowance for lone parents	Yes	Yes	Yes	Yes	Yes
Childcare leave, flexible parental leave scheme	Yes	Yes		Yes	Yes
Home care allowance		Yes		Yes	
Support for lone parents	Yes	Yes	Yes	Yes	Yes

Source: NOSOSKO 8: 1998.

sick child, has increased dramatically. The introduction of the father's quota in Norway meant that the share of men who took up the paternity leave increased from 4 per cent in 1993 to 55 per cent in 1996 (Barne- og familiedepartementet 1996a). A major problem exists with the Norwegian reform, despite the country being the first in the Nordic area to introduce a father's quota. The root of this problem is that the right to parental allowance and the size of the financial compensation it provides depends upon the mother's attachment to the labour market. No matter which parent stays at home, the amount of parental allowance is strongly reduced if the mother works part time. The negative effect of this on the family finances strongly contributes to the maintenance of a traditional family order. In those cases where the mother has not been active on the labour market during six of the ten months prior to the birth, the father has no independent right to parental allowance. When the father's quota was introduced, instead of changing these rules, a number of exceptions to them were granted so that families would not be adversely affected financially. In Sweden, about 30 per cent of fathers take up some part of the parental leave. In Denmark and Finland, the proportion of fathers who take up the parental allowance is very small, but an increasing number take up their entitlement to fathers' days. In Iceland, the phenomenon of paternity leave is still unusual.

A Danish study reveals that during 1985, 41 per cent of new fathers took up their right to paternity leave immediately following the birth of a child. In 1991, the proportion had grown to 55 per cent. The study emphasises that the law is formulated in such a way as to encourage many mothers to take the whole of the leave themselves for breast feeding and other purposes. "The problem seems to be that if the total leave period is not prolonged, the way the parental leave is used will not change" (Carlsen 1994:89). The article also emphasises that the statistics undervalue men's participation in the care of children. Due to the fact that the parental leave is so short in Denmark, many fathers take holiday leave or other forms of leave in order to be with their families. Furthermore, as is shown by Swedish data on the household tasks which fathers participate in, statistics on parental leave do not reveal everything about the changing role of fathers. Today, 85 per cent of fathers participate in tasks such as changing nappies, and feeding and clothing children. This compares with a figure of around one per cent in the 1960s (SOU 1998: 6:49). As pointed out in the Danish study, the length of the total parental leave itself may play a role in deciding whether fathers use it or not. The higher uptake of parental leave by Swedish men can be explained in these terms, because Swedish parents have a right to a total of 450 days of parental leave that may be taken up until the child reaches eight years of age.

"Let the Cry Ring Out: Daycare For All"

Organised childcare outside the home has been a fundamental demand of women struggling to realise the right to paid work and gender equality. "Daycare for all" was a slogan of the women's movement of the 1960s and 1970s. It may be asked whether or not this demand has been achieved in practice. The answers to this question would appear to be both yes and no. There are big differences in childcare policies between the Nordic countries. Denmark, Finland and Sweden have come the furthest in guaranteeing different forms of childcare to everybody through public means, while Norway and Iceland have differed so much from the other countries that the concept of the "Nordic model" could be questioned in this respect. According to Leira, the example of childcare shows that the universal principles usually connected with the Scandinavian model do not apply in this field. In contrast to Denmark and Sweden, Norway has invested relatively little with regard to both the care of children under three years of age and full time care. As in Iceland, childcare provision still seems to be based on the assumption that most mothers of small children remain at home. According to Leira, one explanation for this in the Norwegian case is that municipalities with their strong autonomy have been able to oppose national goals for more universal childcare. Here we find several similarities with Iceland, where the opposition from local politicians to public childcare was one of the reasons behind the decision of Icelandic women to found a women's party (see the next chapter). In Denmark, Finland and Sweden, public childcare has been formed both by considering pedagogical aspects and by making it possible for employed parents to have all their needs for childcare met by one and the same form of provision. In Norway and Iceland part time pre-school care has meant that all those mothers or fathers with small children who work full time, or more than a certain number of hours on a part-time basis, must complement the municipal provision with other forms of care. When Norway had a social democratic government during the 1990s, however, it followed a set of childcare policies more in line with Denmark, Finland and Sweden than was the case during the period of time covered by Leira's study. A Norwegian government report on gender equality (Barne- og familiedepartementet 1992) emphasised that equal responsibility for caring was a prioritised area. Improved conditions for parents with small children were demanded to facilitate the combining of paid employment and care for both women and men. A goal to ensure the "full coverage of daycare centres" before the year 2000 was set out. During the 1990s, a growing proportion of children ranging from under one to six years of age have received a place in a daycare centre (see Table 7.3).[54] Moreover, several initiatives to increase full-time care have been taken in Iceland, especially in Reyjavik.

The term "childcare policies" is used here to refer to publicly financed or subsidised arrangements for the care of children up until school age.[55] We distinguish between collective and individual forms of childcare policy. The most collective form of childcare is that of the daycare centre, but a group of children may also be looked after by a home based child minder. Individual forms of childcare are mostly linked to the different forms of home care allowance that are available to parents for the purpose of arranging private daycare in the home. Collective provision for childcare, which is in line with the dual breadwinner model, is especially favoured by the left, social democrats and many liberals. The home care allowance finds its strongest support amongst conservatives, especially the centre parties and the christian parties, and is a kind of modified male breadwinner-model, as the person who stays at home (usually the mother) is not totally dependent in financial terms on the breadwinner-spouse.

Forms and Scope of Collective Childcare

Between 45 per cent and 67 per cent of all children in the Nordic countries up to six years of age are registered in some form of collectively organised and publicly financed childcare. The highest figure is for Denmark, closely followed by Sweden, with the other countries lagging quite a way behind. All countries show an increase over time (Table 7.3). This rather crudely simplified picture nevertheless reveals some of the scope and development of collective childcare provision in the Nordic area. The tendency is for increasingly larger proportions of children under school age to participate in group-based care. Only Finland experienced a decline in group-based care in the mid-1990s, which, amongst other things, was connected to higher levels of unemployment in the country and the introduction of a home care benefit. We cannot go into detail concerning the economic situation here, all we can do is to briefly state that in recent times all Nordic countries, with the exception of Norway, have been hit by economic

---

54. In 1995, a decision was made to expand the number of the daycare centres, and in 1997 an elementary school reform was introduced that resulted in a transfer of six year olds to school. As a result, resources have been made available for younger children (Barne- og familiedepartementet 1996a).

55. Children start school at the age of six in Iceland and Norway and at seven in Denmark, Finland and Sweden, although a school starting age of six is becoming more common in the latter group of countries as well. Public care of school children after the close of the school-day is most common in Denmark and Sweden, but such a measure will not be discussed further here. Childcare can be organised by municipalities, privately, through parents' cooperatives, etc., but they are largely publicly financed with a fee payable by parents.

problems, unemployment and the restructuring of their general welfare systems. The empirical findings that we present here, do not, however, indicate any change in the principle of public responsibility for childcare. On the contrary, this responsibility has actually been strengthened through different kinds of legislation, childcare guarantees and expansion. For example, in Finland all parents with children under school-age have a so-called subjective right to a place in the municipal childcare system. As an alternative to municipal childcare (collective childcare), parents can receive home care benefit or financial support for the private care of a child. The home care benefit is aimed at families with at least one child under the age of three who does not receive municipal childcare. Financial support is also given for any other children in the family who are looked after in the same way. The child or children in question may be cared for by one of the parents, by a relative, or by another care giver. Support received for private care is meant for children under school-age, who are looked after by a care giver approved by the municipality (for example, a recognised private nursery, private child-minder registered with the municipality, or a care giver employed by the family).

Even if these aggregated figures suggest increasing similarities between Nordic countries and *a single* Nordic model for childcare, they also reveal a number of differences. One problem that we have encountered, however, is that of obtaining comparable figures that are up to date for all countries.[56] Another problem concerns how to interpret those figures that are available. The development of childcare provision over more than a decade is shown in Tables 7.4 and 7.5, including differences between age groups, the extent of full time and part time care, and whether care is provided by a daycare institution or by a child minder. The data confirm the picture of childcare as having developed strongly, but almost totally around the institution of the daycare centre. The proportion of children cared for by child minders is generally lower and approximately at the same level it was in 1981.

There are large differences between the countries in respect of the average age at which children enter daycare and whether or not they are registered as receiving full or part-time care. The tables show children in receipt of public daycare as a percentage of all children in the age groups 0–2 and 3–6. The observed differences are greatest within the age group 0–2 years, because of the effect of the different systems of parental leave and home care benefit. On the one hand, the availability of parental leave has meant that it is uncommon for babies to receive institutionalised daycare in the Nordic countries. On the other hand, variations are large in respect of the 1–2 year-old children. The relatively high figures for Danish children in the group 0–2 years are, amongst other things, to be explained by the shorter parental leave. The lower figures for the youngest group in Finland are related to the home care benefit, which is available after the

---

56. A deterioration in the quality of statistics on childcare is evident in the most recent editions of both the Nordic Statistical Yearbook and the Nordic Social-Statistical Committee (NOSOS-KO).

termination of the parental leave. The tables also indicate the differences mentioned above between, on the one hand, Denmark, Finland and Sweden, where full-time places have been supported and, on the other hand, Iceland and Norway, where part-time care has been prioritised. In Norway, however, this has begun to change somewhat and full-time places are becoming more common. During the 1990s, Iceland has continued to expand part-time care, but a certain shift is taking place towards full-time care.

More Possibilities for Childcare in the Home

Collective forms of childcare have been the most common, but individual forms have been gaining ground during the 1990s. As already noted, Finland has a home care benefit for children under the age of three and support is available for the private care of children. Since 1994, there has been a special arrangement in Denmark, giving parents a right to six months leave with compensation for loss of earnings, which can be prolonged for an additional half a year with the employer's approval. This childcare leave applies to children up to nine years of age. For a short time in the 1990s, Sweden also had a home care benefit. In Norway a similar arrangement was introduced in January 1999.

The above-mentioned entitlements apply to lone parents as well, but they also enjoy other benefits. Only in Norway, however, is there a benefit that makes it possible for a lone parent to stay at home for a longer time without being dependent on an income from paid employment. In other countries, the employment principle applies in the first instance, but lone parents usually have a right to a child maintenance allowance, housing allowances, priority in respect to daycare places, etc. Thus, the public sphere compensates for the absence of one of the breadwinners in the household. Table 7.6 gives an overview of the different arrangements in the other countries. We also include the basic child allowance, which is given as a universal benefit for each child, except in Iceland, where it is means-tested.

Conclusion

The idea that fathers may also stay at home with small children is integrated into legislation in all the Nordic countries, despite large variations in the way caring arrangements are structured. Clearly, a vision of equal parenthood through the application of public policies does exist, but this vision is still far from being a reality. Parental leave has been one, albeit relatively weak, instrument to increase the participation of fathers in the care of small children. Over time, however, the legislation has contributed to changes in attitudes and resulted in more participation by fathers in the care of their small children. The alternative to these kind of policies in other countries has usually involved the public sphere refraining from introducing any forms of paid parental leave or restricting such entitlements to women only.

Our overview has shown that the parental leave scheme is not strictly speaking an individual entitlement like sickness benefit or other similar benefits. A completely gender-neutral and individually based entitlement to parental leave would, for example, mean the mother and the father each taking up half of the leave period, but as parents may transfer leave entitlement between themselves, in practice entitlement is based upon the family as a collective unit rather than on the individual parents within a given family unit. In the transition from a maternity-based insurance for employed mothers to a parentally based insurance for employed parents some of the gender-specific rules have been kept to a greater or lesser degree (the debate around this transformation will be analysed in the next chapter). Thus, the more radical idea of shared parenthood has been undermined by the way in which parental leave has been constructed. Norway, Sweden and Denmark have introduced a kind of quota thinking into the framework of the present system in an attempt to change the low uptake of parental leave by fathers. Either this will mark a step towards a more individualised form of parental insurance, or a view that about one month's paternity leave is "enough" will become de facto institutionalised as a new norm.

In summary, our discussion of parental leave and childcare shows that to a certain extent there are clear similarities and "diffusion effects" between the countries. This concerns, for example, the desire to give fathers the same social rights in respect of paid leave to care for small children that earlier were reserved solely for mothers. These possibilities have been successively increased, which also holds true for other forms of public support for childcare. In spite of this, three different patterns can be discerned. Although these patterns have weakened, they nevertheless broadly imply that since the 1970s Denmark and Sweden have had childcare policies that have strongly prioritised the development of collective full-time care. The starting point has been to make it possible for both women and men to combine paid employment with family responsibilities. As a result of developing part-time "pre-school" care, Norway and Iceland have not linked childcare to gender equality and women's employment as explicitly as the other Nordic countries have. In Norway and Iceland the reforms in this field have been characterised more by traditional gender ideology than in Denmark and Sweden, which have to a larger extent taken the demands of the women's movements of the 1960s and 1970s and integrated them into their legislation. Finland has developed a model of its own, which can be combined with both new and traditional gender roles.

Conservatives and neo-liberals sometimes claim that large public investments in childcare and cash transfers, such as parental leave, etc., have resulted in the state taking over responsibilities that earlier belonged to the family (particularly to the mother). In practice, however, the Nordic experience points in another direction: towards increased opportunities for the parents (especially the mothers) to stay at home with compensation for loss of earnings. The Swedish arrangement, for example, allows one to extend the number of days of entitlement to the parental allowance by proportionately reducing the amount of the allowance payable on a daily basis. The reform is also structured in such a way as to encourage an increase in the birth rate. In practice, this means that Swedish mothers of small children can stay at home for a number of years without having to leave the labour force whilst enjoying financial compensation for loss of earnings. Primary responsibility for the care of children remains in the hands the mothers, even if the economic responsibility still lies, to a relatively high degree, with the public sphere. What may result from these very generous leave arrangements is not quite clear from a gender equality point of view. Yet other models have also failed to contribute to very radical changes in gender relations.

8

The Debate on Childcare Policies

Christina Bergqvist, Jaana Kuusipalo and Auður Styrkarsdóttir

The previous chapter discussed the organisation of parental leave and childcare as well as some of their consequences for changing gender relations. Many women may be found at work behind the policies that have been advocated. This chapter analyses the political activities of women in the Nordic parliaments in respect of these issues, and it explores how different political views have developed since the 1960s. As a rule, earlier research has focused *either* on women's participation and representation in politics *or* on the structuring of welfare policies and their impact upon gender equality. Yet, Helga Hernes' book *Welfare State and Woman Power: Essays in State Feminism*, represents an example of how to fruitfully analyse within the same framework both the entry of women into political decision making and the contents and development of the welfare state. A key argument in Hernes' book is "the way in which advanced Nordic welfare states, through their policies, have 'pulled' women into the public sphere, and how women then began to 'push' developments in accordance with their own interests" (1987:9). Hernes further argues that welfare policy together with labour market policy constituted the institutional framework that "drew" women onto the labour market. At the same time, the opportunities open to women increased and they became more motivated to raise demands or become politically active.

This chapter presents an analysis of the policy debate on childcare in Finland, Iceland and Sweden – countries that have followed somewhat different paths. Its central focus is on the political actors and some of the most important questions that have figured in discussions leading to today's systems of parental leave and childcare. This means that we will stress the importance of *politics* and *actors* over and above that of structures. Which political ideas and reforms have lain behind the organisation of parental leave and childcare provision? Which political actors have been important? What role have women played in the formation of these policies? An actor-orientated perspective does not mean that we must deny the existence of structural and/or institutional restrictions. It merely recognises that the institutions constitute the frames for the formal and informal norms that limit or enhance political agency. We cannot claim to be able to cover the whole debate or all actors. Consequently, our goal is limited to analysing the parliamentary debates in this area. Thus, for example, we cannot explore the impact exerted by groups as diverse as the women's movement, childcare educators, and psychologists. Instead, we will focus on the role of women as politicians and the positions of the different parliamentary parties. The three countries can be seen as examples of how different models of childcare and parental leave have developed at different historical points in time in accordance with both the prevailing political power relations and the impact of women.

Sweden: The Vision of Gender Equality

The prevailing view of gender relations found at a normative level in Swedish welfare policies since the end of the 1960s is summed up in *Jämlikhet* ("Equality"), a report published by a social democratic and trade union-based working group led by Alva Myrdal.[57] In the society of the future, the report states, the practical barriers to the attainment of equality will be eliminated and the starting point for policy will have to be that

> every adult individual is given responsibility for his or her own maintenance. Entitlements that earlier were tied to marriage have to be abolished or tied to children. Children ought to have legal and economic security, irrespective of whether their parents are married, lone parents or cohabiting. Adult individuals – whether they live on their own or in some form of partnership – ought to be treated in a similar manner by society (Jämlikhet 1969:95).

The Party Debate and the Decision to Expand Childcare Provision

At the beginning of the 1960s a line of division emerged within the arena of party politics between those who wanted to promote policies aimed at strengthening the *male breadwinner model*, and those who wanted to shift the policy emphasis towards an *individual model* with two breadwinners. The main lines of this division concerned whether to support housewives through the provision of a home-care allowance or, alternatively, whether to promote a dual breadwinner model by expanding publicly provided childcare. This line of division was also initially present within the governing Social Democratic Party[58] and its women's federation. Housewives were said to be an undervalued group in society, despite efforts in the 1940s and the 1950s to give this group a more professional image. The 1950s had been the "golden age of the small nuclear family", when

---

57. The title of this section is inspired by a book called *Visionen om jämställdhet* ("The Vision of Gender Equality") by Annika Baude 1992.

58. See Appendix 2 for party designations.

even a working class family could live on a single wage (Karlsson 1996:226 ff.). Lisa Mattson, an MP and president of the National Federation of Social Democratic Women in Sweden, advocated the introduction of a home-care allowance in a parliamentary debate in 1965. However, like Ulla Lindström, the cabinet member responsible for family policies, Mattson was not actually opposed to expanding public childcare provision. Rather, she wanted to see a simultaneous expansion of both policies (Hinnfors 1992:108 ff.).

The Right Wing Party, subsequently the Conservative Party, issued a statement in 1963 asserting that it was "in principal disgusting that the natural function of parenthood should be financed by the state". The statement went on to oppose the idea of a home-care allowance (quoted in Hinnfors 1992:99). At the beginning of the 1970s, the party changed its standpoint and came out in favour of a home-care allowance. At approximately the same time, the Social Democrats adopted a negative attitude towards a home-care allowance and instead backed an expansion of the publicly financed system of daycare centres. Support for the introduction of a home-care allowance led to an alliance between the Conservatives and the Centre Party. The Liberal Party had also advocated a home-care allowance in some contexts during the 1960s, although the party did not counterpose this type of benefit to an expansion of daycare centres. Later, the Liberals shifted their position and started to prioritise daycare centres. Thus, there was no obvious clear-cut line of division between the bourgeois parties and the socialist bloc. The Centre Party, which receives much of its support from farming communities, has been a warm advocate of a home-care allowance since the 1960s and remains so today. None of the bourgeois parties, with the partial exception of the Conservatives, is opposed in principle to public measures designed to facilitate the combining of family responsibilities with paid work for women. The principal arguments used in favour of a home-care allowance concerned the notions of freedom of choice and of justice. In respect to the former question, it was argued that the freedom of women (not men) to choose between home and work should be increased. The argument relating to justice implied that families ought to be entitled to social transfers to enable housewives to perform their homemaking duties, just as subsidies were provided to families to enable them to make use of public childcare. Initially, the discussions only dealt with women, but later a more gender-neutral form of language was adopted and one started to talk about the "parent staying at home" (Hinnfors 1992).[59]

According to the other line of thought, the individual model, independence and freedom depended upon every adult, irrespective of her or his sex, having an opportunity to be economically self-supporting. Thus, old sex roles should be abandoned and replaced by new, equal sex roles. Women and men ought to shoulder an equal responsibility for care and family finances, and they ought to have the same opportunities to combine parenthood with paid employment. At the ideological level, radical reforms were demanded to make this new and mod-

---

59. The economic support that the proposed home-care allowance would provide cannot be compared with an ordinary income.

ern life style both possible and free from the fetters of traditional sex roles. One such reform involved the massive expansion of public childcare to facilitate women's participation in the labour market. The report *Jämlikhet* claimed that "a strong, sustained expansion of the daycare centres" was one of the most important reforms needed in order to achieve gender equality (Jämlikhet 1969: 97).[60]

Since the sex-role and gender equality debates entered Swedish politics, none of the political parties in Parliament have unambiguously advocated a strong male breadwinner model or have consistently opposed public measures in this field. The employment rate amongst women with children less than seven years of age increased from 32 per cent in 1960 to 50 per cent in 1970, and 60 per cent in 1975. Despite political support for daycare centres and the strong increase in the employment rate of mothers with small children, the actual expansion in the number of daycare centres did not start until the 1970s. In 1966, for example, more than 90 per cent of children under school age received no care outside of their families. In 1979, the corresponding figure was 61 per cent (Hinnfors 1992).[61] Thus, many mothers with small children entered the labour market long before public childcare became widely available.

Women exercised a powerful influence over the content of the political documents and debates that led to the parliamentary decision to prioritise public childcare provision. Many of the women who contributed to the massive state reports on the expansion of daycare centres favoured their expansion, not only for reasons of gender equality, but also for social and pedagogical reasons. At this time, women were also relatively well represented in politics compared with non-Nordic countries. Between 1965 and 1970 about 20 per cent of social democratic MPs in the Lower House of the Riksdag were women.[62] The government that took office in 1970 contained two renowned advocates of equal opportunities and treatment for women and men, namely Alva Myrdal and Camilla Odhnoff. Even if gender equality arguments were important for women's groups, it was the need for labour force that instead dominated the debate (Hinnfors 1992:9 ff.).[63]

There was also an astonishing degree of political consensus about the public finance of childcare. Even if the bourgeois parties often questioned various aspects of childcare policies, as a rule, they did not express reservations about the

---

60. The report was presented to the Social Democratic Party Congress in 1969. The same views were expressed in the Party's Women's Federation's programme "Towards Socialist Family Policies", 1969.

61. The figures include children in part-time groups and in nursery schools.

62. The Upper House was elected by indirect means, while the members of the Lower House were directly elected at general elections.

63. Thus, whereas strong forces were behind the expansion of daycare provision, in many ways labour market policy viewed women and men as different kinds of employees. Married women were referred to as employed housewives. Workplaces considered to be especially suitable for part-time employed housewives were even politically created. This was common, e.g. in respect of the care of the elderly (Möller 1996:454).

increasing public costs of such policies. It was actually only during the latter part of the 1980s that the bourgeois parties, mainly the Conservative Party, began to question the expansion of publicly funded childcare (Uddhammar 1993:250 ff.). This unity can be understood better if we consider the structural conditions that prevailed at the time. Favourable economic prospects and labour force shortages constituted the main structural backdrop to the formulation of these policies. Earlier, part of the demand for labour had been met by immigration. As the public sector started to expand, a political decision was made to encourage women instead onto the labour market. For this reason, the expansion of childcare became an issue that was supported by all key political actors from the employers to the labour movement (Hinnfors 1992; Kyle 1979). Thus, the consensus in favour of more daycare centres was linked to the rapid economic growth of the time and the growing demand for labour. However, the existence of favourable structural conditions should not obscure the fact that an expansion of public childcare provision was also supported by, as well as in the interests of, large groups of women. Public childcare was seen as a "women's issue" of long standing. Moreover, as Rianne Mahon shows in her comparative study of Sweden and Canada, an "automatic" connection between a high female rate of employment and the availability of childcare does not exist, either.Women's labour market participation is high in both countries, although childcare policies are totally different (Mahon 1997).

From Maternity Benefit to Parental Insurance

The introduction of the general sickness insurance scheme in 1955 led to a reform of maternity benefits that made them more universal in character. It also led to the introduction of an income-related insurance scheme. In principle, this represented a shift in policy that was potentially favourable to employed women. The maternity insurance scheme was further improved, and the means-tested benefit for mothers was abolished. As a result of the growing interest in gender equality, and as a consequence of the debate on the merits of daycare centres as opposed to a home-care allowance, the issue of who should take care of newborn babies and infants came to the fore. The opportunities for the growing numbers of employed mothers to obtain daycare places for their children had increased in accordance with the idea of the dual breadwinner family. Given these circumstances, was it not outdated to hold the view that only mothers should stay at home with small children?

In January 1974, the maternity insurance scheme was replaced by a parental insurance scheme upon the birth or adoption of a child. This provided an income-related allowance, payable for a period of up to six months, to enable one of the parents to stay at home. Under the scheme, which parent should stay at home and for how long was a matter for the parents to decide. This reform strongly reflected the shift in the relationship between the sexes that was under way. The reform both highlighted and institutionalised two radically new ways of looking at the relationship between the sexes. Firstly, it implied that fathers –

and not just mothers – could and should also be responsible for the care of small children. Secondly, another step away from the idea of the male breadwinner model was taken, in favour of the idea of the dual breadwinner family (Bergqvist 1990). The reform of the taxation system in 1970–71, which introduced individual taxation of spouses, represented a first step in that direction. The issue of parental insurance had been thoroughly examined by the Public Committee on Family Policies in a report published in 1972 (*Familjestöd* 1972). The Committee emphasised the positive benefits of shared parental responsibility both for the children, who would have more contact with the father, and for the parents. A parental insurance scheme, it was argued, would probably contribute to an increased division of labour within the home and, thereby, to greater opportunities for women to strengthen their position on the labour market. Hope was expressed in the Committee report that more fathers would stay at home, but it was realised that the mothers would probably take the biggest responsibility. Yet, no proposal was made for the sharing of the parental allowance between parents in a regulated way. Instead, it was left up to the parents themselves to decide upon this (SOU 1972: 34).

The Discussion on Shared Parental Leave

As noted above, everybody seemed to agree that it should be left up to the parents themselves to decide how the parental leave should be shared. Thus, it is interesting to note that women MPs were amongst the first parliamentarians to argue against this view. As early as 1972, the Centre Party MPs Karin Andersson and Elvy Olsson tabled a private member's bill to structure entitlement to parental leave in such a way as to prevent one of the parents in a family from taking up the whole of the parental leave period.[64] Without such a restriction, they argued, it was probable, given existing gender differentials in wages and salaries, promotion chances, etc., that mothers would mainly be the ones to stay at home. As a result, it was argued that an essential part of the reform would be lost (Private Members' Bill 1973:1586). Later, the issue was investigated by aa public committee on family policies. Following a request from the Federation of Social Democratic Women, the investigation was, amongst other things, given the task of examining whether an extension of the allowance period could be combined with a requirement that part of the period be taken up by the child's father. In its report, the committee, in accordance with the suggestion put forward by the federation, proposed that the allowance period be extended from seven to eight months on condition that neither of the parents take up more than seven months (SOU 1975: 62).

During the spring of 1976 the social democratic government prepared a bill on the extension of the parental insurance period to eight months. The bill did not consider demands for this extension to be combined with the proposal to in-

---

64. This measure had also been proposed by the Social Democratic Women's Federation in 1972 in the report *Familjen i framtiden* ("The Family of the Future") (Karlsson 1996:292).

troduce a "father's month", as had been suggested. A large group of social democratic women MPs viewed this omission as a betrayal of gender equality and this in turn led to a "women's coup" in Parliament. The "coup" is described in detail by the historian Gunnel Karlsson (1996, 1998), who characterises it as a very unique event. In short, this event produced a strong protest from women against the party leadership. In a complete break with the prevailing norms of the social democratic government and parliamentary group, eighteen of the thirty-six women members of the social democratic party group (of MPs) joined together in support of a private member's bill on the "father's month". The "coup" involved the submission of the bill to the parliamentary office without giving prior notice to the party leadership and despite the leadership's stated opposition to such a move. According to Prime Minister Olof Palme, this was the first time that an important fraction within the group had ignored the objections of the party council and, thereby, the leadership of the parliamentary group (see, Karlsson 1996:293).

Gunnel Karlsson describes the women's coup as

> a strategy of disobedience that created a sensation within the party, where party loyalty and unity normally were also paramount values for women. The fact that the "coup" took place in the context of the "lottery parliament", where the position of the socialist and the bourgeois blocs was evenly matched at 175 seats apiece, did not make the event any less sensational. Olof Palme viewed the action more or less as a stab in the back... (Karlsson 1996:293 f.).

There was insufficient time for the Social Democrats to make any changes to the parental insurance scheme before the autumn of 1976, when new elections resulted in the bourgeois parties assuming governmental office for the first time in forty-four years. Yet, fundamental changes did not occur in the direction of family policies despite the shift in political power. Rather, the line that the Social Democrats had started was reinforced. For example, no bills were presented on the introduction of a home-care allowance by bourgeois coalition governments between 1976 and 1982 (Hinnfors 1992:166).

The Act on Childcare, the Home-Care Allowance and the "Father's Month"

The expansion of public childcare continued during the 1980s and an extensive preschool reform of a more general character was carried out in 1985. The demand for childcare places has never been satisfied despite a continuous expansion of the system. The 1985 reform of childcare reflected the new political goal of being able to offer daycare places by 1991 to all children from eighteen months of age and upwards, whose parents so wished. After the good years of the 1980s, the 1990s have turned into a decade of retrenchment and public sector cuts. All the basic social insurance systems have suffered cutbacks, and benefit levels have been reduced. Given the increasingly harsh economic situation of recent years and the rise of neo-liberal market currents, it is hardly surprising that questions concerning the organisation of childcare and, more generally, which type of welfare regime is to be preferred, have again become politically controversial. A home care benefit was introduced for a first time in 1994 by a bourgeois government. This action effectively marked the end of the relatively widespread consensus that had prevailed since the end of the 1960s, when the present dual-breadwinner model began to be institutionalised. The introduction of a home-care allowance represents a move towards the male breadwinner model, even if the current version is formulated according to gender neutral principles.

A bourgeois coalition government was formed after the 1991 general election. In contrast to earlier tripartite governments during the 1970s and 1980s, the government that took office in 1991 was the first to include the Christian Democratic Party within its ranks. Thus, the Centre Party gained an ally for its campaign to introduce a home-care allowance. The 1991 general election also resulted in a decline in female representation in Parliament, from 38 per cent of parliamentary seats to 33 per cent.[65] In this situation a window of opportunity opened up for Centre Party and Christian democratic MPs to win over the government to the idea of introducing a home-care allowance. A government bill (1993/94:148) on home care was proposed at the end of 1993 and finally introduced in July 1994, just as new elections were approaching. The idea was for the parent who stayed at home during the first year to receive the income-related parental allowance. Thereafter the parent who stayed at home would be entitled to claim the home-care allowance for a period of up to two years. The allowance could also be used to "purchase" other forms of childcare. The most frequently used argument in favour of the allowance was that it increased the freedom of choice of parents with respect to how their children should be cared for. Even if the advocates of the allowance tried to disguise their arguments using gender-neutral language, it is obvious that the roots of the proposal lay in the idea that the sexes inhabit separate spheres. The idea of a home-care allowance was strongly opposed by the Social Democrats and the Left Party (Parliamentary minutes 1993/94:105, 108). However, the history of the home-care allowance was very short, due the fact that the Social Democrats regained governmental office in the autumn of 1994 and promptly abolished the allowance.

Another debate, more in line with the "vision of gender equality", was carried out in parallel with the discussion on the home-care allowance. This discussion concerned the low level of uptake of the parental allowance by fathers. The proportion of fathers who shared the parental leave with their spouses also re-

---

65. The reason for this was partly that the Conservatives, who for a long time had had a lower level of female representation than other parties, increased their share of the seats and partly that two new parties with a low proportion of women MPs entered Parliament. Apart from the Christian Democratic Party, New Democracy , a populist anti-immigrant party, entered Parliament for the first time. Women made up a smaller proportion of the parliamentary groups of these two parties than was the case for other parties in Parliament. Despite the party's defeat in the elections, women's representation within the Social Democratic Party's parliamentary group exceeded 40 per cent (Bergqvist 1994:41 ff.).

mained low at the beginning of the 1990s, despite substantial efforts to inform fathers of their rights in this area and opinion-forming campaigns designed to encourage them to make use of these rights. It is interesting to note that the issue was driven more by the men (fathers) themselves than by the party-political women's federations. The group of men known as the "daddy group" within the gender equality unit of the government was also of crucial importance here.[66] In a report, they discuss their "vision of the father who is close at hand". Amongst other things, this vision implies that children should learn "that masculinity can also be warm, caring and responsible", that "from the beginning both parents share responsibility and joy", and that "a new role for parents shall be considered a merit on the labour market and shall revolutionise working life". One of the public measures that the daddy group suggested was a minimum of three months' obligatory paternity leave (Ds 1995: 2:109 f.).

In February 1994, the same bourgeois coalition government that had sought to introduce the home-care allowance put forward a proposal for an obligatory sharing of the parental allowance between the parents. According to the proposal, which duly passed into law, a minimum of one month's parental leave had to be taken by the father. As a result, this measure was popularly known as the "daddy month" (see the discussion of the fathers' month in chapter 7). The Liberal Party, in the person of Bengt Westerberg, the Minister for Social Affairs and Gender Equality, was the driving force behind this policy in the bourgeois government.[67] The social democratic government has, in this case, retained the "daddy month". The same is true for the Act on Childcare that had been prepared by the previous bourgeois government and which was introduced in January 1995. The introduction of the "daddy month" and the Act on Childcare can be seen as evidence that the basic principles of gender equality and the dual breadwinner model have not been rejected.

Finland: The Home-Care versus Daycare Debate

Women in Finland have long played a central role in the maintenance of the family income, whether within agriculture or within industry. A single earner-model centred on a male primary breadwinner, with the wife as a homemaker or a part-time employee, has not been as common in Finland as in the other Nordic countries. The improved economic conditions that existed at the start of the1960s encouraged the view that Finland could also adopt the male breadwinner model. The married women's employment rate was expected to decline. The European single breadwinner-model was presented as part of a future orientated process of modernisation. Married women's paid employment was considered to be some-

---

66. It consisted of seven men, some with a connection to politics, others to the mass media or other areas of activity.

67. Westerberg himself is one of a growing group of well-known men who have taken up their entitlement to parental leave. Today, to show that one does not put work above everything else enhances one's political credibility. The present party leader for the Liberal Party, Lars Leijonborg, has also been on parental leave.

thing negative that was seen as more appropriate to a poor, agrarian society. This attitude led to proposals for a "wages-for-mothers" scheme and other forms of social policy that were intended to support women in their roles as mothers and housewives (Kuusi 1963:204; Julkunen 1994:185). Yet, no overarching reforms were carried out in practice to support housewives, and women's employment rates continued to rise. This situation soon led to an even deeper decline in the availability of public childcare places. Calculations showed that only 10 per cent of children who were in need of care had a full-time place in a daycare centre in 1970 (Suonoja 1992:536). A grey zone of unregulated and insecure childcare expanded to fill the gap for those children who lacked municipal daycare.

Mothers' employment was clearly rising despite the negative views that were frequently expressed about it. This gave rise to a comparatively early debate on gender equality, in which childcare was an important issue. During the 1960s, for example, Association 9 (Yhdistys 9), a sex-role organisation, placed the issue of childcare on the political agenda. The association called on the state to take greater responsibility for the expansion of daycare. Association 9 has been characterised as a middle class orientated movement and, to a large extent, the demand for organised daycare arose precisely from the growing number of well-educated middle class women. Anna-Liisa Tiekso, the Minister for Social Affairs, (People's Democratic League) pointed out in 1970 that a lack of adequate childcare had long been a problem for working class women. The left and the trade unions had also pointed out the problem, but the lack of childcare facilities was not seen as a serious social problem until middle class women began to protest (Julkunen 1994:195 f.).

In Finland as in Sweden, two main lines of thought emerged in debates within the political arena – left-wing supporters argued for one line and the supporters of the centre/right argued for the other. The left was in favour of collective care, while the other camp advocated some form of cash benefit for mothers. The Finnish social democratic women's federation, like its Swedish sister organisation, had gradually come to advocate the dual earner model (Lehto 1980:43 ff.). But, above all, it was Association 9, together with a state committee on women's position that placed the issue on the political agenda. Municipal daycare centres became guarantors of women's employment opportunities. In particular, the left-wing women's organisations advocated legislation to guarantee places in municipal daycare centres (Tyyskä 1993:151 ff.). The issue of childcare also brought together women from more traditional organisations for children's welfare, from Association 9, and from political and the trade union organisations. Together, they put pressure on the decision makers to pursue an expansion of public childcare. As a result of this pressure from women's organisations, several public committees were appointed at both the local and central levels. Women participated both at grass-roots level movements and as members of public committees as well as in Parliament and at governmental level. Women's presence on decision-making bodies in this field was already considerable during the 1960s and 1970s. For example, female cabinet ministers with connections to the women's organisations were able to place the issue on the political agenda (Kuusipalo 1989). A "movement for daycare" was in full swing, which had a strong influence on the political process.

During the period 1966–1987 coalition governments dominated by the Social Democrats and the Centre Party mostly led Finland. During these years the bulk of the social reforms that transformed Finland into a modern welfare state was introduced. Several public committees were appointed between the years 1966 and 1972 to investigate the issue of childcare. Initially, support for the single-earner model dominated, but this situation was soon to change. The above-mentioned state committee on women's position was especially significant in shaping opinion in favour of the dual-earner model. Another parallel with developments in Sweden was that the inquiry fully supported the new line on gender equality, in particular, by calling for an expansion of childcare and shared parenthood (Komiteanmietintö 1970: A8).

Following the publication in 1970 of a report by the National Board of Social Welfare, the debate began to take on major proportions. Alli Lahtinen, a supporter of increased public support for childcare chaired the report, which came out in full support of the demands expressed by the "daycare movement". This resulted in accusations that the proponents of collective childcare were intent on destroying the health of the nation's children, and that mothers who placed their children in daycare centres were selfish careerists (Suonoja 1992:537 ff.; Kiuru 1994:191 ff.). Thus, as in Sweden, there was a line of differentiation between the left-wing parties, which together with the liberal parties advocated gender equality, a dual breadwinner model and daycare centres, and the right-wing parties that supported a more traditional model. In contrast to the situation in to Sweden during this period, where governments were formed solely by the dominant Social Democrats, governments in Finland consisted of coalitions of several parties that advocated different policy approaches.

In 1970, the government appointed a committee to examine the issues of public childcare and home-care allowance (that earlier had been called the "wages-for-mothers" scheme). The Minister for Social Affairs, Katri Helena Eskelinen (Centre Party), was a proponent of a home-care allowance. The committee decided to endorse the principle of a public responsibility for the upbringing of small children, just as the public sector accepted a responsibility to guarantee an education to all children. Equality of access to education was a political goal, and it was acknowledged that there should also be public support for the care of small children. The choice was between whether this care should take place in the home by the mother (the home-care allowance option) or outside the home (the daycare centre/private-minders option). The inquiry focussed upon the home-care allowance.

Changes in the composition of the government meant that the proposals put forward by the inquiry did not meet with a great response. The new government was a caretaker government, but the new Minister for Social Affairs, Alli Lahtinen (Social Democratic Party), was a proponent of daycare centres. Lahtinen was critical of the inquiry and appointed a new committee (Suonoja 1992:542). The report of the new committee made proposals for legislation in

1972 to increase the level of support for collective childcare. This resulted in a proposal from the social democratic minority government to expand childcare provisions until the demand for daycare centre places could be met in full. The government won a majority for its proposal in Parliament, but the parliamentary debate that preceded the vote was stormy. Although only 22 per cent of Members of Parliament were women, a majority of the 102 participants in the debate were women. However, no opposition was raised during the debate to the proposal to increase support for public childcare. Once again the conflict had more to do with what the public sector ought to develop first and foremost: childcare in a home environment or in a daycare centre. The Centre Party insisted that it could only approve of the proposal if the home-care allowance was also introduced alongside it. The party failed to achieve its demands, with the result that the eventual decision dealt only with collective childcare. The legislation on daycare that entered into force in April 1973 was universal in coverage and in principle applied to all children less than seven years of age. The legislation placed responsibility for organising and controlling childcare upon the municipalities (Rauhala 1996:170 ff.). In practice, the demand for childcare grew more rapidly than the supply of places, so that a general shortage of childcare provision continued to be felt. In this situation it was decided that priority should be given to children from low-income families and to lone parents (mothers). The problem of a lack of places in daycare centres largely remained for middle class women, who perhaps had been among the staunchest campaigners for the reform (Kurikka 1992:97).

Parental Leave – Women's Political Project

Possibilities for longer maternity leaves and for public childcare had, to a large extent, changed the relationship between women and the state, and the demand for shared parental leave brought to a head relations between the sexes. A new conception of the implications of universal citizenship and the successive institutionalisation of a dual breadwinner model also put new demands on men and the male role. However, the breakthrough of this conception into the policy sphere occurred somewhat later in Finland than in Sweden. A universal maternity leave allowance came into force in 1964; it was available to all mothers irrespective of whether they had been in paid employment. The income-related element was low, reflecting the fact that women were primarily seen as mothers.

A number of changes to the maternity allowances were successively introduced. In 1974, for example, mothers were given a right to twenty-nine weeks of maternity leave, whereas the introduction of paternity rights was delayed until 1978, when twelve fathers' days were granted in connection with the extension of the period of paid maternity leave. A decision to further extend the maternity leave was made a year later, and in cases where the parents were married to one another, the father could, with the mother's permission, take up a maximum of four weeks' parental leave. Some form of "daddy month" has also been discussed in Finland, but this has not yet led to any concrete measures. Women have been particularly active in seeking changes in this field.

Towards a Finnish Childcare Model 1985–1996

As we have seen, since the end of the 1960s the debate on childcare has focussed upon a choice between publicly funded collective childcare and some form of maternity pay, currently widely referred to as "home-care allowance". Although the initial skirmish was won by those on the left who had advocated a dual bread-winner model with municipal daycare as an important ingredient, their opponents continued to press for a home-care allowance. The demand for a home-care allowance was especially strong among women from the Centre Party. They argued that those women in rural areas, who did not need daycare centres, should receive their fair share of public support for families (Tyyskä 1993).

Once again, the coalition government of the Social Democrats and the political centre pursued a "typically Finnish" policy of compromise in the field of childcare, as it did in so many other fields. These policies were characterised both by social democratic values of gender equality, similar to those that were predominant in Sweden, and by the more traditional values of the Centre Party. During the 1980s, the issue of a home-care allowance found its way back onto the political agenda. This time, however, the political impact of the debate was more explosive because of the palpable failure of municipal childcare provision to meet the demand for places. As a result, dissatisfaction was rife among families with small children. During the latter part of the 1970s, temporary public contributions were forthcoming to establish a home-care allowance as an alternative to other forms of childcare for any parent who was caring for a child less than three years of age. A number of municipalities began to experiment with different forms of home-care allowance. The opinion was expressed increasingly strongly that one alternative should not exclude the other. Rather than concentrating solely on collective childcare, attention should also be given to individual forms of childcare. The earlier conflict between advocates of the different models had led to a situation that was not good for either side. To proceed further, some sort of political compromise was seen as necessary (see Palmunen 1992; Suonoja 1992; Tyyskä 1993).

In 1983 the Social Democratic Party and the Centre Party dominated the government. More than 30 per cent of parliamentary seats were held by women, the majority of whom were drawn from the bourgeois parties. However, the two ministerial portfolios for social affairs were held by women with different views on the issue of childcare, Eeva Kuuskoski from the Centre Party and Vappu Taipale from the Social Democratic Party. A Centre Party initiative to introduce a home-care allowance met resistance. Kuuskoski and Taipale ended up on opposite sides during the negotiations, which led the media to deploy epithets such as "the quarrelling female ministers" to describe the situation (Kuusipalo 1990:32). When Parliament finally approved the government's proposal for a home-care allowance in 1984, it was the outcome of a series of negotiations and agreements between the party leaderships of the Centre Party and the Social Democrats. The leader of the Centre Party, Paavo Väyrynen, even claimed to be the "father" of the home-care allowance. Väyrynen is on record as saying that he had threatened the then social democratic Prime Minister, Kalevi Sorsa, with a Centre Party boycott of the budget negotiations unless the issue of home care was resolved (Väyrynen 1993:115 f.).

If the 1973 childcare legislation was a triumph for the Social Democrats, the 1985 home-care allowance represented a victory for the political centre, albeit one tempered by the need to make certain concessions to the Social Democrats. In particular, the Social Democrats refused to accept the proposal before the Centre Party committed itself to increased public support for collective forms of childcare (Kurikka 1992:99). The legislation stipulated that from 1 January 1990 municipalities ought to be able to guarantee either childcare provision or a home-care allowance to the parent who had elected to stay at home with a child less than three years of age, or who had children in non-municipal childcare. The right to home care allowance and public childcare enters into play once the parental leave expires.

One problem was that the goal of meeting needs in full only concerned children less than three years of age, which resulted, for example, in Helsinki trying to redistribute places for older children to the younger ones. The legislation was amended in 1991 in response to such practices, and a new goal was set, namely to provide all children less than seven years of age with an individual right to a place in public childcare. This goal was to be achieved by August 1995. It was a hard struggle for the social democratic Minister for Social Affairs, Tuulikki Hämäläinen, to win support for this suggestion (Interview with Tuulikki Hämäläinen). The adverse economic situation and pressure to prepare Finland for membership of the EU and the EMU had led the centre-right government of Prime Minister Esko Aho (1991–1995) to make cuts in social expenditure. During 1994, the Government sought to postpone the implementation of the decision to expand the individual right to childcare for all children less than seven years of age. This move did not succeed, however, due largely to the efforts of the parliamentary women's network.

One consequence of the 1991 Finnish general election was that women's representation in Parliament rose to what was then a world record high of 39 per cent. After the general election women MPs decided to form a network across party lines. This gave female MPs a platform with which to oppose the proposed delay in the childcare reforms (Ramstedt-Silén 1998b). As a result, it was decided, with only minor amendments to the original proposal, that from January 1996 children under school age were to have an individual right either to a place in public childcare or home-care allowance. Despite conflicts between the Left and the Centre/Right, a consensus exists today on the need to maintain childcare policies that offer freedom of choice and flexibility. This is a consequence of women's high degree of representation within political institutions and organisations. The choice between collective and individual childcare is dependent upon parliamentary power relations. Yet it is clear that irrespective of party affiliation, female politicians have played a significant role in the formation and carrying out of extensive childcare policies based upon the terms, needs and wishes of various groups of women.

Iceland: Voluntary or Public Childcare?

Iceland has a long tradition of independent childcare institutions created and led by voluntary organisations (Broddadóttir et al. 1997). Often these institutions only functioned during the summer months, when the fishing industry required women's labour force participation. The massive entry of women onto the labour market during the 1960s raised the pressure on local authorities to organise and expand childcare facilities. As a result, public childcare increased at local level, but it was often dependent upon the earlier work of the organisations. Thus, the daycare centres run by voluntary organisations sometimes became a basis for the public system. In some towns with a strong dependence upon the fishing industry, a certain degree of daycare activity was organised by the enterprises themselves. Public daycare activity in such towns was relatively marginal in character and was primarily orientated towards children whose mothers were living alone or who, for other reasons, were "forced" to find employment. By the end of the 1960s it was increasingly obvious that childcare demanded both trained personnel and a more general system of regulation. This coincided with the demands of both the old and the new women's movements for more and better daycare centres. In Iceland, as in the other Nordic countries, daycare was seen as a core element of gender equality policy.

The new coalition government that assumed office in Iceland in 1971 included all parties represented in Parliament with the exception of the two parties that comprised the previous coalition government, the conservative *Sjálfstæðis-flokkur* (Independence Party) and *Alþýðuflokkur* (Social Democratic Party). The parties making up the coalition government had promised to expand childcare provision during the election campaign. In December of the same year, the Minister for Education appointed a committee to draw up a proposal to the *Alþingi* for state measures to establish daycare centres. The committee consisted of four women and a man. The man, a junior civil servant from the Ministry of Education, was appointed chairperson. The members represented a broad range of social experience pertaining to childcare provision: one of them was a social worker, another was a Member of Parliament, yet another was a housewife and one was a director of a daycare centre. The appointment of the MP Svava Jakobsdóttir, a well-known author and feminist, was a signal that the government took the gender equality aspects of the issue seriously.

It was clear from the committee report that the need for daycare centre places was very big. The committee had conducted an investigation of the prevailing situation in Iceland and had also compared it with the other Nordic countries. The drift of the committee's proposals was that the state should contribute to a substantial financing of the expansion and running of the daycare centres. The committee differentiated between full-time care and part-time care and advocated a strong increase in the former. The suggestion was that the state should finance 50 per cent of the building costs and 30 per cent of the running costs associated with the provision of full-time daycare. The corresponding figures for part-time daycare were 25 per cent and 20 per cent respectively; the remaining costs were to be met by the municipalities.

A number of arguments were raised in support of these suggestions. The drift of the *pedagogical arguments* was that the existing way in which children were cared for was old-fashioned and outdated. Expanding public provision would be of direct pedagogical, social and economic value to society. Iceland, it was argued, should learn from its Nordic neighbours and create the conditions necessary for all children to receive a place in a daycare centre, irrespective of the social situations and labour market attachments of their parents, because daycare centre activities have an independent pedagogical value for children. *Gender equality* was another important reason for expanding childcare provision, because equal relations between the sexes could hardly be attained if the mother alone was responsible for the home and children. It was also argued that there were strong *economic* grounds for a state responsibility in this field, because statistics showed that many women were already in paid employment and contributed to the economic growth of society, despite the shortage of childcare places.

The Debate in the Alþingi on the Expansion of Daycare Centres

In April 1973, the *Alþingi* debated the issue of daycare. Its decision was largely in accordance with the line of the committee. The proposal for an expansion of public daycare provision was not extensively debated and only eight of the assembly's sixty members actually participated in the debate. The strongest axis of division, however, was between the government parties and the opposition. Those few MPs from the governing parties who expressed an opinion on this matter supported the committee's line.

Svava Jakobsdóttir reported on the committee's recommendations. In particular, she emphasised that as far as the government was concerned, the proposal outlined by the committee was a clear repudiation of the view, commonly held at the local level, that daycare centres were intended for children from problem families. Now the government's intention was to give a high priority to the expansion of the system of daycare centres, whilst simultaneously linking it to the issues of education and gender equality. Auður Auðuns, an MP from the opposition party *Sjálfstæðisflokkur*, opposed this orientation. She followed her party's line by expressing traditionally conservative arguments questioning the principle that the state should support women's employment outside the home through the provision of public childcare. She also claimed that daycare centres could harm children, creating more problems than they solved. Along with the male opposition speakers in the debate, she was additionally of the opinion that the costs of an extensive system of daycare centres were too high. Opposition speakers stated, amongst other things, that the municipalities could not afford to operate extensive daycare activities. Instead, one speaker advocated resources for child minders in a homelike environment, which he claimed would be a cheaper alternative.

· The final decision represented an important deviation from the committee's proposal. Instead of primarily focussing upon full-time care, it was decided to structure the benefit in such a way as to encourage the municipalities to a build up the cheaper alternative of part-time care. For example, the part-time daycare centres did not require cooking facilities. In principle, full-time care was only given to groups with special needs, such as the children of single mothers and students. As a rule, the children of married and cohabiting parents only had access to four hours of childcare per day, a practice that has continued until the present day.

The Debate on Childcare Continues

Thus, the 1973 decision failed to produce satisfactory results. A lack of childcare places continued to be a problem for many women. *Rauðsokkahreyfingin* (the Redstockings movement) continued its struggle for an expansion of daycare centres, amongst other things, through efforts to influence the trade unions. During the mid-1970s, *Alþýðusamband Íslands* (ASÍ, the Icelandic trade union confederation) and the employers' federations, issued a joint resolution calling on central government and the municipalities to build more daycare centres. In doing so, they argued that women's employment is a vital resource for the national economy and individual families alike (Guðmundsdóttir 1994:64).

In 1981, the government appointed a new committee on childcare. The following year the committee came up with a proposal for a national ten-year plan for the expansion of the system of daycare centres (Menntamálaráðuneytið, 1982). Despite this initiative, the development of childcare provision was in practice very slow throughout the 1980s. The lack of daycare centre places was one of the main reasons for the growth of a "women's party" in Reykjavik and Akureyri at the local elections in 1982. In Reykjavik, the left-wing parties had won a majority of the seats on the local council in 1978, after forty-eight years of *Sjálfstæðisflokkur* rule. It was a disappointment for many, however, that the opportunity was not seized to carry out more radical changes in the childcare system. Instead, a reform of childcare provision became one of the most important issues for the newly formed women's list in the run up to the local elections in Reykjavik and Akureyri. Given that the lists were totally new, and that the idea of a "women's party" was something totally novel, to win 10.9 per cent of the votes in Reykjavik and 17.4 per cent in Akureyri indicates considerable support for more women-friendly policies (Styrkársdóttir 1986:149). However, *Sjálfstæðisflokkur* nevertheless regained power in Reykjavik, and thus a new orientation in childcare policies failed to emerge. Instead, the established focus upon part-time institutions continued.

Not until *Sjálfstæðisflokku*r lost power at the 1994 elections, after almost six-ty years of dominance, did it become politically possible to carry out a more rad-ical reform of childcare policies in Reykjavik. Ingibjörg Sólrún Gísladóttir, a well-known feminist, now led the town council. Additionally, two women from the *Kvennalistinn* gained seats on the town council. Nowadays, even cohabiting and married couples can receive full-time daycare places for their children and the town strives to ensure that all parents, who wish to, should be able to obtain daycare places for their children.

The Development of the Maternity Allowance

As we have seen in respect of childcare, resistance to breaking up the traditional male breadwinner model has been stronger in Iceland than in other Nordic coun-tries, even if there are some parallels to the situation in Norway. This is also ev-ident when it comes to discussions about maternity allowance. In contrast to other Nordic countries, Icelandic legislation has for a long time made a sharper distinction between married and unmarried mothers' rights and between private and public employees. When the first maternity allowance was introduced in 1946, it was in principle given only to unmarried employed women. Married women could only receive the maternity allowance if their husbands were una-ble to support them. Those who were entitled to the allowance received benefit for up to three months' from the national social insurance system for the purpose of taking care of their newborn babies. A decade later, female employees within the public sector enjoyed better conditions than women working within the pri-vate sector because women in the public sector enjoyed a right to claim up to three months' maternity leave with full compensation for loss of earnings. These measures equally covered married women. During the following two decades women in the private sector also fought to obtain better entitlements. Although their efforts were not rewarded until 1970, when both married and unmarried women within the private sector obtained a right to one week of paid leave in connection with the birth of a child. In 1974, this right was extended to three weeks (Alþingistíðindi, 1974–1975, B-hluti, 2905).

During the 1970s, the period in which the new women's movement devel-oped in Iceland, the maternity leave issue was high on the agenda. Demands for a longer leave period were presented both to the *Alþingi* and to the trade unions. A powerful argument used in the debate was that all the other Nordic countries had introduced better and more generous rules for maternity leave. Furthermore, in 1975 the *Alþingi* had ratified a UN resolution concerning three months' paid leave in connection with the birth of a child. Thus, it was clear that the issue would soon appear on the domestic political agenda.

The Debate in the Alþingi on Maternity Allowance

In 1975, two of Iceland's three female MPs put forward different maternity leave proposals to the *Alþingi*. One of the MPs, a representative of the opposition parties, proposed a system according to which maternity leave would be financed through the general system of social insurance. The proposal was intended to apply equally to women employed in the public and private sectors (a similar proposal had been put forward by the same MP two years earlier). A member of one of the government parties, *Sjálfstæðisflokkur*, presented the other proposal. It also stipulated that employed women would be entitled to three months' leave. But it further stipulated that this should be financed by the fund for unemployment measures. (At this point in time unemployment was virtually nonexistent, the financial resources of the fund were in good shape and the government had already used money from the unemployment fund for other projects.)

The first proposal never went any further than the Committee for Social Insurance, while the second proposal led to agitated debates both within and outside of Parliament. Twenty-two of the sixty MPs expressed their views on the matter, which may be considered an unusually high number. The controversy was not, as such, primarily about maternity leave. Rather, it mainly concerned how such leave was to be financed. Basically, everybody agreed that reform was necessary. Thus, the debate in the *Alþingi* was mostly about whether the reform should be funded by the social insurance system or by the unemployment fund. Ragnhildur Helgadóttir, the author of the proposal, also pointed out the large differences that existed between women in the public and private sectors. In addition, she argued that the trade unions had shown themselves to be worthless in respect of this issue, as they had come no further despite twenty-one years of negotiations. Only four MPs discussed what was best for the children. For example, one medical doctor said that a longer maternity leave would enable Icelandic women to breast feed for longer than the two to three weeks that was common at that point in time.

Three women's organisations expressed opinions about the proposal: *Kvenréttindafélag Íslands, Kvenfélagasamband Íslands* and *Rauðsokkahreyfingin*. The first two organisations supported the proposal, despite being sceptical. The third organisation, the Redstockings, was unable to support it, because they were of the opinion that the reform should be financed by social insurance rather than by the unemployment fund. The executive board of the unemployment fund and *Alþýðusamband Íslands* (ASÍ) were both opposed to the way in which the proposal was to be financed. In the end, the much debated proposal was approved by the *Alþingi* thanks to the fact that Ragnhildur Helgadóttir received support from two "heavy weight" trade union leaders and party colleagues and thereby managed to overcome the resistance to its financing.

Later Changes of the Maternity Reform

A good deal of discontent was expressed during the 1975 debate over the exclusion of housewives and rural women from the terms of the maternity reform. After negotiations between the ASÍ and the employers, a revised proposal was put together that included the groups mentioned above as well as students. The proposal was adopted by Parliament in 1981 and gave women outside the labour market one month's paid maternity leave. The level of the maternity allowance was the same for everyone, which is to say it was not related to previous income. Thus, it did not offer financial protection in respect of any loss of income in excess of the basic allowance. Further, the reform meant that the father could take one of the three months with the agreement of the mother. Interestingly enough, strong domestic opinion was not the reason for the introduction of this measure. Rather, a desire to emulate policies found in other Nordic countries seems to have been the principal motive.

Intensive debates and pressure from women's organisations and the *Kvennalistinn* has since brought Iceland even closer to the other Nordic countries. Better benefits for both parents were introduced in 1989, including the introduction of entitlement to six months' parental allowance. The first month is nowadays reserved for the mother, but the remaining five months can be shared between the parents. The allowance is still universal in coverage and corresponds to the norm for other social benefits. The full allowance is paid for six months for employed persons and students, while full-time homemakers and women who work less than 50 per cent receive half the allowance. Women employed in the public sector continue to enjoy an additional right to full compensation for loss of salary. However, this additional right is not applicable to those fathers employed in the public sector who decide to take up their entitlement to parental leave. Instead, such fathers only receive the universal allowance.

Both Similar and Different

This chapter has focussed upon the role of women as political actors in the parliamentary debate on childcare and parental leave. Irrespective of whether the level of female representation has been relatively high, as in Finland and Sweden, or relatively low, as in Iceland, female politicians have strongly advocated the need to acknowledge a political responsibility for the care of small children. In all three countries the issue of childcare has generated highly contentious debates and conflict within the parliamentary arena. In Finland and Sweden, women pursued their policies at an earlier stage and to greater effect, whereas resistance to public childcare measures has been more significant in Iceland. Yet, a reversal of attitudes is, however, also taking place in Iceland due largely to a combination of competition from *Kvennalistinn* and increased pressure from female politicians and the political left. This lends support to the positive interpretation of women's integration within the political arena, namely that integration has an impact upon the nature of the political process and that the political system can be made more women-friendly through the efforts of more female decision-makers. This also implies that these countries will continue to experience a certain, limited, convergence.

Despite differences between the Nordic countries, there are several common characteristics that distinguish them from non-Nordic countries. This makes it possible to generalise, to a certain extent, about Nordic features. We have seen that women's position on decision-making bodies within the political arena is exceptionally strong in precisely those policy areas that most concern them. In all three countries (Finland, Iceland and Sweden), this has led to a form of politics that has striven, albeit at variable speeds, to realise a shared responsibility for the care of small children. Women's demands in respect of this responsibility have not only been directed at the *state* but also towards *men* as fathers. Despite several differences in economic, historical and political conditions, which have become apparent during our scrutiny of the three Nordic countries, we cannot deny the ties and similarities that also exist between them.

Yet, a more deep going analysis shows that the three Nordic countries differ in so many ways that it is difficult to talk of a uniform model, even if the countries have borrowed features from each other. Sweden has made the greatest effort to provide places for children with employed parents in collectively formed, standardised childcare centres. Finland has put effort into providing both collective forms of childcare and a home-care allowance, while Iceland has prioritised part-time childcare and nurseries for older children. In Sweden, discussions and political measures to encourage fathers to participate more in the care of children have also been given greater prominence since the mid-1970s. But the vision of equal parenthood has influenced the debate and policy in the other countries as well.

In all three countries, the social democrats and the left have, to paraphrase the literature on welfare, been seen as standing for all that is "typically Scandinavian" – that is to say a large public sector with well developed and equipped daycare centres. Other forms of childcare measures, such as the home-care allowance, have been preferred by the bourgeois parties and were originally intended to maintain an essentially male breadwinner model. The Finnish case complicates this simple division. A characteristic of the home-care allowance in the Nordic countries, especially in Finland, which has the longest experience of this type of benefit, is that it is no longer consistent with the male breadwinner model because it is given to the person who takes care of the child. Thus, the person who stays at home receives a certain degree of economic independence, which is not present in the typical single breadwinner model. In addition, the benefit has not been seen as being either in conflict with or an alternative to collective childcare. The uniqueness of the Finnish model is that the strong influence exercised by female politicians from different political parties has led to a search for the most encompassing solution – in other words, a compromise that offers something to everybody. This does not mean, however, that the conflict between the left/social democracy and the centre/right in respect of the most appropriate forms of care for small children has totally vanished.

PART III
Institutionalised gender equality

Theme editor: Anette Borchost

9

What is institutionalised gender equality?

Anette Borchorst

Defining and delimiting gender equality policies

In this chapter we examine the gender equality policies of the Nordic countries as one of the main political arenas in which the relationship between the sexes is addressed. It goes without saying that the way in which we define and delimit gender equality policy will determine which factors will be included in the comparative analysis of the five countries. One of these ways could be to include all policies pertaining to the relations between the sexes. In practice, however, this would result in too wide a definition because almost all political initiatives bear on the relationship between the sexes, if not directly then indirectly. We will therefore lay down as a first principle that only measures which are *expressly* aimed at promoting gender equality will be considered. This was the also basic premise of the book *Unfinished Democracy*, which applied the following definition of gender equality:

> A policy which is pursued by public bodies whose aim is to work for equality between the sexes, together with other official measures motivated by equality considerations. (Eduards *et al.* 1985:134)

The last part of the definition opens up too large a field for our analysis because gender equality today is part and parcel of a considerable number of policy areas in the Nordic countries, and it would be impossible to include them all in a meaningful way.

Another alternative would be to delimit equality policy on the basis of what is dealt with in the countries' relevant legislation. This, on the other hand, would result in far too constricting an understanding of national policies in general and the scope of equality policies in particular. Public institutions in the Nordic countries which address equal status issues embrace a far wider range of activities whose explicit aim is to promote gender equality than are referred to in the legislation.

A third alternative then, and the one adopted here, is to include – in addition to gender equality legislation – initiatives connected to the official bodies charged with furthering gender equality. But in addition to this we also examine the institutions themselves, and, in one particular case, the debate on gender equality. This mode of delimitation means that the boundaries of our subject area will vary in the Nordic countries according to the extent of the various institutions' remits. There are also variations in the extent to which there exist commitments to promote gender equality in other sectors of the public administration, but due to our self-imposed restrictions these will not be addressed in the analysis.

Equality and gender terminology in the Nordic languages

In this section we examine the terms that have been used to characterise government policies aimed at promoting gender equality. As gender equality issues became institutionalised in the three Scandinavian countries, a particular terminological distinction emerged between equality between social classes on the one hand, and the sexes on the other. In the Finnish and Icelandic languages, however, no new special terms were coined to express a commitment to gender equality.

Nevertheless, there is in Finnish an expression for equality, namely *tasa-arvo*, which is used in combination with other terms to create a variety of meanings. In the seventies *tasa-arvo* was applied mostly in the areas of economic or political equality, while in the eighties and the nineties it has been used mostly in the context of gender equality (Holli 1991).

In Iceland the term *jafnrétti* has been used both to denote equality between the sexes and between classes and social groups. Nowadays, however, the word is strongly associated with gender in general terminology. In the mid-seventies, the meanings ascribed to both *jafnrétti* and *jafnréttisbarátta* (the campaign for equal rights) were gender-neutral, but they gradually became associated with women's rights. Most recently a change has taken place in the direction of greater gender-neutral applications, in line with the increasing tendency for equality issues to relate to both sexes. Another term, *jafnstada*, which means equal rights or equal status, is also linked to disparities between women and men, but it does not appear as frequently in the public debate. This notwithstanding, the Icelandic Sex Discrimination Act is called "lög um jafnan rétt [equal rights] og jafna stö karla [between women and men]".

During the sixties and seventies a terminological distinction emerged in the Swedish, Norwegian, and Danish languages which differentiated between class equality and gender equality. The Swedish terms were *jämlikhet* and *jämställdhet*; the Norwegian *likhet* and *likestilling*; and the Danish *lighed* and *ligestilling*. Semantically, the word *lighed* means that two or more parties are perceived as being equal. The term *lighedspolitikk* or *equality policy* needs then to be considered in light of the social democratic view that differences between the social classes are socially determined in general and by market forces in particular. On the other hand, the term *ligestilling* or *gender equality* suggests that measures are taken to make two parties, deemed unequal, more equal (Hirdman 1990:106). The way in which these expressions are used seems to indicate that total equality between men and women is an impossibility. There may be a connection here with the notion that gender differences – as distinct from class differences – not only are socially determined, but biologically determined too. Unfortunately, the Nordic languages lack the faculty of the English language to discriminate between sex and gender. The latter term is used to denote gender relations which are socially determined and susceptible to market forces or political action. There is, however, little consensus concerning what these socially and biologically determined differences between the sexes are supposed to be, in whatever language. But English does at least permit a more differentiated discourse. In Sweden the term *genus* – signifying gender – has found approval in academic circles, but not in general usage (Eduards 1995:60 ff.).

This terminological variety with reference to equality of gender and class has been interpreted as an expression of dissimilarities in power and interests between gender and class. Hernes argues that, in consequence, women's interests become defined as special interests which, according to the precepts of the prevailing ideology, should not be confused with the dominant and common interest (1987:19). Hirdman is of the opinion that the term *jämställdhet* (gender equality) was coined because there was a desire to reserve *jämlikhet* (class equality) for the conflict between class and capital (1990:106). There is little doubt, however, that efforts made in the name of gender and class equality have not enjoyed equal measures of political attention, and class inequalities have been perceived as a far more urgent matter than gender inequalities. The institutionalisation of class co-operation meant that the class-based organisations, represented by the workers' and employers' federations, played a decisive role in the formation of the Scandinavian welfare states, while the impact of gender-based organisations has been very limited. This must also be seen in relation to the fact that men only to a limited degree have organised themselves on the basis of issues of gender.

Changes in linguistic usage have gradually crystallised in the application of *jämställdhet–likestilling–ligestilling* in political measures for purposes other than achieving gender equality, and especially measures aimed at securing ethnic minorities conditions on a par with other social groups. It is here that the term "ethnic equality" is applied.

In all of the Nordic countries, albeit in contrast to certain other countries and to the UN system, gender-neutral terms were chosen for the various measures, even though they were initially women-oriented and responsibility for them was shouldered by women as players on the political stage. This signalled that the promotion of gender equality should apply both to women and to men. One of the changes which the gender equality policies of the five countries have undergone during the past decade is that initiatives in this area increasingly address men, just as men have become more and more visible as actors in the field of gender equality politics.

The term "women's policies" has been used on occasion to denote policies designed especially to influence the situation of women. Hernes employs it in connection with public income transfers and services which played a crucial role in changing living conditions for Scandinavian women in the sixties (1987:25 ff.). These policies were closely linked to the expansion of the welfare state in the sixties and seventies, and they were adopted prior to gender equality legislation. Today, the expression is hardly ever heard in public debates in Denmark and Sweden. In Norway an application remains for it in the field of regional policy, the intention being to persuade women to stay put in sparsely populated areas by enhancing their living conditions. In Finland, "gender equality politics" and "women's politics" are frequently used interchangeably. In Iceland, terminology has been influenced by the particular dynamic generated by the Women's Alliance. The term *kvennapólitik* (women's politics) was directly associated with the party from its formation in 1983, and in some ways the party has monopolised the term.

State feminism and femocrats

Various concepts have been formed in women's studies to describe government efforts in the field of gender equality. The term *state feminism*, which was introduced by Scandinavian workers in women's studies, has become extremely popular as a designation of such initiatives. Hernes defines it as "feminism from above in the form of gender equality and social policies" (1988:201 ff.) and she posits as its basis the interaction and alliance between the state and women (1987:162). Siim believes that it refers both to feminists as administrators and to female politicians who work to advance gender equality (1991:189). Since then the term has gained international credence in the literature. Stetson and Mazur define it as "activities and government structures that are formally charged with furthering women's status and rights" (1995:1 ff.).

The term requires further clarification on two points. The first concerns its delimitation, i.e., the factors it can be said to embrace. As mentioned above, Hernes stresses the political content, both in the area of policies for women and gender equality. In contrast to this, Siim lays greater weight on the actors both in the form of civil servants and politicians. Stetson and Mazur base their definition on the activities of official bodies set up to further gender equality. In our opinion, the choice of definition must depend on a concrete assessment. As already mentioned, gender equality policies are increasingly being targeted at men and their interests. These interests correlate with those of women in some areas but far from all. Our conclusion is therefore that gender equality initiatives can be pro-feminist or non-feminist, and we will not exclude the possibility that they can also be anti-feminist. But as to determining what is what, we need a definition of feminism, and, in our view, as a minimum requirement it should build on an acknowledgement of the structural background to gender differences.[68]

An expression occasionally used to denote civil servants whose responsibilities include the promotion of gender equality, is *femocrat*. It originated in Australia (Yeatman 1990:65 ff.), but is also used in a Nordic context to designate people of both sexes working to further gender equality. Van der Ros employs "femocrat" to refer to public employees whose work relates to women's policies or gender equality, and she defines the difference between their tasks and their attitudes distinguishing between femocrats who hold feminist views, and those who do not (1996a:200 ff.). Thus we are getting close to a solution to the problem to which the term "state feminism" gave rise; however, the expression has other weaknesses. It implies that women comprise its focus, but since gender equality increasingly involves issues of concern to men it lacks the necessary precision. In this section of the book, the term will be applied in the chapter on efforts to promote equal status at the level of local authorities; for the remainder, we will refer to public employees or civil servants in the area of equal status.

Between *Unfinished Democracy* and the present volume

At the start of the eighties, less than a decade after the institutionalisation of equal status in the Nordic countries, the book *Unfinished Democracy* presented an analysis of gender equality politics in the Nordic countries. The similarities found by the contributors between the Nordic countries were remarkable (Eduards *et al.* 1985, chapter 7). Today, as we look back over twenty years of gender equality politics in action, the time has come to appraise what has been achieved. In this part of the book we will focus on developments that followed in the wake of *Unfinished Democracy*, with a few detours to the period prior to 1983, and we address various aspects of the institutionalisation of gender equality in the five countries.

The theme of the following two chapters is gender equality policies at the national level. The national effort has tended to be more focused and systematic than local-level undertakings. Our main questions relate to whether significant similarities can still be found between the countries, or whether the situation is characterised by increasing divergence. In Chapter 10 we look at organisational structure and the distribution of functions and authority in government undertakings. We also consider the equality institution actors. What interests us is whether differences in the priority and weight accorded gender equality policies by the individual countries are detectable and, that being the case, discuss possible explanations. Chapter 11 addresses the content of equality legislation in relation to decision-making processes and implementation in each of the countries. In Chapter 12, we analyse local-level equality efforts which have enjoyed increasing political attention in the Nordic countries. This applies to Sweden and Norway in particular, to which the last part of the chapter is devoted. The themes

---

68. For a definition of feminism, see Halsaa 1996; Van der Ros 1996a; and Dahlerup 1998.

here are the loyalty and marginalisation of personnel in the area of gender equality promotion, and male opposition to gender equality. In Chapter 13 we concentrate on the perception of equality in the gender equality debate on the basis of an extreme case, namely two Finnish debates on the role of women in the military. The analysis focuses on the manner in which arguments have changed as well as the manner in which gender equality is perceived.

10

Equal status institutions

Anette Borchorst [69]

We analyse in this chapter the organisational structure of the Nordic states' efforts to promote gender equality as well as the division of tasks and allocation of authority among their various bodies and institutions. In addition we focus on the actors that have been associated with and represented on the bodies set up to promote gender equality. The analysis is both synchronic and diachronic, i.e., its subject matter covers developments that have taken place over the past two decades in all five countries. This means that reading the chapter may be laborious at times, but we believe that there is a great and unmet need for this type of analysis. In addition, systematic comparisons are a precondition for theoretical advances in this field. The overall aim of the chapter is to ascertain whether the organisational approaches in the countries under investigation have converged or, on the contrary, diverged. This leads into a discussion of the weight and effect of equal status policies.

Organisational models

During the seventies all of the Nordic countries set up permanent equal status institutions. [70] The Norwegian Equal Pay Council of 1959, and the corresponding Icelandic body set up in 1973, may be considered forerunners of these institutions. The Icelandic body, however, lacked both business premises and staff to carry out its duties. In 1972 the Equal Pay Council in Norway was transformed into the Equal Status Council, [71] while in Finland the Council for Equality be-

---

69. This chapter is extensively based on verbal and written contributions from Anne Maria Holli (Finland), Ingrid Pincus (Sweden), Janneke van der Ros (Norway), and Stefania Traustadóttir (Iceland). Other references will be found in the text and bibliography.

70. Appendix 3.1 provides an overview of the organisational models used by the Nordic countries in their promotion of equal status.

Figure 10.1 Organisationsal models in the national efforts to promote gender equality in the Nordic countries

	Policy-advisory function	Law-enforcing function	Administrative function within the ministerial hierarchy	Minister for Gender Equality	Ministerial location
DK	Secretariat — Equal Status Council			–	Office of the Prime Minister
FN	Council for Equality between Men and Women / Equality Bureau	Equality Ombudsman / Equality Board		+	Varies
ICE	Equal Status Council / Secretariat for Equality Issues	Equal Status Complaints Committee	Section for Gender Equality / Liaison Committee for the Minister for Gender Equality	–	Ministry of Social Affairs
NO (after restructuring)	The Centre for Gender Equality / Board	Gender Equality Ombudsman / Secretariat / The Equal Status Board of Appeals		–	Ministry of Children and Family Affairs
SWE	Council on Equality Issues	Equal Opportunities Ombudsman / Equal Opportunities Commission	Equality Affairs Division	+	Varies

tween Men and Women was formed. In the same year Sweden founded its Council on Equality Issues – which consisted of a smaller and a larger sub-unit. Equal status councils were set up in Denmark in 1975 and in Iceland in 1976. This means that at the end of the seventies, equal status bodies had been formed in all of the Nordic countries, the primary purpose of which was to render advice to policy-makers. The emphasis was on initiating public debates, a strategy which was in line with the contemporary view that the problem of sexual discrimination was above all a question of attitudes, attitudes which would be altered through effectuating a general change of mentality (Halsaa 1995a:25).

Hence, at the end of the seventies there was a large measure of correspondence between the bodies set up by the Nordic countries to promote gender equality both with regard to number and functions. Since that time, however, they have diverged. In most of the countries the original assignments have been portioned out to separate bodies whose scope of operation has also widened. Several countries formed bodies to monitor the implementation of the legislation, and in some countries autonomous administrative units were set up within the ministries. These bodies were officially independent of other gender equality bodies.[72]

Finally, this depiction of the division of functions would not be complete without mentioning the issue of political leadership in the field of gender equality and the appointment of ministers to administer gender equality. A schematic rendition of the division of functions among the five countries' national equality apparatuses can be found in Figure 10.1.

The figure shows that the greatest number of equal status bodies are to be found in Sweden and Norway, and that these two countries also have adopted the clearest division of political, judicial, and administrative functions and tasks. At the other end of the scale is, with one solitary body dedicated to promoting gender equality between men and women. The larger number of institutions concerned with equal status in some countries may well indicate a higher sense of priority and, moreover, give rise to healthy competition. On the other hand, the creation of a multitude of bodies can also result in dissension, and, if their areas of jurisdiction are unclear, resource use and management may become inefficient. In what follows we shall take a closer look at the differences in the coun-

---

71. The Norwegian Equal Status Council changed its English name in the mid-nineties. As the Beijing conference on women drew near, it was felt that the term "equal status" did not reflect the gender aspect of the Council's work, so it was duly dubbed the Gender Equality Council. The Equal Status Board of Appeals was similarly renamed the Gender Equality Board of Appeals as part of the same process. The Equal Status Ombudsman first redesignated itself the Gender Equality Ombud. Dropping the suffix "man" in "Ombudsman" was an attempt to reflect the gender neutrality or equality of the office. After the conference, however, as the realisation dawned that "Ombud" on its own was not understood by many English-speaking people, it was renamed for a third time, and is now referred to as the Gender Equality Ombudsman. Throughout this book, the original names will be applied to avoid confusion, apart from when context demands the employment of current appellations (transl. note).

72. These gender equality bodies have had secretariats either on a joint basis or individually (cf. Figure 10.1).

tries' gender equality institutions, their observance of their responsibilities, and their respective terms of reference.

Policy-advisory and law-enforcing bodies

After the formation of equality bodies with a policy-advisory role in the seventies, all countries apart from Denmark witnessed the establishment of institutions to enforce equal status legislation. The mandate of these bodies was to oversee the observance of the new equal status laws. Norway was the first country, not only in the Nordic region but in the world, to appoint an Equal Status Ombudsman and an Equal Status Board of Appeals. This happened in 1979. Following in Norway's footsteps Sweden appointed an Equal Opportunities Ombudsman and established an Equal Opportunities Commission in 1980, with Finland following suit in 1987 with its own Equality Ombudsman and Equality Board. In 1991 Iceland set up an Equal Status Complaints Committee, but without an ombudsman, something which can be put down to the lack of a tradition for ombudspersons in Iceland (NK Tema 1994d:16). This tendency to appoint equality ombudspersons and appeals boards clearly spread through the Nordic countries by means of diffusion. One of the reasons why Denmark never set up corresponding institutions of its own may be that what was then the EEC (and its member countries) wielded greater influence in the area than Denmark's Nordic neighbours.

In Norway, the main responsibility of the Equal Status Ombudsman is to oversee compliance with gender equality legislation, especially in the handling of complaints, and she is also charged with informing the public about legal requirements. The Ombudsman is obliged to seek voluntary compliance with the law, and she has no authority to impose fines. She can either handle complaints submitted by others, or address cases on her own initiative. If voluntary compliance cannot be achieved she is authorised to submit the case to the Appeals Board which in turn may either prohibit certain acts or order certain steps to be taken. In practice, however, very few cases get as far as the Appeals Board. In 1996, it convened five times and handled nine complaints. The Board is not authorised to adjudicate in matters concerning collective agreements, which come under the purview of the Labour Court. Cases concerning the Gender Equality Act can be brought before the courts, but this is a very infrequent occurrence. Contravention of the Gender Equality Act may render the persons or bodies involved liable in damages, but only if the case is brought before a court of law.

In Sweden it is the duty of the Equal Opportunities Ombudsman to oversee the observance of the provisions of equal opportunity legislation, in particular with regard to the prohibition of discrimination and efforts to promote equal status. She must try to get employers to observe the law voluntarily, but she does have the authority to order cases involving sexual discrimination brought before the Labour Court, whose jurisdiction also covers matters related to collective agreements. The Ombudsman is authorised to conduct sexual discrimination cases before the Labour Court if the parties concerned do not wish to do so themselves. In 1992 and 1994, the regulations concerning the obligation to actively pursue the promotion of equal status were tightened; the law was amended to include provisions setting out the obligations of the unions' and employers' organisations in the area. This meant that collective agreements no longer had precedence and that the Ombudsman now had the power to enter all workplaces and carry out inspections to ascertain that action was being taken to promote equal status in all enterprises with more than nine employees. In this connection the office of the ombudsman was allocated a much larger budget. The Ombudsman has the authority to refer cases concerning violations of the law to the Equal Opportunities Commission, which may impose fines. However, this has only happened on rare occasions.

In Finland the Equality Ombudsman monitors observance of the equality law, and especially the Act on Equality between Women and Men. Her responsibilities embrace furthering gender equality in society as a whole, rendering advice, disseminating information, and handling complaints. In addition to this she has the authority to inspect workplaces. Since the Act on Equality between Women and Men is not subsidiary to collective agreements, it follows that the authority of the ombudsman is not limited by such agreements. She cannot impose sanctions, but the Equality Board has the authority to prohibit actions and give fines. The Ombudsman and the Board are entitled to order the surrender of information. The Board is of little practical significance, and has only dealt with a single case. The Ombudsman may assist complainants in bringing their cases before a court. Previously the decisions of the courts and the Ombudsman have often clashed: in 1989 the decisions of the courts tallied with those of the Ombudsman only 20 per cent of the time (Vuosikertomukset 1990; Holli 1996). According to the present Ombudsman, the courts have generally begun to take gender equality issues more seriously, particularly after Finland joined the EU.

According to the law in Iceland, a government minister is responsible for the implementation of the law. The decisions made by Equal Status Complaints Committee are given in the form of recommendations and have no legal force. There is a legal obligation to disclose information to the Committee when required. In cases in which actions are considered punishable by law, they may be pursued further in courts of law. From 1991 to 1996, twelve such cases reached the courts.

The ombudspersons thus have only limited authority, but in Norway, Sweden, and Finland, they have meant a great deal to the creation of legal precedents in the area. In particular, the Swedish and the Norwegian gender equality ombudsmen have become decisive for the implementation of the gender equality laws since their decisions only on rare occasions are reversed by the courts. On the other hand, while the authority wielded by the ombudsmen in relation to collective agreements is limited in Norway and Sweden, this is not the case in Finland. In all of the Nordic countries, the requirement to disclose information to the enforcing bodies has been made more rigorous, and jurisdiction of these bodies has been widened. In Denmark the Equal Status Council may grant dispensation from the equal opportunity legislation to enact affirmative action. In addition to this, the Council may of its own accord examine cases, and submit when requested recommendations concerning violations of the Equal Pay Act and the Equal Treatment Act. The Council has the authority to order the surrender of information and to inspect workplaces. The final decision concerning violations of the equal status legislation resides with the courts or industrial arbitration councils.

The establishment of bodies to oversee observance of the law transformed the tasks of the advisory bodies. In Norway, the existence of an Equal Pay Council resulted in priority being given to equal pay issues in the new Equal Status Council. When the office of the equality ombud was created, the equal pay section was attached to it. According to the provisions, the Equal Status Council was intended to function as a liaising and co-ordinating body between the public authorities, organisations, and the public at large, and was given an advisory role *vis-à-vis* local-level efforts. In Sweden, the role of the Council on Equality Issues is more restricted. It works primarily as a point of reference for the minister for equal status and meets only four times annually. In Denmark, Finland and Iceland, the tasks of the councils consist in providing advice, promoting equal status, and monitoring developments. They are required to publish information on equal status issues and to function as a watchdog in the area. In Denmark, the Equal Status Council also runs an advisory service for private and public enterprises.

Administrative responsibility and political leadership in the area of equal status

Independent administrative bodies for equal status in the ministries are only to be found in Norway and Sweden. Norway was the first country to establish one: in 1978 it set up the Section for Equal Status and Family Affairs (at the Ministry for Consumer and Family Affairs). The original cause was that a majority in the Norwegian national assembly, the Storting, wanted to see a strengthening of equal status initiatives in the central administration (Halsaa 1995a:27). In 1994, this administrative unit was renamed the Section for Gender Equality, and placed under the Department for Kindergartens and Family Affairs (at the Ministry for Children and Family Affairs). The Section for Gender Equality is responsible for co-ordinating and implementing equality policy. It has no overall responsibility for gender equality efforts in the other ministries but may intervene in specific areas.

In Sweden the Equality Affairs Division was formed in 1982. It assists the minister in the development of principles of gender equality policy and co-ordinates the policy of the government in this area. It also sees to the distribution of funds to relevant projects. Since 1994, the Division has reviewed all bills and reports from public inquiries to ascertain that consequences for gender equality policy have been taken into account.

In none of the Nordic countries does gender equality comprise a separate province of its own headed by a government minister; it is always tagged on to some other area of responsibility. Until recently, only Sweden (since 1976) and Finland (since 1980) actually appointed a minister for gender equality, however, in 1999 Denmark also appointed a minister with responsibility for gender equality issues. Since responsibility for gender equality has always lain with a minister, this suggests that the area is awarded a certain measure of priority at government level. In Sweden, moreover, an under-secretary is appointed with responsibility for gender equality, and Norway has followed suit under the centrist coalition government which came to power in 1997. It is the duty of the ministers in Norway and Sweden to co-ordinate their respective governments' gender equality policy. In Finland, the minister's functions are less clearly defined, but since the end of the eighties the minister for gender equality has had the job of securing support for reforms in the area at the national level. In all countries, the visibility and significance of this position depends greatly on the person holding it, and the various ministers' enthusiasm for and aspirations on behalf of gender equality have a great effect on the work in general. This point is nicely illustrated by Bengt Westerberg who was Swedish minister for equal status from 1991 to 1994 in a non-socialist government, and Mona Sahlin, who held the post from 1994 to 1996 in a social democratic government. Both functioned as deputy prime ministers, and during their incumbencies gender equality issues gained a far higher place on the agenda of their respective governments than had previously been the case. On the other hand, the appointment of a person with slim regard for gender equality or who lacks the required authority to set his or her stamp on the debate can result in periods of stagnation or lowered priorities.

The way in which the governments of the five countries view the issue of gender equality varies considerably. The independent position of the Danish Equal Status Council means that it is also independent of governments which come and go. This can be an advantage, but it is also a drawback in that access to governments and ministers is not particularly good. Concomitantly, the Danish government has no gender equality programme. In Norway and Sweden, political leadership in the field of gender equality has been much more consistent and distinct; what is more, their governments have an explicit and visible gender equality policy. In addition to this, the administrative sections for gender equality means that administrative responsibility for equal status is located within the ministerial hierarchy which in turn means that the minister in question can find a measure of support in the underlying bureaucracy. In Finland, gender equality issues are guaranteed a certain degree of recognition by the government because a minister for equal status is always appointed and the government has a gender equality programme. In Iceland the situation resembles that of Denmark which has no independent administrative section. Nor does Iceland have a minister whose portfolio includes responsibility for gender equality issues. However, when the law was amended in 1991, the Minister for Social Affairs was given responsibility for the implementation of gender equality legislation, and this has ensured a certain level of accountability in the government.

Organisational restructuring in the Nordic countries

In this section we review the way in which the organisational structures have functioned in each of the five countries as well as the reasons behind the steps to restructure the area that have been implemented in some countries or are on the drawing board in others. In Sweden the apparatus set up to deal with gender equality issues has been subject to continuous restructuring. Relations between the numerous equal status bodies have generally been unproblematic, not least thanks to clear-cut jurisdictional boundaries. Disagreements have arisen with regard to details, but there have been no great conflicts to speak of (Pincus 1998:14). The life span of some bodies has been relatively short. Instances of such bodies are the Council for Equal Status Research (abbreviated to *Jämfo*), which existed from 1983 to 1991, and the Council on Equality Issues, which was set up by Mona Sahlin and only functioned during her incumbency as minister with responsibilities for equal status from 1994 to 1996.

In Iceland, the allocation of political and administrative functions has also worked well since 1991, even though the office housing the secretariat of the Equal Status Council also doubles as the office of the Equal Status Complaints Committee. The Equal Status Council was given new duties in 1991 in connection with a review of the law. One of its new tasks consisted in arranging an equal status conference every third year, and its advisory capacity was upgraded as well. Statements made in connection with this amendment were thus of far greater significance to the Council's undertakings, and efforts were made, with some degree of success, to galvanise the interest of the Minister for Social Affairs in issues to do with gender equality. This was the case, for instance, in respect of the priority given to the action plans for gender equality, for which the minister is accountable to the Alþingi. The Council has never uttered any criticism of the minister's actions, however.

In Finland, the founding of the ombudsman's office initially resulted in the Council being sidelined and its tasks transferred elsewhere. This generated a number of problems so that the administrative components of the two bodies were both placed under the leadership of the ombudsman (Holli 1996). In 1994 a study was conducted into the allocation of authority. It concluded that although there was a clear separation into a law-enforcing and an advisory function, the combined administration of the two areas was problematic precisely because no clear division between them existed at this level. The study recommended that either the administrative functions of the two institutions be clearly separated, or that a real integration of them be carried out under the leadership of the ombudsman (Tasa-arvoelinten työnjako 1995). These structural considerations have not resulted in any real administrative separation of duties, but their budgets have been separated.

In Norway, the gender equality apparatus has generally worked without problems. The government has proposed dismantling the Equal Status Council several times, but on each occasion the Council has been saved by a majority in the Storting (Halsaa 1995a:27). In the beginning of the nineties, the role of the Council's secretariat, which also doubled as secretariat for the ombudsman, had become steadily more independent of the Council, and the Council was having a very difficult job carrying out its advisory responsibilities, not least because it met only four times a year. In 1992, the government criticised the Council for not having found a niche for itself in the work to promote equal status and for its apparent lack of ability to influence the political agenda; in addition the government found its composition too limited (Barne- og familiedepartementet 1992:71 ff.). In 1994 what is known as the Hatland Committee was appointed. It concluded in 1995 that the mandate of the Equal Status Council was too wide-ranging, its area of responsibility poorly defined, and the allocation of authority between the ministerial level and the Council unclear. It recommended clearer divisions of responsibilities and tasks. It additionally stressed the necessity of expertise in the area of information and dissemination. The committee majority proposed a three-way division of functions; the minority was satisfied with two. Both of the recommended models went in for the abolition of the Equal Status Council, but the first alternative proposed the setting up of a competence centre, independent of the ministry and the government, whereas the second did not (NOU 1995: 15:8). Following this, a committee appointed in 1996 by the Ministry of Children and Family Affairs considered the proposals (Barne- og familiedepartementet 1996), and in the autumn of 1997 the restructuring process got under way. The Equal Status Council was shut down and the secretariat converted into a Centre for Gender Equality, in line with the majority recommendation. It has a board of directors which functions independently of the ministry, and consists of members selected on the basis of managerial competence and insight into the issues and politics of gender equality. Among other things this squares with the wishes of the Storting for an independent body capable of critically assessing government policies (NOU 1995: 15:9 ff.). The Centre has been located together with a women's research and documentation centre called *Kilden* ("The Source"). In addition, a liaison body has been set up. This body is summoned to annual meetings with the minister responsible for equal status. It is still too early in the day to judge whether the allocation of authority between the many institutions in the new Norwegian structure is sufficiently clear in practice.

Denmark is the only country not to have made any changes to the organisational structure of its national commitment to gender equality since its establishment in 1975, but a restructuring of the equality apparatus is presently on line. Against a background of protracted criticism of the Equal Status Council, the Socialist People's Party submitted a proposal to the Folketing, the Danish national assembly, that an Equal Status Ombudsman be established. The proposal questioned whether the composition of the Equal Status Council and its tasks were in keeping with the times, and whether it had any real chance of influencing the political agenda (Beslutningsforslag nr. B 34 1995). After a debate in the

Folketing which reflected the limited support for the creation of an ombuds-man's office (Folketingstidende 1995, sp. 1901–1910), a broad-based commit-tee was appointed to address the way in which equal status efforts in Denmark were organised, and the tasks that should be given priority in the future. The committee issued a report with recommendations for a totally new structure of Danish gender equality work. These recommendations were accepted by and large by the Folketing and are being considered by the government.

In summary then, one may conclude that the organisational structure of ef-forts to further gender equality have been undergoing change in Sweden, which together with Norway has implemented the clearest division of functions in the area, and has given it highest priority at the governmental level. In Finland, tran-sitional problems arose in connection with the separation of the law-enforce-ment function from the advisory, while this process went smoothly in Iceland. From 1975 to 1999 no changes were made to the Danish apparatus, but a restruc-turing process got under way in 1999.

Allocating responsibility for equal status issues

As Figure 10.1 indicates, the institutions of equal status in the five countries have different areas of responsibility, and equality issues are incorporated into the ministries in different ways. Each of the Nordic countries has its own partic-ular model in this area. We will present these in turn, after which we will con-sider both their advantages and their drawbacks.

The ministerial responsibility for equal status in Sweden has alternated be-tween ministers with different portfolios. Thus, the ministers for immigration, the labour market, home affairs, culture, social affairs, and the office of deputy prime minister have all shouldered responsibility for gender equality at one time or another. The minister for equality between women and men as this book was being finalised was the Minister of Agriculture. The administration of gender equality from 1976 to 1989 was conducted by the Ministry of Labour but from 1990 followed the various ministers and their changing ministries. These loca-tional shifts implied a potential danger in the form of lost knowledge and expe-rience. On the other hand, the potential advantage, which we believe applies to Sweden, comes from the educational effect of introducing considerations of gen-der equality into a variety of contexts (Pincus 1998).

In Finland, which of the ministers is allocated responsibility for gender equality promotion is determined by the government. The secretariat is always under the Ministry of Health and Social Affairs. The minister for gender equality has also generally been the Minister of Health and Social Affairs, as was the case as this book was in its finishing stages. Rather uniquely, from 1991 to 1995 the minister in charge of equal status was the Minister of Defence.

In Norway it is the Minister for Children and Family Affairs who attends to gender equality matters, but there was an under-secretary of state with responsi-bility for gender equality at the Office of the Prime Minister at the time of writ-ing. Gender equality matters were originally administered by the Ministry of

Consumer and Family Affairs,[73] which in 1991 was transformed into the Ministry of Children and Family Affairs. The administrative responsibility for gender equality remained with the ministry.

In Iceland, gender equality work has been under the jurisdiction of the Minister of Social Affairs since the time of the Equal Status Council, and it is also that minister who functions as a minister for gender equality in a Nordic context.

In Denmark, the Equal Status Council is the preserve of the Office the Prime Minister, but it is a free-standing organisation with its own secretariat. Various ministers have acted as ministers of equal status in different contexts. In 1999 the Minister of Housing was appointed Minister of Equal Status.

In Sweden and Finland, and to a lesser extent in Norway, the allocation of responsibility for equal status has changed as political leadership and ministerial functions have changed. When gender equality became institutionalised in the seventies, it was placed under the Office of the Prime Minister in Denmark, Sweden and in Finland. This might have been an indication that it was considered to be of some importance as well as demonstrating that gender equality issues transcended all sectors and should not be associated with just one of them. In Iceland, the Independence Party has proposed moving responsibility for gender equality to the Office of the Prime Minister, precisely on the grounds that gender equality should affect all areas of responsibility. Also the Norwegian Hatland Committee expressed the potentialities which lay in a placement under the Office of the Prime Minister (NOU 1995: 15:29).

It is difficult, however, to draw any unequivocal conclusions regarding the effect of a connection to a prime minister's office. When the non-socialist government removed responsibility for gender equality from the prime minister's office in Sweden in 1976, and when the social democratic government did the same in 1997, it was an expression of the reduced importance attached to gender equality policies. That the social democratic governments transferred the responsibility to the prime minister's office in 1972 and the deputy prime minister's office in 1994 may, conversely, be interpreted as a strengthening of its legitimacy (Pincus 1998). In Denmark, on the other hand, being part of the province of the prime minister has not given gender equality work a particularly high or general significance. Only once has a prime minister mentioned gender equality in an opening speech to parliament (Dahlerup 1998:589), and the prime minister only addresses gender equality issues when bills concerning gender equality or action plans are part of the business of the Folketing. As mentioned above, other ministers represent Denmark when gender equality ministers come together in international fora. The Danish Equal Status Council, contrary to other equal status councils, has only met the minister in charge of gender equality on special occasions and at intervals of several years. When responsibility for gender equality policy was moved from the Office of the Prime Minister in Finland in 1986, this was not an expression of declining significance either. It hap-

---

73. Which later changed its name to the Ministry of Consumer Affairs and Government Administration.

pened at the same time as a number of other public councils were being relocated (Holli 1996). Situating responsibility for equal status within the province of prime ministers' offices might well entail in the current situation a certain degree of isolation since the international tendency is towards a restructuring of prime ministries. Nowadays, individual areas are being relocated outside the office of the prime minister as general governmental co-ordination and top-level international meetings are gaining in importance.

Conversely, if gender equality is permanently anchored within a specific jurisdictional area, it might lead to such a great identification with this area that it loses some of its applicational compass. The primary emphasis in the gender equality legislation, to which we shall return in the next chapter, is related to labour market factors in all of the Nordic countries, but in Norway gender equality is often identified with policies related to children and the family simply because responsibility for it has been located in the Ministry for Children and Family Affairs. This has had the effect in recent years of reorienting policy towards men and childcare (cf. Barne- og familiedepartementet 1992, chap. 3). There is also a certain inconsistency in locating responsibility for gender equality policy here in that Norwegian gender equality legislation does not apply within the home. The Hatland Committee raised the likelihood of a conflict of interests between family policy interests on the one hand and gender equality interests on the other (NOU 1995: 15:29). In 1997 the Equal Status Ombudsman suggested separating gender equality policies and family policies, because gender equality policy had become too family-centred (Nytt om likestilling 1997). This should be considered in light of the fact that the freshly appointed centrist government's Minister for Children and Family Affairs from the Christian Democratic Party has decided to implement a cash benefit scheme for families with pre-school children who do not have a place in a daycare establishment (see Chapter 7). This, according to the Social Democrats and the left-leaning parties, conflicts with the purpose of gender equality, because, in their opinion, it will force women back to the family and result in a lower construction rate of new daycare institutions due to lowered priorities. In Finland too, the day-to-day exercise of gender equality policy is affected by its placement under the Ministry of Social Affairs and Health. In Iceland, the location of the policy field within the domain of the Ministry of Social Affairs does not have the same constrictive effect, since the same ministry also has responsibility for labour market policy, local authorities, housing policy and family policy.

Thus, we can conclude that when responsibility for issues pertaining to gender equality remains in the same place for a considerable time, the interests of that sector tend to influence gender equality policy. Being part of a prime minister's office may signal a general application of gender equality policy, but the Danish example shows that a top priority does not necessarily follow from such a location.

Actors in the field of institutionalised gender equality

Gender equality policy is characterised by different configurations of actors and interests. Although some of these actors have remained the same, they are not of equal significance. In what follows we shall look at different groups of actors and discuss their position within the equal status institutions in the individual countries.

Politicians are principal actors in the politics of gender equality, not least because they ensure a line of communication to the legislature, and, in the countries in which gender equality issues are not located in close proximity to the executive branch, as is the case in Denmark for instance, also to the government. In terms of direct representation on gender equality bodies, Finnish politicians are the most centrally placed in that members of the Council for Equality are nominated by the political parties; the smaller parties are represented on a rotational basis, however. This mechanism means that the Council tends to reflect the relative strength of the parties in the national assembly. If the members have access to the Eduskunta, this can influence the interest shown by the politicians in political decision-making, but key politicians with an interest in gender equality at the start of a political career can also lend weight to the work of the Council. Until recently, the majority of the Council's members were parliamentarians, but today they make up less than half, and they are not particularly influential members either. In Iceland, when the law was amended in 1991 a proposal was put forward to the effect that the political parties should be represented on the Equal Status Council; there was no majority in the Al(ingi for the idea, however. Nevertheless, the Council's chairperson has been appointed by the minister since 1991, and the minister has invariably elected to give the post to politicians, though not to parliamentarians. In addition to this, some of the representatives of the women's organisations are key politicians. In Norway, some of the larger parties have been represented on the Equal Status Council by personal selection, and the same applies to the Swedish Council on Equality Issues. In Denmark, the connection between the Equal Status Council and the executive has been ensured because the Council's chairperson is a government appointee. The chairpersons have thus far been either future, present, or former Folketing politicians.

Civil servants working in the secretariats and administrative divisions of the gender equality apparatus are also major actors in the gender equality institutions, though they are not directly represented. They have grown in number since the beginnings of a politics of gender equality. During the first decades, most of the people working in the sphere of gender equality were women, but in all countries the tendency has been to employ more and more men as gender equality officials. The empirical data which would allow us to conduct a comparison of the role they play in the various countries is unfortunately lacking.

The *principal social partners* have held key positions within the gender equality apparatus in several of the Nordic countries since the start. This needs to be understood not only in the context of the wish to make them accountable and to ease the implementation of gender equality policy, but also because gender equality policy is generally targeted at the commercial and industrial sector, which is the traditional playing field of these parties. Their presence on gender equality bodies has given them the opportunity to delay gender equality initiatives when they have seen fit. In the beginning, both the employees' and the employers' associations were sceptical of gender equality legislation, and first and foremost of the equal pay provisions in it. However, workers' organisations throughout the region have gradually adopted a more positive stance to gender equality, not least in response to pressure exerted by a rising female membership. Many trade unions have also adopted gender equality programmes, and gender equality measures are included in main agreements or co-operation agreements between management and workers in several countries. Nonetheless, the employers still seem to harbour a certain reservation when it comes to dealing with too many gender equality initiatives.

In Norway, the power of the workers' and employers' federations was particularly strong between 1979 and 1997. During this period the Norwegian Federation of Trade Unions and the Confederation of Norwegian Business and Industry were the only organisations to have permanent seats on the seven-seat Equal Status Council. However, an evaluation of the Council's activities revealed that the views voiced by these representatives tallied only relatively seldom with those of their organisations. Nor were these representatives particularly diligent in reporting back to their organisations decisions made by the Council (Skjeie *et al.* 1989:66 ff.). The Norwegian Federation of Trade Unions and the Confederation of Norwegian Business and Industry are also represented on the board of the new Centre for Gender Equality. They play a significant role in the enforcement of gender equality in that two of the seven seats on the Board of Appeals belong to them. In Denmark, of the Equal Status Council's total of nine seats, three are occupied by representatives of the Danish Employers' Confederation, the Danish Confederation of Trade Unions, and the Salaried Employees' and Civil Servants' Confederation. Since 1992, as we shall see below, these representatives have been free to veto decisions granting dispensations for special treatment. In Iceland, the workers' and employers' organisations have three of the Equal Status Council's seven seats, and, until 1991 when the Equal Status Complaints Committee was founded, they exerted a great influence on the Council's law-enforcement function. From 1991 to 1995 their position on the Council was particularly strong due to a powerful constellation of personalities and contacts. In Sweden, the representatives of the unions and employers' organisations comprise only a small number of the thirty-two-seat Council on Equality Issues, but they also have places on the Equal Opportunities Commission. In Finland, the workers' and employers' organisations have been associated with the Council for Equality via its subsections, but they have had no direct representation on the Council. They are represented on the Equality Board, although, as mentioned, the Finnish ombudsman has greater authority relative to collective agreements than his counterparts in Norway and Sweden.

Women's organisations played a crucial historical role in the institutionalisation of gender equality in the Nordic countries through their demands for legislative changes. Nonetheless, there was far less consensus concerning what needed to be done. Contention was especially rife in Norway among some of the larger feminist organisations regarding their demands in the area of gender equality policy (Eduards *et al.* 1983:196; Halsaa 1995a:24). With the founding of permanent gender equality bodies women's organisations gained permanent representation on state bodies, but compared with the workers' and employers' organisations their power has been very limited. Their representation has varied over the years, and has varied in nature in the five countries. In some countries, it has been the women's sections of the political parties which have wielded influence, while in others it was the organisations on the outside of the parties which set the tone.

Denmark is the country where the women's organisations are currently most centrally placed. Since 1988 four of the nine members of the Equal Status Council have come from the Danish Women's National Council and the Danish Women's Society. In Sweden, many of the women's organisations have a seat on the Council for Equality Issues. In Iceland, the women's organisations were not represented on the Equal Status Council before 1985, at which time Iceland's Women's Rights Association and the Women's Association of Iceland each gained a seat on the seven-seat Council. In Norway, the women's organisations lost their permanent seats on the Equal Status Council by statuary provision in 1979, but a report of a1989 inquiry recommended strengthening co-operation between them (Skjeie *et al.* 1989). In connection with the most recent restructuring, there was a proposal to include women's (and men's) organisations in a liaison group under the relevant minister. In Finland, the women's organisations have had no direct representation on the Council, but they have co-operated with NYTKIS, a network of women's organisations, for instance in connection with efforts to increase women's representation at elections (NK tema 1994c:10).

In most of the countries under consideration, the attitude of the *new women's movements* towards the state was one of scepticism, and there are only a limited number of instances in which it has advanced concrete demands for government action. It has, however, played an indirect role in gender equality politics, apart from in Sweden where it was neither as strong nor as visible as in the other countries. In Iceland, the Women's Alliance became the symbol of the new women's movement. It was initially extremely critical of the gender-neutral formulations in the legislation and of the Equal Status Council. Since 1990 the Women's Alliance has worked more actively with the Equal Status Council on questions to do with gender equality policy. In Denmark, where the women's movement was anti-authoritarian and very critical of state institutions, it did not directly demand changes to the legislation. According to Dahlerup, this was because it was too specialised and legalistically oriented. She believes, however, that the movement brought about a radicalisation and strengthening of the state's gender equality policy (1998:238 ff.). In Norway, the movement was very active indeed

Table 10.1 Financial resources and number of people working in the field of gender equality in the Nordic countries. Advisory, monitoring and administrative functions 1996

Country	Staff	Budget	Budget in DKK	Budget per head[a] in DKK
Sweden	28 persons	17.6 m. SEK	15.2	1.72
Norway	22 persons	15–17 m. NOK	14.8	3.39
Denmark	18 persons	7.4 m. DKK	7.4	1.41
Finland	13 persons	1.8 m. FIM	2.3	0.45
Iceland	6 persons	24.0 m. ISK	2.1	7.84

a.   Exchange rate as of 2.1.1997.

Source: Data from the gender equality bodies of each country

in presenting demands *vis-à-vis* the substance of the first anti-discrimination act, and it was extremely critical of the final outcome.

The links between *women's studies* and the institutions of gender equality vary considerably. In Denmark, a feminist scholar (appointed by the rest of the Council), has been a member of the Equal Status Council since 1988. In Finland women's studies are linked to the Council for Equality through one of its sub-sections, and since 1981 a co-ordinator for women's studies has been attached to the Council. In Sweden the link between the politics of gender equality and academic studies during the time of the Council for Equal Status Research (*Jämfo*, 1983–91) was very direct indeed. It was supposed to initiate, co-ordinate, and keep track of research. In Norway a female academic had a seat on the Equal Status Council from 1983 to 1992. After this a male academic occupied the place until the Council was wound up. Co-operation with research will probably be strengthened with introduction of the new Norwegian model and the founding of *Kilden*. However, the question of whether the research councils' women's secretariat should move from the research councils into the new gender equality centre has given rise to much controversy. A number of feminist scholars felt that such a move would weaken the position of women's studies relative to the research councils, so the idea was not put into practice. In Iceland the Equal Status Council has never counted feminist scholars among its members.

During the first years of a politics of gender equality there were no *men's organisations* which could function as an organised counterpart to the women's. Since that time, however, a number of organisations have been formed,[74] and men have become more visible actors in the political arena of gender equality, also in consequence of a number of government initiatives. In Sweden the Men's Role Working Group was founded in 1983 by the Minister for Equality Between Men and Women; in Norway the Men's Role Commission was appointed in 1986 by the Ministry of Consumer Affairs and Government Administration; and in Finland a men's committee was set up as a section of the Council for Equality. In Iceland, the Minister of Social Affairs appointed a men's committee, and in Denmark the Idea Group for Men was established by the Equal Status Council in 1994. In Sweden, Norway, Finland, and Iceland the men's role committees have been opinion-shapers in relation to men and gender equality, and they have activated men in this area. Among other things, they have addressed the position of men in the family and particularly the role of the father; in addition they have deliberated paternity leave, alcohol-related problems and acts of aggression. In these four countries, the collaboration between the men's groups and the institutions of gender equality has functioned relatively well. In Denmark developments took a different path. The Idea Group for Men disbanded only a year after its establishment following a fight with the Equal Status Council over the size of the group's budget. Today, men's committees still operate under the Finnish and Icelandic councils. There is a link between these initiatives and the establishment of *men's studies*, which in several countries have received support from the equality bodies. In addition, in several countries, scholars working in the field of men's studies have been attached to the policy-advisory bodies.

International influences

Since the dawn of a politics of equality, outside influences have been crucial to developments in the area, and there is widespread agreement that the United Nations Year of the Woman in 1975 effectively catalysed the institutionalisation of gender equality in most countries. But international influences are of particular significance in countries whose internal driving forces are too weak to fan innovative thinking and gender equality policy development. *Unfinished Democracy* thus concluded in 1983 that obligations in relation to international organisations have meant more to the institutionalisation of gender equality in Finland, Denmark, and Iceland, and less in Norway and Sweden (Eduards *et al.* 1983:202 ff.). This, we believe, is still a correct appraisal. In Finland it was international obligations, among other things, which was the driving force behind gender equality until the adoption of anti-discrimination legislation in 1986. In Denmark, a conscious attempt has been made to use international co-operation as a locomotive pulling equality efforts forward in the eighties, during which the Equal Status Council strongly emphasised the value of arranging global women's conferences (Ligestillingsrådet 1990:67). There are far more examples of Sweden influencing the formulation of the international organisations' objectives. This is true, for instance, of the dominant equality strategy of the nineties, 'mainstreaming', which the Council of Europe, the UN and EU have recommended. Main-

---

74. There are mainly three types of organisations (Oftung 1995): treatment-oriented groups; rights-oriented groups; and pro-feminist groups. An instance of the first type is the therapy groups for men which can be found in most of the countries; an example of the second is the Father's Association in Denmark. And an example of the last group is the "Male Front Against Male Abuse", which is the strongest men's organisation in Sweden.

streaming is based on integrating gender equality objectives into all areas of administration and policy.[75]

Sweden has led the field in putting this strategy to work, among other things by means of mechanisms to make equality issues more visible, comprehensible and mandatory. The Equality Affairs Division's review of the equality aspects of all parliamentary bills is part and parcel of this approach.

Nordic co-operation has encouraged a mutual process of diffusion between the countries with regard to gender equality policies. Political collaboration between the Nordic countries was initiated in 1974 with the founding of *AK-Jäm*, a liaison body attached to the Nordic Council of Ministers. This, together with the Nordic action plans, has strengthened this coordination. The action plans cover the periods 1989–1993, and 1995–2000, while the action plan for men covers 1997–2000. In addition there are the joint Nordic projects, for instance on workplace cultures, men and equal status, and equal pay. The arranging of women's conferences (NORDISK FORUM) as well as the setting-up of the Nordic Institute for Women's Studies and Gender Research (NIKK) represent other instances of this collaboration.

The EEC/EU has meant different things to the different countries in that Denmark was the sole Nordic member country between 1973 and 1995, when Sweden and Finland became members. EEC/EU directives must be implemented in the member countries and the EU Court's decisions take precedence over decisions of national courts. There have been a number of initiatives in this area and the impact of membership on gender equality legislation has thus been quite considerable. In Norway the EEA (European Economic Area) agreement also generates a certain amount of conformity between EU regulations and national legislation. The organisational collaboration within the EEC/EU's Equal Opportunities Unit and the Advisory Committee on Equal Opportunities together with the community programmes for equal opportunities, which have covered the periods 1982–1985, 1986–1990, 1991–1995, and 1996–2000, have also influenced equality policies in the member countries.

Cost levels

The level of expenditure in the area of gender equality policy is indicative of the priority accorded the undertaking, but it is not simply that the larger the allocated resources, the greater the effectiveness of the efforts made. This depends, among other things, on the presence of a clear allocation of authority and efficient use of resources. To give an impression of the level of expenditure, we have compared the total means made available for budget and staff of the policy-advisory, law-enforcing, and administrative functions.

---

75. Mainstreaming is defined in the manifesto of the UN's world conference on women as "promoting an active and visible policy by integrating a gender perspective in all policies and programmes, so that, before decisions are taken, an analysis is made of the effects on women and men, respectively" (Ministry of Foreign Affairs 1995).

The overall conclusion is that personnel expenditure on gender equality work is greatest in Sweden and lowest in Iceland, and that the allocated budgets are far greater in Sweden and Norway than in the other countries. Taking into account differences in population size, we find that expenditure is markedly higher in Iceland than in the other countries, and least in Finland.

Importance and impact

Thus we are able to establish that gender equality policy has acquired greater significance viewed in relation to the organisational models, division of functions and allocation of authority, and the importance accorded gender equality issues at government level. At the same time, the differences between the countries have widened throughout the eighties and nineties. We find that Sweden and Denmark constitute the extreme cases with greatest importance given to gender equality in Sweden and least in Denmark. Norway follows close behind Sweden. After these two comes Finland, while Iceland lies closer to Denmark. This finding conforms with the assessment in *Unfinished Democracy* (Eduards *et al.* 1983:208). In short, although the paths have diverged over the years, the positions of the countries relative to one another have remained unchanged.

The political agenda of gender equality is far more inclusive in Sweden and Norway both in the political arena and among the general public, and gender equality today is an integral aspect of many policy areas. In Denmark, on the other hand, equal status policy is confined to a niche both organisationally and with regard to content (Borchorst 1995). Topics such as sexually discriminating advertisements, prostitution, and sexual violence are more or less absent from the Danish debate at the same time as topics such as these are debated and are the object of initiatives not only in Sweden and Norway, but in Finland and Iceland, too.

In *Unfinished Democracy*, the economic upswing was viewed as an important factor behind the institutionalisation of gender equality. We agree that periods of prosperity tend to provide the best conditions for equality politics as the need for female workers nurtures the forces promoting gender equality. However, we have not found that the differences in economic growth between the Nordic countries during the eighties and nineties have influenced the importance accorded to gender equality by them today. Nor have we found that economic downturns have resulted in significant cutbacks in the initiatives to promote gender equality. Nevertheless, the coincidence of economic crisis and increasing unemployment and the institutionalisation of a politics of gender equality in Denmark does partly explain the relatively poor opening performance of Danish gender equality policy.

The reason for the increasing divergence between the countries over the past ten to fifteen years is to be found, we believe, in five other factors positioned at different levels relative to the political system and its environment. We do not, however, suggest that there is any one-to-one cause-and-effect relationship between them. The factors we have found to be of greatest significance are: 1) party-political profiling; 2) mobilisation of women; 3) the men's issue; 4) documentation, research, and evaluation; and 5) regulatory tradition and political culture. In what follows we will address each of these items in turn.[76]

We focus first on *party-political profiling in relation to gender equality* which we consider to be a factor internal to the system. In Sweden in particular the political parties have competed to subscribe to gender equality values, a situation which has helped to keep the issue high on the political agenda. The Social Democrats and the Liberal Party in particular have competed to promote an image of themselves as equality-friendly. It is unusual in the Nordic countries for a non-socialist party to take such a positive stance in this area, and also for a social democratic party to oppose gender equality legislation, although this was only in the beginning. Apart from these factors, the main trend has been that Social Democrats and parties to the left have evinced the greatest enthusiasm for gender equality. It is also remarkable for a party to declare that, in addition to being a socialist party, it is also is a feminist party, as did the Swedish Left Party in 1997. The political parties in Norway have also competed among themselves to be seen as supporters of gender equality. This has not been as pronounced as in Sweden, but here too, distinctive initiatives have been taken by the non-socialist parties in the area of gender equality. For instance, a number of key women politicians in the Conservative Party came out as Conservative Feminists during the seventies. What is crucial in our opinion is that most parties, both in Sweden and Norway, have included equality issues in their manifestos. This does not apply, however, to the Norwegian Progress Party, which has always been against equality legislation and differential treatment.

In Finland, where party discipline is high but not as universally applied as in the other countries (Jenssen 1999), politicians are often free to act according to the dictates of their conscience when voting on matters concerning gender equality. This could indicate that the issue represents a political minefield or that it is not considered as a particularly important policy area. On the other hand, however, it does create the space for gender-based differences of opinion to be expressed more clearly in the legislature, and it allows women the freedom to form alliances across party lines. The women's network within the parliament has also taken initiatives on equal opportunity policies. For instance, it played a role in the adoption of radical quota regulations for publicly appointed committees and boards in 1995 (Ramstedt-Silén 1998b). Finland, too, has a party, the Rural Party, which is against equality legislation.

No parties in Denmark have a strong position on gender equality issues, and in general there is very little mention of equal status in the parties' election man-

---

76. The phrase "to profile oneself" in Danish and Norwegian has quite a different ring about it than the term "profile" in English usage. In fact it is difficult to find anything in English which gives precisely the same associations in as few words. The meaning of "party-political profiling" is that of a political party taking active measures to create an overall impression that it espouses, wants to be known, and will work for a particular policy stance, in this instance, gender equality (transl. note).

ifestos. In the seventies nearly all parties had prominent women politicians who were actively engaged in the women's organisations and who initiated equal status reforms. In the eighties, too, women politicians across the political spectrum launched initiatives for gender equality reforms and action plans, but there are few instances of this nowadays. In the non-socialist parties the young women who oppose gender equality rights are more to the fore than those who support them. Nor are any left-leaning parties willing to take a serious stand on gender equality issues. The Danish Progress Party distinguishes itself in its continued opposition to gender equality from the time the issue was first raised in the Folketing in 1973, and has consequently voted against all motions and bills favouring the promotion of gender equality (Dahlerup 1990; Borchorst 1999).[77]

In Iceland, the existence of the Women's Alliance and its demands for a radicalisation of women's policy has helped galvanise the other parties in the area of gender equality, and there is a long-standing tradition for co-operation between women parliamentarians in the Alþingi, for instance with regard to issues such as the physical abuse of women, rape and incest. In the 1995 election, gender equality and equal pay emerged as two of the main themes of the election and were topics about which all the parties had something to say. Moreover, one of the chief items on the agenda of the national congress of the largest party in the country, the Independence Party, was gender equality.

We can conclude, then, that, as far as Sweden, Norway, and Denmark are concerned, there is a link between the importance accorded gender equality politics and party-political profiling, but that this does not seem to apply in the case of Iceland. Another factor, which pertains to the input to the political system "from below" is *the collective mobilisation of women*. Historically this mobilisation was an absolutely essential factor in the creation of a critical public forum for women and the formulation of women's demands for an institutionalisation of gender equality. None of the Nordic countries today can be said to host a women's movement of any significance, but in some of them a mobilisation of women is taking place through the political parties. In Norway, Sweden, and Finland, this is happening through the parties' women's sections, thus opening a conduit to the political system for women's demands "from below". In Denmark hardly any form of mobilisation in the political parties can be detected. We believe that the crucial factor at this point is the cessation of the new women's movement as a vital social movement with the capacity to bring pressure to bear for a radicalisation of the national gender equality policy. A Nordic study of the contacts between MPs and women's organisations shows that Swedish and Norwegian parliamentarians (of both sexes) have far more contact with women's organisations that Danish MPs (Wängerud 1999).

The third factor, which also relates to the input "from below", is the men's issue. We find that the emergence of conflicts or new alliances in relation to the question of *men and gender equality* has affected the importance accorded gen-

---

77. This also applies to the Danish People's Party, an offshoot of the Progress Party.

der equality policies. This topic appeared on the gender equality agenda firstly in Sweden and Norway and lastly in Denmark, where the incidence of conflicts surrounding the men's issue has been higher than in the other four countries. These conflicts have crystallised around the issue of child custody in particular, and in recent years women's and men's organisations have started to compete for the attention of politicians. In the other countries there has been a greater degree of co-operation between men and women in forming priorities in the area of gender equality.

The fourth factor to affect the importance and efficacy of gender equality policies has been the production of *documentation, research and evaluation* in relation to the national gender equality commitment. This we consider to be a crucial overall factor because it determines whether the political system receives information on the effect of its policies and measures taken. It is thus an essential precondition for the adjustment, amendment and further development of the instruments of governance in the area of gender equality policy. The role played by this factor is greatest in Sweden and Norway, where the use of gender-separated statistics, independent evaluations, and research for the purpose of detecting problems related to gender equality is far more systematised. In the other countries it is often difficult to find any historical documentation against which to compare the sexes' present status. These differences between the countries must also be seen in light of the larger allocations made by Sweden and Norway to research and evaluative studies in the area. Thus the Norwegian Gender Equality Section has funds to conduct research and has initiated several independent evaluations of the efficacy of policy instruments with a view to future modifications (see for example Skjeie *et al.* 1989; Halsaa 1995a and 1995b). In Sweden the office of the State Commission of Inquiry has carried out investigations, often with the help of independent academics specially recruited for the job (see for example SOU 1987: 19; SOU 1990: 41; SOU 1995: 110; SOU 1998: 6), and during the eighties the way in which relevant questions on gender equality issues were formulated was radicalised after critical women academics had been invited to participate in the writing of these reports (Pincus 1998). Bergqvist found that an alliance was formed between the researchers carrying out a study of women's representation and the relevant ministers, the aim of which was to increase women's representation (1994:107).

In Finland and Denmark, even though funds have often been made available for women's and gender studies, the research commitment in relation to public gender equality policy has been far more limited than in Sweden and Norway. Iceland has no strong tradition in the field of women's studies and gender studies, and efforts in relation to evaluations of gender equality policy have therefore been limited.

The fifth factor of significance affecting the importance currently accorded equality policies is the *regulatory tradition and political culture* to be found in the Nordic countries. These aspects could also be described as framework structures within which gender equality policy is rooted. Swedish political culture is more centralised, and in some areas there exists a stronger regulatory tradition than in Denmark for example, whose political culture has had a larger liberalist bent. These differences can be illustrated by the ongoing efforts to promote gender equality which in Sweden also extend to the private sector and which are policed by the Equal Opportunities Ombudsman. In Denmark gender equality promotion is limited to the public sector and there are no mechanisms in place to monitor compliance. In addition it is characteristic that Denmark has concluded that rather than more legislation in this area, what is needed is the creation of "an understanding of the benefits of equal status work in the local community" (NK tema 1994b:8).

In our opinion, then, the weight and impact of gender equality policies depends on an interplay between internal and external systemic factors, and in a synergy between the inputs from below as well as from above in the political system. Of the five above-mentioned factors, we would emphasise two as having a greater effect on variations in the importance and impact of gender equality policy. The two are party-political profile and women's mobilisation. We also believe that the trend of increasing divergence between the countries must be viewed in connection with the different implications these two factors have in the different countries. Moreover, what we are talking about are to a certain extent self-reinforcing processes in that the more passive and narrowly defined gender equality policy becomes, the lower its priority and degree of underlying support. Conversely, there is a tendency that the greater the activity and energy in the development of gender equality policies both organisationally and contentwise, the greater their perceived importance. We view the fact that the countries under investigation have not experienced significant changes relative to one another as an indication that early developments significantly affected later efforts to promote gender equality.

11

Gender equality law

Anette Borchorst[78]

A central element in the efforts to promote equal status has been regulation by means of legislative action.[79]

In this chapter we analyse differences and similarities in the five countries' legislation. We address firstly the main principles in the laws. After this we examine in greater detail three gender equality policy instruments, namely positive discrimination or differential treatment; provisions related to the composition of publicly appointed committees; and national action plans, all of which have played a major role in Nordic politics of gender equality. We focus on differences in the make-up and use of these instruments in the various countries. Finally we ask if the decision-making processes were characterised by conflict or consensus and what distinguishes the subsequent implementation of the adopted legislation.

We do not focus on the effects of gender equality policy. Thus, we do not consider whether it leads to a narrowing of the wage differential between men and women, to a less sexually segregated labour market, or to a more equal division of housework and home-based care. This is also because it is impossible to isolate the effect of equality policies from other types of policies, such as economic policy or social and labour market policy. It is also the case that other elements such as market conditions and ideological factors also affect the differences between the sexes.

While the establishing of organisations dedicated to promote gender equality took place more or less simultaneously in the Nordic countries, the adoption of gender equality legislation was far from simultaneous, and the actual volume of

---

78. This chapter is extensively based on verbal and written contributions from Anne Maria Holli (Finland), Ingrid Pincus (Sweden), Janneke van der Ros (Norway), and Stefania Traustadóttir (Iceland). Other references will be found in the text.

79. Appendix 3.2 provides an overview of the legislation of each country.

legislation also varied. Iceland was the first country to adopt an equal pay law in 1973. In 1976 this law was replaced by an Equal Rights Act. In Denmark, the Equal Pay Act was adopted in 1976 and the Equal Treatment Act in 1978. Following in their wake, the Act on Equal Opportunities for Men and Women on the Appointment of Members of Public Committees, Commissions etc. was enacted in 1985, the Sex Discrimination Act in 1988, and the Act on Equal Opportunities for men and Women on the Appointment of Members of Certain Executive Committees or Governing Bodies in 1990. The Norwegian and the Swedish gender equality laws were adopted in 1978 and 1979 respectively. The Finnish Equality Act was passed in 1986 together with a separate law providing for the setting up of an ombudsman's office and an Equality Board. The reason Denmark has five laws relating to equality while the other countries have just one is probably that the first two Danish laws on equal pay and equal opportunities were implemented against a background of two different EEC/EU directives, while the circumstances surrounding the remainder were purely national. We do not believe, however, that the actual number of laws makes any practical difference.

The contents of equality legislation

There is a certain variation in the legislation of the Nordic countries with regard to the use of gender-neutral formulations and specific references to women, and between proscribed and prescribed activities, and it is precisely this that has given rise to disagreements during the course of the decision-making processes. Legislation normally denotes the enactment of gender-neutral prohibitions. At the heart of equal status legislation in all countries is thus a *prohibition against discrimination on the basis of sex*. What is more, anti-discrimination laws were adopted in relation to gender in the Swedish Constitution of 1974, and in the Icelandic and Finnish constitutions of 1995. The ban against discrimination has an additional underpinning in that all of the Nordic countries, apart from Iceland, have enacted laws against indirect discrimination, i.e., differential treatment resulting from some other circumstances. The Danish, Norwegian, and Finnish gender equality laws contained right from the beginning a provision banning indirect discrimination. In the Norwegian Act such differential treatment is defined as "treatment which *de facto* results in an unreasonable disadvantage for one sex compared to the other" (Act no 45 of June 9th 1978 on Gender Equality: §3). The Finnish law referred initially to discrimination which "*de facto*" resulted in differential treatment (Ministry of Social Affairs and Health 1989: §7), but in 1992 a ban against indirect discrimination was incorporated into the law directly. This happened in Sweden in 1991.

In all of the Nordic countries, apart from Denmark, the gender neutrality of the legislation related to gender equality has been modified through the adoption of provisions stating that the aim of the laws is to improve the position *of women in particular* and it is precisely these formulations and demands for pro-active measures that have represented the bones of contention in the decision-making processes and split organisations and parties. The Norwegian Act stated from the outset that it "aims in particular at improving the position of women" (Gender Equality Act: §1). This formulation was a compromise solution arrived at by the contending parties who were arguing over whether a law banning discrimination against women should be enacted at all. The strong opposition on the part of the Norwegian Federation of Trade Unions to an anti-discrimination law moved the Labour Party to propose a gender-neutral bill, which, in the event, was adopted, primarily thanks to the support of the Conservative Party. Although the Conservatives were strongly opposed to the inclusion of any formulations specifically referring to women, such formulations were indeed incorporated into the final Act because it's passage was assured thanks to the votes of the Socialist Left Party (Skjeie 1982). In Finland, where the Act on Equality between Men and Women was endorsed unanimously, the Act's object clause stated that one of its aims was to improve the status of women, particularly in working life. In 1985 it was decided that, on the basis of the Icelandic anti-discrimination law, measures of a limited duration aimed at improving women's status would not constitute a violation of the law. When the law was amended in 1991, there was general consensus that its main aim should be the improvement of women's status (The Equal Status Council of Iceland 1992:26). In Sweden, a passage was introduced into the object clause of the Equal Opportunities Act stating that "the intention of the Act is to improve in the first instance the conditions for women in working life" (Act on Equal Opportunities 1997: §1).

Proscriptive legislation has been supplemented in all five countries with a statutory requirement to take positive action in relation to equal status. The strongest formulation of this obligation is to be found in the Swedish legislation, though it was this prescriptive element along with the creation of an ombudsman's office to which the Social Democrats (and the trade unions) were most opposed as the bill went through the final stages. When the first version of the bill came up in the national assembly the party voted against these provisions. The non-socialist government, in which the Liberal Party was the most powerful driving force for gender equality, were therefore obliged to omit this part of the law first time round. After a subsequent election resulting in a non-socialist victory, a law demanding the institution of pro-active measures was adopted by a margin of a single vote (Dahlberg 1984:51 ff.; SOU 1990: 41:59 ff.). According to this law, every commercial company and enterprise were obliged to take steps to promote gender equality (§6). As mentioned previously, this obligation and its enforcement were tightened up even more with the amendments to the law in 1992 and 1994. It was a non-socialist government which supervised these amendments too, in spite of strong criticism from the Swedish employers' camp. In addition the ombudsman was given the authority to carry out checks to ensure that firms were in fact taking steps to promote gender equality.

Since the law came into force in Norway, the public authorities have supposed to have been implementing measures to "promote gender equality in all sectors of society" (Gender Equality Act: §1). The Finnish law contained from the outset a formulation stating that systematic measures on behalf of gender equality did not represent a violation of the law (Ministry of Social Affairs and Health 1989: 9, subsection 4), and in 1995 the requirement relating to positive action was tightened, after which both public and private employers were obliged to initiate measures to promote equality, and employers with a work-force of more than thirty had to make gender equality plans (Act on Equality between Women and Men 1986: §4, §6). Similarly, new provisions stating that equality should be pursued were added to the Finnish Constitution. When the Danish Act on Equal Opportunities for Men and Women was adopted in 1988, the public authorities were also obliged to commit themselves to promoting equality (§1, subsection 2; Andersen et al. 1996:227). The draft law was carried – as were most of the other equality laws – after a fairly rapid passage through the Folketing, with little dissent and with the support of all parties barring the Progress Party. In Iceland, since 1991 the law has also contained a provision requiring the promotion of equality by the unions and employers' federations (The Equal Status Council of Iceland 1992:26).

Gender equality legislation in the Nordic countries is primarily aimed at the labour market and embraces advertising practices, employment, promotions, dismissals, equal pay, etc. The Swedish legislation specifically covers only the labour market, while the Norwegian, Icelandic, and Finnish laws address the community as a whole. Both the Norwegian and Finnish laws, however, have incorporated exceptions with regard to implementation within the family (and religious communities as well). The Danish laws primarily focus on the labour market.

The main conflict surrounding the adoption of equality legislation concerned the regulations on equal pay. This was especially the case in Norway, Sweden, and Finland where the trade unions actively attempted to limit the provisions, even though equal pay had already been agreed to in the collective agreements between the employees' and employers' organisations in the early sixties. The Swedish law initially contained no provisions for equal pay at all, so in Sweden equal pay was not regulated by law unless the parties' organisations found that the law covered equal pay for work of equal value anyway. In 1992 the law was amended with the inclusion of a provision obliging the workers' and employers' organisations to take positive measures to promote wage equality and avoid wage differences on the basis of sex (§2), and from 1994 the employers have been obliged to make efforts to narrow the wage differential between men and women (§9a). In Denmark the Equal Pay Act regulated the parts of the private sector that were not included in the collective agreements in which the principle of equal pay had been enumerated since 1973. It was adopted by all parties with the exception of the Progress Party, which voted against. The formulation in the Act requiring "equal pay for the same work" was based on formulations taken from the collective agreements. This formulation was tightened in 1986 after the Court of the European Community had cited Denmark for breach of treaty. This resulted in the incorporation of the words "of equal value" in the main provision (Andersen et al 1996:39 ff.).

Developments have tended towards the inclusion of fresh areas such as the gender composition of public committees, to which we shall return below. Even though there are a few minor differences in the substance of the laws, such differences have less bearing in practice. Sexual harassment is specifically mentioned in the Swedish and Finnish laws[80] and reference is made to the way the sexes are represented in textbooks in the Norwegian and Icelandic laws. Sexual discrimination in advertisements is regulated through the Icelandic Equal Rights Act, but through marketing legislation in the other countries. In Denmark the Act on Parental Leave was incorporated into the Equal Treatment Act in 1989.

Regulations on differential treatment

Equality legislation in the Nordic countries also allows for *the preferential treatment of women or of the underrepresented sex*, and this is the most controversial policy instrument of them all. The opponents of positive discrimination or preferential treatment are of the opinion that this constitutes a violation of the principle of individual rights, and that biological sex should not be made a criterion in the allocation of jobs or places of study. An often-used argument is that gender quotas clash with the principle of selecting the best qualified applicant. Advocates of positive discrimination find it an appropriate tool to achieve *de facto* equality between the sexes because structural gender biases can be corrected by treating the two sexes on a differential basis. A frequent argument is that structural barriers stand in the way of a genuine selection according to qualifications.

Positive discrimination can be divided into gender quotas on the one hand, and other measures such as active recruitment through advertising on the other. Gender quotas can in turn be divided into moderate and radical forms in addition to earmarking. When moderate quotas are applied the underrepresented sex is given preference when qualifications are similar. The radical form means that a man or woman is selected even though the person in question does not have the best qualifications, and this approach is applied until a predetermined quota of the underrepresented sex has been achieved. An essential requirement in the radical version is that a person must possess a minimum of the qualifications necessary for the actual job or study in question (Teigen and Steen Jensen 1995). When earmarking is applied, a certain number of jobs or places in educational institutions are reserved for the underrepresented sex, again with the basic requirement that necessary qualifications in the area must be met. Earmarking can be considered as the most extreme expression of the radical form of positive discrimination.

There are wide differences in the extent to which legislation in the five countries allows positive discrimination. Swedish and Norwegian laws are the most permissive. Finland lies in the middle followed by Iceland while Denmark has the most restrictive legislation. From the start the Gender Equality Act in Nor-

---

80. Cases of sexual harassment can be brought before the courts according to the Danish Equal Treatment Act.

way stated that "Differential treatment which promotes gender equality in conformity with the objective of this Act, is not in contravention with the [objective of the Act]. This also applies to special rights given to women based on the biological differences between the sexes." (§3 no. 3). This formulation has indirectly opened up for positive discrimination, but the Gender Equality Act does not regulate directly the use of quotas in working life. After the government had argued in a white paper on gender equality in the nineties that the law should permit differential treatment of men (Report to the Storting no. 70 [1991–92]), the Storting amended the Gender Equality Act: it is now explicitly permitted to treat men differentially in relation to the education and care of children (§3). What is more, the law allows for a moderate use of quotas in admission to educational institutions (§6) and a radical practice *vis-à-vis* representation on publicly appointed boards and committees (§21).

According to the Swedish law, differential treatment is permissible if it takes place in the shape of planned action with a view to promoting equality (§3, subsection 2). In practice this means that positive discrimination must be linked to pro-active gender equality initiatives and the implementation of gender equality plans. The employer must also promote an equal balance of the sexes in relation to training, improvement of qualifications, etc. (§6). Regulations relating to pro-active equality-promoting measures also provide indirectly for the application of moderate differential treatment. The Swedish Constitution permits differential treatment of the one sex for the purpose of achieving gender equality (Chapter 2 §16).

The Finnish gender equality law indirectly provides for the practice of differential treatment to improve women's position in working life in particular (Act on Equality between Men and Women 1986: §1), though with certain exceptions as set out in §9. Both Finnish and Swedish legislation state that planned activities constitute a necessary requirement, that is, as elements of gender equality-promoting plans. Both formulations allow for the use of moderate differential treatment. In 1995 the provisions in the Act regulating nomination to committees and boards etc. (§4) were amended, now prescribing the radical form of quotas in nomination procedures. The government's proposal was originally less far-reaching, but the women's network in the Riksdag made efforts to change it (Ramstedt-Silén 1998b), after which the standing committee for labour affairs tightened the formulations.

In Iceland a motion was passed in 1985 stating that measures of limited duration aimed at improving the status of women did not represent a contravention of the law (§1, subsection 3).

In Denmark the Equal Opportunities Act of 1988 permits public authorities to "implement special measures in order to promote equal opportunities for men and women" (§1 subsection 2), but this wording has not affected the practising of differential treatment. Of greater significance is that it is not permitted, according to the Equal Treatment Act, to implement positive discrimination unless an application for dispensation from the law is made. Thus the Danish laws differ not only from the legislation in the other Nordic countries but also from that in the rest of the EU where differential treatment is permitted under certain circumstances. Until 1989 the authority to grant dispensation from the Act on Equal Treatment of Men and Women lay with the Minister of Labour after consultation with the other relevant ministers and the Equal Status Council. According to the procedural rules this should take place at the recommendation of the Council's committee for labour affairs which consists of representatives of the employees' and employers' federations and the chairperson. In 1989 the Equal Status Council was given authority to grant dispensations after consultation with the minister involved. The law was amended so that dispensation is now conditional on the approval of the workers' and employers' organisations, and in practice any of the parties may veto the granting of dispensation. According to the Equal Treatment Act the authority to handle dispensation applications lies with the appropriate minister after consultation with the labour minister and the Equal Status Council in cases in which gender is crucial to the performance of the job (Andersen *et al.* 1996: 210 ff.).[81]

Practising positive discrimination

In this section we address the way in which positive discrimination or differential treatment is practised in the Nordic countries; we have found significant variations between the countries, Iceland and Norway standing at either ends of the spectrum. When the Icelandic Constitution was amended in 1995, gaining in the process a ban against discrimination on the basis of gender, religion, etc., the Alþingi specified that this did not exclude the application of positive discrimination (Ministry for Foreign Affairs 1995:16). This mechanism has never been used in Iceland, however. Two political parties represent an exception but their practice is not covered by the law.

Norway applies differential treatment more than all the others. In the 1981 government action plan for gender equality, a wide application of quota systems in the areas of education, representation on public committees and public appointments was recommended. Quite a lot of experience has been gained in the use of quotas in higher education, in the appointment of public committees, and within some of the political parties, although these do not come under the law. As already mentioned, the Gender Equality Act does not specifically prescribe the use of quotas in working life, but the main agreement between the government and public sector employees does permit their use. An analysis of the use of quotas in accordance with this agreement concluded that they are seldom used when selecting people for employment (Teigen and Steen Jensen 1995). There has been some discussion about whether moderate quota forms harm women more than they help. The erstwhile Equal Status Ombudsman Ingse Stabel has argued that positive discrimination nourishes the myth that women get jobs be-

---

81. This type of dispensation has been granted, i.a., to religious communities which disallow the appointment of women priests, as well as to crisis centres for abused women, which don't allow men on the staff (Andersen *et al.* 1996:210 ff.).

cause of their sex rather than their qualifications (1994:38) and that this has led to a devaluation of women's qualifications in some areas (Fürst 1988).

Positive discrimination in Sweden has also been practised in connection with selection procedures for committee members and in the political parties, but these areas are not regulated in the Swedish legislation. In addition to this comes the application of differential treatment in parts of the private sector. However, there are no comprehensive studies of the extent to which differential treatment is practised in Sweden. The instance most frequently referred to in Sweden in recent years is the 1995 initiative by Minister of Education Carl Tham, in which thirty professorships and ninety assistant research posts were reserved for the underrepresented sex. On top of this, funds were made available for 120 posts for doctoral candidates and forty post-doctorate scholarships for female scholars.

In Denmark, a dispensation order made in 1989 allowed for certain exceptions to the dispensation regulations. Permission was given to carry out short vocational training courses for women with a view to creating equal opportunities between women and men in the public sector, and advertisements seeking women applicants were also permitted if the wording did not deter men from applying (Ligestillingsrådet 1997a:161 ff.). Within the ambit of the Equal Status Council's authority to grant dispensations, dispensations have been granted particularly in relation to active recruitment, long-term vocational training courses, and, to a much smaller extent, job selection and promotion. In 1996 twelve dispensations were granted, of which six were for men and five for women, while one involved both sexes (Ligestillingsrådet 1997a:60 ff.). The dispensations which caused the greatest consternation were related to four applications between 1992 and 1997 to set apart scholarships and temporary posts for women in the area of research. The Danish Employers' Confederation vetoed two of these dispensations; in the one case the Salaried Employees' and Civil Servants' Confederation also voted it down. The differential treatment of men, which is practised especially in the provision of care and primary school sector, has proved far less controversial than steps taken on behalf of women. While dispensations for employing men have been given relatively infrequently in the past, there is clear evidence that the number is increasing.

In Finland, quotas have been used for admission to educational institutions, the appointment of public bodies and in the political parties. The latter are not included in the gender equality legislation. Positive discrimination has not been applied in relation to job selection. Until Finland's membership of the EU in 1995, the law was interpreted to mean that only the differential treatment of women was permitted in working life, but it is now also permitted in respect of men. Studies conducted on the use of gender quotas in the education sector in the eighties prior to the enactment of the Gender Equality Act showed that men had been favoured in all cases, and that differential treatment had not been proposed for sectors with a low proportion of women (Sukupuolikiintiöt koulutuksessa 1986).

The extent of differential treatment in the Nordic countries has thus varied greatly; this should partly be seen in connection with the fact that legislation permits preferential treatment to varying degrees in the countries, and partly because there are great differences in customs and traditions related to quotas, some of which are not regulated by any legislation. Norway, followed by Sweden, are the two countries to have applied this gender equality instrument to the greatest extent; in Denmark and Iceland it has been used the least. Iceland therefore represents a special case in that even though the law permits differential treatment, it is not practised.

Regulations concerning the gender composition of public bodies

Since the moment gender equality emerged as an item on the political agenda there has been a focus throughout the Nordic region on the dominance of men in the corporatist sector, due, among other things, to the fact that the increase in equality between the sexes that had been achieved in the area of parliamentary politics was barely discernible in the corporate sector. Since the corporatist arena is of crucial political significance in most countries this gave rise to the hypothesis that what women were gaining entry into was shrinking political institutions (cf. Chapter 1). The low level of women's representation on public councils, committees and boards, which make up part of the corporate structure, was questioned in all of the countries, not least by the equal status councils,[82] and in some of the countries warnings were given that steps would be taken to legislate in this area if the situation showed no signs of improving. When this had no effect provisions were incorporated into the law stipulating how public committees in Norway, Denmark, Finland, and Iceland should be put together with respect to gender. In Sweden this was enacted by an order of government.

Norway was the first among the Nordic countries to adopt a provision in the Gender Equality Act (§21) stipulating that both sexes should be represented on all publicly appointed boards and committees by at least two members (Horgen 1983:157). In 1988 this provision was further refined to permit a radical quota system which entailed a minimum representation of 40 per cent. The measure's passage through the Storting was stormy; the Conservative Party was especially critical, but it was divided on the issue.

From its inception, the Danish Equal Status Council focused on the gender imbalance of public committees (Dahlerup 1990:209 ff.). Since the representation of women showed no signs of increasing to any significant degree, in 1985 the Committees Act was adopted, and, in 1990, the Boards Act. In both cases it is stated that a balanced gender composition should be sought (Ligestillingsrådet 1997a:163 ff.). The authorities and organisations are required to propose equal

---

82. It should be pointed out, however, that the present discussion about the representation of women presupposes that women are appointed as women rather than as representatives for women's interests or as experts in gender and equality issues (Van der Ros 1996b:235).

numbers of men and women when nominating committee members, after which the minister under whose remit the committee falls, makes the actual appointments. The manner in which the provisions have been formulated means that their implementation depends largely on how seriously the ministers concerned view failure to comply with them. There are instances of some ministers refusing to approve a committee because the nominations did not include both men and women (Dahlerup 1990:211 ff.), while other ministers have reacted with greater leniency. The law has been met with great opposition from the social partners and particularly the Federation of Danish Trade Unions.

In Finland there was a provision in the first law of 1986 which stated that public committees, barring self-evident reasons to the contrary, should consist of both male and female members. The provision also comprehended municipal committees (Ministry of Social Affairs and Health 1989: §4, subsection 2). In 1988 municipal councils were excepted. The provision gave rise to a good deal of discussion, especially in relation to the municipal sector. It was debated whether the presence of a single woman on a committee would suffice, and in practice the provision lost much of its force. As mentioned above, in 1995, after a great deal of controversy in the Eduskunta, a radical form of differential treatment was introduced whose aim was a forty-per-cent representation of both women and men. On governing boards, in public institutions and enterprises with a majority state holding, the law now requires equal representation of women and men (Equal Status Act 1986: §4).

In 1985 the Icelandic law was amended (§12) with a call for a balanced gender composition corresponding to the Danish provision concerning the nomination of both sexes. Moreover, in the government's action plan for gender equality for the period 1993–97, a target was set for the end of 1997 by which time a thirty-per-cent representation of women was supposed to be met (Ministry for Foreign Affairs 1995:29).

In Sweden, the low level of women's representation in the corporatist channel claimed attention in response to the report entitled *Varannan Damernas* (cf. Chapter 4) (SOU 1987:19). There was a general consensus among women politicians and in the organisations that the level of female representation had to be increased (Bergqvist 1994). A plan was subsequently contrived consisting of three stages of which the first consisted of documenting the gender imbalance by means of annual statistics. The second dealt with the setting up of goals for future developments, and a decision was made to achieve a thirty-per-cent representation of women during the course of 1992, 40 per cent in 1995, and parity in 1998. Failing this, according to the plan, a system of quotas would be introduced by law. Funds amounting to nine million SEK were set apart for projects by organisations willing to take action to increase their women's representation, and later on a further five million SEK were channelled into increasing women's representation on government committees and boards.

Thus the instruments chosen to influence the gender composition of public committees differ among the Nordic countries. These differences relate firstly to whether the issue concerns actual quotas in the resulting composition of the body involved, as in Norway, Finland, and Sweden, or merely proposals to put forward nominees of both sexes for appointment as committee members as in Denmark and Iceland. The two instruments may also be characterised as equality of result over equality of opportunity. The observance of the regulations is overseen in Norway by the Gender Equality Section and in Sweden by the Equality Affairs Division, which ensures a co-ordinated and uniform practice. In Finland and Denmark different ministers are responsible for overseeing compliance with the regulations, an arrangement which can result in wide-ranging applications of the regulations. Secondly there is a difference between legislation, as in Norway, Denmark, Iceland, and Finland, and a government order, as in the Swedish case. Finally, the Norwegian, Swedish and Icelandic governments have set numerical targets for women's representation. The most powerful instrument, all else being equal, is to be found in the legislation on quotas as in Norway and Finland, but targets set by a government can represent a clear policy instrument too, as in Sweden. The weakest policy instrument is found in Denmark and Iceland, where legislation only regulates nominee proposals.

In all of the countries the representation of women has risen in the wake of these measures. The highest percentage has been achieved by Norway and Sweden; the lowest by Iceland. In 1995, the figure for women's representation on public committees, etc. was 39 per cent in Norway, 42 per cent in Sweden in government administration, and 38 per cent in regional government. In Finland and in Denmark, the number on public committees was 28 per cent. In 1996 in Iceland it was 23 per cent. In all five countries, the lowest rates are to be found among women representing organisations, while among politicians and the civil service the percentage is higher. The number of women chairing committees remains very low, and there are large variations in the gender composition of different types of committees in keeping with the traditionally gendered make-up of political committees. Our analysis thus indicates that a correlation does exist between the type of policy instrument applied and the outcome in Sweden and Norway, on the one hand, and Iceland and Denmark, on the other. However, the statutory system of gender quotas in Finland has yet to produce results of any significance.

National plans of action

All of the five countries have implemented national action plans for equal status as a gender equality promoting tool. It was an appeal by UN and the adoption of a document on "forward-looking strategies" by the world conference for women in Nairobi in 1985 that ignited the work on action plans in the Nordic countries. International organisations such as UN, EU, and the Nordic Council of Ministers have also adopted action plans as policy instruments. In the Nordic zone, national plans of action appeared in Sweden in 1979, Finland in 1980, and Norway in 1981. Iceland and Denmark followed suit in 1986.

In Sweden a five-year national action plan to improve women's representation was adopted in 1988. The 1991 plan of action included, among other things, a decision to prevent violence against women, while the 1994 plan of action focused on the distribution of power (Ministry of Health and Social Affairs 1994:11). All of these plans have originated as Government Proposals which have subsequently gained the approval of the Riksdag.

In Finland, the government committed itself in 1980 to implementing the first plan of action for the years 1980–1985. It aimed at improving the observance of equality legislation in Finland and the ratification of the UN Convention on the Elimination of All Forms of Discrimination Against Women – CEDAW. The plan was not put before the parliament (Räsänen 1994:8). The government plan of action for 1997–2001 addresses mainstreaming, and the biggest project concerns violence against women. Since 1990 government ministries have been obliged to implement internal action plans with respect to staffing policies. This was tightened further in 1992.

In Norway, the first action plan – which was adopted by the Storting – covered the years 1981–85. The next one, implemented by the government, was for the years 1986–90, and the third from 1992 covers the nineties. The first plan of action specifically addressed the position of women in relation to education and working life, and quotas made up a significant part of the plan's profile. The second plan was more gender-neutral. It embraced the same concerns as the first, but did not involve quotas to the same degree. The role of men now had a place on the agenda, and a programme for mainstreaming throughout government administration was launched (Skjeie et al. 1989:126; Halsaa 1995a:30). The third plan of action perpetuated these efforts and laid even greater weight on men and the provision of care, as well as the implications of gender equality legislation for children. In addition it addressed polarisation between women, equal pay, and the abuse of women.

After the equal rights law was amended in Iceland in 1985, the task of preparing four-year action plans fell to the Minister of Social Affairs, and when a new round of amendments were due in 1991, it was decided that such plans must be approved by the Alþingi. There have been four action-plan periods, 1986–89; 1990–92; 1992–93; and 1993–97. A fifth, which began in 1998, is currently in progress. The plans have partly concerned themselves with government personnel policy, for which targets for women's representation have been formulated, and partly with policy content, especially social, educational, and cultural policy (NK Tema 1994d).

In 1985 in Denmark, women across the political parties banded together to initiate a debate the outcome of which was that the Folketing directed the government to prepare an action plan for gender equality, something the government duly did in 1986. Since then there have been three subsequent action plans: 1987–90; 1991–93; and 1994–96, all of which have primarily addressed personnel policy. The actual content of the various ministries' policies has only represented a marginal concern in these plans. The plans advocated that all ministries and enterprises with a workforce in excess of fifty persons should prepare annual plans of action. In the second period, it was decided that the plans should contain numerical targets to work towards. The Equal Status Council has assessed the progress of each planning round, and has submitted the results to the Folketing. The Folketing has voted on each occasion to continue working with the plans. These decisions have also included signals to the government to tighten up the rest of the legislation. As this book was being finalised, the assessment of the last planning round had yet to be submitted to the Folketing. The action plan commitments have also been extended to include the municipal sector (cf. next chapter). Fiig concludes in an evaluation of the work carried out in association with the action plans that while this policy instrument has some potential, it is not functioning to full capacity due to the lack of built-in powers of sanction (1998).

Thus, the difference between the plans of action is in whether their primary goal has been personnel policy in the civil service, as in Denmark, or policy content, as in Norway and Sweden, or both, as in Iceland. In Norway, Sweden, and Iceland, the action plans have mirrored the respective governments' equality programmes, and as such have served as a mould for their initiatives in the area. We may conclude that in all of the Nordic countries work carried out in connection with the plans of action has in many respects been a driving force behind efforts to promote gender equality during the eighties and nineties.

Gender equality policy and decision-making processes

Conflicts have arisen as gender equality legislation has made its way through the decision-making processes. These conflicts have been related in particular to the opposition to gender equality legislation as demonstrated by the trade unions and the employers' organisations. In addition, in some of the countries conflicts of a party-political nature have surrounded the adoption of the laws. The issues here have especially turned on equal pay, formulations referring specifically to women, and differential treatment, as well as requirements to engage in pro-active equality-promoting work. The level of conflict has been greatest in Sweden and Norway and least in Denmark.

In Norway the disapproval on the part of the Federation of Trade Unions of any law specifically aimed at women caused the Labour Party to neutralise its original proposal. Skjeie believes that the Federation of Trade Unions actually vetoed a possible anti-discrimination law, and that the resulting compromise served mainly to amputate the chance held by the new women's movement to wield any influence (1982).

In Sweden the Social Democratic Party was the only party in the Nordic countries to oppose legislation and it blocked attempts to get bills through from 1970 to 1975. According to Dahlberg, one of the causes of this opposition was that a non-socialist party, the Liberal Party, had been playing the part of spokesman for the legislation; another was the strong opposition prevailing in the trade unions (1984:51). The general opinion was that legislation represented an expression of bad faith in the ability of the workers' and employers' organisations to solve the problems on their own. Even though the Social Democrats and trade unions' federation eventually relented, in 1978 the employers still had not budged, and they also were strongly opposed to the legislative amendments which came up 1992 and 1994.

In Denmark, the social partners were also sceptical of legislation, but this opposition was less vociferously expressed when the first law was passed, possibly because EU directives on equal pay and equal treatment had to be incorporated into national legislation, thus limiting their scope for action. The general conclusion is that most Danish decisions on gender equality policy have been met with a large measure of consensus among the political parties (Dahlerup 1998; Borchorst 1999). The reason for this lies in the powerful culture of consensus and high level of party discipline in the Danish national assembly (Jensen 1999). More far-reaching proposals dealing with, for instance, specific formulations about women or the radical form of differential treatment, were not proposed in this legislation.

In Iceland a climate of consensus characterised the passing of the first equality law, and all members of the Alþingi apart from two voted in favour of the Act in 1976. There was greater unrest in 1985 and 1991 when the two formulations specifically referring to women were incorporated into the law. The employers opposed the founding of the Equal Status Complaints Committee in 1991 because they were not represented on it, among other reasons.

In Finland the strong opposition of the employers to legislating on equal pay and positive discrimination resulted in a long-drawn-out process to determine the procedures for the first gender equality bill. In addition to this, the influence and weight of the employers enabled them, by means of the corporatist channel, to veto legislation (Bruun 1982; Koskinen 1983). As we saw in the previous paragraph, the employers had no position of any significance on the equal status bodies. The labour movement in Finland, on the other hand, has been more positive to legislation than in the other countries. In the Eduskunta conflicts along gender lines have been more in evidence than in the other countries because party discipline is enforced as strictly (Jensen 1999). This was the case, for instance, when the quota regulations relating to committees were approved in 1994: all female ministers and a large number of female MPs voted in favour of the proposal and against the government's motion (Roos 1995).

As a rule the parties to the left and the Social Democrats have been inclined to favour the most comprehensive policies, while in Sweden the Liberal Party and the Social Democrats have competed in profiling themselves as the most gender-equality-friendly. At first this resulted in a rather unusual situation, namely that of a non-socialist party leading the field in promoting gender equality legislation. As we saw in the preceding chapter, this state of affairs has continued to keep equality issues high on the agenda.

In comparison with a number of other policy areas, gender equality policy is characterised by a poorly defined and fragmented configuration of interests, and this has also affected the decision-making processes. This is related to the newness of the policy area as well as its many points of contact with labour market policy. On the other hand, labour market policy is an old policy area with long-standing traditions of institutionalised dealings between the employers, trade unions, and central authorities. The opposition voiced by the labour movement to gender equality legislation in Norway, Sweden, and partly in Denmark too, was noteworthy simply because the movement had supported all other types of labour-related legislation. According to Nielsen and Halvorsen, the fact that the crucial breakthrough for the gender equality issue happened via legislation rather than via the collective bargaining routines of the social partners was due to the comparatively higher proportion of women in the national parliaments in contrast to the lower level of female representation in the decision-making bodies of the labour movement (1988:3 ff.). The women's organisations in several countries represented the views of women, but their position was weak compared to that of the powerful social partners, and they had no counterpart in officialdom. It would not be unreasonable to say that, in the early days of a politics of gender equality, the organisations actually functioned effectively as men's organisations, given the gender composition of their topmost levels, their scope of interests, and, in part, their membership.

The broad collective mobilisation of women in the seventies and the demands set forth by the women's organisations played a role in the institutionalisation of gender equality issues through legislation. However, according to conventional choice theory so-called majority politics – by which both benefits and expenses are spread across large segments of the population – should not be conducive to a powerful mobilisation of organisations (Winter 1994:54). In the nineties there is not the mobilisation of women to the same degree. But in spite of this, women's demands are picked up "from below", partly by political parties which have women's sections. In Iceland the Women's Alliance served much the same purpose during its time in the Alþingi.

The politics of gender equality have largely been characterised by token policies in which the authorities show signs of willingness to think in new ways and carry out restructuring measures, but without pursuing the matter with unambiguous policy instruments to achieve the expressed objectives (Halsaa 1995a and 1995b). It is our opinion, however, that this description suits Iceland, Finland, and Denmark rather more than it does Sweden and Norway. Indeed, Halsaa notes the existence of a distinct political will fuelling the Norwegian gender equality commitment, even though she finds that there is greater breadth, weight and method in the state-driven effort than that of the local authorities (1995a). We should also point out that token politics can play quite a significant role, as, for instance, a demonstration of the commitment of the Nordic governments to promote gender equality and a signal that to dismiss equality issues or to ridicule them is simply not on any more. Our analysis of the dissimilarities among the Nordic countries has partly undermined conclusions to the effect that conflict-ridden decision-making processes often end up in compromises which in turn result in vague formulations and fuzzy objectives in the legislation. On the contrary, the Swedish and Norwegian decision-making processes have been the most contentious but it is in these countries that legislation and practice are most far-reaching. At the other end of the scale, the decision-making processes in Denmark have enjoyed the largest degree of consensus, but that country has the least radical laws.

Implementing equality

Because the political processes of decision-making and the subsequent implementation of the decisions made generally lie in the hands of different sets of actors, this naturally affects outcomes. We lack the empirical material to carry out a comparative analysis of the way in which legislation has been implemented in the five countries; we will simply offer a few comments of a general nature. In the next chapter we will address the question at the local level in Sweden and Norway. The implementation of gender equality policies in most of the countries has depended to a far greater degree on individuals than other policy areas. Thus, it has an impact if the civil servants appointed to implement the policy are personally in favour of the objectives laid out in the legislation, against them, or simply apply themselves dutifully to their implementation. However, it does appear that individuals' whims and fancies is a smaller factor in Norway and Sweden than in Denmark because in the former countries implementation is based on a clearer division of responsibilities and clearer organisational structures than in the latter (as shown in the preceding chapter).

If the laws contain vague formulations and there is no correspondence between ends and means, implementational problems can arise. One instance of this is in the legal requirement to actively promote gender equality: there are many examples of plans not being made, or of them getting no further than the blueprint stage. This requirement is weakened even more when, as in Norway, Finland, Iceland, and Denmark, there are absolutely no institutions at all with the authority to police its implementation, or no powers of sanction available to enforce it. This can be further illustrated by the relatively large number of Danish ministries which do not comply with the Folketing's requirements for specific targets in their action plans, sins of omission about which the Folketing has been unwilling to enact sanctions.

The problems associated with the implementation of gender equality policies are also due to the fact that, because there are no clear-cut ideas about the underlying means and ends involved, there is little clearness as to the causes of inequality. The question of whether gender equality is a win-win situation in which all involved stand to gain from increased equality, or whether there are structural inequalities which can be changed by treating the sexes differently is also in need of clarification. The outcome would then be that men would have to surrender positions and power in some areas and women in others. Eduards finds that gender equality policy (and gender equality studies) rests on a premise that a duty to keep the peace obtains between the sexes. This is based in turn, she explains, on a political desire to remain neutral in a complex and difficult matter, and she believes that this has led to the development of antagonisms and conflicts in the area of equality (1995:59). Disputes related to positive discrimination reflect this lack of precision in which the discrepancy between women's interests as a group contrasts with the violation of individual men's rights. At the same time there seems to be far less disagreement about treating men differentially to increase the proportion of men in women-dominated areas. In practice, however, we cannot really say that there has been a duty to keep the peace in the politics of gender equality, because by formulating direct references to women in particular, legislation has indeed been targeted especially at women.

Conclusion

The politics and policies of gender equality have deepened and broadened in all of the five countries under investigation, and the trend has been towards the empowerment of bodies administering and promoting gender equality to such an extent that they are now in a position to take legal action on their own initiative; a requirement to actively promote equality has become law. Several more areas have been included in equality legislation, and laws have been tightened, for instance in relation to surrendering information to the monitoring bodies. In addition, policy instruments have multiplied and become more efficient, such as action plans for equality and quotas in the nomination of committees etc. In this sense, then, we believe that real changes have taken place since the publication of *Unfinished Democracies*. That volume concluded that gender equality targets are maintained only when they do not come into conflict with other objectives (Eduards *et al.* 1983:231). Legislation and the implementation of equal status measures are pursued with greatest avidity in Sweden and Norway, and least in Denmark. Viewed in the context of corresponding differences in the organisational structure of work to achieve gender equality (cf. Chapter 10), this indicates that the organisational aspect interacts with the substance of the policies, though we are not in a position to ascertain a closer causal link.

Our analysis of the decision-making processes has shown that specific references to women in the legislation, the application of quotas, and an active effort to promote equality have represented bones of contention, but the conclusion is that in the countries where issues have spawned the greatest controversies, the resulting legislation in fact is the most comprehensive. Opposition to legislation in the area has been particularly prevalent among the employers, but in Sweden and Norway the trade unions have also represented an oppositional front. In Sweden the Social Democrats stood out in the Nordic context with their initial opposition to legislation, which, apart from the scepticism among the worker's organisations, needs to be understood in light of a non-socialist party espousing gender equality. In Finland and Iceland conflicts along gender lines in some areas have been more discernible in the respective parliaments than in Denmark, mainly due to the relatively lower level of party discipline in Finland and the efforts of the Women's Alliance in Iceland. The explanation for the Danish situation lies partly in the strict party discipline and the absence of women's organisations in the political parties, and, for the last part of the period, the lack of a radical women's movement.

Thus it is that some forces contribute to widen the gap between the countries, to maintain the status quo, or to narrow it. With regard to the first of the three, Sweden's, Finland's and Denmark's membership of the EU and Norway's and Iceland's EEA membership have produced a certain level of correspondence between their respective legislations, among other things because the European Court's decisions concerning the implementation of EU directives have an immediate bearing on the former three countries and an indirect bearing on the latter two. The institutional disparities, the differences in political culture, and the character of women's mobilisation may work in an opposite direction, namely towards maintaining or even magnifying the differences.

12

A question of political will? The state, local authorities, and equal status policy

Ingrid Pincus and Janneke van der Ros

In this chapter we discuss aspects of the organisation and implementation of equal status policy at the level of local authorities in the Nordic countries. The main emphasis will be on the home countries of the two authors, namely Norway (Janneke van der Ros), and Sweden (Ingrid Pincus). In the post-war period, the municipality has taken on greater importance as an arena for efforts to promote gender equality. Increasingly, tasks which were previously the responsibility of central government, or which were regarded as purely private matters, came under the widened remit of local government. As a result, the way the municipality meets its responsibilities has considerable influence on the opportunities women and men have to create a more equitable everyday life for themselves (as well as influencing the problems they face) (Johansson 1997; Nagel 1998). In addition to this, the local authorities are significant employers, especially of women. The evolution of the welfare state has brought about an increase in jobs for women in particular. At the same time, the devolution of government responsibilities, including issues relating to equal opportunities or gender equality policies, means that the "struggle" has been decentralised, raising the spectre of fragmentation. In all of the Nordic countries, developing the machinery to implement equal status seems to run more smoothly at the national level than at the municipal, and it takes a considerable time for the goals of gender equality to percolate down from the government to local authorities (Halsaa 1995a; Van der Ros 1997a, b).

One of the themes of this chapter is the relationship between central government and local authorities in the area of gender equality initiatives. In Nordic political culture the notion of local self-governance is highly prized and considered one of the cornerstones of democracy (Kolam 1987:1). National considerations related to political objectives such as equality, law and order, and fair distribution of wealth, as well as factors related to the national economy mean, however, that the term "local self-governance" is a relatively elastic concept. On the one hand, the local authorities are independent political-administrative entities. On the other hand, they are supposed to act as extensions of the state. These factors play a role in the way gender equality policies are addressed at the local level, and in the ability of central government to influence policies at the local level. The way in which *national* bodies associated with the policies of equal status are organised also affects the *actions of the local authorities in the area* (Halsaa 1995a; Pincus 1996; Van der Ros 1996a, 1997a).

While our first theme focuses on the relationship between central and local government from the point of view of administering and organising the equal status commitment, our second theme is concerned with factors at the local level. There, we address first of all the situation of the government employees whose job it has been to promote gender equality – the femocrats. Secondly, we examine men's ambivalence, and even opposition, to the introduction of gender equality. Janneke van der Ros has studied femocrats, while Ingrid Pincus is responsible for the section on men and opposition. We thus focus on structures – in the sense of the relationship between central and local government – as well as on the players involved at the local level. We concentrate on what are explicitly designated as gender equality policies at the local level. This means that the potential gendered aspects of other policies – welfare policy for instance – are neither addressed nor assessed.

Legislation and organisation of local-level equal status efforts

Local authorities wear several hats. They are employers – and women make up a large section of their employees. They are political communities which citizens can influence directly through elections and indirectly through elected representatives to political bodies. They are service providers, and "companies" to which the citizens relate as "customers" or "clients". The activities of the local authorities in the area of gender equality should comprise three types of undertakings and roles. A fourth local authority role is in the transfer of payments from the state to the individual, for instance in the form of social security payments including housing allowance and other types of benefits. A woman's relationship with the authorities, and this applies to central government as well as to local authorities, can thus be as employee, citizen, and/or customer/client (Hernes 1982, 1987).

There are two ways to perform analyses of the means available to central authorities to govern local authorities: We can ask, firstly, if the state's objective is to control the local authorities' *resources*; the way in which they are *organised*; or the *outcomes*. Secondly we can examine the mechanisms – i.e. judicial, financial, or moral – the state is willing to apply to attain its objectives (Kommunal- og arbeidsdepartementet 1993; Halsaa 1995a). In the following paragraphs we review the state's judicial instruments. Legislation is regarded as a powerful governance mechanism available to the state. We also consider the relationship between state and local authorities by examining the state bodies in charge of policing local authority efforts to promote gender equality. Thirdly, we present briefly the way in which local authorities have adhered to state guidelines and proposals as to how equal status policies should be organised.

Finland

In Finland, the Act on Equality between Women and Men w as adopted in 1986 and has since then been amended on three occasions – in 1988, 1992 and 1995. Finland was the last of the Nordic countries to pass such legislation. The provisions of the Act extend to the municipalities, both as local authorities and as employers. As local authorities they are responsible for promoting gender equality in their municipalities, and as employers they are obliged to follow the law both in regard to the ban on sex discrimination and in regard to working actively for gender equality within their organisations. Sanctions can be levied against municipalities that fail to comply with the provisions of the Act regarding sex discrimination. The Act on Equality was strengthened first in 1988 and then again in 1995 when women's representation did not increase in local government. In 1988 the obligation to ensure that both women and men are represented in all municipal bodies (with the exception of municipal council executive committees) was made explicit. In 1995 the Act was further strengthened in this respect when rules on quotas were added. The revised Act also includes: 1) a provision banning sexual harassment and 2) a sharpening of the provision concerning employers' obligation to work actively for gender equality by making it obligatory to include concrete measures for furthering gender equality in their planning documents.

In 1979, the Council for Equality urged the municipalities to establish committees for gender equality within their organisations as part of the UN's Decade for Women. A special unit was established within the Council during the first half of the 1980s to assist the municipalities in this respect. During the 1980s, the number of municipalities that had gender equality committees grew (from fifteen municipalities in 1981 to thirty municipalities in 1986); but the number declined again at the beginning of the 1990s (to fourteen municipalities by 1997). The municipalities that have kept their gender equality committees are found, above all, in the larger urban areas. Some of the municipalities that disbanded their gender equality committees transferred the responsibility for these issues to other municipal committees, primarily to those that dealt with personnel issues. The proportion of municipalities and towns with committees for gender equality never exceeded 10 per cent during this period (Holli 1992:272).

At the end of the 1980s, state responsibility for the coordinating of the municipal level gender equality work was transferred, without much debate, from the Council for Equality to the three central associations of municipalities. These associations were never particularly active in promoting municipal gender equality work, however. Today, municipal gender equality work is co-ordinated by the Association of Finnish Local and Regional Authorities. The Association arranges some educational activities but, above all, assists the municipalities with advice and legal expertise on gender equality issues.

Iceland

In Iceland the Equal Rights Act has also been amended and the responsibility of the local authorities to promote equality between the sexes has been more clearly defined. When the Icelandic equal rights law was revised in 1991, it resulted in the establishment of the Equal Status Council (§13). The new ordinance replaced an older one relating to local authority councils and committees which merely recommended the setting up of standing committees for equal status. The statutory requirement from 1991 covers local councils with a population of more than five hundred people (of which there are fifty-two). The supervisory role of the committees is set out in the provision. The job of these committees is to ensure that the local authorities act in compliance with the equal rights legislation. The national responsibility to oversee compliance is in the hands of the Equal Status Council – which also has an obligation to advise and guide the local committees. The Council arranged the first national congress for local standing committees for equal status in 1992, and since 1994 has organised national congresses on an annual basis.

With regard to organisation at the local authority level, Iceland got its first four equal status committees in 1975, the UN Year of the Woman. The largest local authorities nominated equal status committees during the seventies and eighties, but the level of activity in several of these was very limited indeed. The Icelandic Equal Status Council is a political body in the sense that representatives are appointed after local elections and according to the relative strength of the parties on the Council. Some local councils have formulated plans to promote equal status, though this is not required by law. An administrative institutionalisation – in the form of equal status consultants – is only to be found in the two largest municipalities in Iceland, namely Reykjavik (since 1994) and Akureyri (since 1991).

Denmark

The Equal Opportunities Act of 1988 directed all public authorities, including local authorities, to take action to advance equality between women and men. In the wake of this legislation, equal status committees started to "trickle forth" – ten years after a similar initiative had been taken in Finland, and thirteen years after the proposal to establish equal status committees in Norway. On the threshold of the nineties, according to a study conducted by Dahlerup, only 20–25 of the 273 local authorities in Denmark had fulfilled their legal obligations (Dahlerup 1991:8). In connection with the work on the report to Beijing, the government conceded that the local authorities remained the weakest link in the efforts to attain equality between the sexes, compared to central government and grass-roots groups. This assessment covered the production of equal status action plans, as well as to efforts made to increase the representation of women on political bodies at the local level and women's share of jobs in top management. In response to these disappointing findings, in 1995 the Danish parliament – the Folketing – approved the incorporation of new provisions concerning the duties of local authorities in this respect into the Local Authorities Act (§62, subsection 3). Local authorities are now obliged to report on their gender equality achievements every other year. The first report was released in September 1997. The reports are supposed to include a "horizontal" as well as a "vertical" picture of the gender composition of the local authorities' workforce, in other words, the legislation stresses that the reports contain information regarding both sexual differentiation in general and senior positions within local government. The reports are used in the context of personnel development. Nearly all of the local authorities have submitted such reports. The Equal Status Council sums up in its report "Kønsgerninger i kommunen" (Gender Exploits in the Municipalities) that

> Even though the reports overall do not warrant undue enthusiasm with regard to the amount of work performed by the local authorities to further gender equality, such issues do tend to attract greater attention today than was previously the case... The Equal Status Council is therefore, generally speaking, satisfied with the effects of the legislative amendment which required local authorities to submit progress reports detailing their efforts in this area. (Ligestillingsrådet 1997b:6)

It seems that the division of responsibilities with regard to local equal status policies between the central authorities on the one hand – represented by the Equal Status Council – and the National Association of Local Authorities, on the other, has been unclear at times. From the mid-nineties, however, the Equal Status Council and the National Association of Local Authorities have collaborated with the Ministry of Home Affairs and other local and regional actors to co-ordinate local government efforts to promote equal status. The establishment of equal status committees is a widely used method of promoting gender equality, but the National Association of Local Authorities in Denmark recommended putting coordinating committees to work on gender equality rather than creating specific equal status committees at the local level. The stance of the National Association of Local Authorities may indicate that the thrust of the local-level commitment to gender equality is mainly confined to personnel policy – the focus is on the local authorities' role as employers. This information was culled, moreover, from the local authorities' progress reports on their gender equality work, and the Equal Status Council corroborates this further: "Equal status policy in the local authorities is essentially personnel policy. The number of local authorities which approach equal status policy from the point of view of the situation in the local community is very small indeed" (Ligestillingsrådet 1997b:19).

About a fifth of the Danish local and county councils have established equal status committees, though there has been an increase from twenty-three in 1992 to twenty-eight in 1994, and to thirty-three in 1997 (Ligestillingsrådet 1997b:11). The make-up of the equal status committees varies:

> Most of the equal status committees at the local and county level are made up of politicians, management representatives and employees' representatives. This is a somewhat unique structure for local committees. (Dahlerup 1991:12)

Norway

The Norwegian Gender Equality Act includes a general clause obliging public authorities to promote gender equality; this applies to authorities at all levels of government. What is more, the Local Government Act points out the responsibility of local authorities for equal opportunities policies. In the past, the Local Government Act had no provisions regulating the composition of council committees; this was the province of the Gender Equality Act (§21). The government wanted to extend its control of local affairs so when the Local Government Act was amended, provisions of a more specific nature concerning gender equality policies were added.[83]

The new Local Government Act's §§36–38 address the balance of the sexes on councils and committees; the wording of the Act has been made more rigorous too (Guldvik 1998:4 ff.). Elections to local boards may be held either according to principles of proportional representation or by majority ballot. The Local Government Act includes provisions regulating the nomination of candidates in elections using proportional representation and the gender balance among the candidates.[84]

In elections by majority ballot the provisions applying to representation are as follows: each sex shall be represented by at least 40 per cent of those elected. In the event that one of the sexes is underrepresented, candidates of that sex shall be moved up as far as possible to ensure balance between the sexes. If a local authority has introduced so-called "continuous representation" – which means that members of working committees are elected from among local council members – then gender biases will spread to the nomination system. The Ministry of Local Government and Regional Development wants a review to be made of these provisions (Kommunal- og regionaldepartement 1998).[85]

---

83. Act of September 25th 1992, no. 107 on Local and County Authorities.

84. In elections to bodies comprising fewer than four seats, each sex shall be represented. If four or more representatives are to be elected, the law stipulates that both sexes must be represented by at least 40 per cent of the proposed candidates on the individual lists. If one of the sexes is underrepresented on a list the regulations concerning the final allocation of votes in proportionally representative elections require that candidates be moved up as far as necessary to achieve such balance. If a list wins five seats on a body, for example, each sex shall be represented by at least two members from the list. In working committees on which each of the lists has only one seat, the balance of the sexes may be biased, however.

85. Ministry of Local Government and Regional Development 1998: Amendments to the Local Government Act – hearing. Hearing Statement of 22 January 1998.

The new Act transferred responsibility for overseeing equal representation from the Equal Status Ombudsman to the County Governor's Office. The advantage of such a move is that the county governor has a power of sanction which the ombudsman lacked. The disadvantage, in the short run, could be a deficiency in expertise and a tendency on the part of the county governor to award lower priority to the control function than the Equal Status Ombudsman (see also Halsaa 1995a:56 ff.).

Of all the Nordic countries Norway has the largest number of equal status committees. The historical reason can be found in the establishment of local women's committees set up for the UN Year of the Woman on an *ad hoc* basis in 1975. The central authorities, represented by the then Equal Status Council and the Ministry of Family and Consumer Affairs, and the grass-roots level represented by women in the local communities, worked very hard to transform the Year-of-the-Woman committees into standing equal status committees. The Norwegian Association of Local Authorities supported these efforts, too. The process was relatively long-winded: it took until the mid-eighties for two-thirds of Norwegian local authorities to establish such committees (Halsaa 1983, 1988a). In recent years, and especially during the nineties, we have witnessed a tendency for equal status committees to be disbanded and for equal status concerns to be passed on to committees with other mandates, mostly committees dealing with administrative affairs (Guldvik 1995). As a result, gender equality issues at the local level have shifted from issues associated with the local authority as a service provider to issues connected with personnel policy (Halsaa and Van der Ros 1989; Guldvik 1995). The action radius of local-level gender equality policies therefore stands in jeopardy of being severely curtailed. One benefit of the change, though, is that the administrative committees are headed by key politicians, which may imply a strengthening of gender equality efforts.

At the national level, the Equal Status Council was responsible until August 1997 for following up, advising and supporting the local committees (Halsaa 1995a; Van der Ros 1996a, 1997). What characterises the state's responsibility for following up gender equality policy and policies aimed at women at the local level is the large number of bodies charged with implementing the policies in the municipalities. In addition to the erstwhile Equal Status Council (and it is not finally decided which agency will take over the Council's responsibility for following up the local committees), various ministries are in charge of policies relating to gender equality and women's issues in their respective areas of jurisdiction. For example, the Ministry of Fisheries is in charge in regions which depend heavily on fishing, the Ministry of Defence in the Armed Forces, and the Regional Department at the Ministry of Local Government and Regional Development has responsibility *vis-à-vis* women in rural areas. The Ministry of Children and Family Affairs is responsible for overall co-ordination. Such an profusion of government actors interfacing with the local authorities represents a "challenge to governance" or even a governance problem. We will here point out three factors which may give an idea of the state's relationship to efforts by the local authorities to promote gender equality and to municipal self-governance. The first of these factors is that the Local Government Department at the Ministry of Local Government and Regional Development, which shoulders extensive responsibilities *vis-à-vis* local authorities, has not given gender equality policy a place. A second factor is that the Equal Status Council's contact with the local authorities was mainly limited to the local equal status committees, leaving out the political and administrative leadership. And thirdly, the Equal Status Council made hardly any efforts to inquire about the local authorities' situation and problems, and in consequence failed to kindle a broader debate at the national level (Halsaa 1995a). Transferring the burden of the state's responsibility for the local authorities' gender equality work to such a feeble body as the (then) Equal Status Council may help explain the poor state of affairs at the local level. To strengthen gender equality work at the local level, the state's handling of both the capacity to govern and the will to govern is fundamental (Van der Ros 1997b, chap. VI). In 1997, a new centrist coalition government took over in Norway: the choice of "gender equality minister" (Valgjerd Svarstad Haugland) may signal that state might be intending to strengthen its control of local-level gender equality work.

The Norwegian equal status committees at the local level consist of politicians elected from among candidates on the parties' election lists. Studies show that many of these elected representatives had only marginal contact with local council politics. This contributed to a marginalisation of the committees (Halsaa and Van der Ros 1989). Following the local government reforms in Norway, many local authorities have made efforts to implement "continuous representation", which means that local council members also sit on key committees such as, for instance, the school committee and the committee for health and social affairs. This change has pushed gender equality issues even further into the outback of local politics, since members of the standing committees on equal status seldom hold other council positions.

Sweden

Municipal responsibility for the implementation of government gender equality policy is not regulated in Sweden. Municipalities are though, like other employers, required to adhere to the Equal Opportunities Act (EqA) which covers the labour market as a whole. The 1979 Equal Opportunities Act (SFS 1979:1118) includes both a ban on discrimination on the basis of sex as well as a provision stipulating that employers pursue goal-orientated gender equality work in their organisations. Thus, the Act is a steering instrument which aims at influencing both personnel and work organisation issues.

The paragraph in the 1979 Act dealing with active measures to promote gender equality did not apply in such cases where employee and employer organisations had included the promotion of gender equality work in their collective agreements. In such cases, supervisory and control functions were removed from the Equal Opportunities Ombudsman (JämO) and the responsibility for ensuring employer adherence to agreements was transferred to the trade unions. By the beginning of the 1980s most of the labour market organisations had included gender equality provisions in their collective agreements. One of the three chapters in the 1980 collective agreement (MBL-KL) covering municipal and regional government organisations was devoted to gender equality issues. The goals and guiding principles concerning the promotion of gender equality in this agreement mirrored in large part those of the EqA. It included provisions for employers to draw up annual plans for their gender equality work and in one respect the agreement went further than the Act itself, namely in recommending the appointment of gender equality officers with the task of developing and coordinating gender equality work within the organisation.

Following a government report (SOU 1990: 41), which evaluated the effects of the EqA during the 1980s, the parliament strengthened the part of the Act which deals with employers' obligations to promote gender equality. According to Margit Kärrström, who conducted the investigation, the evaluation results pointed to "a powerless Equal Opportunities Ombudsman, passive trade unions, and a lack of interest on the part of employers" (Svenska Dagbladet 10/9 1990). The new Equal Opportunities Act (SFS 1991:433 amended in 1994) stipulates that all employers with more than ten employees are obliged to actively promote gender equality in their organisations and that collective agreements between the labour market organisations can no longer replace this legal obligation. They are further obliged to draw up goal-orientated gender equality plans which, amongst other things, must, in accordance with the European Community's equal pay directive (Directive 75/117/EEC), include documentation of wage differentials between the sexes. The Equal Opportunities Ombudsman (JämO) is now responsible for ensuring employer compliance with the EqA on the whole labour market and it has further been given increased resources for this purpose. Today all municipalities have a gender equality plan, even if their ambitions to follow the provisions that state what should be included in these plans vary. The strengthening of the EqA and of JämO indicate that the state has increased its ambitions in respect to promoting gender equality work on the labour market. At the same time it seems as if the labour market organisations have lowered theirs. In their latest collective agreement (U-92 Agreement of Cooperation) the issue of gender equality is only briefly mentioned in a section on personnel development where it is noted that: "Personnel development policy includes paying attention to men's and women's special conditions, experiences and perspectives in working life. This will increase the prospects for taking advantage of the organisation's total competence" (U-92:39). These vague and noncommittal formulations indicate that the labour market organisations have not paid attention to, or taken seriously, the criticism that has been levelled against them over the years for their lack of interest in promoting gender equality work at work.

The establishment of local gender equality committees in Sweden is solely a matter of municipal discretion. At the beginning of the 1980s, around fifty municipalities had gender equality committees in their political organisations (Eduards *et al.* 1983:212). In addition to the political representatives, the trade unions were often represented in these committees (Dahlberg 1984:196). Trade union representation in these committees points to the close connection between gender equality issues and personnel issues. Some municipalities followed the recommendations in the 1980 collective agreement between the labour market organisations and established gender equality groups comprised solely of employer and employee representatives (MBA-KL: § 14). A few municipalities created civil servant positions (gender equality officers) for the purpose of organising and developing gender equality activities within the administrative organisation.

Since the 1980s some municipalities have established gender equality committees while others have disbanded theirs. Today approximately sixty to seventy municipalities have gender equality committees. This means that although it is still the case that only a small proportion of municipalities have committees, this proportion has increased from 18 per cent of the total in the 1980s to 25 per cent today. The committees are often established at the initiative of female politicians who are engaged in gender equality issues. However, the Swedish gender equality committees, like their Norwegian counterparts, are for the most part allocated limited resources and committee posts are often given to relatively inexperienced or peripheral politicians who lack an interest in these issues. This has made gender equality work quite ineffective and difficult in these organisations. Gender equality work has, on the other hand, taken important steps forward in those few municipalities where: 1) gender equality committee chairs have been given to politicians with both an interest in and a commitment to promoting gender equality and with a relatively high post in the political hierarchy and 2) gender equality officers have been appointed to work with these issues in the administrative organisation (Pincus 1998). In an effort to increase municipal interest in the promotion of gender equality issues the Equal Opportunities Ombudsman has, since 1994, conferred the title of "the gender equality municipality of the year" upon municipalities that have distinguished themselves in this respect.

Summary

In the preceding sections we have given a short presentation of the legislation relating to gender equality and the way in which gender equality concerns are organised in the Nordic countries. Equality between the sexes has little or no place at all in local authority legislation in the Nordic countries, and, conversely, local government concerns are only to a limited extent reflected in national anti-discrimination legislation. We have noted that the Nordic countries have opted for partly dissimilar organisational models and legal remedies. Some legal provisions concern women's representation (such as in Norway), some address the way in which local authorities organise the work (as in Iceland), while others prescribe plans of action or status reports (as in Denmark and Sweden). In none of the countries do these obligations involve any great infringement of the local authorities' right to self-governance. What is more, we believe that the similarities between them are relatively extensive with regard to the responsibility of the state to follow up local gender equality efforts: in most of the Nordic countries, this responsibility lies in the hands of a national Equal Status Council. As a rule, these councils have access only to relatively mild control mechanisms, i.e., recommendations, information, and advice, in other words, "soft" control mechanisms.

However, we note that during the nineties weak control mechanisms are giving way to stronger ones in all of the Nordic countries, simply because the former have not produced the desired level of local authority involvement and action throughout the past ten to fifteen years. Finland and Norway have tightened up their legislation in the area of positive discrimination. Iceland has given statute form to the establishment of equal status working committees in local councils covering more than five hundred inhabitants. In Sweden, the Equal Opportunities Act has been made more stringent vis-à-vis employers' obligations to promote gender equality, and it is the state – in the shape of JämO – the Equal Opportunities Ombudsman – that is responsible for overseeing compliance with the legislation in the public sector, including the local government sector. Denmark has decided that local authorities must prepare gender equality progress reports every second year.

In most of the Nordic countries, equal status measures focus on the local authorities *as employers*, in the form of personnel policy guidelines, through agreements between the workers' and employers' organisations, and in the form of legislation. In Norway we have witnessed an organisational shift towards personnel policy, responsibility for gender equality being transferred from equality committees to administrative committees. Because of this shift in focus, the state is in danger of clashing with another weighty principle of the Nordic countries' political culture, namely the freedom of the workers' and employers' organisations do as they will in "matters of internal concern". The local authorities as employers and the associations of local authorities bargain with the employees' organisations on wages, the working environment, and equal opportunity agreements. It seems as if both parties – the employers' and the employees' organisations – have wanted to dilute directives issued by the state and the regulatory and control authorities.

Another similarity in the Nordic countries' policies of gender equality lies in the commitment to enhance the representation of women both on political bodies and in local authority administration. In Norway and Finland, for instance, local authorities as *political entities* have legislation on positive discrimination which can help ensure a balanced distribution of the sexes on local councils and committees etc. The argument generally advanced in this context is the resource argument, i.e., that women's experiences and "expertise in care management" represent crucial resources in local community development. In other words, it is not the conflict perspective – that the interests of women and men as social groups may be dissimilar and in conflict with one another – that is emphasised when arguing for an increase in women's participation in the organisations of local government. In addition it appears that gender equality policies in local authorities very frequently are initiated and run by enthusiasts: "Everywhere it has been the few enthusiastic souls who got the work started" (Dahlerup 1991:13). We will take a closer look below at the conditions under which such "enthusiastic souls" are obliged to work with gender equality and women's issues.

Looking at the way in which the work is organised there are few perceptible dissimilarities among the Nordic countries. Equal status committees have been established at the local level, even though the extent to which this applies varies considerably. In most of the Nordic countries, the committee members are politicians, and the job of the committees is to work as initiators, watchdogs, and advisory bodies. Their mandates are wide-ranging and vague. Their members are often inexperienced politicians and marginal in relation to the local councils. The committees seem to occupy rather marginal places in the local political landscape in all of the Nordic countries and dispose in general over limited independent resources (Guldvik 1995; Dahlerup 1991; Halsaa and Van der Ros 1989; Pincus 1996). It might be apposite to ask whether this organisational form is an appropriate mechanism to promote gender equality at the local level. In Sweden and Iceland, we are witnessing the appointment of equal status officers in the local administration. This is viewed by a number of feminist academics as a more efficient tool for implementing equality policies, provided that they are given a position of some authority in the local administration (see also Dahlerup 1991:13 and Pincus 1997a). These officers who have gender equality as their main responsibility – the so-called femocrats – encounter a number of challenges, to which we shall return below.

The means employed by central government to control and steer administrative bodies further down the line – in our case the local authorities – vary. Legislation is one such device. Other instruments can be found in the legal requirement to promote equal status locally and the provision related to methods of implementation and the use of policy instruments. A common feature of the Nordic countries has been a disinclination on the part of central government to interfere in matters pertaining to local authorities' gender equality policies, to mention one example, or with agreements between the workers' and employers' organisations, to mention another. Legislation has been imprecise and ways to organise gender equality issues have been left the local authorities to decide. We have noted that all of the countries have tightened up their legislation, making it more specific, and that less of the organisational aspect of the work is left to the discretion of the local authorities. We seem to be witnessing a greater inclination on the part of the state to actually exercise its instruments of control. A third type of implementation mechanism over which the state disposes, i.e., financial instruments, is used only in exceptional circumstances for one-off pilot schemes and projects.

Femocrats – marginalities and conflicts of loyalty

In the introductory chapter Anette Borchorst elucidated the rationale behind the choice of the term "femocrat" which is defined as a bureaucrat working to further gender equality, equal rights and/or women's issues. The definition does not necessarily mean that the person holding the position has feminist attitudes and perspectives.[86]

The "femo" part of the term reflects the bureaucrat's area of responsibility, which comprises concerns related to women and/or gender issues. In Norway and Sweden, projects and trials under the auspices of the public authorities are a much-used strategy to bring about change and stimulate developments, and in the eighties and nineties we notice an increase in the number of projects related to women and equal status issues. In the early nineties in Norway consultants or advisers responsible for women's issues were employed by the county councils for project periods of three to five years. In what follows we shall highlight some of the common problems these femocrats or project leaders had to deal with.[87]

This presentation of some of the conditions under which these femocrats worked is based on studies carried out by Van der Ros of femocrats in the county councils, the so-called county femocrats (1996a, 1997b).[88]

Their area of responsibility in the county councils consisted of implementing the aspect of regional policy that was aimed at improving women's conditions. The reason why these jobs came into being at all was the demographic imbalance between the sexes in rural areas which in turn was an outcome of what soon became known as the "flight of the girls" (*jenteflukten*) from the countryside. The femocrat's task was to devise strategies to make rural areas more attractive to women as places to live, as well as to assist women create their own workplaces.

Three forms of marginality

The principal aim of regional policy is to sustain dispersed settlement patterns, and a commitment to improve women's general situation in rural areas was one of the elements of that policy's implementation. Thus, policies aimed at improving women's living conditions in the regions were not a goal in themselves, but a means in a larger policy. The allocations made available were modest in comparison to other regional initiatives. The fact that strategies and measures to enhance women's living conditions were accorded low priority in regional policies

---

86. Which is contrary to the manner in which Australian scholars apply the term. There, femocrat denotes a feminist bureaucrat (Calvert 1987; Franzway 1989; Levi and Edwards 1990; Eisenstein 1990, 1991).

87. These positions can be translated as "county officer for women's issues" or "women's issues co-ordinators". For the sake of simplicity in what follows we shall simply use the term "county femocrat" or just "femocrat".

88. Van der Ros studied the work of the county femocrats. She followed a network project and its project leader in the county of Oppland very closely over several years. She supplemented the analyses with a questionnaire distributed to all of the project leaders who were funded by the SND (Industrial and Regional Development Fund) and who headed schemes targeted at women (in fifteen counties). Added to this came observations and interviews. A presentation of the work can be found in Van der Ros 1996a and 1997b. Previous studies of femocrats working in the county agricultural offices support her findings (Vaagland and Van der Ros 1992).

we have termed *political marginality*. These strategies had their heyday in the late eighties and early nineties.

The county femocrats were *administratively marginal* inasmuch as their position was limited to a period of three to five years. This administrative marginality found further expression in that their jobs were tied in with the national government's efforts to improve women's conditions, and in the early years funding was made available by central government.[89]

The femocrats' duties consisted in the organisation of women-oriented projects, and they often applied methodologies typical of projects centred on process orientation and user participation. Working methods were often what we could call of a "bottom-up" type (Lotherington *et al.* 1992). This contrasted with the usual methods of working found in the county departments of planning, industry or development, where procedures follow established rules and routines, and are typically organised "from the top down".

All the county femocrats were women and they worked in very male-dominated environments – such as the county's planning, regional development or industry departments – and with male superiors. Their situation was thus also one of *gendered marginality*: they were women in an organisation run by men, primarily for men, in which male values and approaches prevailed.

Cumulative marginalisation

Marginalisation is *cumulative*: some of the problems femocrats had to deal with were not very different from those facing all civil servants from time to time, such as the requirement of loyalty to political decisions. But what put an additional strain on the femocrats in this respect was the fact that they were employed by *central government* to ameliorate women's living conditions in the regions at the same time as they were part of the *county government*. This involved them in a working relationship with two different sorts of political decisions and signals. This illustrates a more general problem in the relationship between state control and local self-government. While it was the local politicians who drew up the guidelines for the county administration, the county femocrats – as both project and pilot scheme – were implementation tools in the hands of the *central* authorities *vis-à-vis* the *county* authorities. Thus they had to relate to two types – occasionally conflicting – of political loyalty claims.

Some of the challenges faced by the femocrats are also common to bureaucrats working with process-oriented methods of implementation. Process-oriented implementation represents a break with a more traditional implementation rationale. And project work – which is often used in developmental issues – involves its own specific types of problems in hierarchical organisations.

The third type of marginality which characterised the femocrats' situation arose from the fact that they were women in highly male-dominated depart-

---

89. Government funds were channelled through what was then the Norwegian Regional Development Fund, now the Norwegian Industrial and Regional Development Fund.

ments. This type of marginality is specific for femocrats and is tied more directly to the type of work involved by women's issues in hierarchic, male-oriented and gender-neutral – that is, often gender-blind – organisations. Femocrats came up against resistance mechanisms consisting of the tendency for male-oriented principles and interests to prevail over women-oriented and women-sensitive principles and interests. These types of resistance were connected to implicit sexual discrimination found in organisations in which positions of power are generally held by men. The county administration resisted women-oriented projects and femocrats because this questioned the self-perception of these organisations as gender-neutral entities. Furthermore, such projects – by addressing the need to focus more sharply on the desires and needs of women in rural communities – might come to pose a threat to male dominance and to the priority given to male-oriented interests.

Three types of loyalty conflicts

This threefold marginality – political, administrative, and gendered – embraces three types of dilemmas or conflicts of loyalty. *Political dilemmas* could arise as considerations of regional policy on the one hand and feminist considerations on the other each pointed in different directions,[90] and/or in situations in which regional policy priorities clashed with the interests of women in rural areas.[91]

Femocrats had to defend regional policy priorities even when these priorities clashed with or ignored the interests of women. The femocrats found that their area of work very frequently did not receive the attention it merited. They met with a great deal of rhetorics from the political side. But because of claims of loyalty they were unable to talk with their user groups – i.e., the women in the regions – about these experiences. The employment of femocrats could even reinforce the marginalisation of women's policies: issues pertaining to women's conditions were left to the femocrats to deal with, while the rest of the bureaucracy could get on with other business.

Administrative dilemmas arose due to varying organisational structures and the employment of two different implementation rationales. There was firstly the organising of the women's projects and process-oriented implementation methods based on extensive user participation and a "bottom-up" approach, and secondly, a "top-down" and regulation-based administration, to which the femocrats themselves belonged and were obliged to remain loyal. The user groups – the rural women – might easily come to view this as disloyalty towards themselves: the femocrats were part and parcel of a "remote" bureaucracy.

The third type of loyalty conflict is connected with the gendered marginality which set its stamp on the femocrats' situation. They were supposed to remain loyal to their male bosses. They could definitely not make public the different

---

90. For instance in the choice between upgrading the county hospital or setting up local maternity units.

91. For instance in the choice between upgrading the road system or improving public transport.

ways in which senior managers, colleagues, or politicians demonstrated opposition against the femocrats' efforts to improve the conditions of rural women.

Feministisation of the bureaucracy

We have noted that femocrats, thanks to their experiences of this threefold marginality – political, administrative, and gendered together with the three attendant conflicts of loyalty – developed women-friendly, or even feminist, attitudes and values. The county femocrats – civil servants whose work concerned women's issues, and who were seldom feminists at the outset – gradually became more sensitive to women's issues or even became feminists. We have called this phenomenon the *feministisation of bureaucracy.*

The structures we have depicted with regard to the femocrats at the county administrative level apply in general to other organisations as well, such as, for instance, officers with responsibility for women's and equal status issues in county agricultural offices and county employment offices. Even though our analyses are based on observations of Norwegian county femocrats, there is reason to believe that more or less the same conditions prevail for co-ordinators and leaders of women's projects at the level of local administrations. In the following section we shall address this question in greater detail, but with a focus on male managers and their opposition, or ambivalence, to gender equality initiatives in local administrations.

Male opposition and ambivalent men

The state's choice of steering instruments is an important factor in the realisation of gender equality policy in general as well as in regard to promoting the development of gender equality work in the municipalities. Weak steering instruments can limit the impact of initiatives and reforms, but it is also important to note that the state is dependent on local political and administrative actors for the implementation and realisation of the different reforms and measures it initiates. The extent to which municipal leadership shows an interest in and supports the development of gender equality work is an important factor in determining the success of its implementation. This is no less true for gender equality reforms than it is for any other policy area. In the Swedish municipalities it is still men who dominate in upper level political and administrative positions even though the proportion of women in politics and middle level leadership positions has increased during the last twenty years (Man är chef 1992; Eklund 1996). This means that on the upper political levels men meet predominantly other men, on the upper administrative levels men meet almost without exception other men and in encounters between leading politicians and administrative officials the arena is once again male dominated. This was also the case in the three municipalities that were chosen to participate in a five-year government initiated gender equality project – the Pilot Project for Municipalities – that was carried out between 1989 and 1993. The evaluation, which focussed on the leadership strata of the municipalities, showed that the interest in gender equality issues amongst groups at this level was very low.

The evaluation of the Pilot Project for Municipalities investigated the development of four different types of gender equality measures, whose aim was to start and/or deepen an organisational process of change, namely: committees for gender equality, plans for gender equality, positions to develop gender equality issues in different parts of the administration (officers, advisors, project leaders) and the development of municipal gender equality projects.[92] With few exceptions, men in the leading strata of the municipalities acted in ways that undermined the implementation of the various gender equality initiatives. Such actions were considered to be forms of resistance, partly because individuals in leadership positions have both an obligation and a responsibility to comply with the laws that concern municipal operations, and partly because the attitudes and actions of leadership have a strong impact upon individuals and groups in the rest of the organisation.[93] The forms of resistance used by these men, individually and as a group, are presented in a summarised form below. The effects of leadership resistance were particularly evident, when contrasted with their opposite, that is when men in leadership positions showed an interest in, and promoted gender equality work. This question will also will be explored below. The final part of this section contains a short discussion of why men in leadership positions, who claim to be supportive of gender equality, not only mostly fail to put their words into practice but also often do the opposite, namely obstruct the development of gender equality work in their workplaces.[94]

Passive and Active Forms of Resistance

The different forms of resistance that were employed to prevent the development of gender equality work in the pilot municipalities were first divided into two categories; passive and active. These were then divided into subcategories on the basis of when in the implementation process they occurred. This is presented in a summarised form in Figure 12.1. Above all, resistance in phase one aimed at preventing gender equality from appearing on the municipal agenda at all. In

---

92. Evaluations of the Pilot Project for Municipalities can be found in the following reports: Pincus 1992, 1995a and 1995b. The evaluations, which covered a period of almost fifteen years (1980–1994), are based upon interviews with key actors in political and administrative positions of leadership in the three municipalities, regular interviews and contacts with the project leaders, documentary studies and a questionnaire that was carried out in 1994, some months after the conclusion of the pilot project.

93. It is important to stress that not *all* men engaged in resistance and resistance was *not solely* a male phenomenon. Yet men predominated within the upper echelons of both the administration and the political bodies of the pilot municipalities. For this reason, male resistance and male ambivalence to gender equality issues were focused upon in the pilot project. It is also important to point out that, as the evaluation showed, even though there were women who were opposed to, or ambivalent about, gender equality reforms, with very few exceptions, women were the ones to initiate and work in order to promote gender equality in these organisations.

94. This section is based on Pincus 1997a and 1997b.

phase two, gender equality was already on the agenda, for example, in the form of a committee for gender equality or a plan for gender equality. As a result, resistance during this phase aimed mainly at preventing the measures from being operationalised and put into practice. In phase three, gender equality work was already in progress and, as a consequence, resistance was directed towards minimising, as far as possible, the potential of this work to effect change within the organisation.

Figure 12.1 Male leaders' forms of resistance against the implementation of gender equality reforms in the pilot municipalities

Forms of resistance:	Passive	Active
Phase in the implementation process:		
Phase one: The gender equality issue is not on the agenda	Silence	
Phase two: The gender equality issue is on the agenda	Silence	Counter-arguments
	Sham-actions	
Phase three: Gender equality work is in progress	Silence	Counter-arguments
	Sham-actions	Subversive activity

The passive forms of resistance were most common amongst leading groups within the three pilot municipalities and *silence*, which was practised during all three phases of the process, was absolutely most prevalent amongst these. Leadership silence meant, for example, that: 1) the issue of establishing a plan for gender equality never came up despite obligations laid down in legislation and collective agreements; 2) decisions that were made about various types of measures for gender equality were never realised. Instead, they were "quietly forgotten"; and, 3) gender equality officers and femocrats were marginalised and effectively "ignored". *Sham-actions* as a form of resistance, specifically actions that only seemingly appear to promote the gender equality work of the municipality, were also relatively common. Examples of sham-actions within the three municipalities included the drawing up of gender equality plans in order to avoid fines, participation in a gender equality project in order to put the municipality on the map, the inclusion of vague and noncommittal gender equality related formulations in various municipal planning documents, and the use of such formulations as protection against accusations of inactivity. In none of these cases were the decisions that were taken genuinely intended to develop gender equality within the municipality.

Municipal leadership passivity towards government initiatives designed to further gender equality is a form of obstruction. This is a way for individuals in positions of power to exercise *power* and *control* and, as such, it is a very efficient steering mechanism (Lukes 1979:18 f., Holter 1992:74). The passivity of these individuals and groups towards gender equality initiatives signals to other politicians, to lower level management and to other personnel, that this is an issue that is not to be taken seriously. This, in turn, means that it becomes legitimate for these groups – and sometimes it may even be in their interest – to ignore or "forget" gender equality initiatives. Passive resistance, in turn, also leads to very problematic working conditions for the femocrats. For example, the project leaders stated that leadership silence seemed to spread to other personnel and colleagues and expressed itself in, amongst other things, an embarrassing silence that arose around them during lunch or coffee breaks. Of course, silence and a lack of interest in gender equality issues among colleagues need not always be attributed to leadership passivity. Yet the connection is not totally a matter of the imagination either as is evidenced from cases of the reverse, that is when individuals in leading positions show an interest in and a positive attitude towards gender equality work. The point is that unfavourable conditions for the development of equality work can be both counteracted and changed. This may be illustrated by drawing upon an example taken from one of the municipalities in the pilot group. A very negative development in the municipality was reversed following the appointment of a new chief municipal administrator half way through the period of the pilot study. The new chief administrator showed an active interest in the issue of gender equality and, with the aid of the project leader, devoted himself to developing gender equality work within the organisation.[95] Amongst other things, he offered all the administrative directors the opportunity to attend a university course on "power and gender". Having made them, as one might say, "an offer they couldn't refuse" all the directors attended this rather extensive course. Very few men in these positions had attended the different and, comparatively speaking, limited educational activities that the project leader had organised prior to the appointment of the new chief administrator. Together with the project leader and the gender equality committee, the chief administrator also strengthened the organisation of gender equality work by ex-

---

95. Pincus 1997b discusses the support of male leaders to gender equality reforms and how, in different ways, this support promoted gender equality work in the municipalities. This work involved both active and passive forms of support. An active form of support was considered to be present when a man in a leading position: 1) publicly showed a positive interest in the development of gender equality work within the organisation; 2) actively promoted such work within the organisation and those leading contexts where he participated; and 3) made active use of the knowledge and competence of the gender equality workers and, in other ways, contributed to the strengthening of their role as agents of change. A passive form of support was considered to be present when a man in a leading position supported the work of gender equality workers but did not combine this with an active or public involvement in the development of gender equality work within the organisation.

plicitly clarifying where political responsibility lay for these matters, and by following up and overseeing the development of this work in the different administrative sectors. The issue of gender equality, the gender equality project, and the position of the project leader were all strengthened in the organisation, and interest in these issues increased both amongst the directors and the personnel. The silence was broken and it became legitimate both to ask about and to question gender equality.

Active forms of resistance, *counter-arguments* against equality measures and *subversive activity* were used only when the issue of gender equality was already on the agenda and the practical work of implementing a decision was about to begin or was already underway. In such cases, resistance consisted of different ways of preventing gender equality measures from influencing the working routines and decision-making processes of the organisation. Men in leadership positions very frequently resorted to the use of counter-arguments as a form of resistance. Despite the existence of legislation and municipal decisions, they argued that gender equality measures were, as a matter of fact, inefficient as steering instruments and therefore that it was meaningless to try to implement them in practice. Some of the men were of the opinion that gender equality problems were actually inaccessible to management action in those contexts in which they themselves worked, because these problems were primarily about how to change people's attitudes, which was best done within the family, in the day-care centre or in the schools. None of the men interviewed seemed to think or realise that their own attitudes might have any importance for, or impact upon, conditions in the organisation, whether in a positive or negative direction. Others claimed that the work with gender equality measures would require a commitment incompatible with other, more important tasks. If they or their colleagues were to devote a great deal of precious time to gender equality issues, this would lead both to a waste of resources and to a decline in organisational efficiency. What is sidestepped in arguments of this kind is that gender equality work is about changing planning and decision making routines, not attitudes. Male leaders, moreover, have personnel capable of conducting the practical side of gender equality initiatives. This means that there is no reason why such leaders could not limit their role to that of supporting gender equality initiatives.

The form of resistance referred to in Figure 12.1 as *subversive activity* was directed both against gender equality measures and femocrats. In one way or another, it involved removing from gender equality measures anything likely to influence routines and the content of work in the organisation. For example, in one of the municipalities suggestions that would have made it possible to develop gender equality work within the organisation were deleted from the gender equality plan. The suggestions in question were threefold, that: 1) the municipality should employ a gender equality officer on a part-time basis; 2) all administrative units should establish their own gender equality plans with goals and resources; 3) local work for gender equality should be followed up on a continuous basis and evaluated by the administrative units, together with the municipality's newly established committee for gender equality. The reason that was given for making these deletions was that gender equality issues should be a "natural part" of the personnel activities of the municipality. As a result, the committee for gender equality was, in practice, denied both the responsibilities and the resources it needed in order to be able to influence the planning activities of the different administrative units. Both gender equality work and gender equality plans were then forgotten by the parties that advocated the deletions and the higher level political bodies that followed their recommendation. Another form of action designed to undermine gender equality initiatives involved preventing persons, mostly women, who had both knowledge and experience of gender equality work from: 1) being included in contexts where personnel and organisational issues were discussed and planned; and, 2) being appointed to posts as project leaders for gender equality projects or as gender equality officers.

When resistance aimed at undermining the implementation of gender equality initiatives was directed against gender equality workers/femocrats, it became more personal in character and in different ways undermined the professional and personal authority of femocrats within the organisation. This was the case when, for example, men in leading positions criticised or expressed negative opinions about the work or personal qualities of staff responsible for gender equality matters, in both informal and more formal contexts. For example, in one of the municipalities a male municipal manager claimed that the gender equality project of the municipality was insufficiently "modern", although, as he also admitted, he did not know very much about the project and was not interested in its development. In another case, the project leader's choice of activities was questioned, because, it was argued, they were directed towards "those already saved", and that they missed those people who really needed to be informed and enlightened. When "subversive activity" was addressed against femocrats as persons, it took the form of a criticism of alleged personality traits. Individual femocrats, it was claimed, were too aggressive, too frivolous, too serious, lacked a sense of humour, or that they were not being serious enough. According to the critics, such character failings could have negative consequences for the development of gender equality work within the organisation. This does not mean that opinions about both gender equality projects and gender equality initiatives could not differ, or that criticism could not be directed against both gender equality reforms and femocrats. Mostly, however, criticism and negative opinions were expressed by individuals who in other contexts failed to show an interest in issues of gender equality or the development of gender equality work. In other words, serious discussion hardly ever preceded or followed criticism of this kind.

The problem presented by active resistance, whether in the form of "counter-arguments" or "subversive activity", could be summarised, somewhat incisively, in the following way: when claims, regarding the issue of gender equality and gender equality measures, are expressed by individuals in superordinate positions, their position in the organisation protects them from criticism and awkward questions. For subordinate groups the reverse is true – they are prevented, amongst other things because of their position, from expressing such criticism because they feel vulnerable. In addition, statements made by individuals in superordinate positions have greater authority because of the status of the persons making them, irrespective of factual content or correctness. The reverse is true for statements made by individuals in subordinate positions.

Finally, it may be concluded that it is important to highlight leadership resistance for somewhat different reasons. One reason is that these groups constitute a well known and a significant obstacle to the work of increasing gender equality within working life. Furthermore, it is not unusual for responsibility for the failure of various gender equality measures to be placed on those measures themselves, with the consequence that discussion of gender equality issues often revolves around the question of whether they should be continued or discontinued. That is, gender equality committees, gender equality plans, and gender equality posts are criticised or considered insufficient as steering instruments when a substantial part of the problem lies elsewhere, more specifically in the resistance of male leaders. Moreover, it is hardly reasonable for individuals/ groups to be assigned tasks and to be paid to carry them out, only to have their efforts undermined at a later stage and, sometimes, even to be penalised by their superiors for doing what they are supposed to do.

Male Ambivalence to Gender Equality Reforms

All the male leaders that were interviewed for the evaluation of the pilot project said that they were positive to gender equality and its promotion. One question that interested me, therefore, concerned how we should interpret the gap between what these men said about gender equality and what they did and, above all, what they failed to do in this respect? This type of man is often referred to as an "in principle man", a concept coined by the Swedish men's studies researcher Lars Jalmert (1984). Here the gap between what the men say and what they do is interpreted to mean that they do not actually mean what they say but, rather, that they are saying what is considered to be "politically correct". Another common viewpoint is that it is more difficult for older men to change their attitudes towards women and female gender roles than it is for younger men. The assumption here is that things will improve once younger men, who have grown up in another era, appear on the scene. Both of these explanations, which often coincide, certainly contain elements of truth. But the picture that emerges from the evaluation of the pilot project, as well as from other studies, is ambiguous. For example, in many respects, male involvement in and backing of gender equality work in the pilot municipalities came from older men. Young men are also capable of opposing the increased competition within the workplace that women's rising labour market participation implies (Kvande and Rasmussen 1993). Thus, the picture is a complicated one, and further research is needed to deepen our understanding of why it is that men who claim that they are positive to gender equality do not act accordingly.

In the pilot project evaluation reports, I took up a discussion about whether the gap between the words and actions of male leaders within the municipalities could be seen as a form of ambivalence brought about when their positive values on gender equality were counterposed to, or came into conflict with, other interests, namely; 1) their interest in strengthening their position and career chances within the organisation; and, 2) their interest in strengthening and maintaining – and, above all, in not threatening – their dignity as men in the eyes of other men. In the first case, we are dealing with relationships of dependency between individuals in leadership positions at different levels of hierarchically organised organisations. In the second case, we are dealing with those principles or mechanisms that influence men's relationships with one another in male-dominated contexts. In this perspective, interest in career development and the confirmation of one's masculinity may come into conflict with a positive attitude towards gender equality. If this is the case, it is easier to understand why the few male leaders who not only said that they were positive to gender equality but also acted accordingly, were found in the highest echelons of the organisation. These men were no longer dependent on men in superordinate positions for their careers and, having made it to the top, they were less concerned, relatively speaking, with gaining the acceptance and confirmation of other men in order to sustain their male identities. Other male leaders who claimed to have a positive view of gender equality had power and status in some situations, but were subordinate to other men in other situations. In the latter cases, they were in a relationship of dependence and could, so they argued, feel relatively powerless. These men felt that they had to adapt to the prevailing norms and culture in order to advance in their careers and in order to avoid being criticised or ridiculed by other men in leadership groups dominated by men and male values. These men did not view work with gender equality issues as a potential merit for career development or in terms of what was expected of them as men.

During the more than three decades that the issue of gender equality has been on the political agenda, few men in leading positions have been openly hostile towards the idea of increasing equality between women and men. Yet very few men have been openly positive towards, or actively involved in, gender equality work during this period of time, either. Passivity and silence on the part of the majority of men seem to be a major obstacle for the development of gender equality work in politics, working life and elsewhere, even if such men say that they are in favour of greater gender equality. Feminist research has sought to shed light on the oppression and subordination of women. Here men and masculinity appear in their most negative forms and many men do not see themselves as oppressors of women. In traditional research "man" as generic human or "norm" has most often been the implicit point of reference with the consequence that our understanding of men – whether as individuals or as a group – has not been recognised or problematised (Brod 1987:40; Kimmel 1987:11). Women's engagement with, and work for, gender equality has often resulted in much progress. But women cannot fully realise the goal of gender equality without the involvement of men and it is becoming increasingly obvious that if gender equality work is to move forward within organisations and working life, men also have to be engaged in this work. In order to proceed it is therefore important to not only uncover the different forms of resistance men in leadership positions use against the development of gender equality work but also to investigate and uncover the world of men in partially new and more subtle ways.

Summary and conclusions

In the first section of this chapter we discussed various ways in which central government steers gender equality work at the local level in the Nordic countries, with particular focus on Sweden and Norway. In the last part, we concentrated on the actors in these structures – the county femocrats in Norway and the male managers in local administrations in Sweden. And we discussed the challenges facing these people working with gender equality and women's issues at the county and local levels in their day-to-day work.

It seems that in general local equal status efforts are far weaker than those at the national level throughout the Nordic region, and that work related to local gender equality policies has to put up with far worse conditions than other welfare policy issues. The will and capacity of central government to steer and control the policies of gender equality in the local authorities is mainly limited to personnel policy, that is, the obligations of local authorities *vis-à-vis* their female employees.

The means available to central government to influence local authorities have become more powerful in some countries, i.e., in the field of legislation and supervision. However, it is characteristic that, for all the Nordic countries, we must report the absence of the state's use of financial mechanisms in the form of allocations, jobs, etc. Our impression is that two other important principles in the Nordic democracies, i.e., local self-governance and the autonomy of the workers' and employers' organisations, take prime place in comparison with the objectives of gender equality policy. In Sweden – and in Norway partly following in Sweden's footsteps[96] – a number of equal status policy tasks are being transferred from the central to the county level, while the national equal status councils in the Nordic countries oversee the responsibility to follow up the local authorities in the area of gender equality. These national councils have access to limited resources only, and lack authority *vis-à-vis* the local and regional decision-making bodies.

Gender equality policy objectives are, in a certain sense, all-inclusive, and mainstreaming or integration is an implementational method which is being mentioned more and more often in the nineties (Guldvik 1992, 1995, 1996). However, policy tools such as competence-building measures, in order to increase our understanding of gender, women's, or equal opportunity perspectives, as well as tools to integrate these perspectives into everyday policy-

---

96. The county of Rogaland has initiated a three-year project with an equal status advisor at the office of the county governor (which is an extension of the state at the regional level).

making, are few in number and poorly developed. In many cases it is deemed sufficient to hand responsibility for these matters over to a female employee. Local authorities expect female politicians and employees, rather than central government, to be responsible for keeping work in the area on the right track and moving forwards. In light of the femocrats' experiences and the ambivalence or even downright opposition to equal status objectives by male administrators, the decentralisation of responsibility from central to local authorities and from (male) managers to female employees seems to be ill-starred. Viewed in the context of male opposition to gender equality measures, the oft-mentioned management approach that has gained ground in public administration, also at the local level, is interesting though possibly alarming. Hedlund asks whether this approach should be considered as a process of masculinisation (Hedlund 1997:55).

Scholars in the field of gender studies have pointed out that the implementation of political objectives in the area of equal status "leaks" from both ends: from the top – that is at the national level – and "further down" – at the local level, as we saw in the relationship between local management and femocrats. Attempts to strengthen local equal opportunity policies require an abundance of measures based on a clear-cut and precise approach on the part of central government – and the channelling of substantial resources to follow-up and monitor such undertakings.

13

The debate on Gender Equality within the Armed Forces – A case study of Finland

Anne Maria Holli

In Finland, the issue of military service for women arose at a later point in time and reform was enacted more rapidly than in the other Nordic countries. Earlier, Denmark, Norway and Sweden had already started to gradually expand the range of military tasks open to women. Women were also given a combat role within the armed forces in Norway in 1985, in Denmark in 1988 (with the exception of the air force) and in Sweden in 1989.[97] In these countries, the topic was not as politically controversial as it was in Finland, either.

The Finnish debate on gender equality within the armed forces started in 1984, when the Act on the Finnish UN Peace Corps was changed so that it also became possible to recruit women to the Corps. The main purpose of this law, as with many later reforms, was to enable the military to deploy women in support roles, for example, as service personnel. By this means male soldiers could be released for actual military duties. The military continued to open up positions (especially those reserved for civil personnel) to women into 1990s. This process culminated in the granting of voluntary military service for women in 1995.

The advocates of the reforms often pleaded their case with an explicit reference to the promotion of gender equality, whereas many feminist and pacifist opponents of the reforms regarded the "militarisation" of women as the antithesis of equality. The traditional lines of division in the debate on gender equality fluctu-

---

97. Iceland lacks an army of its own. Instead, the defence of the country has been organised by means of a bilateral defence pact with the United States. Icelandic men or women who wish to enter military service, e.g., in NATO, can receive military training in one of the neighbouring countries, such as Denmark, Norway or Great Britain. Hitherto, approximately 10–15 men have received a military education in this way. However, so far no women have made use of the possibility.

ated so much that one of the participants was finally forced to describe the ab-
surdity of the situation as follows: "The best friend of a pacifist feminist in the
struggle against female military service is the good old male chauvinist" (Laxén
1992:2).

In contrast to the previous chapters, where we analysed and compared Nordic
gender equality policies in respect of their institutions, strategies and actors, we
will now change both the perspective and the method employed. This chapter
will focus upon gender equality, as a concept and as a political ideology, as well
as on an individual country, namely Finland. Due to its more conservative attitude towards the participation of women in the armed forces, Finland can be
considered an extreme case within the Nordic community in this respect.

Three questions will be posed in this chapter. Firstly, is it at all possible to
speak of gender equality when referring to such a patriarchal institution as the
military? Secondly, which gender ideologies have been promoted and legitimated using the concept of gender equality? Finally, is gender equality of necessity
associated with progressive lines of thought, as is often assumed, or has it become a conservative slogan, as has also been claimed?

The data for the analysis consist of two Finnish parliamentary debates on the
position of women and gender equality within the armed forces for the years
1984 and 1994/95, as well as some press material and official defence policy
documents for the same period.

First, we will introduce some theoretical perspectives on the relation between
gender equality and the military. We will concentrate here on the question of
whether it is possible for patriarchal institutions such as the army to change. After this, we shall present our framework for the analysis of different gender and
equality ideologies. Finally, we will present the empirical material.

In summary we conclude that "gender equality" has been utilised for many
different and conflicting political purposes in Finland: it has legitimated both
conservative gender ideologies and feminist efforts. The analysis also shows that
the gender ideology of the Finnish military has become more "progressive"
within the time period in question. We have our doubts, though, about the claim
that this implies a more significant transformation of the patriarchal character of
the institution.

Gender Equality and the Military: Some Theoretical Reflections

The question of whether it is possible for a patriarchal institution to change is
one that has engaged both feminist activists and researchers during the past few
decades, especially where the relationship of women to the state is concerned.
This question becomes even more of a challenge if – instead of concentrating on
the Social Democratic Welfare State with all its redeeming, in-built maternal
characteristics – we focus on other, "more" patriarchal institutions such as the

military. Can the army ever be women-friendly – let alone an institutional model of equal opportunities?

The army has traditionally been a male bastion that has excluded women from all positions other than those strictly reserved for the female sex: as civilians in need of protection, as mothers, girl friends, wives or as hierarchically subordinated service and care personnel. In this respect, the army has been organised as an emphatically male-dominated work community. As such, it has had to face new challenges when recruiting women. Is it women who will adapt to the military or is it the system that will change?

Cynthia Enloe (1988a, 1988b) has stressed the ideological importance of the army for the construction and reproduction of gendered identities. According to Enloe, the military has a special role in the ideological structure of patriarchy, since the notion of "combat" is so closely intertwined with the construction of "manhood". If one could not associate the male with the roles of "protector" and "warrior", one would not be able to justify the subordinate role ascribed to the woman as "the protected", either. This hierarchical distribution of gender roles provides the basis for the organisation and legitimacy of the army. It also partly explains why the question of arming women has been so problematic for the military itself. A woman with a weapon in her hands obliterates gender difference as defined by military logic. Simultaneously, something crucial in the self-image of the military is shattered.

Yvonne Hirdman's theory of the gender system and its transformation (1988, 1991) offers us another means to analyse the tensions between gender equality and the military. According to Hirdman, the gender system is based on two fundamental principles, namely dichotomisation and hierarchy. Dichotomisation implies the differentiation and separation of the sexes, something that is also expressed, for example, in the division of labour between the sexes. Gender relations are also regulated by the rule of hierarchy, which is revealed in the primacy of the male norm. Hirdman claims that the more extensive the separation of the sexes is, the more legitimate the male norm appears. The reverse of this situation is equally true: if the separation of the sexes breaks down, the male norm is also revealed and called into question. At the same time, gender conflicts latent within the system escalate into more open conflicts.

However, Hirdman (1991:194) argues that the structural conflicts that appear as a result of weakened dichotomisation, for example via the integration of women into the military, are automatically modified by the system into more acceptable and useful forms, that basically strengthen the primacy of the male norm. Crudely put, patriarchy succeeds in restoring its balance even when under threat. Thus, the change does not represent a genuine transformation of the system, but just a renegotiated form of the gender contract, based on the same old principles.

Mary Fainsod Katzenstein (1990) has analysed the spread of feminism to conservative and male-dominated milieus, such as the church and the army. She regards the emerging women's activism within these institutions as the newest form of feminist politics. Katzenstein points out that during the 1980s, feminist values spread from the women's movement to new groups in society. At the same time, a kind of blending of values, even contradictory values, took place. She calls the result of this process "a complex consciousness". An example of this "complex consciousness" is provided by Finnish women's magazines, in which feminist demands began to appear alongside diet programmes – apparently without conflict.

During the 1980s, those women's groups that embraced feminist beliefs and values began to mobilise for the realisation of specific goals in their own communities. However, the ways in which these groups operated were not necessarily copied from the feminist movement. Rather, their strategies developed context-bound and have to be judged accordingly. Katzenstein (1990:53) makes the following comment when describing the changes that took place within the U.S. military:

> Feminism in the armed forces has set its sights largely on making the military sex-blind. In another institution, at another time, such an objective might be thought conservative. In the U.S. military at this time, the vision is deeply challenging.

Thus, in a way, Katzenstein and Hirdman can be regarded as representing opposite points of view on the ability of patriarchal institutions to be transformed. Can, for example, the army demonstrate a genuine desire for gender equality and work for improved positions for women? Hirdman's response to this question is more or less in the negative, while Katzenstein displays more optimism. Katzenstein emphasises that changes within institutions are always context-bound and gradual, and she also underlines the role of women as agents of change.

The Conceptual Framework for Analysis: Different Ideologies of Gender and Equality

The purpose of the following section is to outline a classificatory model, a framework for our analysis of different ideologies of gender and equality, which can be used for structuring and analysing opinions and ideas present in the debates on the role of women and gender equality in the armed forces. By "ideologies of gender and equality" we refer to conceptions of women and men and the relations between them.

Gender ideologies are usually divided into two categories: ideologies of sameness and ideologies of difference. In the former category women and men are seen as fundamentally *similar*, whereas in the latter they are presented as being fundamentally *different* (see, e.g., Eduards *et al.* 1983; Bacchi 1990).

Ideologies of difference emphasise women's and men's different essence, different characteristics or different functions. They can be seen as either inherent (biologism) or as internalised (theories of socialisation). In earlier research in particular, ideologies of this type were considered expressions of a conservative attitude to gender issues. Yet, they were in tangential contact at several points with those *difference feminists* that have emerged especially in the Romance countries. In the spirit of liberalism, *the ideologies of sameness* emphasise women and men's universal and similar human nature and also, by extension of this argument, their right to equal treatment in society. Historically, the strategy of connecting sameness with the concept of equality has also been used to justify the political demands of different new groups. By stressing their similarity with other already accepted political actors, new groups have been able to appeal to the principles of democracy and equality, and thereby to justify the extension of existing rights and privileges to themselves.

One consequence of the existing conceptual links between sameness, equality and political rights is that ideologies of sameness have long been regarded as inherently progressive and reform-orientated. For example, for a long time this trend was evident in attempts to classify different women's movements. More recently, however, research into feminist ideologies has produced new interpretations on the "conservatism" of ideologies of difference and the "progressiveness" of ideologies of sameness and, sometimes, it has even reversed them.

For example, Bacchi's (1990) analysis of the ideas of the women's movement shows that external pressures affect the construction of feminist debates in terms of the form they take in respect of the opposition between sameness and difference. Feminist debates have tended to orientate towards either end of this sameness-difference opposition. The central factor has been the political environment and its demands, which have required strategic responses, found only by turning to arguments that stress either women's difference or similarity with men. Bacchi, like Melby (1991), who studied some of the Norwegian women's movements of the inter-war period, questions the view that an emphasis either on women's difference from men, or on their similarity to men, would *per se* say anything about the nature of gender ideology or the women's movement. As a matter of fact, feminist movements have often been a mixture of both approaches.

Thus, the problem that remains is how to differentiate conservative gender ideologies from progressive ones. This problem has most often been solved by focussing on either of the following questions: Firstly, what is the standpoint of the ideology at issue with regard to the relation between women and men on the conflict-harmony axis (see, e.g., Berggren 1987)? Secondly, what is its standpoint with regard to the prevailing situation on the preservation-change axis (see, e.g., Eduards *et al.* 1983)? In both cases the question concerns the acceptance or rejection of the prevailing gender hierarchy.

However, we will adopt another typology here; one which originally derives from Julia Kristeva's (1986; see also Moi 1987) categorisation. According to Kristeva, different gender ideologies can be divided into three types:

(1) ideologies where the man is the norm, and in which the woman is regarded as a deviation from this norm. As a result, "similarity" and adaptation to the prevailing (symbolic) order is demanded of women.

(2) ideologies that reverse the patriarchal power relation and, in other words, extol femininity or utilise the female as the norm. This orientation strives to find

support for this new feminine vision of the world and to change the male in line with its values.

(3) postmodern gender ideologies, which reject metaphysical divisions that are based on the dichotomisation of the masculine and feminine. In a sense, this perspective implies a deconstruction of our prevailing ways of thinking, which are based on oppositions and hierarchies. It also implies novel ways of approaching concepts such as identity and gender (Moi 1987:122 f.).

Perhaps it is also necessary to point out that the dimension of preservation and change lies behind Kristeva's division, as well – at least if we assume the primacy of the male norm as our starting point for the analysis of the prevailing order. To replace the male norm with the female norm, as such, already implies a questioning of the old system and a demand for change. Postmodern gender ideologies, for their part, reject the present gender divisions *per se*. For that reason, one has to treat them as a category of their own, which cannot be equated directly with the ideologies of sameness or difference.

Starting from the division presented above, we can create a system for categorising different ideologies of gender and equality. This model will be used in this chapter for structuring and analysing the different actors' contributions to the debate on the role of women and of gender equality in the Finnish armed forces.

Figure 13.1. Classification of gender ideologies

	The normative starting point for an ideology		
The conception of gender	Man as norm	Woman as norm	Rejection of gender dichotomies and hierarchies
The difference of the sexes	(1) The ideology of complementarity	(2) Cultural feminism	
			(5) Postmodernist gender ideologies
The similarity of the sexes	(3) Patriarchal liberalism	(4) Matriarchal liberalism	

The Controversy over the UN Peace Corps in 1984

Throughout the whole period since independence, Finnish legislation has structured the armed forces along gender lines: compulsory military service has been stipulated solely for men, whereas the obligation to defend the country has been gender neutral. This has made it possible in periods of crisis to require women to carry out support and maintenance tasks, while armed defence has only been obligatory for men. The gendered division of tasks has been repeated within the army in respect of the distribution of military and civil tasks and, further, within civil posts, in respect of the division into female and male-dominated fields. The male-dominated posts have, of course, been better paid than the female-dominated ones (Kurkela 1991:6 ff.).

· During the1960s and 1970s several committees had already considered how to better include women in the emergency preparations of the defence forces. The committees typically suggested that armed military service be strictly left outside women's sphere of activity. This also became the official, as well as the unofficial, view of the Finnish armed forces until the beginning of the 1990s, when this policy underwent a rapid about-turn.

During the first half of the 1980s, armed military service for women was still not subject to public debate. Neither was there any pressure in society in that direction. Rather, the opposite was the case: the Finnish peace movement was in its heyday and attracted support especially from women (see chapter 6). The more critical attitude of women towards the question of defence was also noticeable in the opinion polls conducted by the Planning Commission for Defence Information (Millaisin toimenpitein 1986:330 f., Table 5).

At the same time, the military was worried about the decline in the male age cohorts. The popularity of the system of community service for conscientious objectors was also on the increase, despite it being difficult to obtain. During the latter half of the 1980s, the Finnish defence debate was largely characterised by discussion of the need to reform the rules covering conscientious objectors. Also, women were more positive than men with regard to this issue. According to the findings of a study by Suhonen (1988: 178), 70 per cent of women and 55 per cent of men in 1984 were in favour of shortening the period of community service for conscientious objectors.

These worrying tendencies encouraged the military to give more thought than before to how women might be provided with both more information and "more accurate" information about defence questions – not to mention the idea of transmitting the "correct attitude" about such issues to them.

In this situation, a proposal to reform the Act on the Finnish UN Peace Corps was submitted for parliamentary scrutiny. The Bill had been prepared by the Ministry of Defence and was primarily of a technical nature. The purpose of the proposed new law was to clarify the role of the supreme state bodies in the decision-making process in respect of peacekeeping and to reorganise the administration of the peacekeeping forces (HE 193/1983). Preparations for the reform of the law by the parliamentary Committee on Defence Matters were initially conducted in a spirit of consensus, until the state Council for Equality between Men and Women issued its report on the matter.

Conflict emerged over paragraph 4, section 2 of the Bill, regarding a reformulation of the wording of the stipulation of the size of the peacekeeping forces from "a maximum of 2,000 men" to the gender neutral form, "a maximum of 2,000 persons". The Government promoted the amendment with the argument that in this way one could remove a legislative obstacle to women's participation in the peacekeeping forces. Thereby, it was argued, equality between citizens could also be increased (HE 193/1983).

The Council for Equality and its representative Heta Tuominen (Centre Party), who had given a statement to the parliamentary defence committee on this issue, opposed the proposed amendment of the paragraph and, thereby, also women's participation in the Finnish UN Peace Corps. The Council rejected the claim that the reform was motivated by a concern for gender equality and proposed a new qualitative interpretation of equality: "To be a soldier is not a question of equality". The Bill was seen as a first step towards militarising women's lives, since, for example, it also extended punitive regulations concerning soldiers to women serving in the military (TANE 15/54/84; Heta Tuominen 1984). In its own interpretation of equality, the Council appealed to the UN Convention on the Elimination of All Forms of Discrimination against Women, which Finland had signed in 1980. In this agreement, discrimination was defined as activity that impaired or nullified a person's or a group's enjoyment of human rights and fundamental freedoms on the grounds of sex. According to the Council, the exclusion of women from service in the military community within war zones was neither an injury to women's human rights nor to their fundamental freedoms. Therefore, it considered that the Act on the Finnish UN peacekeeping forces could not be justified on the basis of gender equality arguments (TANE 15/54/84).

Both the passage of the Bill in Parliament and the lively public debate that followed concentrated upon whether the reform was about gender equality or not. Those in favour of the Bill, a majority within all parties except the Finnish People's Democratic League (a left-wing socialist alliance) emphasised the consequences of the reform for equality. The reform would give women an opportunity to take part in a sphere of activity that previously was closed to them – and in this way, it ought to clearly improve equality between women and men. In addition, women already held civil posts within the domestic defence forces and they were active in the peacekeeping troops of other countries. The message of the supporters of the Bill was both simple and direct: if women elsewhere could engage in a full range of military activities, they argued, why not also in our country? There were no formal obstacles in domestic legislation or in international law. Finnish peacekeeping forces suffered from a lack of professional personnel in the care and service sectors: it was not easy to find men to undertake these tasks. In addition, it was argued that recruitment to the peacekeeping forces was a voluntary matter of choice for women – not an obligatory duty.

Anna-Kaarina Louvo, MP (conservative National Coalition Party) summed up the gender ideology of the Bills' proponents in the following manner during the third reading of the Bill:

> As far as I can see, the Council for Equality has now started a war against women's equality through its decision to oppose the participation of women in UN peacekeeping activity. It is not only a question that many of the tasks of the Finnish UN peacekeepers suit women better than men, but also that, on the grounds

of gender, the law has hitherto forbidden the carrying out of these tasks for those citizens who are best suited for them (1984 Diet, 10.5–27.5.1984:1233–34).

The *ideology of complementarity* that was employed was based upon the notion of differences between women and men and the different tasks they performed, both in society and, more narrowly, within the armed forces. The prevailing order and the male norm were taken for granted. It was the role of women to assist and undertake caring work within the armed forces so that men could be released for their hierarchically privileged tasks as soldiers. This acceptance of women in the army was explicitly motivated by the army's increased demands for manpower with the required skills. In addition, women's own needs for self-realisation within the field of defence were mentioned as an argument for reform by the Bill's proponents.

Even if the defenders of the Bill continuously emphasised their concern for formal equal rights between women and men with regard to certain tasks, they simultaneously stressed that this goal did not, under any circumstances, imply that women should bear arms. That is, the aim was not to put women and men on an equal footing where military service was concerned.

> Those tasks that have been outlined for women should be totally non-military, assisting and maintenance duties, which should not require any kind of military education in the use of weapons. To give women weapons for possible use during peacekeeping duties, and to educate them in the use of weapons – even for purposes of self-defence – has not been considered necessary during any of the preparatory phases of this matter (Mauri Miettinen, Chairperson of the Parliamentary Committee for Defence (National Coalition Party), 1984 Diet 1.2–9.5.1984:884).

For the advocates of the Bill, "equality" solely came to mean women having the possibility to gain employment with the same employer as men, that is, the Peace Corps, even if they were to be given different tasks.

Again, the opponents of the Bill wanted to deny the gender equality implications of the proposed legislative reform with the help of arguments that were mainly borrowed from the Council for Equality. To give women maintenance duties in military communities would not make a big difference to women's position. This point of view was summarised by Ulla-Leena Alppi (Finnish People's Democratic League):

> Gender equality, women's liberation, does not mean similarity, or that we women should do everything that the male part of society does now or has to do (1984 Diet, 10.5–27.5.1984:1165, see also Jaakonsaari op.cit.:1164).

It would seem that the opponents of the proposition largely drew upon a *cultural feminist ideology*, which took the female sphere of activity as its starting point. Women's desire for peace, both as mothers and educators of the new generation, was offered up as a model for men to follow:

> In the name of equality we ought to demand that armies be totally abolished. Then, men would be equal to women, who, today, do not need to bear weapons (Arja Alho, MP, Social Democratic Party, 1984 Diet, 1.2–9.5.1984:893).

Thus, the gender ideologies of both the supporters and the opponents of the Bill were based upon the same notion of gender difference, but they valued the sexes in different ways. What essentially differentiated the ideologies, was their relationship to the current order and the primacy of the male norm. The proponents of the Bill regarded entry into the male preserve of the peacekeeping forces as progress for women, irrespective of how illogically "similar rights" might be realised in practice. For their part, the opponents questioned the prevailing order and were searching for plausible alternatives to it.

Moreover, it should be noted that while both sides argued about gender equality, they understood the concept differently. Equality was defined in broader and more "feminist" terms by the Council for Equality and other opponents of the Bill, than it was by the Bill's proponents, whose standpoint on gender equality – as our analysis suggests – may, with good reason, be called conservative-masculine. For their part, the opponents of the Bill even saw gender equality as equalling "women's liberation" (see Alppi above).

When discussing the new and contradictory interpretations of gender equality found in the debate on the peacekeeping troops, we also have to consider the more general attitudes to defence policies and the military, which to a great extent structured the ins and outs of the debate. The Bill on the Finnish UN peacekeeping forces was supported by practically all political groups as well as by the public. The common factor uniting the proponents of the Bill lay in their general acceptance of armed defence and the ideology underpinning it. The Bill's opponents came from pacifist and feminist circles or from the Finnish People's Democratic League, the party that had been the most consistent critic of all on defence matters in the post-war period (see Matilainen 1984). Once the issue basically became one of accepting or rejecting the machinery of war and of armed defence, in other words once it became a choice between "militarism" and "pacifism", gender equality became an element in the service of these prioritised goals.

On the whole, the legislative proposal from the defence ministry and the government thus represented an extremely conservative view of gender relations. In this view, women were explicitly regarded as an exploitable human resource (cf. Jónasdóttir 1992:211 ff.) as well as a cheap solution to the recruitment and manpower problems of the peacekeeping forces. The Bill did not have much to do with gender equality, either, at least not with the standard interpretations of the concept. Appeals to gender equality during the promotion of the Bill were nothing more than a rhetorical device, designed to increase its acceptability.

Despite this, paragraph 4 of the Act on the Finnish UN peacekeeping forces was adopted in a gender neutral form by the Finnish parliament in the spring of 1984, by eighty-nine votes to twenty-three. The parliamentary group of the Finnish People's Democratic League and some persistent peace activists and feminists voted against the government proposal.

When Parliament adopted the Act in 1984, it stipulated that "before recruiting women for peacekeeping tasks, the government should undertake measures tó ensure that women's activities in the peacekeeping organisation are limited to civil tasks and to exclude them from regulations applying to military punishment" (Parliamentary Reply to the Government's Bill 193/83, 1984 Diet). These concessions to the pacifists were "forgotten" in 1988, when some of the regulations in the military crime act were also expanded to include women in the UN peacekeeping forces. In practice, however, the first women were not recruited to the peacekeeping forces until 1991. Before this, they had enjoyed a short period of weapons training, referred to as "sport shooting", together with the female civilian professional staff of the Finnish army. Once again, this explicitly contravened the will of Parliament.

Between the passage of the Act and women's assumption of duties in the peacekeeping forces, both the decade and, with it, attitudes towards military service for women had nevertheless changed.

The Controversy over Voluntary Military Service for Women during the Years 1994–95

The controversies over the relationship between gender equality and the military appeared clearly for the first time in the Finnish context during the reading of the Bill on the Finnish UN peacekeeping forces. The debate on this theme continued during the latter half of the 1980s and beginning of the 1990s. During this period, the role of women within the armed forces was also discussed in several political committees and working groups on defence matters. Some reforms were also realised concerning, amongst other things, the legislation on military preparedness in crisis situations and the position of female personnel in the armed forces. In spite of the reforms, the attitude of the military towards armed military service for women remained unchanged, at least until the early 1990s.

The Ministry of Defence experienced the career advance of women in a concrete way in 1990, when Elisabeth Rehn, MP (Swedish People's Party), became the country's first female defence minister. In addition to her post as Minister for Defence, Rehn acquired the portfolio for gender equality affairs in 1991. Giving both the portfolios of defence and gender equality to a single woman minister led to these themes becoming linked, at least in the eyes of the public. Rehn also used her position as the minister in question to call for more information and research on the position of women within the armed forces. Yet, Rehn did not personally support military service for women (see, e.g., Helsingin Sanomat 1990; Rehn, 1994 Diet, 20.9.1994:2896).

In 1992, the defence ministry appointed a committee to investigate whether women should be allowed to undertake voluntary military service, and to what extent they should be permitted to enter the military professions. The committee published its report in 1993. The report stated that there were no grounds for excluding women, not even from armed military posts (KM 1993: 9).

The decade-long debate on gender equality within the armed forces had at least fulfilled one function; the defence committee explicitly abandoned any attempt to defend its point of view by reference to gender equality arguments.

> ..."gender equality" cannot be defined unambiguously. Therefore the committee will not rely on gender equality arguments to support its views, but will instead build its proposal upon the general developments in women's situation and the positive effects of cooperation between women and men within other fields in society and working life (KM 1993:9:40).

Individual characteristics should be the decisive factor in recruitment to posts in the armed forces as well. It would also be to the advantage of the armed forces to obtain the most suitable individuals for the functions they have to perform (KM 1993:9:39).

Even if the report explicitly abandoned the use of gender equality arguments to promote the reforms, these arguments continued to play a backstage role. For example, the emphasis on individual characteristics and aptitudes instead of gender, originates clearly in that liberal ideology of gender equality that traditionally has emphasised the similarities between women and men. The arguments outlined in the committee report on women's usefulness for the military were also modified to include more up-to-date formulations that were better suited to the *patriarchal-liberal gender ideology* that was now adopted by the armed forces.

What was the reason, apart from a lack of personnel, for the changed attitude of the armed forces to military service for women? We can think of three possible explanations, each of which has probably contributed to the change.

Firstly, Ministry of Defence studies indicated that women did not constitute a "weak link" for military organisations, as was perhaps feared earlier (see, e.g., Kauppinen and Huida 1993). On the contrary, it looked as if women could have a positive effect on the army as a working community.

Secondly, the political climate became more conservative and defence-friendly as a result of the collapse of the Soviet Union and the domestic economic recession. At the same time, attitudes towards female military service changed. Whereas in 1986 there was approximately as many opponents (50 per cent) as supporters (49 per cent) of military service for women, supporters had gained a clear majority (68 per cent) by 1992 (PLM-tiedote 9.3.1987; MTS-tiedote 13/1992). The young, particularly young women, were the group most favourably disposed to opening up military service to women. Indeed, according to one study, support among young women for this position was almost total (Laisi 1994).

The third explanation is that arguments for "gender equality" in the context of the army may have produced unexpected "side-effects" for the military. In the face of criticism, the army was forced to modernise, at least superficially, its conservative and inconsistent ideology regarding gender and equality.

The government bill (HE 131/1994) to introduce voluntary military service for women was tabled in Parliament at the beginning of the autumn of 1994. It was largely based upon the committee report "Women and Military Defence". Both the report and the government proposal expressly avoided using gender equality arguments, even though the liberalistic view of gender equality could be read into other motivations. However, despite the defence ministry's wish, reflected in this strategy, to avoid disputes over the meaning of gender equality, this became the central theme in the parliamentary process. In the plenary sessions of Parliament the different conceptions of the gender equality character of the proposed law constituted a clear line of division between the proponents and the opponents of the reform.

In contrast to the debate on the peacekeeping forces that took place in 1984, this time the opposing parties mostly used arguments based upon the notion of sameness and *the liberalistic view of gender equality*. According to the mostly non-socialist proponents of female military service, the gender equality character of the reform was undeniable. It would remove the occupational ban that had restricted women's activities, and it would open up new professional career opportunities for women within the military. In addition, the proposed law only sought to remove obstacles that prevented women from seeking employment with the military – women would not be forced to do so.

The Left Wing Alliance (a successor party to the Finnish People's Democratic League), the Greens and other, pacifist and feminist, orientated MPs[98] strove in turn to deny the gender equality character of the reform because of the internal controversies and transgressions against gender equality which they detected in the proposal. In contrast to male conscripts to the army, for example, female recruits were required to undergo psychological tests.

The opponents of the reform now defined the notion of gender equality in a new way: Equality came to mean offering both sexes the same choice between obligatory community service (including a choice to do it by way of military service) and voluntary military service (in practice, the creation of a professional army). The opponents concentrated upon showing that the suggested reform would violate men's right to equality, as military service would continue to be obligatory for them:

> Voluntary military service for women does not promote their position, neither does it advance gender equality in society, if military service or community service for conscientious objectors remain a duty for male citizens (2nd minority position, PuVK 4 – HE 131/1994:6).

---

98. The Council for Equality between Men and Women did not play as large a role in this debate as it did in 1984, because it was divided over the question of voluntary military service for women. For example, in the Council's 1993 statement to the Committee on Women and Military Defence, three different opinions were expressed: one opinion primarily represented a cultural feminist view reminiscent of 1984, another opinion defended women's military service on patriarchal-liberalistic grounds, and a third opinion opposed military service for women on the same grounds as later opponents of Act were to do in the 1994–95 debate (TANE 3/43/93).

It is interesting to note that the proponents of the law reform also seem to have adopted the opponents' definition concerning "the ideal type of gender equality", that is to say they acknowledged the same choice between obligatory community service and voluntary military service for both sexes. "Of course, none of these alternatives are relevant here", explained the chairperson for the parliamentary defence committee (Lamminen, 1995 Diet, 19.1.1995:6742). The working committee of Parliament and several of the participants in the debate opposed obligatory community service for both sexes, because of what they saw as the "natural, biological" functions of the woman:

> Motherhood, birth giving and the care of children are important reasons why compulsory military service for women cannot be defended solely on the narrow basis of a gender equality perspective (1994 Diet, PuVK 4 – HE 131/1994, appendix).

Thus, it was not possible to demand that men and women be treated similarly with regard to social *obligations* when women were already fulfilling a gendered obligation within the reproductive sphere. A parallel initiative from the Greens on gender neutral community service also failed to receive any support in Parliament.

Consequently, the gender ideology of the advocates of female military service clearly represented a form of *patriarchal liberalism,* while the alternative put forward by the opponents of the reform combined *elements of both patriarchal and matriarchal liberalism.* Obligatory community service for all citizens, women and men alike, which constituted one of the ideal solutions offered by the opponents of the reform, took its normative model from the existing system of compulsory military service for men. In this way it can be regarded as a patriarchal-liberalistic approach. The other ideal, voluntary military service for both sexes, was modelled upon the prevailing situation of woman, and thus it represents a form of matriarchal liberalism. This latter ideal was also the most frequently striven for alternative.

Moreover, the *ideology of complementarity* also had a role in this debate – even if a lesser one. This time, only those with conservative views about gender roles talked about gender difference, while opposing military service as an "unnatural" and unsuitable task for women.

In the debate on the peacekeeping forces in 1984, gender equality was primarily defined as being subordinate to the conflict between militarism and pacifism and also, as dependent on it. During the parliamentary debates of 1994–95 the fundamental attitudes towards defence also influenced the standpoints of the participants, although not to the same extent. The reason for this might be that this time the definitions of gender equality that were used also correlated better with the actors' general attitudes towards defence policy.

Military service for women was intensively debated in Parliament, partly during the same sessions where the amendments to the Act on Equality between Women and Men were discussed in 1995. Many of the women and men who most eagerly supported the inclusion of new, radical quota rules in the Act on

Equality simultaneously opposed the suggestion to introduce voluntary military service for women. Despite their efforts, the Bill on Voluntary Military Service for Women was passed with the backing of the right wing parties and the Centre Party, in a slightly amended form, by 103 votes to 66. The Left Wing Alliance, the Greens and a part of the parliamentary group of the Social Democratic Party voted against the Bill. In addition, some MPs from the Christian League, the Swedish People's Party, the Centre Party and the smaller groupings also voted against the proposal.

Conclusions

In this case study we have analysed two Finnish parliamentary debates on gender equality in the military that took place at an interval of ten years.

In the 1984 dispute over the UN peacekeeping forces, both the proponents and the opponents of a reform of the law used gender difference as their starting point to define the role and functions of women, but they interpreted it in different ways. The conservative complementarian ideology of the militarists was confronted by cultural feminist perspectives. However, it was the conflict between militarism and pacifism that constituted the central line of conflict in the debate. It was this basic conflict that largely determined how the concept of gender equality was defined and interpreted by the different parties.

In the 1994–95 debate on military service for women, both parties based their arguments on the liberalistic ideology of sameness, once again with opposing normative starting points for analysis. The patriarchal liberalism of the defence ministry and the proponents of the Bill were confronted with the opponents' combination of patriarchal and matriarchal liberalisms. By this we refer to a choice between obligatory community service and voluntary military service for both sexes. However, the latter alternative, with its normative model taken from women's situation was the solution to the problem preferred by the opponents of the Bill.

As the above presentation shows, gender equality arguments were used to justify and legitimate all the gender ideologies (other than postmodernist) that were outlined in our original analytical model. The content of the gender equality that is referred to in the debates varied considerably, depending on who used the concept and to what purpose. Gender equality arguments were deployed to advance both gender conservative and feminist agendas. This, to us, indicates that the utilisation of gender equality as a concept or as an argument – at least in the Finnish context – does not as such say anything about the potential radicalism or conservatism of the user or of the gender ideology promoted.

The assumption of a connection between gender equality and progressive ideologies affected at least the trajectory and outcomes of the debates so that the boundaries between the gender conservative and the gender radical became blurred. It was extremely difficult to assess which of the parties to the debate actually represented a genuine desire for equality or a progressive ideology from a gender perspective. For example, in the debates analysed above, it looked as if

public opinion largely concurred with the conservative standpoints of the defence ministry and the government, while the feminist-pacifist front was criticised for nothing less than exhibiting conservative and hostile attitudes towards
gender equality.

The analysis appears to confirm Bacchi's (1990) observation that feminist
discourses are formed by a choice of orientation towards either "sameness" or
"difference", particularly in the face of an external political pressure. In the debates analysed above this was especially apparent in the feminist-pacifist arguments that sought to prevent the integration of women into the military
apparatus. Arguments based upon difference were used to challenge notions that
assumed gender differences; and arguments based upon sameness were used to
counteract arguments that assumed gender similarities.

However, one cannot, on the basis of the previous analysis, give a definite
answer to the question of whether it is possible for a patriarchal institution, in
this case the military, to genuinely be transformed. The study has shown that a
change occurred in the gender ideology of the Finnish armed forces during the
period in question. The conservative ideology of complementarity of the 1980s,
with its idea of the specificity of the sexes, was replaced in the armed forces at
the beginning of the 1990s by a more modern and liberal way of understanding
gender, even if it still remained a patriarchal variation of liberalism. The amount
of data available for the analysis is, however, insufficient for more far-reaching
conclusions. Consequently, we cannot exclude the possibility that the change
noted in the military is an exception to the rule. As a matter of fact, many of the
recent statements and policy measures initiated by the Finnish armed forces give
cause to suspect precisely this.

Drawing upon the approach developed by Hirdman (1988:91), we may conclude that the patriarchal basis of the Finnish military has not fundamentally
changed, despite it modifying its thinking with regard to military service for
women and actually recruiting female conscripts into the service. Indeed, the patriarchal institution may just have succeeded in dealing with the challenge of
change by moulding new female recruits to its own culture. The presence of
women within the system does, however, constitute a continuous basis for new
gender conflicts.

According to Katzenstein's (1990) more optimistic interpretation, the change
apparent in the ideology of the Finnish armed forces can represent the beginnings of something new. In evaluating the process of change we must consider
the context in which it occurs and acknowledge the fact that changes that eventually take place, happen slowly and in a step-wise fashion. We have to bear in
mind that Katzenstein, like Hirdman, underlines the significance of the presence
of women in the army as well as their role as agents for change.

Those women who are currently serving in the Finnish army have not yet fulfilled the expectations for change from within that are part of the Katzenstein hypothesis. The share of female recruits has been very small since the army was
opened up to women in 1995. Moreover, those women are to be found at the

lower end of the hierarchy and thus do not constitute a "critical mass" within the institution (see Moss Kanter 1977; Dahlerup 1988b).

Still, the critical mass may well be on its way, at least if the studies carried out by the armed forces themselves are to be trusted. According to the MTS-gallup (MTS-tiedote 4/1995), 4.5–20.1 per cent of young women will either enter voluntary military service, or at least consider this option. If all of them were to seek admittance during the same year, we would soon see 22,000–98,400 women knocking at the gates of the garrisons ...

PART IV

Women on the Self-governing Islands

Theme editor: Susanne Jungerstam-Mulders

14

Women's Representation and Gender Equality on the Faeroes, Greenland and Åland

Susanne Jungerstam-Mulders[99]

Major differences exist between the Åland Islands, the Faeroe Islands and Greenland. But what they all share in common is that, to some degree or other, they have developed separately from their respective "mother lands"– Denmark with regard to the Faeroes and Greenland, and Finland with regard to Åland. Isolation, the sea and relatively harsh living conditions are also common features that have characterised the development of these island communities. At the same time, the smallness and insularity of these communities has been combined with a certain degree of pride and self-awareness, which in all three cases has manifested itself in the exercise of extensive autonomy.[100]

Gender equality policy belongs to those questions that fall within the competence of the institutions of self-government of the Faeroes, Greenland and Åland. Women in the three island communities have traditionally borne a large part of both the caring and financial responsibilities associated with the family. Despite this and the fact that self-government has not formally hindered the entry of wom-

---

99. The author wishes to thank all those who have contributed to this chapter. A special thanks is addressed to Vivan Nikula, from the Council for Equality on Åland, and to Turið Debes Henze, the chairperson of the Equal Status Council on the Faeroes, for their invaluable assistance with the compilation of the research material. I also wish to thank participants at the seminar on the development of gender equality on Åland, held on 5 June 1997, for their valuable comments on an earlier draft of this chapter.

100. Greenland cannot, of course, be considered small in the literal sense of the word. Rather, what is meant here is that it is perceived as being small because of its relatively small population (approximately 55,000) and its remote geographical position with respect to Danish power structures (cf. Anckar 1996:421).

en into the public arena, all three island communities show a considerably smaller share of women among popularly elected representatives than the rest of the Nordic area (with the exception of Iceland until recent elections). At the same time, the development of "institutionalised gender equality" in the form of a public machinery for the promotion of equality between women and men, started considerably later on the self-governing islands than in the rest of the Nordic area. Is this pattern of development based upon a struggle for autonomy and national identity that has overshadowed all other aspects of life, so that no space has existed for other internal conflicts? Or is the explanation for the relatively low percentage of women elected to political bodies and the comparatively late development of a public "machinery of gender equality" within the self-governing island communities to be found in other aspects of their history, culture, social structure and/or political conditions?

Without claiming to provide the answers to all aspects of the above mentioned problematic, we aim here to describe the development of the self-governing island communities with respect to *women's political representation and the institutionalisation of gender equality policies* in the light of a Nordic perspective on gender equality. Two features are seen as basic to "the Nordic view". Firstly, there is an acceptance of the legitimacy of the demand that women constitute approximately half of popularly elected representatives. Secondly, there is the recognition of an obligation on the part of the authorities to promote equality of status and rights between women and men in different areas of society and to ensure that such aims are observed. The linking of these two, as such, separate themes is based upon the view that an interaction exists between two factors. The first factor concerns the way in which state policy – in this case, the policy of the self-governing island authorities – is formed. The second factor concerns political reality and the claim that the increased representation of women in politics and the integration of gender equality issues into the public sphere are connected (see, e.g., van der Ros 1996b:197). Furthermore, earlier studies have shown that the political parties have played a major role in mobilising groups of women. They have also shown that it is particularly within the party-political arena that discussions about gender and women's interests have largely been problematised (cf. chapter 4). This suggests that women's mobilisation within the framework of the political parties and their increased share of positions within the political arena has helped to place gender equality on the political agenda. It also implies that there has been an interaction between the greater level of representation achieved by women and the more thorough integration of gender equality concerns within the public sphere. However, as the discipline of women's studies and gender research is still in its infancy when it comes to the self-governing island communities, this assumption is not open to empirical verification. Nevertheless, it does provide a certain speculative starting point for our study.

In what follows, women's representation and the institutionalisation of gender equality will first be outlined for each of the three self-governing island communities. The autonomous status of these three regions is often emphasised in connection with the themes we focus on here. Yet differences exist both amongst the regions and between them and the rest of the Nordic area in respect of the establishment of self-government and the party systems. For these reasons, the section dealing with the regions will begin with a short introduction on the establishment of self-government and the party system in each respective region. Finally, the concluding section sets out to analyse the two themes that have been the focus of attention here with the aid of a comparative perspective.[101]

The Faeroe Islands

Self-government on the Faeroes

The Faeroese nationalist movement emerged during the latter half of the nineteenth century. At first, debate centred on the status of the language as a guarantor of Faeroese identity. Voices were raised in support of the introduction of Faeroese as a language of educational instruction, religious devotion and judicial justice. Gradually, rising nationalist sentiment led to demands for independence from Denmark. At the turn of the century the nationalist awakening manifested itself in the emerging political parties, which represented different standpoints on the issue of independence. In 1946, a referendum on independence was held on the Faeroe Islands, which somewhat surprisingly showed that a majority of the Faeroese people were in favour of independence. This, however, could not be approved by Denmark and, instead, in 1948 negotiations with Denmark led to the establishment of self-government (Debes 1993:27 ff.).

By means of the Home Rule Act of 1948, the Faeroes were given a considerable degree of autonomy. Today, this means that the Faeroese authorities have full autonomy regarding, for example, questions of culture, communications and industrial policy. Responsibility for other issues, such as education, and social and health care, is shared jointly by the Faeroes and Denmark. However, in practice, most administrative concerns have been transferred to the Faeroese authorities. The administration of justice, monetary and banking policy, and defence and foreign policy are the only areas of decision making that cannot be transferred to the Faeroese authorities (Debes 1993:32; Internet 1997a).

The legislative assembly and supreme decision-making body on the Faeroe Islands is the Løgting, the thirty-two members of which are elected every four years through a system of direct and proportional representation.[102] In turn, the executive power, the *Landsstýri*, consists of between three and seven members

---

101. The chapter is based upon material compiled during 1995/96. Therefore, the description of the "current situation" also refers to this period. The section on women's political representation has, however, been complemented with new data on the 1998 elections to the Faeroese parliament (*Løgting*).

102. The parliament has 27 members chosen in 7 constituencies plus a maximum of 5 supplementary seats. The supplementary seats aim to ensure proportional representation. Therefore, the number of seats in the *Løgting* can vary between 27 and 32. Since 1978, however, the number of representatives elected to the *Løgting* at each election has remained stable at 32.

led by the Løgmaður, the head of government. In addition, the Faeroe Islands have fifty municipalities with relatively extensive municipal autonomy. The Faeroes also elect two representatives to the Danish *Folketinget* (Petersson 1995:29).

The Party System

Faeroese politics has always been characterised by two developmental dimensions: matters relating to the relationship of the Faeroes to Denmark have often evoked nationalistic responses, while economic interests have often been expressed in terms of competing class ideologies. The traditionally largest parties on the Faeroe Islands are schematically placed according to these dimensions in Figure 14.1.

Figure 14.1 The Faeroese Party Systems

	Left		Right
Independence	Tjóðveldis-flokkurin		Fólkaflokkurin
		Sjálvstýrisflokkurin	
Union	Javnaðarflokkurin		Sambandsflokkurin

Source: Jákupsstovu 1996:39, see also Appendix 2.

However, the nationalist dimension declined in importance during the 1980s, while the deep-going economic crisis that hit the Faeroes increasingly dominated politics during the 1980s and into the 1990s. The 1984 elections were primarily characterised by the defeat of the Social Democrats, while several of the smaller parties, which do not easily fit into traditional categories, were strengthened, and the newly formed Workers' Front made its entrance into the *Løgting*. At the same time, the economic crisis also breathed new life into the debate on Faeroese independence, and revelations about a controversial bank deal shortly before the April 1998 elections contributed to the renewed prominence that the issue of self-government attained during the election campaigns. Moreover, those parties that traditionally had supported the unionist cause now began to emphasise the need for changes in the relationship with Denmark (Jespersen 1993:177 f.; Jákupsstovu 1996:51; Internet 1997c; Internet 1998b).

Women's Political Representation

The women's association in Tórshavn was founded in 1952. It focussed mostly on social and cultural issues during its early years. But prior to the municipal elections in 1956 the association sought to make its presence felt politically by putting together a cross party-political women's list. As a result, the association obtained the election of one of its candidates to Tórshavn municipal council.

However, by 1960, when the next election was held, the women's list was no longer in existence (Jensen 1989:117 f.). Despite this, a woman from *Javnaðarflokkurin*, the Faeroese social democratic party, sat on the municipal council during the period 1968–72, but this seat also ceased to be held by a woman when she stood down as a candidate at the following elections. At the same time, however, the electoral system on the Faeroes was changed so that the electoral chances of candidates on a party list were directly related to the number of votes they individually received. Earlier, by contrast, a given candidate's chances of being successfully elected had not been based directly on the number of votes they received but, rather, on a combination of their ranking order on their party list and the total number of votes cast for all candidates on that list. Yet this change in the operation of the electoral system actually seemed to inhibit women's opportunities for election (Jákupsstovu 1996:39 and 46).

During both the 1980 and 1984 municipal elections attempts were made to relaunch women's lists in Tórshavn, but these efforts attracted only 4.6 per cent and 6.1 per cent of the votes respectively, which was not enough to win seats for the candidates that stood on those lists. At the same time, however, the other parties had begun to include women on their own lists, perhaps out of fear that votes might otherwise be lost to the women's list. Thus, the number of female candidates standing in Tórshavn on the list of *Tjóðveldisflokkurin*, the republican party, increased from none at all during the previous elections to five in the 1980 elections. By contrast, the social democrats of *Javnaðarflokkurin* stood six women at the 1984 elections compared with two at the 1980 elections. In both elections, however, the votes for women candidates were split to such an extent that no women were elected in 1980 and only one was elected in 1984. Yet, the woman who was elected in 1984 was neither associated with the women's list nor the Social Democrats. Rather, she was a candidate for the conservative party, *Sambandsflokkurin*. Although no further women's lists were put up in Tórshavn after the 1984 elections, the share of seats held by women on municipal councils increased to 23.1 per cent following the elections in 1988 and rose again to 30.8 per cent in 1992. One reason why the motivation to maintain a women's list was less than it had been earlier was that it seemed as if women had after all gained a foothold within the established parties (Jákupsstovu 1996:43 f.).

Just as women in Tórshavn had decided against reestablishing a women's list for the 1988 elections, interest in women's lists was rising in other parts of the Faeroes. Women's lists were put up in seven of the fifty-three municipalities. The elections resulted in thirty-four female candidates being elected onto different municipal councils (corresponding to an average of 11 per cent of all councillors elected compared with 5 per cent earlier); one in four of whom had been a candidate on a women's list (Hanusardóttir 1994:51). However, the most sensational result was in the medium-sized municipality of Vestmanna, where the women's list won three out of the seven seats and became the largest political grouping after the election. As a consequence, the position of chairperson of the municipal council also went to a councillor from the women's list (Joensen 1989:118).

Despite individual women being elected onto the local councils during the early years of autonomy, it was not until the 1978 elections that the first female member was elected to the *Løgting*. Only in 1988, the year that women both recorded their breakthrough within the established parties in Tórshavn and achieved successes in several other municipalities, did the number of women in the *Løgting* increase to three. However, a women's list was not put up to contest the 1988 elections to the *Løgting*. Instead, those women who were elected gained the support of the voters by standing as candidates for their respective parties. In this context, furthermore, it is worth noting that the women elected in 1988 received the highest number of votes cast for a candidate of their respective parties (*Javnaðarflokkurin* and *Tjóðveldisflokkurin*) (Joensen 1989:118 f.; Hanusradóttir 1994:50).

At the following elections of 1990 and 1994, this modest but rising trend for women to be elected to parliament continued. The number of women in the *Løgting* remained at three after the 1990 elections, but rose to five following the 1994 elections (Appendix 1, Table 7.1). Moreover, at the beginning of the 1990s, women occupied several important posts. For example, a woman was appointed Head of Government (*Løgmaður*) after the 1994 elections and, at the moment of writing this article, the highest civil servant is a woman (Debes Hentze 1996:9). Despite this situation, the 1994 elections did not pave the way for more women to gain election to public office at the following elections. Instead, the number of women in the *Løgting* declined to four in April 1998.

An examination of electoral behaviour reveals that voting activity amongst the Faeroese people is generally higher than amongst either Greenlanders or Åland islanders (Appendix, Tables 7.1–7.3). But as is the case on Åland, it appears that participation in elections has been higher in rural communities than in the major cities on the Faeroes. Yet, in the period between 1972 and 1992, the highest participation rates in elections in Tórshavn were recorded during the elections of 1980 and 1984, when respectively 77.2 per cent and 75.6 per cent of registered voters went to the polls. This compares to roughly 69 per cent in the two preceding elections and 69 per cent and 65 per cent respectively in the subsequent elections. Thus, one may speculate as to what motivated these voters to turn out in such large numbers when they had manifestly failed to do so in either earlier or subsequent elections. Was it possible that it was the women's lists that generated the debate and roused the voters – even if the women's lists themselves were unable to harvest the fruits of their labour? (cf. Jákupsstova 1996:45).

The Institutionalisation of Gender Equality

If we now turn to the institutionalisation of gender equality in the form of a public machinery for the promotion of equality between the sexes, it may be noted that as early as 1976 the *Landsstýri* decided to appoint an Equal Status Committee (initially called the Committee for Equal Rights). However, the appointment of the first committee was delayed until 1981. Moreover, it was not given any terms of reference and never actually functioned. As a consequence, a new com-

mittee for equal rights was appointed in 1986, and only in 1988 did this committee present a proposal for a law on gender equality (Årsberetning 1995:4). This
proposal aroused strong emotions on the Faeroe Islands. Amongst other things,
it led a representative from the right-wing Christian People's Party, which had
been a part of the government coalition at the time, to demand the immediate
withdrawal of the "immoral proposal". The party left the *Landsstýri*[103] when the
latter refused to withdraw the proposal. Eventually the issue was decided on a
free vote in the *Løgting* as a so-called matter of conscience (Joensen 1992).

However, for many people on the Faeroe Islands gender equality is more a
question of belief than it is a political issue, and the nuclear family is considered
holy by many. During the debates for and against the proposed law on gender
equality, for example, it was argued in the *Løgting* that the proposal constituted
a major threat to family life, to the moral health of women and to vulnerable
young girls. Furthermore, it was claimed that gender equality was guaranteed by
the legal and governmental systems of the Faeroe Islands, and that such legislation was therefore unnecessary (Joensen 1992). It was claimed that the attainment of equality was only a question of whether women used the possibilities
that were available to them. It was also claimed that the introduction of gender
equality legislation would restrict the human rights of other individuals. It was
even suggested that women would find such legislation demeaning (Equality in
Denmark 1995:36; Hanusardóttir 1994:52). As a result, the legislative proposal
was rejected and it was not until April 1994 that the necessary majority for its
approval was finally put together – and even then it was passed by majority of
only one vote.

The delay in approving the Act on Equality between Women and Men was
remarkable in two senses. Firstly, because the UN Convention on the Elimination of All Forms of Discrimination Against Women had, in practice, become
binding on the Faeroes already in 1983, and secondly, because the *Løgting* had
ratified the Convention in March 1987. However, ratification of the Convention
took place without any debate and without any measures being undertaken to ensure its enforcement. Indeed, the *Løgting* is said to have been of the opinion that
discrimination against women did not exist on the Faeroe Islands and, as a consequence, that the Convention could be adopted without any problems arising.
This view was prevalent despite, for example, the employer having a right at this
time to give a pregnant woman as little as three months' notice to quit, or to dismiss her with immediate effect if she had failed to reveal her condition within
the first six months of the pregnancy. Another example is that until 1988 women
did not have rights to inheritance equal to those enjoyed by men. (Joensen 1992;
Hanusardóttir 1994:52; Equality in Denmark 1995; Årsberetning 1995).

---

103. It has to be added that at this time cooperation between the governing parties was not without
friction in other respects, either. Therefore, it is possible that greater importance was attached
to the issue of gender equality than would have been the case under different circumstances
(Debes Hentze 1996.)

The adoption of the Act on Equality between Women and Men in 1994, confirmed the legal status of the Equal Status Committee just as the Committee's tasks were defined for the first time. Today, the Committee's tasks include, amongst other things, working for the elimination of discrimination against women in all spheres of society, ensuring that the Act is followed, and acting as an advisory body for public institutions in respect of gender equality questions. It is also responsible for taking up gender discrimination cases, either on the Committees's own initiative or as a result of complaints received by it. In special cases, the Committee can grant an exemption from the Act. The main focus of Committee activity lies in ensuring that the Act is adequately enforced as well as in publicising and investigating alleged cases of gender related infractions of the law within different spheres of society. The latter task is considered central, because the Committee is often the only public institution that is concerned with gender equality issues (Årsberetning 1995).

The Committee is comprised of five members. A Chairperson represents the *Landsstýri* and the employers and employees are each represented by one member. Of the two remaining places, one member is chosen to represent the Faeroese women's associations and the other to represent the educational health care and social care spheres. Furthermore, the Committee is under the jurisdiction of the minister responsible for labour market issues – whereas administrative communication has taken place through the *Landsstýri's* Department of Social and Health Care. Currently, the committee does not have a secretariat run by employed personnel. For this reason, it is the chairperson who is responsible for the daily management and administrative work of the committee (Årsberetning 1995).

Greenland

Self-government on Greenland

Greenland is the only self-governing region in the Nordic area to have experienced conditions of downright colonisation. Despite this fact, however, for a long period of time it developed in relative isolation from Denmark. Thus, the national awakening did not take place until the 1960s and 1970s, and then primarily as a reaction against the rapid modernisation that had begun in the 1960s. Modernisation was mainly aimed at developing the Greenlandic economy and implied, amongst other things, that the traditional fisheries should be made more efficient and that the population needed to be more concentrated. At the same time, the health-care system was improved, and the population increased explosively. The division of labour and social roles changed – and soon rapid modernisation was also expressed in the spread of rootlessness, disillusionment and a loss of cultural identity (Søvndahl Petersen 1994:139 f.).

Once all the consequences of modernisation started to emerge, a reaction to these developments began to take shape in the form of a new consciousness of Greenlandic national identity, culture and language. During the 1970s, this new consciousness resulted in demands for increased autonomy. Since the mid-1970s, the nationalist flow has assumed, for the first time, the form of an established Greenlandic party system with some degree of stability. In 1979, negotiations with Denmark resulted in self-government for Greenland (Agerskov 1989:122; Thomsen 1991:127 f.; Petersson 1995:29).

Self-government on Greenland has been organised on a similar pattern to that of the Faeroes, even if the Greenlandic parliament was not established until the Home Rule Act was passed in 1979. Thus, reminiscent of the role of the *Løgting* on the Faeroes, different administrative fields relating to the administration of Greenland have been transferred from Denmark to the Greenlandic authorities. The Greenlandic parliament nowadays comprises thirty-two members, who, in a similar way to the Faeroese *Løgting*, appoint the executive body, the government. In addition, Greenland, again like the Faeroe Islands, elects two members to the Danish parliament (Petersson 1995:29).

The Party System

In contrast to the situation on the Faeroes, the political system on Greenland did not take shape until the 1970s; for a long time politics had been dominated by individuals rather than by ideologies or political views, and self-government did not become a central political issue until the mid-1970s. Even if the development of the party system was not just a consequence of the interests that different demographic groups had in self-government, the nationalist issue has also undoubtedly played an important role within Greenlandic party-politics.

Today, five main parties dominate the political arena: *Siumut*, a left social democratic party that advocates Greenlandic autonomy under the Danish crown, *Atassut*, a liberal-conservative party that favours stronger links to the mother land, *Inuit Ataqatigiit*, a left-socialist party that wants total independence from Denmark and opposes the presence of American military bases on Greenland, *Iissitup Partiia*, a conservative party that advocates minimal state intervention by both the Danish and the Greenlandic authorities and increased privatisation of business life, and *Akulliit Partiiaat*, which won seats in the Greenlandic *Landsting* for the first time in 1991. In terms of ideology, this last-mentioned party can be placed between *Atassut* and *Siumut*.[104] (Petersson 1995:49; Internet 1998c; Appendix 2).

Women's Political Representation

Greenlandic women achieved full rights of suffrage only in 1948, which is to say several decades after women in other parts of the Nordic area gained these rights. But at the first set of elections open to women – the 1951 elections to the Greenlandic parliament and the municipal councils – their representation remained virtually nonexistent. No women were part of Greenland's thirteen-member par-

---

104. However, it should be noted that one cannot easily apply features found in Western European party systems to the Greenlandic party system. Therefore, placing Greenlandic parties on a left-right ideological axis is only indicative.

liament, and only one council seat (out of a total of one hundred) went to a woman. At the same time, however, some women had started to organise in local women's associations, which initially resembled housewives' groups, but which came to play an important role in women's future mobilisation (Agerskov 1989:122 ff.).

Arnat Peqatigiit Kattuffiat, the Greenlandic women's association, was founded in 1960, when several local women's groups merged. During the 1960s and the 1970s, the association played an increasingly central role in public debate. It represented women's interests to the authorities, especially on matters relating to family planning, free abortion and housing, but it also began to have an impact on the process of nominating candidates for election to public office. This is thought to have contributed to the election of thirteen women councillors out of a total of 146 councillors in 1967 (9 per cent of the total), sixteen women councillors out of a total of 148 councillors in 1971 (11 per cent of the total) and twenty women councillors out of a total of 163 councillors in 1975 (12 per cent of the total). Women were less successful in elections to the Greenlandic parliament: in 1959, one woman was indeed elected, but when she lost her seat at the 1975 elections it was not until 1984 that a woman was again elected to the assembly (Agerskov 1989:122 ff.).

The role played by women both in and during the negotiations on self-government with Denmark was largely invisible. For example, only three of the fifty-six participants in the conference on self-government in Sisimiut were women, including women representatives of *Arnat Peqatigiit Kattuffiat*. Female representation was totally absent on the Home Rule Commission that was appointed in 1975 to represent Greenland in the negotiations with Denmark on self-government. This situation upset a number of young and well-educated women, who at the same time began to sharply criticise the public authorities both on Greenland and in Denmark: they claimed to be oppressed in a double sense, culturally by the Danes and politically by both Danish and Greenlandic men. Despite cases of such discontent, most Greenlandic women expressed solidarity with their menfolk. It was often said that the new awakening of nationalist consciousness and the struggle for self-government did not allow space for internal conflicts or splits between the sexes. At the same time, the sense of distance from so-called Western feminism, which was often associated with "Western" culture and with Denmark as a "colonial power", was strong among inuit women, irrespective of age (Thomsen 1991:1331 ff.).

The introduction of self-government in 1979 was associated with the establishment of the system of party politics and an increased ideological polarisation that together raised fears of a further decrease in the extent of women's representation. In the run-up to the 1983 elections, *Arnat Peqatigiit Kattuffiat* therefore adopted a unified programme designed for a cross-party audience and directed to issues that were considered especially relevant to women. But this programme was not very popular with the voters. Consequently, a large part of the association's role as a political body was undermined, just as the new women's associations that were emerging during the 1970s and the 1980s indicated that both a generational change and an ideological shift were underway. Thus, *Kilut*, one of the first of women's organisations of the new generation, whose members were largely young, educated and politically conscious women, may be regarded as an opposite pole of attraction to the Association from the 1970s until the mid-1980s (Agerskov 1989:122 ff.; Thomsen 1991:128 ff.).

The fear of a decline in women's representation was, however, not entirely justified. There was some decline in the number of female councillors in the first elections after the introduction of self-government. However, two of the twenty-seven members elected to Parliament at the 1984 general election were women (representing 7.4 per cent of total seats), and in 1991 the number rose to four (equivalent to14.8 per cent of seats) (Appendix 1, Table 7.2). Following the 1991 elections, two of the seven posts in the Greenlandic government were also held by women. If statistics are used as an indicator of attitudes, then it appears that voter confidence in female candidates remained greater at the level of municipal elections. For example, at the 1991 elections, women won a record number of six out of the seventeen seats in the municipality of Nuuk. Moreover, several municipalities also have had female mayors (Thomsen 1991:157).

Of all the parties that currently contest elections, only *Inuit Ataqatigiit* has expressed a commitment to the goals of gender equality during recent decades. According to a party decision dating back to 1978, this commitment concerns both the responsibilities of women and men in the home and in society, and the question of equality of political representation. The party has made an effort to ensure that both women and men are represented within its bodies as well as externally, through the adoption of female candidates for both municipal elections and at the level of the government. Women have been active in *Siumut*, the largest Greenlandic party, since it was founded, and the party has appointed women to posts within the government, but for a long time the party's attitude towards gender equality was strictly theoretical. However, at the general election held in 1995, the number of seats won by *Siumut* women increased from one to four, compared with a change in total party representation in the Greenlandic parliament from eleven to twelve. As a result, the share of *Siumut* seats won by its female candidates rose from 9 per cent to 33.3 per cent, which is the largest female share of elected representatives of any party in the Greenlandic parliament by a wide margin. Prior to 1991, the other parties had yet to officially initiate active measures to promote numerical gender equality, even if individual women had been represented on some of their internal governing bodies (Thomsen 1991:153 f.; Appendix 1, Table 7.2).

The Institutionalisation of Gender Equality

Turning now to the institutionalisation of gender equality on Greenland, we find that it was not so long ago that the Danish concept of *"ligestilling"* (equivalent to the English term "equal status" or "equality") was used solely in the context of relations with Denmark. In fact, it is only since the end of the 1970s that the concept has also been applied to the relationship between the sexes. Despite this fact, Greenlandic women did cooperate in various ways with women and women's organisations from Denmark, the other Nordic countries and the Arctic regions before the introduction of self-government. In particular, cooperation with the Danish women's organisations is said to have been an important source of inspiration for *Arnat Peqatigiit Kattuffiat* during the 1960s and the 1970s. Furthermore, the association also had a representative on the Danish Equal Status Council (*Ligestillingsrådet*) during the period 1975–1988. By contrast, the introduction of self-government in 1979 implied that Greenlandic women became, to some degree, isolated from the outside world (Thomsen 1991:145 ff.).

At the beginning of the 1980s, *Arnat Peqatigiit Kattuffiat* took the lead in establishing a committee for gender equality. This initiative was formally supported by, amongst others, the Greenlandic employers' association (SIK) and the National Association of Municipalities (KANUKOKA). *Kilut* also supported the initiative, but it did not actively participate in the preparatory work. In 1985, broad, if rather passive, support for the establishment of the committee was forthcoming in the parliament. In 1986, the Committee for Gender Equality became a reality. The primary task of the Committee was to offer support and back up to enable women to achieve a broader engagement in politics. Since 1990, the Committee has also been working on a proposal designed to improve the conditions of families with children in areas such as municipal family guidance, childcare and parental leave opportunities for fathers. However, the Committee has largely been forced to promote these issues without the involvement of either the political establishment or the trade unions. As a result, no legislation on gender equality had been approved by 1996 (Thomsen 1991:150 ff.; Lund 1992).

The commonly held view that women and men enjoy equal rights and are equal in a legal sense as well as with respect to their work and educational attainment, may also contribute to the passive way in which gender equality has been promoted on Greenland (cf. the Faeroes and Åland). In practice, the extensive modernisation of Greenland during the 1960s has meant that the traditional social structures and division of labour have changed. However, such change has by no means resulted in the traditional division of labour being forgotten. Rather, modernisation has resulted in many women today being both in waged work and responsible for care of home and household. In many cases, women have even continued to take care of chores related to the hunting and fishing activities of their menfolk. Many of today's Greenlandic women have also been educated in different branches, but only a few have taken a higher academic degree (Equality in Denmark 1995:38).

Åland

Self-government on Åland

Once Russian tsardom began to waver, it appeared quite natural for the Swedish speaking Ålandic people, with their long traditions of self-government (although suppressed for much of the time), to lay claim to the basic principle of nationhood – the right of a people to self-determination. Voices were raised in support of secession from Finland and for union with Sweden. When Finland and Sweden failed to agree upon the status of Åland, the matter was finally decided by the League of Nations. In 1921, Åland was granted autonomous status within Finland and guarantees were given regarding the maintenance of the Swedish language, culture and customs on the islands, and in respect to their demilitarisation and neutrality. The Autonomy Act of Åland has been revised on two occasions since then, in 1951 and 1993. On both of these occasions, self-government has been further strengthened. Thus, in many areas today the province functions as an independent state with its own legislation and administrative apparatus. For example, Ålandic autonomy extends to the police and postal services, social and health care provision, transportation, culture, and the promotion of industry. Self-government does not, however, extend to matters relating to foreign policy, the judicial system, the customs service or monetary policy (Petersson 1995:27 f.; Internet 1998a).

The Ålandic legislative assembly, the *Lagting* (previously known as the *Landsting*) is made up of thirty members, who are elected once every four years. The *Lagting* appoints the *Landskapsstyrelse*, which is the executive body on Åland. Until 1987, the *Landskapsstyrelse* took the form of a "mandatory grand coalition" government, where all parties were represented in proportion to their share of seats in the *Lagting*. Today the *Landskapsstyrelse* is formed on the basis of government negotiations, either as a majority coalition or as a grand coalition including all parties. If neither a majority coalition government nor a grand coalition can be formed as a result of negotiations, the government is appointed according to the principle of proportionality that formed the basis of the old system. One Ålandic representative is also elected to the Finnish parliament. Furthermore, the local administration on Åland is divided into sixteen municipalities that are run by municipal councils, which are elected every four years (Petersson 1995:28 and 95).

The Party System

In general, one can say that while both the Faeroese and the Greenlandic party systems emerged in the wake of nationalist awakenings, the reverse seems to have been the case on the Åland Islands, where the introduction of self-government predated a developed party system by many decades. Indeed, the emergence of a fully-fledged party system on Åland did not take place until the 1970s. A possible explanation for this is that because Åland has always been a homogenous society, it has lacked the social, economic and regional conflicts that otherwise might have given rise to the formation of political parties (Nousiainen 1991:328). Moreover, there was less need for a party system to emerge in the same way as occurred on the Faeroes or Greenland, as the direct threat to Åland's identity was already removed by the attainment of self-government in 1921. The absence of political parties up until the 1970s (in the sense in which party-political activities are generally understood today) means, however, that politics on Åland, as on Greenland and certainly also on the Faeroe Islands, was for a long time very much centred around individual personalities (Steinby 1994:69; Högman 1994:131).

The oldest party currently contesting elections is the Social Democratic Party (*Ålands socialdemokrater*), which was founded in 1935 and has functioned in its present form since 1971. The party's main base of support is in the capital, Mariehamn. However, it has never gained as strong a position within Ålandic politics and society as its sister parties have achieved within the different Nordic countries. This relative weakness of the Ålandic Social Democrats is, perhaps, due to the fact that wage workers comprise a comparatively small proportion of the total workforce on Åland. Currently, the largest political party in the *Lagting* is the Ålandic Centre Party (*Åländsk center*). It receives its main support from the archipelago and countryside areas, while support for the second largest party, the Liberal Party *(Liberalerna på Åland)*, is distributed fairly evenly across Åland. The third largest party in the *Lagting* is the conservative party, *Frisinnad Samverkan* (Harriet Tuominen 1984:66 f.; Steinby 1994:68).

Women's Political Representation

Ålandic women achieved suffrage as early as 1906, simultaneously with women on the Finnish mainland, but until the 1980s they were almost completely invisible in politics. It is true that a woman was elected to the first *Landsting*, and that the Ålandic Martha Association (a housewives' association) has also supported female candidates since the municipal elections of 1954. However, at no point in time prior to 1983 did more than three women sit in the thirty-member *Landsting/Lagting*. The practice of voting directly for individual candidates on party lists has not resulted in a high degree of female representation within the Ålandic *Lagting*, any more than it has within the Faeroese *Løgting* (Dahlerup et al. 1985: 1989).

In the past, efforts have been made to stand candidates on women's lists during elections to the *Lagting*; in 1964 social democratic women put up a list of their own, and in 1979 the Liberal Party's women's group had a list of its own. Yet neither of these efforts met with success. At the 1987 elections, however, the share of *Lagting* seats accounted for by women increased markedly (to 26.7 per cent of the total, compared to 16.7 per cent in 1983 and never more than 10 per cent prior to 1983), following the election of eight women to that body. As a result, two female candidates were elected to the *Lagting* from each of the Liberal, the Social Democrat and the Conservative parties, while the two successful candidates representing the Green Party (*De Gröna*) at the assembly elections were both women. However, until 1995 the largest party in the *Lagting*, the Centre Party, did not have any female members in the assembly.[105]

However, a certain dualism between the political parties is discernible in respect of attitudes towards gender equality. In particular, the Liberals and the So-

---

105. In 1995, none of the Centre Party's female candidates were elected to the *Lagting*, but when the party joined the *Landskapsstyrelse* one woman entered the *Lagting* as the replacement for a male representative who had been elected to the *Landskapsstyrelse*.

cial Democrats, on the one hand, and the Centre Party and *Frisinnad Samverkan*, on the other hand, have generally defended somewhat different visions of society and women's roles within it. The former parties seek to promote structures that enable women to actively participate in the labour market and in public life. By contrast, the starting point for the latter parties, is individual free choice. This dualism has also been apparent among the female members of the parties (see, e.g., mass media reports of the Women's Parliament in Mariehamn, 1983).

The increase in women's representation in the *Lagting* in 1987, was unexpectedly reversed at the 1991 elections, when the share of women in the *Lagting* fell by half. Women won only four seats in the assembly (equivalent to 13.3 per cent of the total), which was the lowest figure since the 1970s. The decline is partly explained, however, by the fact that the Greens lost both of their seats at the election, and partly by the fact that the personal attributes of candidates still affect voting behaviour on Åland, despite the strong move towards a system of party politics in recent decades. Such a personal dimension to voting practice can have considerable political consequences, because small differences in the number of votes cast for individual candidates can result in large differences in the distribution of seats.

At the 1995 elections greater efforts were made, however, to improve the electoral performance of women. This led to a doubling of the proportion of candidates who were women at the 1995 elections compared with the elections held in 1991; all together ninety- three female candidates stood for election to the *Lagting* in 1995 compared with forty-seven in 1991. The number of female candidates standing in the 1995 elections corresponded to nearly 42 per cent of all candidates and represented the highest female share of candidates ever achieved on Åland. But despite high expectations the result did not go quite as anticipated; only seven women were elected to the *Lagting*. The number of votes cast for female candidates within all parties did, however, increase. In total, 32.9 per cent of the votes cast went to female candidates (cf. 20.8 per cent in 1991), although this is not fully reflected in women's share of candidates elected to the *Lagting* in 1995 (23.3 per cent) (ÅSUB 3/1995; Appendix 1, Table 7.3).

Interestingly, women's representation at the municipal level has always been higher than in elections to the *Lagting*. This is in contrast to the situation on the mainland, but rather similar to the experience on both the Faeroes and Greenland. For example, the proportion of seats on Åland's sixteen municipal councils held by women averaged 19 per cent in 1979, 20 per cent in 1983, and approximately 37 per cent subsequent to the 1995 elections. There has also been a trend for the rural areas with their traditionally lower levels of female representation on local councils to catch up with the towns. This is producing a rather equal geographical distribution of women across the municipalities, whether in villages, hamlets or the archipelago. Following the 1995 municipal elections, women constituted more than one quarter of the councillors in all but one municipality. Furthermore, the increase in the share of seats won by women at the 1995 municipal elections means that there is now a better correspondence between the proportion of women candidates standing in municipal elections (40.9 per cent in 1995) and the proportion of women councillors actually elected (36.7 per cent in 1995), than has been the case for the *Lagting* (Dahlerup 1989:120 f.; ÅSUB 3/1995).

The growth in the female share of candidates in both elections to the *Lagting* and at the municipal level in 1995 can certainly be regarded as a consequence of an ongoing process of change across the whole of Ålandic society. It is also probable that these results are indirectly connected to the introduction of quotas in the Act on Equality between Women and Men in 1995 (see below). The 1995 elections on Åland were the first to be held in Finland following the decision to introduce a minimum quota of at least 40 per cent for both sexes in state and municipal committees. It is feasible that the changes of the Act also indirectly affected the electoral result.

Furthermore, it is characteristic of Ålandic politics that participation in elections has been considerably lower than in the rest of the Nordic area (including Greenland and the Faeroes). This indicates a certain indifference towards elections and thereby a low level of trust in the importance of politics. In this, however, large differences are discernible between the urban and rural communities (cf. the Faeroe Islands). Mariehamn, for example, had the lowest participation rates for the elections to the *Lagting* in 1991 and 1995 of 58 per cent and 57 per cent respectively. By contrast, participation rates in respect of the archipelago population were on average 75 per cent and 72 per cent, respectively, for the same elections (Steinby 1994:69; ÅSUB 3/1995).

The Institutionalisation of Gender Equality

Compared to the situation on the Faeroe Islands and Greenland, the institutionalisation of gender equality was discussed at a relatively early stage on the Finnish self-governing province of Åland. In June 1977, all political parties were asked whether they would be prepared to submit a joint request to the *Landsskapsstyrelse* for it to take the initiative in setting up a committee for gender equality. According to the request, the foremost tasks for the committee were to be the investigation of the position of women on the labour market, in the educational sector, in associations and within political bodies. The majority of the responses from the various parties were favourable to the idea of a committee (see, Anhållan till Ålands Landskapsstyrelse, undated). The only directly negative response to the proposal at this time came from the Centre Party, which argued that it already sought to ensure that women and men enjoyed the same opportunities. In addition, it claimed that the appointment of a committee for gender equality would result in women being less equal and that those unsatisfactory states of affairs that the committee was supposed to investigate were already so well-known that further investigations were unnecessary (Åländsk center 1977).

In July 1978, a committee for gender equality was appointed consisting of five members, one from each of the parties represented in the *Landsting*, and in September the committee adopted a plan of action. The committee's terms of reference as set out by the *Landsskapsstyrelse* largely follow those laid down for the Council for Equality between Women and Men on the mainland (see, Jämställdhetskommittén 1979). Although, in principle, the *Landsskapsstyrelse* had been positive towards the founding of the committee, the committee was not always received sympathetically by the central authorities on Åland. For example, at the beginning of the 1980s it proposed an extensive programme to promote gender equality within the system of self-government (see, Jämställdhetskommittén 1980). However, the programme was not received quite as well as the committee had hoped for. The proposal was officially noted without any further action being taken by the authorities, and when the committee sought clarification on the matter, the response was that "gender equality prevails within the administration" (see, Ålands landssskapsstyrelse 1981, 1982; Svensson 1982).

In November 1981, a private member's bill was presented to establish a council for gender equality prescribed by law. The council was to be appointed by the *Landskapsstyrelse* every two years in line with the latter body's biannual periods of office. Administratively, the council was to be subordinated to the "Department of Government" (*kansliavdelningen*). A "Secretary for Gender Equality", answerable to the Department of Health and Social Affairs, was also to be employed. The bill was passed by the *Lagting* in June and came into force on 1 October 1982. The appointment of the council followed in January 1983, although no separate provision was made for it in the budget at the time. Since its establishment, however, the position of the Council for Gender Equality on Åland has strengthened considerably. Its enhanced status is manifested, for example, by the fact that a gender equality act has been adopted, that relatively extensive activities of different kinds are carried out, and that the Council currently also employs a full-time secretary for gender equality.

The provincial Act on the Application of the Law on Equality between Women and Men on Åland, which was formally adopted in March 1989, is based on Finnish gender equality legislation dating from 1986. The Act is specifically adapted to the workings of the Ålandic system of government. The biggest difference, however, between the Ålandic Act and the corresponding piece of legislation in Finland is that, following the Norwegian model, the Ålandic Act also takes up cases of alleged sex discrimination in advertising. The Act includes a paragraph that prohibits businesses on Åland from carrying advertisements that contain images of women or men of an insulting or a degrading nature (see, Landskapslag 27/89).

The March 1995 amendment to the Act on Equality between Women and Men implies that a minimum quota of 40 per cent for both sexes should be introduced in all municipal and state bodies, including civil service departments and institutions where the state or municipality has a majority holding. Only elected assemblies, such as the *Lagting* and municipal council assemblies, are exempted from this stipulation. According to the amendment to the Act, quotas should apply "if special reasons do not dictate otherwise". The amendment was not enforced on the mainland until after the municipal elections of October 1996, whereas the Ålandic authorities sought to apply the amendment on the islands as early as the municipal elections held during the autumn of 1995. In most municipalities the quota principle also means that the letter of the law is followed in the appointment of people to all new municipal bodies; only a few municipalities have deviated from the principle. In these latter municipalities this has mostly been justified on the grounds that "the population basis is insufficient" (Hufvud-stadsbladet 1996). It remains unclear, however, whether municipalities may use the small size of a population group as grounds to invoke the "special reasons" clause in the Act to legally set aside the quota principle. Even if they may do so, it is unclear how small such a population would need to be to qualify for an exemption.

The Importance of Self-government for Women's Political Representation

A comparative perspective on women's political representation on Greenland, the Faeroes and Åland, reveals a number of interesting parallels. Firstly, in all three island communities the entrance of women into the political arena has been relatively late. At the same time, women still account for a lower share of elected representatives in the legislative assemblies of the self-governing islands than they do in the different national parliaments within the Nordic area (with the exception of Iceland in relation to Åland, until recent elections). The first steps towards a more equal representation of women and men within the legislative assemblies of all three island communities occurred approximately at the same time. Since these initial steps were taken the proportion of assembly seats held by women increased, albeit at varying speeds and to varying degrees.

The low share of seats held by women in the legislative assemblies of the three island communities has often been explained in terms of two related factors. Firstly, it has been argued that the question of self-determination has not left any room for a struggle for gender equality. Secondly, it has been claimed that in respect to national identity and the struggle for self-government, women have chosen to emphasise their feelings of solidarity with their menfolk. But if we consider for a moment that the Åland islands achieved self-government as early as 1921, the Faeroe Islands in 1948 and Greenland only in 1979, this looks like an incomplete explanation, at least in the case of Åland. In addition, because throughout history Åland has had a unitary Swedish speaking population and administration, it has not experienced the same kind of lengthy struggle for linguistic and cultural identity that has marked Greenland and the Faeroe Islands.

However, there may be a possible link between the thesis that the struggle for autonomy has had important consequences for women's political representation and the assumption that the political parties have performed a "gender function", in the sense of playing a decisive role in mobilising women. In this context we have seen that, on the one hand, the national awakening and the struggle for independence, directly or indirectly, led to the establishment of political parties on both Greenland and the Faeroe Islands. Although these developments did not in themselves favour women's political representation. On the other hand, we may also assume that the late emergence of a process of "party-politicisation" on

Åland and Greenland inhibited political mobilisation in general, including women's mobilisation. If the formation of the political parties has had a decisive impact on women's political mobilisation and representation, the only plausible explanation for the approximately simultaneous entrance of women into the political arena in all three island communities is that the struggle for a "sense of self" did indeed favour the formation of parties at a time when national identity was under threat. But, at the same time, nationalist sentiments and the struggle for a "sense of self" have also explicitly hampered women's participation because of the impact of conflicts in the world around them. Thus it appears as if the tug-of-war over the question of self-government alone does not explain the delayed, but simultaneous, entry of these women into politics.

Furthermore, when it comes to women's representation at the local level, all three island communities have undergone a noticeable "reverse" development to that experienced in the rest of the Nordic area. In most cases, Nordic women first gained election to the legislative assemblies and then, somewhat later, to the "local" municipal councils. By contrast, women in the autonomous regions generally entered the local power structures first and thereafter, the legislative assemblies. Given the importance of self-government for the autonomous island communities, the supposed tendency of the nationalist struggle to hamper women's political mobilisation may have been weaker at the municipal level, where local issues have long constituted the primary sphere of interest for the interplay of politics, than at the provincial level. At the same time, the principal differences of political culture between the "small" island communities and the rest of the Nordic area basically seem to derive from the distinctive features of the person-orientated politics that has characterised these communities – and to a certain extent continues to do so.

The strength of the personal factor in politics on the islands may well have legitimised the entrance of individual women into the political arena. But, as such, this need not imply that there was a striving for, a demand for, or otherwise expectations concerning representation based on gender or even expectations linked to gender interests. That women have been less well represented in rural areas than in the more urbanised areas may be due to peasant and fishing communities – partly for practical reasons – being more closely tied to traditional roles and values than communities of town-dwellers. In turn, this has resulted both in a smaller number of women being active politically and in a reduced inclination on the part of electors in the countryside to vote for women. Naturally, this voting behaviour has been reflected at the level of the legislative assembly as well. In particular, it has been even more difficult to combine a political career with the traditional female role at the provincial level than at the municipal level because political work at the former level demands an engagement on a full-time basis. In addition, an indirect connection may be discerned in sparsely populated areas and the archipelago between the comparatively small share of elected representatives accounted for by women and the comparatively high voter turn-out in elections. This phenomenon is probably also affected by the greater presence of traditional views in the rural communities concerning duties and obligations in respect of both the private and the public spheres.

When it comes to local power structures, differences between the municipalities with respect to the proportion of elected representatives who are women have, to a large extent, been equalised in recent elections, especially on Åland. At the same time, the female share of elected representatives has also increased considerably on both Åland and the Faeroe Islands during recent years. If elections to legislative assemblies also follow the same trend that is evident in local elections, it is probable that the political representation of women in the autonomous island communities will slowly, but surely, approach the level found in the rest of the Nordic area.

The Growth of Gender Equality Institutions in a Comparative Perspective

It is apparent that in all three island communities the debate on gender equality and related institutional developments, such as the establishment of committees for gender equality and the introduction of legislation for the promotion of equality between the sexes, started later than in their respective "mother countries". On Åland and the Faeroe Islands, the idea of a committee for gender equality emerged during the latter half of the 1970s, whereas on Greenland it emerged some years later. However, the first committee for gender equality on Åland was appointed in 1978, while the decision to set up a similar committee on the Faeroe Islands was take two years earlier, in 1976. Yet it was not until 1986 that a committee for equal rights was up and running on the Faeroes. On Greenland, a committee for gender equality was appointed somewhat later than elsewhere, in 1986. But as the Greenlandic authorities only acquired the necessary competence to act on such matters through the introduction of the Home Rule Act in 1979, it is not surprising that this policy initiative did not take place earlier.

It is a characteristic feature of the debates on the institutionalisation of functions that promote gender equality on the three island communities that similar arguments have been put forward both with respect to a committee for gender equality and with respect to the introduction of legislation on gender equality. One feature common to these debates is that opposition to the committees and/or legislation was initially based upon the claim that action was unnecessary as women and men were already in principle treated equally. Gender equality was primarily seen as a question of whether or not women used the opportunities that were available to them. Furthermore, it was suggested that committees for gender equality and/or the adoption of laws on gender equality would actually undermine gender equality – leaving women less equal in practice. In addition, the debates have also in certain respects followed religious lines of reasoning, with the emphasis placed upon the role of women in the family. This was especially important in the Faeroese debate on the introduction of gender equality law. Another question – where Greenland differs from the Faeroes and Åland – concerns the debate as to whether gender equality has also been strongly influenced by the relationship of the population of Greenland to Danish and Western culture. For a long time the concept of equality was mainly invoked in the context of Greenland's relationship to Denmark, while feminism came to be associated with the "Western" influences that the struggle for national identity was pitted against.

A further feature common to the gender equality committees in the respective autonomous territories has been that they were initially forced to work under rather unfavourable conditions. They lacked financial resources and political support, and they faced a certain amount of political opposition. On Åland, the political opposition seems to have been more moderate and less prolonged than on the Faeroe Islands and Greenland. Amongst other things, this is reflected in the fact that when Åland adopted its gender equality Act in line with the Finnish model in 1989, the Act also contained a paragraph prohibiting sex discrimination in advertising, which was not included in the Finnish Act. Åland also assumed a pioneering role within Finland in respect of the implementation of the new gender quotas included in the amended Act on Equality between Women and Men because of differences in election timetables for municipal elections.

It also looks as if the role of the Ålandic Council for Gender Equality was more strongly institutionalised in respect of other issues than similar bodies on the Faeroes and Greenland. This is reflected, amongst other things, in the Ålandic Council being the only gender equality institution on the autonomous islands to have permanently employed staff. Greenland, by contrast, has yet to adopt legislation on gender equality – whereas the Faeroese law was only adopted in 1994. However, as a consequence of this legislation, activities to promote gender equality on the Faeroes gained judicial legitimacy and increasing numbers of women are being appointed to high level political posts. Taken together, these developments suggest that Faeroese society will also change and that gender equality will become ever more politically and institutionally anchored.

Given that institutionalised gender equality has undergone a degree of change proportionate to women's rising share of seats in the legislative assemblies of the three island communities, it is tempting to conclude that gender equality as an ideology is starting to take root, especially on Åland and the Faeroes. At the same time, one may assume that a diffusion of ideas and an interaction between the various societies has also taken place. As a result, the level of female representation, the degree of institutionalisation of gender equality issues, and the prevailing attitudes and values in society have developed symbiotically: prevailing attitudes influence the degree of female representation, which in turn plays a decisive role in the integration of gender equality issues into the public sphere. Such an institutionalisation will, in turn, have an impact on both the anchoring of attitudes in society and the opportunities open to women. At the same time, the extent of women's share of elected representatives not only affects how gender equality is institutionalised, but it also influences the formation of attitudes in society.

Conclusions

Equal democracies? Conclusions and perspectives

Anette Borchorst, Ann-Dorte Christensen, and Nina Raaum

In this book we have considered two fundamental questions. Firstly, how is gender equality manifested in terms of policies, institutions, and political participation? Secondly, are the differences between the Nordic countries so large that they represent a challenge to the notion of a homogeneous Nordic gender model? The book *Unfinished Democracy*, which presented the first large study of women in Nordic politics, found in 1983 that politics was still a man's world, and that, with only a few exceptions, the percentage of women sinks the higher one gets in the hierarchy of power (Haavio-Manila *et al.* 1983:241). It was this fact which provided the inspiration for the book's title. During the fifteen years that have passed since its publication, gender equality has become more widespread. This development was depicted in a subsequent book, *Women in Nordic Politics – Closing the Gap*, which addressed the political participation and attitudes of women, but, as with *Unfinished Democracy*, it was mainly concerned with the features that were common across the Nordic region (Karvonen and Selle 1995).

The title of the present book, *Equal Democracies?*, refers to our two overriding questions: How equal are women and men in the Nordic countries and how homogeneous are the Nordic countries? The question mark in the title thus relates to both of these issues. There is still a great deal that needs to be done before we can say that men and women can influence societal decisions on an equal basis. It may be the case that, in some areas, equality between the sexes has steadily improved while in others it has stagnated or even deteriorated. We ask whether we legitimately can speak of a homogeneous model for all the five countries.

From an outsider's point of view, it seems as if Nordic women improved their status and gained power in a number of areas earlier than women in many other countries, not least due to government initiatives. This empowerment was one of the things highlighted by Helga Hernes in her conclusions regarding the woman-friendly potential of the Scandinavian welfare states (1987). In doing so, she and other feminist scholars thereby broke with the new women's movement's relatively negative perception of the state. The large number of ensuing studies also broke with the movement's earlier reluctance to concern itself with the state. In an international context, Scandinavian women's studies played a part in challenging feminist theories about the state as a tool for oppressing women. Equally importantly they increased awareness about the differences between welfare states dominated by a liberal, conservative or social democratic ideologies, respectively (Borchorst 1998a). Scandinavian feminist scholars also created the term "state feminism". The term was supposed to imply that a woman-friendly potential on the part of the state had become manifest from an interplay between a broad mobilization of women "from below" and political decision-making "from above" (Hernes 1987; Siim 1988).

However, not all feminist scholars shared this positive portrayal of Scandinavia and the Nordics which Hernes in particular promoted. Recent research has reflected a contradiction – but also a dialogue – between those who view the effects of the welfare state on divisions of labour between men and women and women's opportunities to influence politics in an optimistic light, and those who are more pessimistically inclined. This controversy has been especially strong in Norway and Sweden. The debate on the Nordic welfare states' equality model is not over; indeed, this book may be seen as a contribution to it. We believe that the terms of reference and concepts in this discussion are in need of further elaboration and clarification. We also have to be clear about which elements to compare with which when we try to determine whether there are grounds for optimism or pessimism. Should we compare women's contemporary situation with that of the past? Should we examine differences between men and women today? Should we be concerned whether the circumstances of certain groups of women have improved more than they have for others? Or should we compare conditions in the Nordic region with those in countries elsewhere? In addition to this we have to decide whether to study overall factors which affect political gender relations, or limit ourselves to specific aspects of policy. It is likely that there will be less disagreement between interpretations if the discussion is related to specific areas, and takes account of uncertainties and the fact that historic developments in the Nordic countries have not happened simultaneously.

So is it possible to find the contours of a specifically Nordic gender model? Well, as far as women's representation in the various parliaments is concerned, we believe that it is. With the exception of Iceland, such a model has existed for some considerable time making the Nordic countries world leaders in the area. The same is true of women's participation in paid work within the OECD countries. There is certain amount of synergy between these phenomena, though we need to be careful about postulating a clear connection between them. However we have not concentrated on these particular factors in this book. Here, we have focused on women as political actors and on mobilisation "from below", and the effect of woman-friendly politics "from above", in the form of policies and political institutions. We should also point out that our empirical analyses are restricted to selected aspects of political life: the political mobilisation of women primarily concentrates on women's integration into the parliamentary system and political participation and less on political attitudes. The analyses of the political institutions concerns the institutions of gender equality, and (b) the analyses of the decision-making processes concentrate on childcare and gender equality.

Until now there has been a tendency to exaggerate features common to the Nordic countries, and to make generalisations about the whole region based on only one or two of the Scandinavian countries. Two examples of this tendency are (a) the generalised statements regarding the expansion of collective childcare which are based on observations from Denmark and Sweden, and (b) observations about the very high number of women in the governments which are based on the situation in Norway, Sweden and Finland. We have tried to modify the common assumption that men's and women's status is uniform throughout the Nordic countries. This we have done by analysing similarities and differences between the countries. We have found many palpable differences between the countries, and they become more and more distinct the deeper one probes, the more one differentiates between developments and the longer the period of time covered by the study. We must, however, point out that our analyses and conclusions not are based upon a systematic comparative study of all five countries in all fields. This is mainly due to the fact that it in several areas it has been impossible to obtain data from all of the countries. Below, we first summarise the results of the different parts of the book, then we outline the five countries' gender profiles, and finally we raise some perspectives for future research.

Mobilising Nordic women

The first part of the book addressed women's political mobilisation. Our analysis of this mobilisation in relation to *general processes of democratisation* in the Nordics over the last hundred years (Chapter 2) has revealed a large measure of correspondence in terms of women's overcoming of the four institutional thresholds in parliamentary politics, i.e., legitimisation, incorporation, representation, and executive power, with the exceptions of Iceland and the self-governing islands (Åland, the Faeroe Islands and Greenland). A shared characteristic of the Nordic countries – again with the exception of Iceland, where the electoral system contributes to hindering the integration of women – is that women are relatively well represented in their respective parliaments. Looking forward from the incipient struggles for democratisation and universal suffrage at the end of the last century, we see that the mobilisation of women in the individual countries has followed quite different paths. These variations are related to the state and nation-building processes specific to each country. It is thus interesting that in all Nordic countries, although less evident in Iceland, there was a high degree of correlation between the first party formations, which primarily involved men, and the establishment of the first women's rights and suffragette organisations. Just as among male farmers and workers, the strong national independence movements in Norway, and especially Finland, contributed to speed up the introduction of the right of women to vote. Another common feature is that women had to wait until the 1970s to make a breakthrough into parliamentary politics. Through the entire period up to the present, however, the mobilisation of women has proceeded at different rates in five countries. Norway and Iceland in particular have had a tendency to lag behind the other countries. Norwegian women have caught up with the others through their very extensive mobilisation between 1970 and 1985, but in Iceland women are still relatively weakly represented.

The other historical point of focus has been the progress of women's mobilisation over the past thirty years. Here, *national surveys on citizenship in Denmark, Norway and Sweden* (Chapter 3) reveal a common characteristic, namely the high level of similarity of women's and men's political participation. Prior to 1970 the situation was marked by great differences between the sexes, but by about 1990 these were in the process of very nearly disappearing. This description is most accurate of the situation in Norway, less so of Denmark and least of all of Sweden. In parallel with the increase in female political participation in Denmark, Norway and Sweden, has been a significant change in the traditional differences in attitudes between the sexes. The tendency to move towards the left among women and towards the right among men is especially striking in the younger generation, but it is too soon to say whether or how such a pronounced "gender gap" will characterise the younger generation in the future. Added to this picture is the fact that many more women than men in Denmark, Norway, and Sweden say that they are sceptical of the EU and the ongoing process of European integration.

The analysis of the *political parties* (Chapter 4) has shown that there are notable differences between Denmark, Finland, Norway and Sweden in terms of the parties' efforts to recruit women and increase female representation. We have depicted the traditional strategies to integrate women in relation to whether or not historically there has been a tradition for independent women's sections in the political parties. We have analysed modern strategies of female integration on the basis of the parties' gender quotas. Both parameters exhibit large variations between the countries. Denmark and Iceland differentiate themselves clearly as the countries in which political parties have the weakest integration strategies for women. Sweden and Finland are probably the countries in which the women's sections historically have made the strongest impact, while Norway, undoubtedly, is the Nordic country in which political parties during recent years have developed the most efficient modern integration strategy for women through the use of quotas. The analysis also shows that developments in political parties over the last twenty years are affected by the extent to which the parties have succeeded in attracting and incorporating the potential represented by politically active women. In Denmark it appears as if the membership crisis in the political parties has been accelerated and reinforced by the low level of women's support of the political parties. In Norway, on the other hand, the crisis has been allayed – or at the very least postponed – by the integration of women into the political parties in that country.

The *Icelandic Women's Alliance* (Chapter 5) presents an interesting example of a mixture between a political party and a movement. The mobilisation around the Alliance contributed to notable progress in the parliamentary representation of women, not only in the form of seats which the Alliance itself obtained, but also because other political parties have felt compelled to recruit more women. The women's movement in Iceland was very active through the 1970s and was radically feminist. The new women's movement on Iceland is unique however in that it engaged directly with the formal political system, which in the end led to the formation of the Women's Alliance. The Icelandic experience shows that the non-hierarchical structure typical of grass-roots movements is hard to combine with political influence, and the ambivalent policy of the Women's Alliance to leadership and structure has been a contributory factor to its declining popularity among voters.

The new social movements (Chapter 6) were a central arena for the mobilisation of new groups of women in the 1960s and 1970s throughout the Nordic countries. Grass-roots participation in the Nordic countries has been more of a supplement than a competing factor to reckon with in relation to other channels through which women have been mobilised. That is to say, that, in the Nordic countries (except for Finland), there has been a strong correlation between mobilisation on the basis of social movements and other forms of political participation. This basic form of interaction between forces "from below" and those "from above" has been a consistent characteristic in developments in all of the countries, but the way in which it has taken place has varied in the different nations and this in turn has created differences in the way in which women have been mobilised. Participation in the new social movements therefore reflects intrinsic political cultures and traditions of social movements in the nations, in which – despite striking similarities in, for example, the phases of development of the new women's movement – clear differences are also to be found, such as in the movements' relations to the formal political system. In Norway and Iceland in particular, the new women's movements have advocated the integration of women into party politics, something that feminists in Denmark and Sweden have condemned. Apart from mobilising new groups for political participation, the movements have influenced policy-making by placing subjects like abortion, sexualised violence, gender equality, the environment, and peace on the political agenda.

Seen from an overall vantage point, it appears that Denmark and Finland represent opposite ends of the scale in terms of the mobilisation models of Nordic women. While the mobilisation of women in Denmark has been strongly oriented towards the social movement model, Finland, and to a more limited extent, Sweden and Norway, have availed themselves of the most party-oriented model. Iceland stands out by its combined grass-roots and party-oriented model. There are indications that Iceland is in the process of moving towards a predominantly party-oriented mobilisation model.

Childcare in the Nordic welfare states

In the second part of the book we focused on policy content. Here we chose to study specific political decisions of vital importance to the combination of work and family life, namely: *rights in relation to childcare and parental leave*. Our comparison of the current situation in the five countries (Chapter 7) has shown that while there are slight differences from country to country, the general tendency is convergence towards greater parental equality with regards to rights. In all five countries, fathers now have the right to take two weeks leave following the birth of a child, and they have also the right to share part of the total parental leave with the mother. Norway, Sweden, and Denmark have introduced in addition a system in which a portion of the total parental leave is reserved for the father. Thus the Nordic countries have abandoned a male-breadwinning model, in favour of a more individually oriented model in which both men and women alternate much more between earning an income and caring for children. The opportunities for combining work with active parental duties are thus improved. Even though many men do avail themselves of their rights, we can not say that parenthood has become egalitarian because the proportion of the total permitted parental leave taken out by fathers is still very low.

With respect to the issue of childcare, we have differentiated between collective provisions in the form of public childcare provisions, and individual arrangements in the form of government assistance to parents who take care of their own children. With regard to the collective solutions it is possible to identify three different models: least is on offer in Iceland and Norway while Denmark and Sweden have the most comprehensive provisions. Finland's model encompasses both collective and individual initiatives. Sweden, Denmark, and Finland have predominantly established full-time childcare facilities, while Iceland and Norway tend to favour part-time childcare. In all Nordic countries the public contribution to childcare has continued to expand, even during periods of economic stagnation and decline. The trends in these countries have converged since Norway expanded its public childcare facilities, and more full-time places became available. It would appear that a similar process is also occurring in Iceland.

We have examined the role played by women in the *parliamentary debates on childcare policy* in Sweden, Finland and Iceland (Chapter 8). A common feature in the three countries across the whole political spectrum is the low level of consensus as to which solutions should be chosen for childcare. Non-socialist parties tend to prefer support to individual parents, while the social democratic and left-wing parties tend to favour the collective approach. In all three countries proposals in favour of the allocation of benefits to individual parents who take care of their own children have led to heated discussions which echo considerable disagreement between female politicians on this issue. Women from the non-socialist parties support a greater freedom of choice between the collective and individual approaches. Women from the left-wing parties regard such proposals as undermining gender equality and supporting a traditional gendered division of labour.

In all three countries women have figured strongly in the debates on childcare. In Sweden, the discussions on the role of the father have been much more public than in Finland and Iceland. In Finland for many years there have been exchanges between supporters of individual and collective childcare. In Iceland, resistance to policies which undermine the male-provider model has been particularly strong, and Icelandic legislation on maternity leave also gives fewer incentives for fathers to involve themselves in childcare.

Institutionalised equality

In the third part of the book we considered equal opportunity policies, as defined by legislation and initiatives connected with official equality institutions (Chapter 9). Since the 1970s, differences in the organisation of the *gender equality institutions* in the Nordic countries (Chapter 10) have grown. Sweden and Norway have accorded greatest weight to institutionalisation, and it is here that its development has progressed furthest. Denmark has accorded least weight to institutionalisation while Finland and Iceland fall within these extremes. The differences are exhibited in the number of gender equality institutions, their jurisdictions, and their available resources. Equality is deeply rooted at the governmental level and in the state administration in Sweden and Norway, but has the lowest prestige in Denmark, where the gender equality policy agenda is also more restricted than in the other Nordic countries. Participants in the institutions of gender equality in the five countries are generally similar, in the sense that the organisations representing the employers and workers in the public sector have key positions. Politicians have played a more important part in Finland than in the other countries, and the women's organisations have played the most important role in Denmark.

As an explanation of the national variations that we have found in the weight and impact of gender equality policies we have shown that Swedish and Norwegian political parties tend to profile themselves far more on gender equality than the Danish parties. In Finland women have formed alliances across party lines on central gender issues, while in Iceland, the presence of the Women's Alliance contributed to stirring the interest of other political parties in matters related to gender equality. We have also found that the continued existence of women's sections in some of the political parties remains an essential factor behind the institutionalisation of equal opportunities in Sweden, Norway, Finland and Iceland. In Denmark the lack of women's sections in the political parties is a crucial factor, as is the lack of an active women's rights movement which once was a driving force in the radicalisation of equal opportunity projects. In Norway and Sweden, equal opportunity work is supported by a far wider research and evaluational efforts than in the other three countries. In a broader sense, we have argued that differences in political culture, e.g. in the will to regulate by means of legislation and institutionalisation, are also of some significance.

Our study of *gender equality law* (Chapter 11) has shown that, although the same issues are more or less common to all Nordic countries, there are differences both in the number of laws and the points in time at which they were adopted and put into force. We have found that legislation is most extensive in Norway and Sweden, where the number of conflicts during the legislative processes also was greatest. In Sweden the People's Party was unique as a non-socialist party in its willingness to push the gender equality issue to the forefront, while the Social Democratic Party was similarly unique among its Nordic sister parties in its initial blanket opposition to legislative measures. In Denmark a culture of consensus has persisted in which the goal has been the attainment of cross-party agreement. This has probably hindered the extension of its equality legislation. In all countries, the social partners have been very sceptical towards such legislation. This is especially true of the employers. In fact this was the reason why the Finnish legislation did not come into place until 1986, some ten to thirteen years after the first equality laws in Iceland and Denmark.

Another factor that we have found to be of some significance is that gender equality is a relatively new policy field large areas of which overlap with the much older and entrenched labour market policy which is characterised by strong management and worker interests. Thus, the unions and employers, which are central actors in the configuration of labour market policy, have also been instrumental in shaping gender equality policies. The implementation of gender equality policy has generally depended very significantly on the persons who carry it out not only because its vague formulations have given room for wide interpretation, but because its scope and range have expanded over time. This has been especially the case in Norway and Sweden, whose enforcement of the legislation is also the most efficient.

The *gender equality efforts at the level of local authorities* (Chapter 12) has had hardly any or no impact at all in the five countries' legislation on local government; nor has it made any detectable difference to the autonomy of local authorities either. We have seen, however, a tightening of the legislation and a stricter control of their implementation in all countries. In most countries responsibility for supervising gender equality measures is located in the national gender equality councils. Their mandates are directed primarily towards personnel management policy in the local government authorities and towards increasing women's political representation. Another feature is that efforts have been focused on local equal status working committees. The number of the agencies varies greatly in the individual countries.

We have examined the work situation of the femocrats in the Norwegian county administrations, a situation characterised by different forms of marginalisation, political, administrative and sexual. This in turn has created conflicts of loyalty. Conflicts connected with political loyalty arise among other things from discrepancies between the goals of the local county councils and more women-oriented political priorities. Conflicts at the administrative level arise from the fact that the femocrats are at one and the same time part of the machinery of the county authority – which is generally managed in a hierarchical "top-down" mode – and working with women-oriented projects – which are often organised in a "bottom-up" manner. The gender-based conflicts arise from the fact that equality femocrats, who are all female, are obliged to remain loyal to their bosses, who are generally male.

    · A Swedish study of male leadership resistance to gender equality initiatives in three municipalities showed that resistance takes both passive and active forms. Passive resistance, which is the most common form of resistance, takes place when men in positions of leadership meet gender equality initiatives with silence or sham-action. Active resistance takes place when they meet these initiatives with counter-arguments as to their capacity to bring about change and when men in leadership positions use different methods to undermine the possibilities for gender equality reforms to lead to change. The ambivalence of men in leadership positions towards gender equality efforts is quite discernible in this study, since they all claim – despite their different forms of resistance – that they are in favour of equality between women and men.

    We have discussed gender equality as it appeared both as a term and as an ideology in the *debate on women's status in the armed forces in Finland* (Chapter 13). This study analysed a case which was extreme in several ways. Firstly because the military is an extremely male-dominated institution and secondly because women were not allowed to enlist for military service in Finland until some time after this had become common throughout the rest of the Nordic region. The controversy was exceptionally heated in Finland. We have compared material from two debates which took place in 1984 and 1994–95. In our analyses we distinguished between ideologies of difference and sameness according to whether the argumentation took the male or the female as the basic point of reference. In addition we outlined a deconstructivist approach to the debate from a gender perspective. The arguments in the debate tended to be based on either a philosophy of difference or of sameness. In 1984, both the supporters and the opponents of the recruitment of women based their arguments mainly on gender differences, but incorporated them in different ways. In 1994–95, both factions approached the debate from the point of view of the principle of sameness. The Finnish military changed its ideological approach to gender and equality between the 1984 debate and the 1994–95 debate. The question to be answered now is whether it is realistic to expect a change in an institution as patriarchal as the that of the military or whether the integration of women will take place on men's premises. According to a pessimistic interpretation, the aim of the Finnish military establishment is to adapt women to the military without making any efforts to change the institution in a more women-friendly direction. According to the more optimistic point of view, however, the changes that have occurred within the Finnish military may reflect a genuine willingness on the part of the institution to transform itself.

Women on the self-governing islands

The analyses of *women's representation and equality policies on the self-gov-erning islands of the Faeroes, Greenland and Åland* (Chapter14) have taken account of the special characteristics of these islands in relation to the rest of the Nordic countries. Each has its individual characteristics and differences, but they share common features in their isolation, their position by the sea, and relatively hard living conditions. Compared with their mother countries, women have been integrated much later into the political system, and women's representation within the political systems on the islands has also been at a lower level than on the mainland. The establishment of bodies to supervise gender equality took place much later too. These factors suggest a correlation between women's representation and the institutionalisation of gender equality. In contrast to the situation in the mother countries, the women on these islands have gained a foothold in local politics before attaining it in central government.

It is important to consider whether one can explain the lower level of gender equality on the islands on the basis that the islands' struggles to achieve political independence have resulted in women's issues assuming a lower priority. We have been able to only partly confirm this, as regions like Åland, which became autonomous relatively early, do not have substantially higher women's representation than the other islands. On the other hand, it would appear that the bodies set up to further gender equality are stronger on Åland than on the Faeroe Islands and Greenland, where legislation also has been adopted rather late.

Five different gender profiles

The conclusions we have drawn in the successive sections of the book with regard to similarities and differences show that the impression of inter-country variations depends on the perspective from which they are considered. Rather than a single monolithic Nordic gender profile, we have identified the existence of five different profiles that need to be perceived in relation to the special characteristics of each country. Here, we will characterise the five country models across the dimensions we have utilised in the book.

The *Swedish gender profile* comes high in our rankings on all the parameters. In welfare and childcare policy a great expansion has taken place from the 1960s, and Sweden has been at the forefront when it comes to the length of parental leave and rights for fathers. The high level of institutionalisation by means of legislative developments and government policies has left its mark on concerns related to women and gender. The level of women's representation in Sweden has been among the highest of the Nordic countries. This is an outcome, we believe of the interaction between women's social and political citizenship, the institutionalisation of women's issues through the women's sections in the political parties, and integration of women into the labour market. These developments have been supported by long periods of social democratic government and the high profiling of women's and gender equality issues in the political parties, not least the non-socialist parties, a phenomenon which was quite unique in the Nordic region. Competition between parties to profile themselves in the area of gender equality has helped to keep these issues high on the political agenda.

The *Danish gender profile* has also been characterised by a great expansion of the welfare state, in particular publicly funded childcare. In comparison with the rest of Scandinavia, until recently, Danish women have had relatively low levels of political representation, there have been fewer women in government, and the institutionalisation of gender equality has not progressed as far. The Danish gender profile is the most "bottom-up" of all the countries. Women's concerns and gender issues were formulated and articulated by the social movements, and women's organisations have occupied key positions in gender equality bodies. On the other hand, concerns related to gender equality have been generally absent from the policies of political parties, and the issue is also granted a low priority today, as no active women's movements presently exist. It is our belief that developments in Denmark should be understood against a combination of a relatively high liberal component together with a relatively undogmatic left wing, which has opposed too much steering "from above". Danish political culture is characterised by a strong orientation towards consensus which has tended to prevent a radicalisation of gender equality policies. This factor is important in explaining why controversial matters such as sexual violence, sexual harassment, etc. have been absent from the political agenda.

The *Norwegian gender profile*, like that of Sweden, is built upon a high level of institutionalisation of gender equality. The issue has figured on the political programmes of successive governments. The integration of women into politics and the workforce has taken place later in Norway than in Denmark and Sweden, but it has been accomplished much faster. In contrast to Denmark and Sweden, however, Norway has lagged far behind in expanding its childcare provisions. There is a trend towards convergence of opinion in this area. In the past decades, political parties have developed the most effective and compulsory strategies to integrate women of all the Nordic countries and gender equality in general constitutes a fundamental element of government and party policies. Another characteristic of the Norwegian gender profile is that the ideology of difference has had a much firmer foothold than in Finland, Sweden, and Denmark, a fact which should be probably understood in terms of a carry-over from a period in Norway during which women's place was generally considered to be the home. The Norwegian example shows that, under favourable political conditions, an ideology of difference can also be conducive to the advance of equality between the sexes.

The *Finnish gender profile* differs from that of the Scandinavian countries in that the number of women in the workforce and their political representation began to rise as early as in the fifties. On the other hand, developments in the labour market were less prominent than in Denmark and Sweden, taking place without a comprehensive expansion of the welfare state's childcare programme. Although public childcare facilities have subsequently increased, policies designed to support childcare in the home on an individual basis have been more central in developments in Finland than the other countries. Political parties play a relatively dominant role in Finnish political culture. Thus, this has allowed for a much more open parliamentary discussion of conflicts which follow gender lines. Finnish women were primarily mobilised through the political parties, and while politicians are central players in gender equality bodies, social movements have played a relatively minor role. Finland was the final country to pass gender equality legislation, primarily because of resistance from employers, and because the workers' and employers' organisations have fewer key positions on gender equality bodies than in the Scandinavian countries.

The *Icelandic gender profile* diverges from that in the other four countries due to its relatively low level of female political representation, and because women's social citizenship in Iceland has not been as broad as in the rest of the Nordic countries. Icelandic society has been characterised by a strong male-breadwinner model. Childcare facilities have been expanded much later, and still remain at a lower level than in Denmark and Sweden in particular. In addition to this, such expansion as has occurred has been mainly in the form of part-time childcare facilities. Iceland was also the final country to introduce parental leave rights for fathers. The Icelandic mobilisation of women takes place predominantly through the parties, and the parties have held the banner of women's and gender issues relatively high. This is thanks not least to the Women's Alliance, the existence of which has obliged the other parties to address these issues and to make policy recommendations. The Alliance's concern with women in politics has also contributed to other parties nominating more female candidates.

Given these national gender profiles, there is no single factor which we can indicate as either facilitating or constraining the development of equal democracies. It is evident that processes of institutionalisation, as they were initiated "from above" combined with the mobilisation of women "from below", have represented important factors in the promotion of gender equality. All of the models just discussed derive from the interplay between these factors, and also reflect different opportunity structures. This is why the models are linked to specific structural, cultural and, not least, political circumstances in the individual countries. The conclusions in this book stress that female mobilisation, the childcare policies, and gender equality policies, not only play a key role in terms of gender relations, but also for the general development of the Nordic welfare states, among other ways by positively influencing the development of political institutions. It would therefore be misleading to conclude that addressing women's rights and gender issues has only taken place in empty, shrinking, or actorless institutions; it is rather the case that women represent a potential political force which has an impact on the strength and efficacy of the political institutions.

As in many other countries, the historical empowerment of women's citizenship in the Nordic countries has been characterized by the attainment of social rights before political rights. This is contrary to the history of the introduction of full rights for male citizens, in which political rights preceded social rights. At a high level of generalisation this conjecture about gender differences in citizenship is no doubt correct. But if we view women's citizenship in the Nordic countries in a more refined way, differences emerge which complicate the picture of a homogeneous pattern of women's place in the citizenries of the Nordic countries. In Norway, for example, we may ask whether women's social participation has been weaker than in the rest of Scandinavia, and whether they have trailed behind in this area compared to their relatively strong integration into parliamentary politics.

It would appear that the classic tension between an ideology of difference and one of similarity is still a key element in defining the significance of gender and in understanding national differences in the Nordic gender profiles. Over the past decades this tension between difference and similarity has characterised the debate about gender quotas in relation to women's political representation and the workplace. The variations which can be found in the Nordic countries with respect to the impact of the difference and similarity approaches on the equality debate must be seen in connection with the significance and impact of religion. The relatively greater weight attached to the difference perspective in Norway can be seen, for instance, in relation to the key role played by religion in that country. In Denmark and Sweden, two of the most secularised societies in the world, the ideology of equality has prevailed to a far greater extent. This is, however, a matter which we have not considered here, and one which has received scant attention in Nordic women's and gender research literature in general.

The development towards more gender-equal democracies in the 1990s requires that equality and gender issues remain on the political agendas and in the public debate. In circumstances in which women's mobilisation "from below" is attenuated it appears that that the maintenance of a certain degree of institutionalisation of gender politics and associated conflicts will ensure that the debate does not die out. It remains to be seen if the politics of women's concerns and gender equality have lost much of their radical thrust and broad impact simply because outside pressure has lost much of its potency.

Perspectives and challenges for further research

The conclusions in this book present the opportunity to consider recommendations for further research, both in terms of perspectives and areas in need of more investigation. The national gender profiles and the individual features of the five countries highlight the need to combine structural approaches with approaches based on actors. We believe that politics is a very important factor, and that the interplay between actors on the political stage and the political institutions cannot be understood merely in terms of the impact of social structures on the labour market or the family. Rather than assigning a deterministic role to structural factors, they should rather be seen in an historical and contextual interplay with political actors and institutions.

In our opinion, caution should be exercised in contrasting optimistic and pessimistic viewpoints too sharply. The various viewpoints have tended to have a synergetic effect and have contributed constructively to more heterogeneous and stimulating research in the area of women's studies in the Nordic countries. It is also necessary to resist the tendency to over-generalize the features common to the Nordic countries. There is a need instead to construct dynamic analytical models, which can incorporate factors associated with the interplay between "from above" and "from below" in addition to the structural and actor-oriented approach. This renders superfluous the issue as to whether we should take the institutionalised political system (e.g. the integration of women into the political élite) or the non-institutionalised (e.g., women's autonomous organisations) as our point of departure. The goal must be to combine different levels and to focus much more on processes, through, for example, analysing concrete mobilisation and decision-making processes in relation to gender. It is therefore not appropriate to hold onto ambitions to construct unitary theories and uniform explanations about gender and politics in the Nordic countries. As far as we can see, there is not "one great narrative" to be told about the Nordic gender model, but rather an extremely variegated patchwork of similarities and differences in the Nordic profiles.

There is much to indicate that developments over the past thirty years have increased the differences between women, both socially and politically. In women's and gender studies (and in this book as well) there has been a tendency to treat women as a uniform entity, and to say "women" when talking about "gender". This has resulted on occasion in the production of essentialist explanations and a tendency to avoid addressing key differences between women, which applies to a certain degree to this volume too. At the same time there is a paucity of research on men, including the effects welfare state developments, gender equality policies, and the political mobilisation of women have had on men's social and political participation, as well as on the emergence of differences between men as a group.

The research literature on the impact of European integration on gender relations is also very limited. A central issue is whether EU regulations will widen the differences in the Nordic countries' gender equality and welfare policies. Another relates to the extent to which the shift in the focus of power from the national parliaments to the institutions of the EU will lead to a worsening of women's political citizenship. These factors have often been identified as contributing to the greater scepticism with which women view increased integration with the EU. However, this has not been subject to systematic research. We have argued that the heterogeneity in the Nordic gender profiles is of interest to an understanding of the subject. However, it is also our opinion that, in a wider comparative perspective, the common factors will continue to generate interest in the political arena and in academia. Comparative Nordic studies on the effects of the relatively high level of female political representation are of obvious importance.

In some areas, such as the interaction between social and political citizenship and between working and family life, developments in the Nordic countries preceded developments in the rest of the West. The Nordic region could hardly serve as a model in the sense that other countries with entirely different political cultures and social conditions might elect to emulate developments in the Nordic countries, or even desire to do so. But gathering both the positive and negative features in one place may none the less contribute to the development of more sensitive strategies for achieving a greater degree of equality in democratic countries. In the nineties, all of the Nordic welfare states have responded to demands for restructuring and renewal, the consequences of which for the balance between the sexes are only partially studied in the five countries.

Appendices

Appendix I

Women in the Nordic countries – a statistical overview

Table 1 Milestones in the history of Nordic women

	Denmark	Finland	Iceland	Norway	Sweden
General					
Equal inheritance rights for women and men	1857	1878	1850	1854	1845
Unmarried women attained majority status	1857	1864	1861	1863	1863
Married women attained majority status	1899	1930	1900	1888	1921
Women may accede to the throne[a]	1953			1990	1980
Politics					
Women are granted the right to vote and become eligible for office:					
in elections to local authorities	1908	1917	1910	1910	1918
in general elections	1915	1906	1920	1913	1919
First woman elected to parliament	1918	1907	1922	1922	1922
First woman minister	1924	1926	1970	1945	1947
First woman prime minister	–	–	–	1981	–
First woman president		–	1980		
First woman parliamentary spokesperson	–	1994	1988	1993	1991
Education and working life					
Women are allowed to enrol for university studies	1875	1901	1911	1884	1873
Women achieve equal rights in appointments to public offices	1921	1926	1911	1938	1925
Women can be ordained as priests	1947	1988	1911	1952	1958
First woman bishop	–	–	–	1993	1997
First woman member of the Supreme Court of Justice	1953	1970	1982	1982	1968
Equal pay for the same work in the public sector	1919	1962	1945	1959	1947
Equal pay for the same work in the private sector	1973	1962	1961	1961	1960

a: Applies only to the Danish, Norwegian and Swedish monarchies
b: Applies only to the republics of Finland and Iceland

Sources: *Women and Men in the Nordic countries 1994*; *Women and Men in Norway 1995*; *Women and Men in Sweden 1995*; Björkhem *et al.*1994; Ligestillingsrådet 1995; Ministry for Foreign Affairs 1995.

Table 2 **The enactment of the right to vote in general elections and elections to local authorities**

Elections to local authorities		General elections	
Men	Women	Men	Women
		1849 Denmark	
1855 Denmark Men with a household of their own who satisfy certain economic criteria		Men with a household of their own; not adjudged incompetent or a recipient of poor relief	
1860 in the market towns 1865 in Copenhagen		1857 Iceland 25 years of age, landowner paying a certain amount of taxes or who has a university degree or license to hold office	
1872 Iceland 25 years of age and tax-payer; not servants			
	1882 Iceland tax-paying widows and unmarried women; not servants	1898 Norway except servants and recipients of poor relief	
1901 Norway	1901 Norway		
	Limited right to vote and limited eligibility to stand for office 1908 Denmark	1906 Finland 1907 Sweden	1906 Finland 1907 Norway limited right to vote, dependent on income
1909 Sweden			
1910 Iceland	1910 Norway		
also male servants	1910 Iceland		
	Tax-paying women or women married to tax-paying men; also female servants		
			1913 Norway
		1915 Iceland	1915 Denmark
		also male servants	1915 Iceland
1917 Finland	1917 Finland	40 years and older	40 years and older
	1918 Sweden		1919 Sweden
		1920 Iceland	1920 Iceland
		25 years and older, not recipients of poor relief	25 years and older, not recipients of poor relief
1926 Iceland	1926 Iceland		
irrespective of tax	irrespective of tax and marital state		

Sources: Haavio–Mannila *et al.* 1983; Björkhem *et al.* 1994; *Women and Men in Norway 1995*; Auður Styrkársdottir 1997.

Table 3 Proportion of women in the Nordic parliaments 1900–1999[a] (%)

Year	DK[b]	Year	FIN	Year	I	Year	N	Year	S[c]
		1907	9.5						
		1908	12.5						
		1909	10.5						
		1910	8.5						
1918	2.9	1911	7.0			1915	0.0		
		1913	10.5			1918	0.0		
		1916	12.0						
		1917	9.0						
		1919	8.5						
1920 I+II	2.1	1922	10.0	1923	2.4	1921	0.7	1922	1.7
1920 III	2.0	1924	8.5	1927	2.4	1924	0.0	1925	2.2
1924	2.0	1927	8.5			1927	0.7	1929	1.3
1926	2.0	1929	8.0						
1929	2.7								
1932	2.7	1930	5.5	1931	2.4	1930	1.3	1933	2.2
1935	2.0	1933	7.0	1933	2.4	1933	2.0	1937	4.3
1939	2.0	1936	8.0	1934	2.0	1936	0.7		
		1939	8.0	1937	2.0				
1943	1.3	1945	8.5	1942 I+II	0.0	1945	4.7	1941	7.4
1945	5.4	1948	12.0	1946	1.9	1949	4.7	1945	7.8
1947	8.7			1949	3.8			1949	9.6
1950	7.9	1951	14.5	1953	0.0	1953	4.7	1953	12.2
1953	9.3	1954	15.0	1956	1.9	1957	6.7	1957	12.6
1953	9.5	1958	14.0	1959 I	1.9			1959	13.4
1957	8.4			1959 II	3.3				
1960	9.5	1962	13.5	1963	1.7	1961	8.7	1961	13.7
1964	9.5	1966	16.5	1967	1.7	1965	8.0	1965	13.3
1966	10.6					1969	9.3	1969	15.4
1968	10.6								
1971	16.8	1970	21.5	1971	5.0	1973	15.5	1971	14.0
1973	15.1	1972	21.5	1974	5.0	1977	23.9	1974	21.1
1975	15.6	1975	23.0	1978	5.0			1977	22.6
1977	16.8	1979	26.0	1979	5.0				
1979	23.5								
1981	23.5	1983	31.0	1983	15.0	1981	25.8	1980	27.8
1984	26.3	1987	31.5	1987	20.6	1985	34.4	1983	29.5
1987	29.1					1989	35.8	1986	30.9
1988	31.4							1989	37.5
1990	33.0	1991	38.5	1991	23.8	1993	39.4	1992	32.9
1994	33.0	1995	33.5	1995	25.4	1997	36.4	1994	40.4
1998	37.4			1999	34.9			1998	42.7

a: includes election years when suffrage was still not universal but included some segments of the female population

b: the proportion of women in the Danish Folketing has been calculated on the basis of 179 seats, that is, including the four seats reserved for Greenland and the Faeroes

c: only comprehends Sweden's Second Chamber until 1971

Sources: 1900–1982: Haavio–Mannila *et al.* 1983; 1982– see Table 4.5.

Table 4.1 – 4.5:
Women's representation in the party groups in the Nordic parliaments

Table 4.1 Denmark. Women's representation in the party groups in the Folketing 1960–1998

Year	Soc. Dem.			Liberal			Cons.			Socialist People's Party			Centre Dem.			Rad. Lib.			Progress Party			others[a]			%[d]
	Tot	W	%	Tot	W	%	Tot	W	%	Tot	W	%	Tot	W	%	Tot	W	%	Tot	W	%	Tot	W	%	
1960	76	7	9	38	2	5	32	6	19	11	–	–				11	2	18				11	–	–	9.5
1964	76	7	9	38	1	3	36	6	17	10	1	10				10	2	20				9	–	–	9.5
1966	69	5	7	35	1	3	34	6	18	20	3	15				13	3	23				8	1	13	10.6
1968	62	3	5	34	3	9	37	6	16	11	1	9				27	5	19				8	1	13	10.6
1971	70	10	14	30	3	10	31	7	23	17	4	24				27	6	22				8	1	13	16.8
1973	46	6	13	22	3	14	16	2	13	11	3	27	14	2	14	20	5	25	28	3	11	22	3	14	15.1
1975	53	6	11	42	7	17	10	2	20	9	2	22	4	–	–	13	4	31	24	3	13	24	4	17	15.6
1977	65	12	18	21	2	10	15	4	27	7	2	29	11	2	18	6	1	17	26	1	4	28	10	36	16.8
1979	68	16	24	22	3	14	22	7	32	11	7	64	6	2	33	10	3	30	20	1	5	16	3	19	23.5
1981	59	11	19	20	1	5	26	9	35	21	9	43	15	6	40	9	3	33	16	1	6	13	2	15	23.5
1984	56	10	18	22	6	27	42	13	31	21	9	43	8	3	38	10	2	20	6	1	17	14	3	30	26.3
1987	54	13	24	19	2	11	38	13	34	27	9	33	9	4	44	11	5	45	9	5	56	12	1	13	29.1
1990	69	24	35	29	9	31	30	7	23	15	6	31	9	5	56	7	3	43	12	4	33	8	1	25	33.0
1994	62	24	39	42	13	31	27	9	33	13	3	23	5	2	40	8	4	50	11	3	27	11[b]	1	14	33.0
1998	63	24	38	42	16	38	16	5	31	13	5	38	8	5	63	7	4	57	4	1	25	26[c]	7	27	37.4

a: Includes two seats each for the Faeroes and Greenland, as well as, i.a.. Left Socialist Party, the Communist Party of Denmark, and the Christian People's Party
b: Six seats for the Unity List, of which one is held by a woman
c: Four seats (one woman) for the Christian People's Party, five seats (one woman) for the Unity List, thirteen seats (four women) for the recently formed Danish People's Party, as well as two seats each from the Faeroes and Greenland, of which one is held by a woman (Greenland)
d: Proportion (%) of women in the Folketing

Source: See Table 4.5.

Table 4.2 Finland. Women's representation in the party groups in the Eduskunta/Riksdagen 1962 – 1995

Year	Soc. Dem.			Centre Party[a]			Nat. Coalition Party[b]			Left Wing Alliance[c]			Swedish People's Party			Finnish Green League[d]			Christian Democratic Party			others[e]			%[f]
	Tot	W	%	Tot	W	%	Tot	W	%	Tot	W	%	Tot	W	%	Tot	W	%	Tot	W	%	Tot	W	%	
1962	40	8	20	53	4	8	32	4	13	47	9	19	14	–	–							14	2	14	13.5
1966	62	13	21	49	6	12	26	5	19	41	7	17	12	–	–							10	2	20	16.5
1970	52	13	25	36	6	17	37	10	27	36	10	28	12	1	8				1	–	–	26	3	12	21.5
1972	55	15	27	35	6	17	34	7	21	37	9	24	10	1	10				4	–	–	25	5	20	21.5
1975	54	13	24	39	7	18	36	9	25	40	9	23	10	2	20				9	2	22	12	4	33	23.0
1979	52	16	31	36	5	14	47	13	28	35	11	31	9	2	22				10	2	20	11	3	27	26.0
1983	57	18	32	38	9	24	45	18	41	27	10	37	11	2	18				3	1	33	19	4	21	31.0
1987	56	18	32	40	11	27	53	22	42	20	7	35	12	1	8	4	–	–	5	1	20	10	3	30	31.5
1991	48	22	46	55	15	27	40	20	50	19	5	26	11	3	27	10	5	50	8	3	37	9	4	44	38.5
1995	63	23	37	44	12	27	39	17	44	22	5	23	11	3	27	9	6	67	7	1	14	5	–	–	33.5

a: Until 1962 the Agrarian Party, 1962–87 the Centre Party; now the Centre Party of Finland

b: Also includes for 1975 and 1983 the Finnish Constitutional Conservative Party

c: 1945–1987 the Democratic League of Finnish People (including the Finnish Communist Party)

d: Not established as a political party in 1987

e: Including i.a. the Liberal People's Party, Smallholders' and Rural Party, Constitutional Conservative Party, Åland Alliance and in the 1995 election the Young Finns Party, the Ecological Party and True Finns; the Green Alliance is also included in 1983

f: Proportion (%) of women in the Riksdag

Source: See Table 4.5.

Table 4.3 Iceland. Women's representation in the party groups in the Alþingi 1963–1995

Year	Independence Party			Progressive Party			People's Alliance			Soc. Dem.			others			Women's Alliance			Proportion (%) women in the Alþingi
	Tot	W	%	Tot	W	%	Tot	W	%	Tot	W	%	Tot	W	%	Tot	W	%	
1963	24	1	4	19	–	–	9	–	–	8	–	–							1.7
1967	23	1	4	18	–	–	10	–	–	9	–	–							1.7
1971	22	2	9	17	–	–	10	1	10	6	–	–	5	–	–				5.0
1974	25	2	8	17	–	–	11	1	9	5	–	–	2	–	–				5.0
1978	20	1	5	12	–	–	14	1	7	14	1	7							5.0
1979	22	1	5	17	–	–	11	1	9	10	1	10							5.0
1983	23	2	9	14	–	–	10	1	10	6	1	17	4	2	50	3	3	100	15.0
1987	18	2	11	13	1	8	8	2	25	10	1	10	8	1	12	6	6	100	20.6
1991	26	4	15	13	2	15	9	2	22	10	2	20	0	–	–	5	5	100	23.8
1995	25	4	16	15	3	20	9	2	22	7	1	14	4	3	75	3	3	100	25.4

Source: See Table 4.5.

Table 4.4 Norway. Women's representation in the party groups in the Storting 1961 – 1997

Year	Norwegian Labour Party			Centre Party			Cons.			Christian Democratic Party			Progress Party			Socialist Left Party			Liberal Party			others			Proportion (%) women in the Storting
	Tot	W	%	Tot	W	%	Tot	W	%	Tot	W	%	Tot	W	%	Tot	W	%	Tot	W	%	Tot	W	%	%
1961	74	11	15	16	1	6	29	1	3	15	–	–				2	–	–	14	–	–	–	–	–	8.7
1965	68	9	13	18	–	–	31	1	3	13	–	–				2	–	–	18	2	11	–	–	–	8.0
1969	74	11	14	20	–	–	29	2	7	14	1	7				–	–	–	13	–	–	–	–	–	9.3
1973	62	12	19	21	3	14	29	5	17	20	1	5	4	–	–	16	3	19	2	–	–	1	–	–	15.5
1977	76	20	26	12	1	8	41	12	29	22	3	14	–	–	–	2	1	50	2	–	–	–	–	–	23.9
1981	66	22	23	11	2	18	53	13	25	15	1	7	4	–	–	4	2	50	2	–	–	–	–	–	25.8
1985	71	30	42	12	2	17	50	15	30	16	4	25	2	–	–	6	3	50	–	–	–	–	–	–	34.4
1989	63	32	51	11	3	27	37	11	30	14	5	36	22	1	5	17	7	41	–	–	–	1	–	–	35.8
1993	67	33	49	32	14	44	28	8	29	13	5	38	10	1	10	13	4	31	1	–	–	1	–	–	39.4
1997[a]	65	32	49	11	4	36	23	7	30	25	11	44	25	2	8	9	3	33	6	1	17	1	–	–	36.4

Source: See Table 4.5.

Table 4.5 Sweden. Women's representation in the party groups in the Riksdag 1961 – 1998

Year[a]	Soc. Dem.			Cons.			Centre Party			Liberal Party			Left Party			Green Party			Christian Dem.			New Dem.			Proportion (%) women in the Riksdag
	Tot	W	%	Tot	W	%	Tot	W	%	Tot	W	%	Tot	W	%	Tot	W	%	Tot	W	%	Tot	W	%	%
1961	114	23	20	39	6	15	34	–	–	40	3	8	5	–	–										13.7
1965	113	24	21	33	3	9	35	–	–	43	3	7	8	1	13										13.3
1969	125	24	19	32	5	16	39	2	5	34	3	9	3	2	67										15.4
1971	163	28	17	41	4	10	71	9	13	58	5	9	17	3	18										14.0
1974	156	35	22	51	8	16	90	22	24	34	5	15	19	4	21										21.1
1977	152	33	22	55	7	13	86	23	27	39	8	21	17	4	24										22.6
1980	154	42	27	73	16	22	64	20	31	38	9	24	20	5	25										27.8
1983	167	57	34	85	22	26	57	19	33	20	2	10	20	3	15										29.5
1986	159	54	34	76	17	22	44	14	32	51	20	39	19	3	16										30.9
1989	156	60	38	66	19	29	42	16	38	44	19	43	21	8	38	20	9	45							37.5
1992	138	56	41	80	22	27	31	10	32	33	12	36	16	5	31	–	–	–	26	7	27	25	3	12	32.9
1994	161	77	48	80	22	27	27	10	37	26	9	35	22	10	45	18	8	44	15	5	33	–	–	–	40.4
1998	131	65	50	82	25	31	18	10	56	17	6	35	43	18	42	16	8	50	42	17	41	–	–	–	42.7

a: In 1971 the Riksdag replaced the bicameral system. Data for the years 1961–1969 refer to the Second Chamber.

Sources: 1960–1981, see Haavio–Mannila *et al.* 1983:259 ff.
Denmark: Nordisk statistisk årsbok; Internet 1998d.
Finland: Norden i tal 1994 and 1996; Statistisk årsbok för Finland, several annual publications.
Iceland: Data from Auður Styrkársdóttir
Norway: Nordisk statistisk årsbok.
Sweden: Bergqvist 1994; *Women and Men in Sweden 1995*; Sveriges riksdag 1998.

Table 5.1 – 5.5:
Female ministers by ministry 1970–1998

Table 5.1 Denmark

Year	Government	Tot	W	%	Portfolio
1971–72	Soc. Dem	19	2	11	Ecclesiastical affairs, social affairs
1972–73	Soc. Dem.	21	2	10	Ecclesiastical affairs, social affairs
1973–75	Liberal Party	12	2	17	Justice, culture, education
1975–78	Soc. Dem.	20	2	10	Social affairs, education
1978–79	Soc. Dem.; Liberal Party	21	3	14	Justice, education, wp (foreign affairs)
1979–81	Soc. Dem.	21	3	14	Social affairs, education, wp (foreign affairs)
1981–82	Soc. Dem.	20	3	15	education, culture, Nordic affairs, ecclesiastical affairs, Greenland
1982–87	Cons. People's Party; Centre Dem.; Liberal Party; Christian People's Party	21	4	19	Ecclesiastical affairs, culture, home affairs, labour
1987–88	Cons. People's Party; Centre Dem.; Liberal Party; Christian People's Party	22	3	14	Ecclesiastical affairs, social affairs, health
1988–90	Cons. People's Party; Liberal Party; Rad. Lib.	21	4	19	Health, housing, environment, social affairs
1990–93	Cons. People's Party; Liberal Party	19	4	21	Industry and energy, health, social affairs, culture
1993–94	Soc. Dem.; Rad. Lib.; Centre–Dem.; Christian People's Party	24	8	33	Co-ordination, finance, development, home affairs, labour, culture, justice, social affairs
1994–98	Soc. Dem.; Rad. Lib.; Centre–Dem.	20	7	35	Finance and Nordic co-operation, employment, home and ecclesiastical affairs, labour, culture, health, social affairs
1998–	Soc. Dem.; Rad. Lib.	20	7	35	Finance and Nordic co-operation, urban affairs and housing, social affairs, employment, transport, culture, education and ecclesiastical affairs

wp - without portfolio, i.e., minister without portfolio, deputy minister or second min-ister, secretary at the office of the prime minister and corresponding positions. The ministry referred to in brackets denotes the ministry to which the minister without portfolio is attached.

NB! The table shows the proportion of female ministers at the time at which the Government assumed office; later changes have not been taken into account.

Source: see Table 5.5.

Table 5.2 Finland

Year	Government	Tot	W	%	Portfolio
1968–70	Soc. Dem.; Centre Party; Swedish People's Party; People's Dem. Party; Swedish People's Party; independent	16	1	6	Health and social affairs – (minister without portfolio 1970)
1970	Independent	13	1	8	wp (health and social affairs)
1970–71	Soc. Dem.; Centre Party; Lib.; Swedish People's Party; People's Dem. Party; independent	17	3	18	Social affairs, 2 wp
1971–72	Independent	15	1	7	Social affairs
1972	Soc. Dem.	17	1	6	wp
1972–75	Soc. Dem.; Centre Party; Lib.; Swedish People's Party; independent	16	2	13	Social affairs, wp (education)
1975	Independent	17	2	12	Justice, wp (finance and social affairs)
1975–76	Soc. Dem.; Centre Party; Lib.; Swedish People's Party; People's Dem. Party	18	2	11	Social affairs, wp (social affairs)
1976–77	Centre Party; Lib.; Swedish People's Party; independent	16	3	19	Social affairs, education, wp (social affairs)
1977–79	Soc. Dem.; Centre Party; Lib.; Swedish People's Party; People's Dem. Party; independent.	15	1	7	Social affairs
1979–82	Soc. Dem.; Centre Party; Swedish People's Party; People's Dem. Party; independent	17	3	18	Social affairs, 2 wp (education, social affairs and industry)
1982–83	Soc. Dem.; Centre Party; People's Dem. Party; Swedish People's Party; independent	17	2	12	wp (education) wp (health and social affairs) (Health and *social affairs 1983–83 and education 1983)
1983–87	Soc. Dem.; Centre Party; Swedish People's Party; Rural Party	17	3	18	Social affairs, education and wp (social affairs) (* home affairs 1984–87)
1987–91	Soc. Dem.; Nat. Coalition Party; Swedish People's Party; Rural Party	18	4	22	Social affairs, 3 wp (finance, education, social affairs) (* defence 1990–91, justice 1990–91, transport 1990–91)
1991–95	Centre Party; Nat. Coalition Party; Swedish People's Party; Christian Dem. Party	17	7	41	Justice, education, defence, environment, housing, social affairs, wp (education)
1995–99	Soc. Dem.; Nat. Coalition Party; Swedish People's Party; Greens; Left Wing Alliance; independent	18	7	39	Foreign affairs, defence, health and social affairs, transport, employment, 2 wp (finance and social affairs – and health)

wp – without portfolio, i.e., minister without portfolio, deputy minister or second minister, secretary at the office of the prime minister and corresponding positions. The ministry referred to in brackets denotes the ministry to which the minister without portfolio is attached.

NB! The table shows the proportion of female ministers at the time at which the Government assumed office; later changes have not been taken into account.

Source: see Table 5.5.

Table 5.3 Iceland

Year	Government	Tot	W	%	Portfolio
1970–71	Independence Party; Soc. Dem.	7	1	7	Justice, ecclesiastical affairs
1983–87	Prog. Party; Independence Party	10	1	10	1983–85 Education, culture
1987–88	Independence Party; Prog. Party; Soc. Dem.	11	1	9	Social affairs
1988–89	Prog. Party; Soc. Dem.; People's Alliance	9	1	11	Social affairs
1989–91	Prog. Party; Soc. Dem.; People's Alliance; Citizens' Party	11	1	9	Social affairs
1991–95	Independence Party; Soc. Dem.	10	1	10	Social affairs
1995–	Independence Party; Prog. Party	10	1	10	Health

NB! The table shows the proportion of female ministers at the time at which the Government assumed office; later changes have not been taken into account.

Source: see Table 5.5.

Table 5.4 Norway

Year	Government	Tot	W	%	Portfolio
1971–72	Labour Party	15	1	7	Consumer affairs/family
1972–73	Centre Party; Christian Democratic Party; Liberal Party	15	2	13	Consumer affairs/ family, social affairs
1973–76	Labour Party	15	3	20	Justice, social affairs, transport
1976–81	Labour Party	16	4	25	Justice, consumer affairs/ admin., environment, social affairs
1981	Labour Party	17	4	24	Prime Minister, consumer affairs/admin., local gov./ employment, commerce
1981–83	Conservative Party	17	4	24	Justice, transport, consumer affairs/ admin., environment
1983–85	Conservative Party; Centre Party; Christian Democratic Party	18	4	22	Justice, consumer affairs, environment, development aid
1986–89	Labour Party	18	8	44	Prime Minister, environment, development aid, justice, ecclesiastical affairs/ education, social affairs, consumer affairs/ admin., agric.
1989	Conservative Party; Centre Party; Christian Democratic Party	18	7	39	Social affairs, ecclesiastical affairs/ science, agric., Justice, Consumer affairs/admin., environment, commerce
1990–96	Labour Party	19	9	47	Prime Minister, employment/admin., agric., Justice, social affairs, ecclesiastical affairs/culture, commerce, development aid, fishery
1996–97	Labour Party	19	8	42	Foreign affairs, children/ family, justice, culture, trade & industry/ commerce, petroleum/ energy, transport, social affairs
1997–	Christian Democratic Party; Centre Party; Liberal Party	19	9	47	Children/family, justice, local gov., admin./ employment, culture, environmental cons., petroleum/energy, social affairs, development and human rights

NB! The table shows the proportion of female ministers at the time at which the Government assumed office; later changes have not been taken into account.

Source: see Table 5.5

Table 5.5 Sweden

Year	Government	Tot	W	%	Portfolio
1969–73	Soc. Dem.	19	2	11	wp
1973–76	Soc. Dem.	19	3	16	wp
1976–78	Conservative Party; Liberal Party; Centre Party	20	5	25	Foreign affairs, housing, 3 wp (housing, social affairs, education)
1978–79	Liberal Party	19	6	32	Communications, housing, 4 wp (employment, budget, social affairs, education)
1979–81	Conservative Party; Centre Party; Liberal Party	21	5	24	Social affairs, housing, 3 wp (employment, social affairs, education)
1981–82	Centre Party; Liberal Party	18	5	28	Social affairs, housing, 3 wp (employment, social affairs, education)
1982–85	Soc. Dem.	20	5	25	Education, employment, 3 wp (employment, industry, social affairs)
1985–88	Soc. Dem.	20	6	30	Social affairs, employment, justice, agric. & industry, 2 wp
1988–90	Soc. Dem.	21	6	29	Justice, social affairs, employment, environment and energy, 2 wp (immigration, civil)
1990–91	Soc. Dem.	22	8	36	Development aid, foreign affairs, commerce, justice, environment, employment, social affairs, 2 wp (home affairs, social affairs)
1991–94	Conservative Party; Liberal Party; Centre Party; Christian Dem.; independent	21	8	38	Justice, finance, culture, civil, foreign affairs, 3 wp (justice, education, environment)
1994–98	Soc. Dem.	22	11	50	Foreign affairs, justice, civil, education, communications, environment, culture, agric., social affairs, 2 wp (deputy Prime Minister, social affairs)
1998–	Soc. dem	20	10	50	Foreign affairs, agric., culture, 7 wp (deputy Prime Minister, justice, social affairs, education, culture, trade & industry)

wp – without portfolio, i.e., minister without portfolio, deputy minister or second minister, secretary at the office of the prime minister and corresponding positions. The ministry referred to in brackets denotes the ministry to which the minister without portfolio is attached.

NB! The table shows the proportion of female ministers at the time at which the Government assumed office; later changes have not been taken into account.

Sources: 1970 – 81/82, see Haavio–Mannila *et al.* 1983.
Denmark: EJPR, Political Data Year Book 1996, Internet 1998d.
Finland: Finlands statskalender 1986–90; EJPR Political Data Year Book 1992, 1993, 1996 and Special Issue Vol. 24 nr 1/93.
Iceland: Data supplied by Auður Styrkársdóttir 1997.
Norway: Nordby 1985; Regjeringer, statsråder og statssekretærer, Oslo: Statsministerens kontor 1993; fr. 1993: Statsministerens kontor, Oslo.
Sweden: Bergqvist 1994; EJPR Political Data Yearbook 1992 and 1996, Regeringskansliet.

Table 6. Representation of women in parliamentary committees; a comparison (in %)

Committee	DENMARK % women		FINLAND % women		ICELAND % women		NORWAY % women		SWEDEN % women	
	1981	1997[a]	1983	1996[b]	1981–82	1996[c]	1981–85	1997	1982–83	1994
social sector/ health	47	50	41	53	14	60	50	48	47	47
education/culture/ecclesiastical affairs	40	41	47	47	14	50	46	47	37	50
parl. budget/admin.	–	–	–	18	–	–	50	–	–	–
local gov./employment/ housing	24	43	–	41	0	–	38	39	33	35
foreign affairs	24	38	18	29	0	50	25	27	27	59
constitution/justice/civil law	36	36	43	29	14	30	28	38	24	49
transport/communications	6	26	12	24	0	20	31	40	13	41
Agric./forestry/fishery/trade & industry	–	38	18	24	0	20	17	29	13	41
industry/energy	24	35	–	–	0	30	7	13	13	41
finance/finance/tax revenues	12	33	31	29	0	28	17	30	7	32
defence	12	18	18	29	–	–	10	30	13	35
environment	–	53	–	65	–	22	–	–	–	–
others	–	44	–	32	14	30	–	–	–	–
Total proportion women	25	37	33	34	6	35	28	35	25	43

a: The Danish committees consist of 17 members, apart from the Procedural Committee which comprises 21 (forms part of the Committee on Constitutional Affairs). The group designated "others" includes the Committee for Electoral Trials and the Committee for Economic Policy. The § 71 Supervisory Committee is not included in the table.

b: The Finnish committees consist of 17 members except the Grand Committee, the Committee for the Future, and the Committee for Constitutional Law. The group designated "others" includes the Grand Committee and the Committee for the Future; the Committee for Constitutional Law is included in the section finance/economy/taxes.

c: Most Icelandic parliamentary committees have 9 members + an extra member with the right to speak but not to vote. Issues concerning the armed forces belong to foreign affairs, consumer affairs are divided among the majority of the committees, while local gov./administration and housing fall within the jurisdiction of the Committee for Social Affairs.

Sources: Haavio–Maanila *et al.* 1983; Internet 1997b; 1998d; Auður Styrkársdottir 1997; *Women and Men in Sweden* 1995; S nr 3 (Report from the electoral committee on the composition of the standing committees in the Norwegian Parliament).

Table 7.1 – 7.3:
Women elected to the parliaments of the self-governing regions 1983–1998

Table 7.1 Women elected to the Faeroese Løgting 1984–1998

Political parties	1984			1988			1990			1994			1998		
	tot	W	%	tot	W	%	tot	W	%	tot	W	%	tot	W	%
Republican Party	6	1	17	6	2	33	4	–	–	4	–	–	8	1	13
People's Party	7	–	–	8	–	–	7	–	–	6	–	–	8	1	13
Soc. Dem.	8	–	–	7	1	14	10	1	10	5	1	20	7	1	14
Unionist Party	7	–	–	7	–	–	6	1	17	8	2	25	6	1	17
Independence Party	2	–	–	2	–	–	3	1	33	2	1	50	2	–	–
Centre Party	–	–	–	–	–	–	–	–	–	2	–	–	1	–	–
Christ. People's Party	2	–	–	2	–	–	2	–	–	2	–	–	–	–	–
Worker's League	–	–	–	–	–	–	–	–	–	3	1	33	–	–	–
Total	32	1	3.1	32	3	9.4	32	3	9.4	32	5	15.6	32	4	12.5
Turnout in %	86.8			87.2			86.1			81.3			d.m.		

D.m. – data missing

Sources: Nordisk statistisk årsbok, various editions; Lagtingets sekretariat.

Table 7.2 Women elected to the Landsting of Greenland 1984–1995

Political parties	1984			1987			1991			1995		
	tot	W	%	tot	W	%	tot	W	%	tot	W	%
Siumut	11	–	–	11	–	–	11	1	9	12	4	33
Liberal Party	11	1	9	11	1	9	8	2	25	10	–	–
Inuit Ataqatigiit	3	1	33	4	1	25	5	1	20	6	1	17
Akuliit Partiiat	–	–	–	–	–	–	2	–	–	2	–	–
Iissittup Partiia	–	–	–	1	–	–	1	–	–	1	–	–
others	–	–	–	–	–	–	–	–	–	–	–	–
Total	25	2	8.0	27	2	7.4	27	4	14.8	32	5	15.6
Turnout in %	66.8			69.6			67.5			67.5		

Sources: Nordisk statistisk årsbok, various editions; Norden i tal 1996.

Table 7.3 Women elected to the Lagting of Åland 1983–1995

Political parties	1983			1987			1991			1995		
	tot	W	%	tot	W	%	tot	W	%	tot	W	%
Centre Party	11	–	–	9	–	–	10	–	–	8	–	–
Liberal Party	9	2	22	8	2	25	7	1	14	8	4	50
Free-Thinking Alliance	5	1	20	5	2	40	6	1	17	6	1	17
Soc. Dem.	5	2	40	4	2	50	4	2	50	4	2	50
Independent Alliance	–	–	–	2	–	–	3	–	–	3	–	–
The Greens	–	–	–	2	2	100	–	–	–	–	–	–
Independent Åland	–	–	–	–	–	–	–	–	–	–	–	–
Total	30	5	16.7	30	8	26.7	30	4	13.3	30	7	23.3
Turnout in %	64.4			64.3			62.4			62.5		

Sources: Nordisk statistisk årsbok, various editions; ÅSUB 3/95.

Table 8. Proportion of women councillors (in %) on local councils in the Nordic countries 1900–1998[a]

Year	DK	Year	FIN[b]	Year	ICE[c]	Year	N	Year	S[d]
1909	1					1901	1		
.						1907	1		
						1910	2		
1913	1					1913	1		
1917	1					1916	1		
						1919	1	1919	4
1921	1					1922	1	1920	3
1925	1					1925	1	1922	3
1929	1					1928	1	1926	2
1933	1					1931	1	1930	1
1937	1					1934	2	1934	2
						1937	2	1938	4
1943	2	1945	5			1945	3	1942	5
1946	3	1947	5			1947	5	1946	7
1950	4	1950	7	1950	1	1951	6	1950	8
1954	4	1953	7	1954	0.4	1955	6	1954	10
1958	4	1956	7	1958	1	1959	6	1958	10
1962	6	1960	8	1962	1	1963	7	1962	11
1966	10	1964	8	1966	2	1967	10	1966	12
		1968	11						
1970	10	1972	15	1970	2	1971	15	1970	14
1974	12	1976	18	1974	4	1975	15	1973	17
1978	18			1978	6	1979	23	1976	23
								1979	29
1981	21	1980	22	1982	12	1983	24	1982	29
1985	24	1984	25	1986	19	1987	31	1985	30
1989	26	1988	27					1988	34
1993	28	1992	30	1990	22	1991	29	1991	34
1997	27			1994	25				
		1996	31	1998	28	1995	33	1994	41

a: The table includes all elected representatives on rural and urban councils.
b: Statistics on Finnish elections do not comprise data on distribution by sex of council members prior to 1945.
c: Data on women's representation on Iceland are lacking prior to 1950.
d: The data for the 1919 and 1920/21 elections are comparable with other data since the latter elections only comprised half the number of members, while the former included members for two-year and well as four-year periods.

Sources: Haavio–Mannila *et al.* 1983; Christensen & Damkjær 1998; Pikkala 1996; Statistik-centralen Finland 1997; Raaum 1995; *Norsk statistisk årbok 1996;* Auður Styrkársdóttir 1997; Bergqvist 1998; Sveriges officiella statistik; *Allmänna valen,* various editions.

Appendix II

Overview of the political parties in the Nordic countries

Denmark

Centrumdemokraterne (CD) – The Centre Democrats; formed by a splinter group from the Social Democratic Party

Denmarks Kommunistiske Parti (DKP) – The Communist Party of Denmark; does not participate in elections as an individual party

Danmarks Retsforbund (DR) – The Danish Justice League; centrist

Dansk Folkeparti (DF) – Danish People's Party; right-wing populist party which ran in the 1998 elections, an offshoot of the Progress Party

Det Konservative Folkepartiet (Cons.) – The Conservative People's Party; formerly the Conservative Party; urban conservative

Det Radikale Lib. (RV, Rad.) – The Radical Liberal Party; moderate liberal

Enhedslisten – de rød–grønne – The Danish Red-Green Alliance; alliance consisting of DKP, SAP and VS

Fremskridtspartiet (FRP) – The Progress Party; right-wing populist

Fælles Kurs (FK) – Common Course; left-wing populist

Kristeligt Folkeparti (KrF) – Christian People's Party; Christian-centrist

Socialdemokratiet (Soc. Dem.) (The Social Democratic Party

Socialistisk Arbejderparti (SAP) – Socialist Workers' Party; Trotskyist, does not participate in elections as an individual party

Socialistisk Folkeparti (SF) – Socialist People's Party; socialist

Venstre, Danmarks Liberale parti (V) (The Liberal Party of Denmark

Venstresocialisterne (VS) – Left Socialist Party; formed by a splinter group from the Socialist People's Party

The Faeroes

Fólkaflokkurin – The People's Party; a conservative party advocating independence

Javnaðarflokkurin – The Social Democratic Party; a social-democratic party favouring increased autonomy though not outright independence

Kristiligi Fólkaflokkurin Føroya Framburðs- og Fiskivinnurflokkur – The Faeroese Christian People's, Progress and Fishery Party; conservative

Miðflokkurin – The Centre Party; formed by a breakaway group from the Faeroese Christian People's Party; Christian-conservative

Sambandsflokkurin – The Unionist Party; advocates continued affiliation with Denmark; liberal-conservative

Sjálvstyrisflokkurin – Independence Party; liberal party advocating independence

Tjóðveldisflokkurin – The Republican Party; a republican party left of centre; advocates gradual separation from Denmark

Verkarnannafylkingin – The Workers' League; protest party founded prior to the 1994 election

Greenland

Akulliit Partiiat (AP) – centrist
Atassut (A) – The Liberal Party of Greenland; liberal-conservative
Inuit Ataqatigiit (IA) – originally Marxist, now left-wing
Iisittup Partiia (IP) – conservative
Siumut (S) – social democratic

Finland

Suomen Keskusta (KESK) – The Centre Party; formerly the Agrarian Party
Suomen Kansan Demokraattinen Liitto (SKDL) – The People's Democratic
League; a left-wing socialist alliance (also comprising the Communist Party;
disbanded in 1990)
Suomen Kommunistinen Puolue (SKP) (The Communist Party of Finland
Suomen Kristillinen Liitto (SKL) – The Christian Democratic League of Fin-
land; Christian-centrist
Suomen Maaseudun Puolue (SMP) – The Rural Party; populist smallholders'
and agrarian party, subsequently dissolved and succeeded by the True Finns Par-
ty (Perussuomalainen Puolue) at the 1995 general election
Suomen Sosialidemokraattinen Puolue (SDP) (The Social Democratic Party
Vihreä Liitto (vihr) – The Green League; formerly the Greens
Perustuslaillinen Oikeistopuolue – The Constitutional Party; formerly the Con-
stitutional People's Party
Liberaalinen Kansanpuolue (LKP) (The Liberal People's Party
Kansallinen Kokoomus (Kok) – The National Coalition Party; moderate con-
servative
Svenska Folkpartiet (SFP) – The Swedish People's Party; Swedish-language
party; liberal-centrist
Nuorsuomalainen Puolue (Nuors.) – The Young Finns Party; neo-liberal
Vasemmistoliitto (VL) (The Left Wing Alliance

Åland

Frisinnad Samverkan (FS) – The Free-Thinking Alliance; conservative
De Gröna (The Greens
Liberalerna på Åland (Lib) (The Liberal Party
Obunden Samling (Ob) (The Independent Alliance
Åländsk Center (C) – The Centre Party; agrarian-centrist
Ålands Socialdemokrater (Soc) (The Social Democratic Party

Iceland

Alþýðubandalag – The People's Alliance; formerly the Icelandic Socialist Party
(Sócíalistaflokkur); socialist party founded by communists and socialists
Alþýðuflokkur – The Social Democratic Party

Bandalag jafnaðarmanna – The Socialist Alliance; founded by a splinter group from the Social Democratic Party in 1983, disbanded in 1987

Borgarflokkur – The Citizens' Party; right-wing populist; founded by a splinter group from the Independence party; disbanded in 1991

Framsóknarflokkur – The Progressive Party; agrarian-centrist

Kvennalistinn – The Women's Alliance

Sjàlfstæðisflokkur – The Independence Party; conservative

Þjóðvaki – The National Party; breakaway group from the Social Democrats in 1995, reunited in 1996

Norway

Det Liberale Folkepartiet (DLF) – The Liberal People's Party; formerly the New People's Party; liberal; formed after the break-up of the Liberal Party in the seventies; reunited with the Liberal Party in 1988

Det norske Arbeiderparti (DNA) – The Labour Party of Norway; social democratic

Fremskrittspartiet (FrP) – The Progress Party; formerly Anders Lange's Party; right-wing populist

Høyre (H) – The Conservative Party; conservative

Kristelig Folkeparti (KrF) – The Christian Democratic Party; Christian-centrist

Norges Kommunistiske Parti (NKP) (The Communist Party of Norway

Rød Valgallianse (RV) – Red Electoral Alliance; alliance between the Workers' Communist Party (Marxist-Leninists) and independent socialists

Senterpartiet (SP) – The Centre Party; formerly the Agrarian Party; agrarian

Sosialistisk Venstreparti (SV) – The Socialist Left Party; formerly the Socialist People's Party

Venstre (V) – The Liberal Party; liberal

Sweden

Centerpartiet (C) – The Centre Party; formerly the Agrarian League; agrarian-centrist

Folkpartiet (FP) – The Liberal Party; liberal

Kristdemokratiska samhällspartiet (KD) – The Christian Democratic Party; formerly the Christian Democratic Alliance; Christian-centrist

Miljöpartiet de Gröna (MP) (The Green Party of Sweden

Moderata Samlingspartiet (M) – The Conservative Party; formerly the Right Party; conservative

Ny Demokrati – New Democrats; populist right-wing party represented in the Riksdag 1991–94

Sveriges Socialdemokratiska Arbetarparti (SAP, Soc. Dem.) – The Social Democratic Party

Vänsterpartiet (V) – The Left Party of Sweden; formerly the Communist Party and the Left Party Communists

Appendix III

Gender equality, bodies and legislation

1. Gender equality bodies in the Nordic countries

Denmark[106]

Equal Status Council (formed in 1975, established by law in 1978). Appointed for a period of four years, convenes at least 8–10 times annually. The Council comprises nine members. Composition (since 1988): The chairperson is nominated by the Government, the Danish Federation of Trade Unions, the Federation of Danish Civil Servants and Salaried Employees, the Danish Employers' Association, and the Danish Women's Society each nominate one member. The Danish Women's National Council nominates three members. A female researcher is nominated by the rest of the Council.

Finland

The Council for Equality between Men and Women (formed in 1972). The Council comprises thirteen members: the chairperson, deputy chairperson and eleven members. The Council is appointed by the Government for a period of three years. The members are nominated by the political parties. Convenes 6–8 times annually.

The Office of the Ombudsman for Equality (established in 1987 for a period of four years).

The Equality Board (formed in 1987), five members (representing expertise in the areas of the law, industrial relations, and gender equality).

Iceland

The Equal Status Council (formed in 1976). The Council comprises seven members. They are appointed after every election to the Alster of Social Affairs has appointed the chairperson (who was previously appointed by the Supreme Court). The Association of Government and Municipal Employees, the Icelandic Federation of Trade Unions, the Icelandic Federation of Employers, the Icelandic Association for Women's Rights, appoint a member each. In addition, the chairperson of the Equal Status Complaints Committee also has a seat on the Council.

The Equal Status Complaints Committee (formed in 1991). Appointed for a period of three years by the Minister for Social Affairs. Convenes twice monthly. Comprises three members, all of whom are jurists. The Minister for Social Af-

---

106.As the book was in its final stages the Danish gender equality apparatus was undergoing a process of restructuring.

fairs appoints one member, while the Supreme Court appoints two, one of whom being the chairperson.

Norway

The Office of the Equal Status Ombudsman (formed in 1979). Renamed the *Gender Equality Ombud* in 1994; renamed later the *Gender Equality Ombudsman*.

The Equal Status Board of Appeals (formed in 1979). Appointed by the government for periods of four years. Seven members (chairperson, deputy chairperson, of which one must be a qualified judge). Seats on the Council are specially reserved for representatives of the Norwegian Federation of Trade Unions and the Confederation of Norwegian Business and Industry. Renamed the *Gender Equality Board of Appeals* in 1994.

The Centre for Gender Equality (formed in the autumn of 1997).

The Board of the Centre for Gender Equality is appointed by the minister for a period of four years. May comprise as many as seven members.

Liaison Committee for the Minister for Gender Equality (formed in 1998).

Kilden (The Source) (formed in 1998).

The Section for Gender Equality (formed in 1994), under the Ministry for Children and Family Affairs.

Sweden

The Council on Equality Issues (formed i 1983). Thirty-one members, the Minister for Equality Issues holds the office of chairperson. Convenes four times annually. Political parties and a variety of other organisations are represented on the Council.

The Office of the Equal Opportunities Ombudsman (Jämo) (formed in 1980). Appointed by the Government for a period of six years.

Equal Opportunities Commission (formed in 1980). Appointed by the Government. Comprises nine members including jurists, representatives of the employees' and employers' federations, and experts in the area.

Equality Affairs Division (formed in 1982); follows the minister in charge of equality issues.

2. Legislation in the Nordic countries

Denmark

1976   *Act on Equal Pay*
       Amendments: 1986, 1989, 1992
1978   *The Equal Status Council Act*
1978   *Act on Equal Treatment* (entered into force 1979)
       Amendments: 1990, 1994
1985   *Act on Equal Opportunities for Men and Women on the Appointment of
       Members of Public Committees, Commissions etc.* (the Committees
       Act).
1988   *Act on Equal Opportunities for Men and Women* (replaced the Equal
       Status Council Act)
1990   *Act on Equal Opportunities for Men and Women on the Appointment of
       Certain Executive Committees or Governing Bodies* (the Boards Act)

Finland

1986   *Act on the Equality Ombudsman and Equality Board* (entered into force
       1987)
1986   *Act on Equality between Women and Men* (entered into force 1987)
       Amendments: 1988, 1992, 1995

Iceland

1973   *Act on Equal Pay*
1976   *Act on Equal Rights between Women and Men* (the Equal Rights Act)
       (from 1985 *Act on Equal Rights and Equal Status between Women and
       Men*)
       Amendments: 1985, 1991

Norway

1978   *Act no 45 of June 9th 1978 on Gender Equality* (the Gender Equality
       Act) (entered into force 1979)
       Amendments: 1981, 1983, 1988

Sweden

1979   *Act on Equal Opportunities* (entered into force 1980)
       Amendments: 1988, 1991 (entered into force 1992), 1993 (entered into
       force 1994), 1995 (reversed burden of proof)

References

Agerskov, Ulla. 1989. Från kvinnonominering till partinominering. Grönländska kvinnor under det nya självstyret. In: Drude Dahlerup, red. *Vi har väntat länge nog*. Köpenhamn: NORD

Albrektsen, Beatrice Halsaa. 1977. *Kvinner og politisk deltakelse*. Oslo: Pax

Anckar, Dag. 1996. Ett självständigt Åland? *Finsk tidskrift*, 7/96, 417–430

Andersen, Agnete, Ruth Nielsen & Kirsten Precht. 1996. *Ligestillingslovene*. Gylling: Jurist- og Økonomforbundets Forlag

Andersen, Johannes, Ann-Dorte Christensen, Kamma Langberg, Birte Siim & Lars Torpe, red. 1993. *Medborgerskab. Demokrati og politisk deltagelse*. Herning: Systime

Andersen, Johannes & Lars Torpe, red. 1994. *Demokrati og politisk kultur. Rids af et demokratisk medborgerskab*. Herning: Systime

Andersen, Jørgen Goul. 1984. *Kvinder og politik*. Århus: Politica

Andersen, Jørgen Goul. 1993. Politisk deltagelse i 1990 sammenlignet med 1979. In: Johannes Andersen *et al.*, red. *Medborgerskab. Demokrati og politisk deltagelse*. Herning: Systime

Andersen, Jørgen Goul 1996. *Membership and Participation in Voluntary Associations in Scandinavia, in a Comparative Perspective*. Project paper no. 8: The Democratic Citizenship in the Nordic Countries. Aalborg University: Department of Economics, Politics and Public Administration

Andersen, Jørgen Goul & Jens Hoff. 1998. *Democracy and Citizenship in Scandinavian Welfare States*, forthcoming Macmillan

Andreasen, Tayo *et al.* 1991. Introduction. In: Tayo Andreasen *et al.*, red. *Moving On: New Perspectives on the Women's Movement*. Atla Jutlandica LXVII:1, Humanities series 66. Aarhus: Aarhus University Press

Bacchi, Carol Lee. 1990. *Same Difference. Feminism and Sexual Difference*. Sydney: Allen and Unwin

Backlash i Norge? 1994. Rapport fra en konferanse om kvinner i 90-åra. 25.–26. oktober 1993. Oslo: Sekretariatet for kvinneforskning, Norges forskningsråd. Arbeidsnotat 1/94

Backlash i Sverige? 1993. Kvinnotribunalen. Stockholm: Norstedts

Barne- og familiedepartementet. 1992. *St.meld. nr. 70 (1991–1992) Likestillingspolitikk for 1990-åra*. Oslo

Barne- og familedepartementet. 1996a. *På vei mot full barnehagedekning!* Statusrapport 1996 for Utviklingsprogrammet for barnehagesektoren. Oslo

Barne- og familiedepartementet. 1996. *Om reorganisering av Likestillingsrådet, herunder en sammenslåing av Likestillingsrådets sekretariat og Sekretariatet for kvinneforskning.* Oslo

Baude, Annika *et.al.*, red. 1992. *Visionen om jämställdhet.* Stockholm: SNS

Berggren, Anne-Marie. 1987. *Likhet eller särart – harmoni eller konflikt? En analys av kvinnorörelsens idéer med utgångspunkt i utvecklingen i USA under 1960- och 70-talen.* Göteborg: Historiska institutionen

Bergman, Solveig. 1995. *Feministisk motkultur och kvinnomakt: "Nya" kvinnorörelser och en studie av feminismen i Västtyskland.* Meddelanden från Ekonomisk-statsvetenskapliga fakulteten vid Åbo Akademi, sociologiska institutionen. Ser. A:432. Åbo: Åbo Akademi

Bergman, Solveig. 1998. Frauen in der finnischen Politik: Auf dem weg zur Hälfte der Macht? In: Beate Hoecker, red. *Handbuch Politische Partizipation von Frauen in Europa.* Kornwestheim Opladen: Leske+Budrich

Bergqvist, Christina. 1990. Myten om den universella svenska välfärdsstaten. *Statsvetenskaplig Tidskrift,* 3:223–233

Bergqvist, Christina. 1994. *Mäns makt och kvinnors intressen.* Acta Universitatis Upsaliensis. Skrifter utgivna av Statsvetenskapliga föreningen i Uppsala, 121. Stockholm: Almqvist & Wiksell International

Bergqvist, Christina. 1997. Korporatismens nedgång – kvinnornas framgång? In: Anita Nyberg & Elisabeth Sundin, red. *Ledare, makt och kön.* SOU 1997: 82. Stockholm: Fritzes

Bergqvist, Christina. 1998. Frauen, Männer und die politische Repräsentation in Schweden. In: Beate Hoecker, red. *Handbuch Politische Partizipation von Frauen in Europa.* Opladen: Leske+Budrich

Beslutningsforslag nr. B 34. 1995. *Forslag til folketingsbeslutning om oprettelse af Ligestillingsombud og ændring af Ligestillingsrådet.* 31. Oktober, København

Bille, Lars. 1995. Medlemsudviklingen i otte danske partier 1953–1993: Et demokratisk problem. In: M. Madsen *et. al.*, red. *Demokratiets mangfoldighed: Tendenser i dansk politik.* Kolding: Forlaget Politiske Studier

Bille, Lars. 1997. *Partier i forandring. En analyse af danske partiorganisationers udvikling 1960–1995.* Viborg: Odense Universitetsforlag

Bjarnar, Ove. 1995. *Veien til velferdssamfunnet. Bd. 2.* Oslo: Norske Kvinners Sanitetsforening

Björkander-Mannheimer, Eva. 1984. Kvinnor i rörelse. In: Mats Friberg & Johan Galtung, red. *Rörelserna.* Stockholm: Akademilitteratur

Björkhem, Barbro, Lisbet Hansing Engström & Lena Wägnerud, red. 1994. *Rätt att rösta. 1919–1994. Så fick kvinnor politiskt inflytande.* Stockholm: Sveriges riksdag

Bjørklund, Tor. 1986. Kvinners og menns partipreferanse. *Tidsskrift for samfunnsforskning,* 27:417–443

Blom, Ida. 1998. Refleksjoner over kjønn og stat. In: Anne-Hilde Nagel, red. *Kjønn og velferdsstat*. Bergen: Alma Mater

Borchorst, Anette. 1994. The Scandinavian Welfare States – Patriarchal, Gender Neutral or Woman-Friendly? *International Journal of Contemporary Sociology*, 31:45–67

Borchorst, Anette. 1995. A Political Niche: Denmark's Equal Status Council. In: Dorothy Stetson McBride & Amy Mazur, red. *Comparative State Feminism*. Thousand Oaks, Cf.: Sage Publications

Borchorst, Anette. 1998. Køn, velfærsstatsmodeller og familiepolitik. In: Jørgen Elm Larsen & Iver Hornemann Møller, red. *Socialpolitik*. Viborg: Munksgaard

Borchorst, Anette. 1999. Ligestillingsrådets historie. In: *Betænkning om det fremtidige ligestillingsarbejde og dets organisering*. Betænkning fra Udvalget ved-rørende det fremtidige ligestillingsarbejde. København

Borre, Ole & Jørgen Goul Andersen. 1997. *Voting and Political Attitudes in Denmark*. Aarhus: Aarhus University Press

Bratterud, Åse. 1994. Blir kvinner velferdsstatens viktigste støttesspillere? In: Anders Todal Jensen & Willy Martinussen, red. *Velferdsstaten i våre hjerter*. Oslo: Ad Notam Gyldendal

Brock-Utne, Birgit. 1981. Kvinner og fredsarbeid. In: Helge Sivertsen, Lise Vislie & Finn Børre Stokholm, red. *Kvinner viser vei: Festskrift til Eva Nordland*. Oslo: Aschehoug

Brod, Harry. 1987. The case for men's studies. In: Harry Brod, red. *The Making of Masculinities*. Boston, Ma.: Allen and Unwin

Broddadóttir, Ingibjörg, Guðný Eydal, Steinunn Hrafnsdóttir & H. Sigurveig Sigurðardóttir. 1997. The development of local authority social services in Iceland. In: Jorma Sipilä, red. *Social Care Services: The Key to the Scandinavian Welfare Model*. Aldershot: Avebury

Bruun, Niklas. 1982. Finsk jämställdhetslagstiftning i stöpsleven? In: Jytte Lindgård & Ruth Nielsen *Årbog for Kvinderet 1982*. København: Juristforbundets Forlag

Calvert, Gillian. 1987. "Feminism in the Public Service", *Hersay,* Newsbulletin from the New South Wales Women's Advisory Council, nr. 4

Carlsen, Søren. 1994. Mænds brug af fædre- og forældreorlov. In: S. Carlsen & Jørgen Elm Larsen, red. *Den svære balance. Om sammenhaengen mellem arbejdsliv og familieliv set i et ligestillingsperspektiv*. København: Ligestillingsrådet

Christensen, Ann-Dorte. 1986. *Kvinder i sociale bevægelser i Danmark* (upubl.)

Christensen, Ann-Dorte. 1990. *Kvinder i fredsbevægelsen*. Forskningsrapport: Aalborg Universitetscenter. Aalborg

Christensen, Ann-Dorte. 1991. Women in the New Peace Movement in Denmark; Empowerment and Political Identity. In: Tayo Andreasen *et al.*, red. *Moving On: New Perspectives on the Women's Movement*. Atla Jutlandica LXVII:1, Humanities series 66. Aarhus: Aarhus University Press

Christensen, Ann-Dorte. 1997. De politisk-kulturelle betydninger af køn. In: Ann-Dorte Christensen, Ann-Birte Ravn & Iris Rittenhofer, red. *Det kønnede samfund*. Aalborg: Aalborg Universitetsforlag

Christensen, Ann-Dorte & Poul Knopp Damkjær. 1998. Frauen und politische Repräsentation in Dänemark. In: Beate Hoecker, red. *Handbuch Politische Partizipation von Frauen in Europa*. Kornwestheim Opladen: Leske+Budrich

Dahlberg, Anita. 1984. *Jämt eller ibland – om jämställdhet*. Forskningsrapport 43 i AJDA-projektet. Stockholm: Arbetslivscentrum

Dahlerup, Drude. 1977. Et selvstændigt kvindeparti? Den danske stemmeretsbevægelse efter stemmeretten var vundet, 1903–18: En historie om stadigt bristede forventninger. *Kvindestudier*. Rødovre: Fremad

Dahlerup, Drude. 1979a. Kvinders organisering i det danske Socialdemokrati 1908–69. For og imod en selvstændig socialistisk kvindebevægelse. *Meddelelser om Forskning i Arbejderbevægelsens Historie*. nr. 13.m

Dahlerup, Drude. 1979b. Udviklingslinier i kvinders politiske deltagelse og repræsentation i Danmark. In: Mogens N. Pedersen, red. *Dansk politik i 1970'erne*. København: Samfundsvidenskabeligt Forlag

Dahlerup, Drude & Haavio-Mannila, Elina *et al.* 1985. In: Haavio-Mannila, *et al.* ed. 1985. *Unfinished Democracy: Women in Nordic Politics*. Oxford: Pergamon Press, pp. 160-169

Dahlerup, Drude. 1986. Is the New Women's Movement Dead? Decline or Change of the Danish Movement. In: Drude Dahlerup, red. *The New Women's Movement. Feminism and Political Power in Europe and the USA*. London: Sage Publications

Dahlerup, Drude. 1988a. *Vi har ventet længe nok – håndbog i kvinderepræsentation*. København: Nordisk Ministerråd

Dahlerup, Drude 1988b. From a Small to a Large Minority: Women in Scandinavian Politics. *Scandinavian Political Studies*, 11:275–298

Dahlerup, Drude. 1989. Kvinnoparlamentet på Åland. In: Drude Dahlerup, red. *Vi har väntat länge nog*. Köpenhamn: NORD 1989

Dahlerup, Drude. 1990. Da ligestilling kom på dagsordenen. In: Drude Dahlerup & Kristian Hvidt, red. *Kvinder på Tinge*. København: Rosinante

Dahlerup, Drude. 1991. Ligestilling i den offentlige forvaltning i 1990'erne – hvordan kommer man fra målsætning til iværksættelse? In: Louise Berntsen *et. al.*, red. *Ligestilling ja! Men hvordan? Ligestillingstiltag i den offentlige forvaltning*. Aarhus: Institut for Statskundskab og Cekvina, Aarhus Universitet

Dahlerup, Drude. 1993. From Movement Protest to State Feminism: the Women's Liberation Movement and Unemployment Policy in Denmark. *NORA: Nordic Journal of Women's Studies*, 1:4–20

Dahlerup, Drude. 1998. *Rødstrømperne. Den danske Rødstrømpebevægelses udvikling, nytænkning og gennemslag, 1970–1985*. København: Gyldendal

Dahlerup, Drude & Brita Gulli. 1983a. Kvindeorganisationerne i Norden: Afmagt eller modmagt? In: Elina Haavio-Mannila *et al. Det uferdige demokratiet. Kvinner i nordisk politik*. København: Nordisk Ministerråd

Dahlerup, Drude & Brita Gulli. 1983b. *The Impact of Women's Liberation Movement on Public Policy in Denmark and Norway*. Paper prepared for the workshop on "The Impact of the New Women's Movement" of the ECPR Joint Sessions, Freiburg, March 1983

Dahlerup, Drude *et al.* 1985. *Blomster & Spark. Samtaler med kvindelige politikere i Norden*. København: Nordisk Ministerråd, NORD 1985

Dahlström, Edmund. *et al.* 1962. *Kvinnors liv och arbete. Svenska och norska studier av ett aktuellt samhällsproblem*. Stockholm: SNS

Debes, Hans Jacob. 1993. Historia – en översikt. In: Hasse Schröder, red. *Färöarna mer än fåglar*. Uppsala: Schröders Ord & Bild

[Debes Henze, Turið, see Henze, Turið Debes]

[della Porta, Donatelle, see Porta, Donatella della]

Diani, Mario & Ron Eyerman. 1992. The Study of Collective Action: Introductory Remarks. In: Mario Diani & Ron Eyerman, red. *Studying Collective Action*. London: Sage Publications

Directive 75/117/EEC

Dominelli, Lena & Guðrún Jónsdóttir. 1988. Feminist Political Organization in Iceland: some Reflections on the Experience of Kwenna Frambothid. *Feminist Review*, 30:36–60

Ds 1995:2. *Pappagruppens slutrapport. Arbetsgruppen (S 1993:C) om papporna, barnen och arbetslivet*. Stockholm

Ds 1996:49. *Samhällets stöd till barnfamiljerna i Europa*. Stockholm

Eduards, Maud. 1977. *Kvinnor och politik, fakta och förklaringar*. Stockholm: Liber

Eduards, Maud. 1992. Against the Rules of the Game: On the Importance of Women's Collective Actions. In: Maud Eduards *et al. Rethinking Change: Current Swedish Feminist Research*. Stockholm: HFSR

Eduards, Maud. 1995. En allvarsam lek med ord. In: SOU 1995: 110, *Viljan att veta och viljan att förstå*. Stockholm

Eduards, Maud. 1997. The Women's Shelter Movement. In: Gunnel Gustafsson, red. Maud Eduards & Malin Rönnblom, *Towards a New Democratic Order? Women's Organizing in Sweden in the 1990s*. Stockholm: Publica

Eduards, Maud, Beatrice Halsaa, & Hege Skjeie. 1985. Equality: How Equal? In: Haavio-Mannila, *et al.* ed. *Unfinished Democracy: Women in Nordic Politics*. Oxford: Pergamon Press, pp. 134-159

Eisenstein, Hester. 1990. Femocrats, Official Feminism and the Uses of Power. In: Sophie Watson, red. *Playing the State: Australian Feminist Interventions*. London: Verso

Eisenstein, Hester. 1991. *Gender Shock*. London: Allen & Unwin

Eklund, Johan. 1996. *Varför så få kvinnor? En studie i kvinnorepresentation*. (Opublicerad uppsats). Stockholm: Statsvetenskapliga institutionen, Stockholms universitet

Elklit, Jørgen & Roger Buch Jensen, red. 1997. *Kommunalvalg.* Odense: Odense Universitetsforlag

Elman, Amy R. 1996. *Sexual Subordination and State Intervention: Comparing Sweden and the United States.* Providence, R.I.: Berghahn Books

Enloe, Cynthia. 1988a (1983). *Does Khaki Become You? The Militarization of Women's Lives.* London: Pandora

Enloe, Cynthia. 1988b. Rambon tuolle puolen: naiset ja sotilaallisen miehisyyden muodot. In: Eva Isaksson, red. *Nainen ja sotalaitos.* Jyväskylä: Suomen Rauhanliitto

The Equal Status Council of Iceland. 1992. *Women and Equality in Iceland.* Reykjavík

Esping-Andersen, Gøsta. 1990. *The Three Worlds of Welfare Capitalism.* Cambridge: Polity

European Journal of Political Research, vol. 24, nr. 1/1993. Special issue: Political data 1945–1990. Party Governments i 20 Democracies. Dordrecht: Kluwer Academic Publishers

European Journal of Political Research. Political Data Year Book. Dordrecht: Kluwer Academic Publishers

Eurostat Yearbook 1996: A Statistical View of Europe 1985–1995. Luxemburg: Office of Official Publications of European Communities

Eyerman, Ron & Andrew Jamison. 1991. *Social Movements: A Cognitive Approach.* Cambridge: Polity Press

Faludi, Susan. 1991. *Backlash: The Undeclared War Against Women.* New York: Crown

Fiig, Christina. 1998. *Evaluering af dansk ligestillingspolitik i 1990'erne.* Ålborg: GEP

Fosshaug, Lene. 1989. *Ubuden gjest i lukket selskap.* Hovedfagsoppgave. Bergen: Institutt for sammenliknende politikk, Universitetet i Bergen

Franzway, Suzanne *et al.* 1989. The 'Femocrat' Strategy. In: Suzanne Franzway, Dianne Court & R. W. Connell, red. *Staking a Claim. Feminism, Bureaucracy and the state.* Oxford: Polity Press

Freeman, Jo. 1975. *The Politics of Women's Liberation: A Case Study of an Emerging Social Movement and its Relation to the Policy Process.* New York & London: Longman

Friberg, Mats. 1984. De nya rörelserna och de gamla. In: Mats Friberg & Johan Galtung, red. *Rörelserna.* Stockholm: Akademilitteratur

Frønes, Ivar. 1996. Revolusjon uten opprør: Kjønn, generasjon og sosiale forandring i Norge på 1980-tallet. *Tidsskrift for samfunnsforskning,* 37:71–86

Fürst, Elisabeth. 1988. *Kvinner i akademia – inntrengere i en mannskultur?* Oslo: NAVFs sekretariat for kvinneforskning

Gallagher, Michael, Michael Laver & Peter Mair. 1995. *Representative Government in Modern Europe.* New York: McGraw-Hill

Gelb, Joyce. 1989. *Feminism and Politics: A Comparative Perspective.* Berkeley: University of California Press

Gidron, B., R. Kramer & L. Salamon, red. 1992. *Government and the Third Sector: Emerging Relationships in Welfare States.* San Fransisco: Jossey-Bass Publishers

[Goul Andersen, Jørgen, see Andersen, Jørgen Goul]

Graubard, Stephen R., red. 1986. *Norden – the Passion for Equality.* Oslo: Norwegian University Press

'Grindheim, Jan Erik. 1991. Kommunene og de frivillige organisasjonene i helse- og sosialsektoren. In: Anne-Hilde Nagel, red. *Velferdskommunen. Kommunenes rolle i utviklingen av velferdsstaten.* Bergen: Alma Mater

Gråt inte, kämpa! 10 år med kvinnorörelsen. 1982. *Kvinnobulletinen.* Enskede: Hammarström & Åberg

Guðmundsdóttir, Ásdís. 1994. Staða kvenna á þingum Alþýðusambands Íslands 1940–1994. B.A. ritgerð við Háskóla Íslands

Guldvik, Ingrid. 1992. *Integrering, tilkobling eller avkobling?* Hovedoppgave i høgere studium i samfunnsplanlegging. Lillehammer: Oppland distriktshøgskole

Guldvik, Ingrid. 1995. *Så gjør vi så ... når vi integrerer.* Hovedoppgave i samfunnspolitikk, Institutt for samfunnsplanlegging, Universitetet i Tromsø

Guldvik, Ingrid. 1996. *Forandring er ikke forvandling! En studie av likestillingspolitikkens integrering i fire kommuner,* forskningsrapport nr. 8, 1996. Høgskolen i Lillehammer

Guldvik, Ingrid. 1998. *Endret lovgivning – endret praksis. Kommunelovens bestemmelser om kvinner og menn i politiske utvalg.* Prosjektbeskrivelse Norges Forskningsråd 1998.

Gundelach, Peter. 1988. *Sociale bevegelser og samfundsændringer.* Århus: Politica

Gundelach, Peter. 1993. New Social Movements in the Nordic Countries. In: Thomas P. Boje & Sven E. Olsson-Hort, red. *Scandinavia in a New Europe.* Oslo: Scandinavian University Press

Gustafsson, Gunnel. 1997. Strategies and Practical Considerations. In: Gunnel Gustafsson, red., Maud Eduards & Malin Rönnblom: *Towards a New Democratic Order? Women's Organizing in Sweden in the 1990s.* Stockholm: Publica

Gustafsson, Gunnel, red., Maud Eduards & Malin Rönnblom. 1997. *Towards a New Democratic Order? Women's Organizing in Sweden in the 1990s.* Stockholm: Publica

Haas, Linda. 1992. *Equal parenthood and social policy: a study of parental leave in Sweden* Albany, N.Y.: State University of New York Press

Haavio-Mannila, Elina. 1979. Kvinnebevægelse og kvinneorganisasjoner. *Sosiologi i dag,* 9:55–67

Haavio-Mannila, Elina et al., red. 1983. *Det uferdige demokratiet: Kvinner i nordisk politikk.* København: Nordisk Ministerråd

Haavio-Mannila, et al. ed. 1985. *Unfinished Democracy: Women in Nordic Politics.* Oxford: Pergamon Press (English edition of the above title)

Hagemann, Gro & Anne Krogstad, red. 1994. *Høydeskrekk. Kvinner og offent-lighet.* Oslo: Ad Notam

[Halsaa Albrektsen, Beatrice, see Albrektsen, Beatrice Halsaa.]

Halsaa, Beatrice. 1983. *Utvalg i motbør,* ODH-Rapport 44/83. Lillehammer: Oppland distriktshøgskole

Halsaa, Beatrice. 1988a. Fra kvinneårsutvalg til likestillingsutvalg. In: *Underveis..., Festskrift til Eva Kolstad.* Oslo: Aventura

Halsaa, Beatrice. 1988b. *En feministisk utopi og veier dit.* Oslo: Alternativ Framtid

Halsaa, Beatrice. 1992. *Policies and Strategies on Women in Norway: The role of women's organizations, political parties, the government.* Oppland distriktshøgskole, skriftserie nr. 74

Halsaa, Beatrice. 1995a. *Sisyfos eller "øvelse gjør mester?".* Dilemmaer ved *statlig likestillingspolitikk og kommunalt selvstyre. En iverksettingsstudie.* Oslo: Barne- og familiedepartementet

Halsaa, Beatrice. 1995b. *Forsøk til nytte? Erfaringer med likestillingarbeid lokalt.* Rapport i forskningsprosjektet "Organisering av kommunal likestillingspolitikk i 90-årene". HiL-Forskningsrapport nr. 1, Høgskolen i Lillehammer

Halsaa, Beatrice. 1996. Variasjoner over et tema: feminisme som teori. In: Harriet Holter, red. *Hun og han – Kjønn i forskning og politikk.* Oslo: Pax

Halsaa, Beatrice og Janneke van der Ros. 1989. *Muligheter og motstand. Rett person på rett sted.* ØF-rapport 9/89, ODH-Skriftserie 81/89, Lillehammer: Østlandsforskning og Oppland distriktshøgskole

Hanusardóttir, Bergtóra. 1994. Úr Føroyum. In: Brit Fougner & Mona Larsen-Asp, red. *NORDEN – Kvinners paradis?.* København: NORD 1994:14

Harðarson, Ólafur Þ. Valgundersøgelser 1983–1995. (upubl.)

Haukaa, Runa. 1982. *Bak slagordene. Den nye kvinnebevegelsen i Norge.* Oslo: Pax

HE 193/1983 = Hallituksen esitys Eduskunnalle laiksi Suomen osallistumisesta Yhdistyneiden kansakuntien rauhanturvaamistoimintaan. Helsinki

HE 131/1994 = Hallituksen esitys Eduskunnalle laiksi naisten vapaaehtoisesta asepalveluksesta ja eräiksi siihen liittyviksi laeiksi. Helsinki

Hedlund, Gun. 1997. Kön, makt, organisation och ekonomi i svenska kommuner. In: *Styrsystem och jämställdhet – Institutioner i förändring och könsmaktens framtid.* SOU 1997: 114, Stockholm: Fritzes

Hedlund-Ruth, Gun & Janneke van der Ros Schive. 1983. *The Impact of the New Women's Movement on Politics. Local Experiences in Norway and Sweden.* Paper prepared for the workshop "The Impact of the New Women's Movement", ECPR Joint Sessions, Freiburg, March 1983

Heidar, Knut & Nina C. Raaum. 1995. Partidemokrati i endring?. In: Nina C. Raaum, *Kjønn og politikk.* Oslo: Tano

Helgadóttir, Herdís. 1996. *Vaknaðu kona! Barátta rauðsokka frá þeirra eigin sjónarhóli.* Reykjavík: Skjaldborg

Hellevik, Ottar & Tor Bjørklund. 1995. Velgerne og kvinnerepresentasjon. In: Nina C. Raaum, red. *Kjønn og politikk*. Oslo: Tano

Hellevik, Ottar & Torild Skard. 1985. *Norske kommunestyrer – plass for kvinner?* Oslo: Universitetsforlaget

Helsingin Sanomat. 11.7.1990. "Aseellinen palvelus ei sovi naisille Suomessa."

Henze, Turið Debes. 1996. Ligestilling på Færøerne, september 1996 (unpubl.)

Hermansson, Jörgen. 1993. *Politik som intressekamp. Parlamentariskt beslutsfattande och organiserade intressen i Sverige.* Stockholm: Norstedts Juridik

Hernes, Helga. 1982. *Staten – kvinner ingen adgang?* Oslo: Universitetsforlaget

Hernes, Helga. 1987. *Welfare State and Woman Power: Essays in State Feminism.* Oslo: Norwegian University Press

Hernes, Helga. 1988. The Welfare State Citizenship of Scandinavian Women. In: Kathleen B. Jones & Anna G. Jónasdóttir, red. *The Political Interests of Gender.* Oxford: Sage Publications

Hernes, Helga & Eva Hänninen-Samelin. 1983. Kvinners representasjon i det korporative system. In: Elina Haavio-Mannila et. al., red. *Det uferdige demokratiet.* København: Nordisk Ministerråd

Hernes, Helga & Kirsten Voje. 1980. Women in the Corporate Channel: A process of Natural Exclusion. *Scandinavian Political Studies*, 3:163–186

Hinnfors, Jonas. 1992. *Familjepolitik. Samhällsförändringar och partistrategier 1960–1990.* Göteborg Studies in Politics, 26. Stockholm: Almqvist & Wiksell International

Hirdman, Yvonne. 1988. Genussystemet – reflexioner kring kvinnors sociala underordning. *Kvinnovetenskaplig tidskrift*, 3:49–63

Hirdman, Yvonne. 1989. *Att lägga livet till rätta.* Stockholm: Carlssons

Hirdman, Yvonne. 1990. Genussystemet. In: SOU 1990: 44, *Demokrati och makt i Sverige.* Stockholm

Hirdman, Yvonne. 1991. The Gender System. In: Tayo Andreasen et al., red. *Moving On. New Perspectives on the Women's Movement.* Acta Jutlandica LXVII:1, Humanities Series 66. Aarhus: Aarhus University Press

Hoadley, Anna-Greta Nilsson. 1989. *Atomvapnet som partiproblem.* Stockholm: Almqvist & Wiksell International

Hobson, Barbara & Mieko Takahashi. 1997. The parent-worker model: lone mothers in Sweden. In: Jane Lewis, red. *Lone Mothers in European Welfare Regimes.* London: Jessica Kingsley Publishers

Hoff, Jens. 1995. *Nordiske Medborgerundersøkelser.* Arbejdspapir nr. 19. København: Institut for statskundskab

Holli, Anne Maria. 1990. Why the State? Reflections on the Politics of the Finnish Equality Movement Association 9. In: Marja Keränen, red. *Finnish "Undemocracy", Essays on Gender and Politics.* The Finnish Political Science Association. Jyväskylä: Gummerus

Holli, Anne Maria. 1991. *Miehisestä tasa-arvosta kohti naisten käsitteellistä tilaa. Tasa.arvoasiain neuvottelukunnan tasa-arvopoliittinen diskurssi 1972–86.* Licensiatavhandling. Institutionen för allmän statslära vid Helsingfors Universitet, december

Holli, Anne Maria. 1992. Kunnalliset tasa-arvotoimikunnat tasa-arvolain jälkeen. In: *Naiskuntavaaleihin*. Social- och Hälsovårdsministeriet, Jämställdhetspublikationer, Serie B: Meddelanden 1/1992, Helsingfors

Holli, Anne Maria. 1996. Equality policies in Finland. Opublicerat manuskript

Holter, Harriet. 1981. Om kvinneundertrykkelse, mannsundertrykkelse og hersketeknikker. In: Kristian Andenæs, Tom Johansen & Thomas Mathiesen, red. *Maktens ansikter*. Oslo: Gyldendal

Holter, Harriet. 1992. Motstand og avverge i sosiale organisasjoner: Fremdeles et aktuelt tema? *Nytt om kvinneforskning* 2/92

Holter, Harriet. 1996. Om kjønn og politikk. In: Harriet Holter, red. *Hun og han – Kjønn i forskning og politikk*. Oslo: Pax

Horgen, Randi. 1983. Ny §21 i den norske likestillingsloven om representasjon av begge kjønn i alle offentlige utvalg mv. In: *Årbog for kvinderet*. København: Jurist- og Økonomforbundets forlag

Hufvudstadsbladet. 11.11.1982. "Jämställdheten inte värt eget budgetmoment"

Hufvudstadsbladet. 21.04.1996."Jämställdheten prövas"

Hultman, Kristina. 1995. Kön och medborgarskap: kvinnan som demokratiskt problem. In: Claudia Lindén & Ulrika Milles, red. *Feministisk bruksanvisning: essäer*. Stockholm: Norstedts

Högman, Gyrid. 1994. Kvinnor på Åland. In: Brit Fougner & Mona Larsen-Asp, red. *NORDEN – Kvinners paradis?* København: NORD 1994:14

Inglehart, Ronald. 1977. *The Silent Revolution*. Princeton: Princeton University Press

Inglehart, Ronald. 1990. *Culture Shift in Advanced Industrial Societies*. Princeton: Princeton University Press

IPU (Inter-Parliamentary Union). 1995. *Women in Parliaments 1945–1995. A World Statistical Survey*. Geneva: Series "Reports and Documents" no. 23

IPU (Inter-Parliamentary Union). 1997. *Men and women in politics. Democracy still in the making*. Geneva: Series "Reports and Documents" no. 28

Jákupsstovu, Beinta Í. 1996. Kvinner ingen adgang? Rekruttering av kvinner til bystyret Tórshavn 1972–1992. In: Dag Ingvar Jacobsen & Idar Magne Holme, red. *Norsk statsvitenskapelig tidsskrift* nr. 1, 35–56

Jallinoja, Riitta. 1983. *Suomalaisen naisasialiikkeen taistelukaudet. Naisasialiike naisten elämäntilanteen muutoksen ja yhteiskunnallis-aatteellisen murroksen heijastajana*. Porvoo: WSOY

Jalmert, Lars. 1984. *Den svenske mannen*. Stockholm: Tidens förlag

Jensen, Torben. 1999. Party Cohesion and Cooperation across Party Lines in Nordic Parliamentary Parties. In: Peter Esaiasson & Knut Heidar, red., *Beyond Congress and Westminster. Nordic Experiences*. Columbus: Ohio State University Press

Jenssen, Anders & Åse Bratterud. 1997. Kvinnenes "nei" til EU. Da den lille forskjellen fikk stor betydning. *Tidsskrift for samfunnsforskning*, 38:359–388

Jenssen, Anders Todal, Pertti Pesonen & Mikael Gilljam, red. 1998. *To join or not to join. The 1994 referendums on membership in the European Union.* Oslo: Scandinavian University Press

Jespersen, Jógvan. 1993. Välstånd tur och retur. In: Hasse Schröder, red. *Färöarna mer än fåglar.* Uppsala: Schröders Ord & Bild

Joensen, Hanna. 1989. Kvinnolistor på Färöarna. In: Drude Dahlerup, red. *Vi har väntat länge nog.* Köpenhamn: NORD 1989

Joensen, Hanna. 1992. Ligestilling på Færøerne. *Conference on Equality.* (upubl.)

Johansson, Ulla. 1997. Den offentliga sektorns paradoxala maskulinisering-stendenser. In: Elisabeth Sundin , red. *Om makt och kön i spåren av offent-liga organisationers omvandling.* SOU 1997: 83. Stockholm: Fritzes

Jónasdóttir, Anna. 1992. Har kön någon betydelse för demokratin? In: Gertrud Åström & Yvonne Hirdman. *Kontrakt i kris. Om kvinnors plats i välfärds-staten.* Stockholm: Carlssons

Jónsdóttir, Sigrún. 1993. Kvinner i politikken på egne premisser: Kvinnelisten på Island 10 år. *Nordisk tidsskrift,* 6:525–532

Julkunen, Raija. 1994. Suomalainen sukupuolimalli – 1960-luku käänteenä. In: Anneli Anttonen, Lea Henriksson & Ritva Nätkin, red. *Naisten hyvinvointi-valtio.* Tampere: Vastapaino

Julkunen, Raija. 1997. Naisruumiin oikeudet. In: Eeva Jokinen, toim. *Ruumiin siteet: tekstejä eroista, järjestyksistä ja sukupuolesta.* Tampere: Vastapaino

Jämlikhet. Första rapport från SAP–LO:s arbetsgrupp för jämlikhetsfrågor. 1969. Stockholm: Prisma

Jämställdhetskommittén, Åland. 1979. Definition av jämställdhet. In: *Verksam-hetsberättelse*

Jämställdhetskommittén, Åland. 1980. *Förslag till Ålands landskapsstyrelses program för främjandet av jämställdheten mellan könen under senare hälften av FN:s kvinnans årtionde 1981–1985.* B.D. 6967/711–79

Jämställdhetslagen. 1997. Stockholm: Jämställdhetsombudsmannen

Jørgensen, Henning *et al.* 1992. Medlemmer og meninger. Rapport over spørge-undersøgelser blandt medlemmer af LO-forbundene. Carma, Aalborg Universitet

Kaasinen, Päivi. Naisten osuus valtion komiteoissa ja työryhmissä sekä valtion virastojen ja laitosten, liikelaitosten ja valtionyhtiöiden johto- ja hallintoeli-missä 1995–1996. Sosiaali- ja terveyministeriö: Tasa-arvon työraportteja 3/ 1996. Helsinki: Sosiaali- ja terveysministeriö

Kalleberg, Annemor. 1979. Kvinnebevegelsen i Skandinavia i sosiologisk perspektiv. *Sosiologi idag,* 9:68–79

Kansan Uutiset 19.4.1978

Kanter, Rosabeth Moss. 1977. *Men and Women of the Corporation.* London: Basic Books

Karlsson, Gunnel. 1996. *Från broderskap till systerskap: det socialdemokra-tiska kvinnoförbundets kamp för inflytande och makt i SAP.* Lund: Arkiv

Karlsson, Gunnel. 1998. Social democratic women's coup in the Swedish parliament. In: von der Fehr, Drude, Jónasdóttir Anna G. & Roisenbeck Bente, eds.: *Is there a Nordic Feminism? Nordic feminist thought on culture and society.* London: UCL Press, pp. 44-68

Karvonen, Lauri & Per Selle, red. 1995. *Women in Nordic Politics. Closing the Gap.* Aldershot: Dartmouth

Karvonen, Lauri & Jan Sundberg, red. 1991. *Social Democracy in Transition: Northern, Southern and Eastern Europe.* Aldershot: Dartmouth

Katzenstein, Mary Fainsod. 1990. Feminism within American Institutions: Unobtrusive Mobilization in the 1980s. *Signs: Journal of Women in Culture and Society*, 16:27–54

Kauppinen, Kaisa & Outi Huida. 1994. *Naiset, rauhanturvaamistyö ja muutos.* Tutkimusselosteita A-S3-2/1994. Pieksämäki: Puolustusvoimien kehittämiskeskus

KM 1993: 9 = *Naisten vapaaehtoinen asepalvelus. Naiset ja sotilaallinen maanpuolustus - toimikunnan mietintö.* Komiteamietintö 1993: 9. Helsinki: Puolustusministeriö, Hakapaino

Kimmel, Michael, red. 1987. *Changing Men, New Directions in Research on Men and Masculinity.* New York: Sage Publications

Kiuru, Sakari. 1994. *Taakan tasaaja: Alli Lahtinen pohtijana ja päättäjänä 1926–1976.* Helsinki: Painatuskeskus Oy

Klausen, Kurt Klaudi & Per Selle. 1995. Frivillig organisering i Norden. In: Kurt Klaudi Klausen & Per Selle, red. *Frivillig organisering i Norden.* Oslo: Tano

Klausen, Kurt Klaudi & Per Selle. 1996. The third sector in Scandinavia. *Voluntas,* 7:99–122

Kolam, Kerstin. 1987. *Lokala organ i Norden 1968–1986.* Akademisk avhandling, forskningsrapport 1987:7. Umeå universitet: Statsvetenskapliga institutionen

Komiteamietintö 1970:A 8. Naisten asemaa tutkivan komitean mietintö. Helsinki, 1970

Komittebetänkande 1996:13. *Vi tiger inte längre.* Social- och hälsovårdsministeriet i Finland. Helsingfors

Kommunal- og arbeidsdepartementet. 1993. *St.meld. nr. 33 (1992–93) By og land: hand i hand. Om regional utvikling.* Oslo

Koskinen, Pirkko. 1983. Finsk jämställdhetslagstiftning – ännu i stöpsleven. In: Jytte Lindgård & Ruth Nielsen, *Årbog for Kvinderet 1983.* København: Juristforbundets forlag

Kramer, Ralph. 1981. *Voluntary Agencies in the Welfare State.* Berkeley, CA: University of California Press

Krasner, Michael & Nikolaj Petersen. 1986. Peace and Politics: The Danish Peace Movement and its impact on National Security Policy. *Journal of Peace Research,* 23:155–173

Kristeva, Julia. 1986. Women's Time. In: Toril Moi, red. *The Kristeva Reader.* Oxford: Basil Blackwell

Kristjánsson, Svanur. 1998. Electoral Politics and Governance: Transformation of the Party System in Iceland, 1970–1996. In: Paul Pennings and Jan-Erik Lane, red. *Comparing Party System Change*. London: Routledge

Kuhnle, Stein. 1994. Norge i møte med Europa. In: Aksel Hatland, Stein Kuhnle & Tor Inge Romøren *Den norske velferdsstaten*. Oslo: Ad Notam Gyldendal

Kuhnle, Stein & Per Selle, red. 1992. *Government and Voluntary Organizations*. Aldershot: Avebury

Kurikka, Minna. 1992. Päivähoidon naispolitiikka, valtio-opin pro gradu-tutkielma. Tampereen yliopisto, politiikan tutkimuksen laitos

Kurkela, Kaija. 1991. *Naiset ja puolustusvoimat*. Helsinki: Sosiaali- ja terveysministeriö, tasa-arvojulkaisuja, sarja C: Työraportteja 4/1991

Kuusi, Pekka. 1963. 60-luvun sosiaalipolitiikka, Sosiaalipoliittisen yhdistyksen julkaisuja 6. Porvoo: WSOY

Kuusipalo, Jaana. 1989. Naisena politiikan huippupaikoille: Naisedustus Suomen hallituksissa ja naisministerien poliittinen ura vuosina 1926–1986. *Tampereen yliopiston sosiologian ja sosiaalipsykologian laitos*. Tampereen yliopisto

Kuusipalo, Jaana. 1990. Finnish Women in Top-Level Politics. In: Marja Keränen red. *Finnish "Undemocracy", Essays on Gender and Politics*. The Finnish Political Science Association. Jyväskylä:Gummerus

Kuusipalo, Jaana. 1992. Finnish Women in Top-Level Politics. In: Marja Keränen, red. *Gender and Politics in Finland*. Aldershot: Avebury

Kuusipalo, Jaana. 1993. Women's position and strategies in political arenas. In: Hannele Varsa, red. *Shaping Structural change in Finland*. Equality papers, series B: Report 2, Helsinki: Ministry of Social Affairs and Health

Kuusipalo, Jaana. 1994. Kvinnorörelsens strategier – igår och idag. *Nordisk Kontakt*. Tema Jämställdhet, 39:26–35

Kvande, Elin & Bente Rasmussen. 1993. Organisationen en arena för olika uttryck av kvinnlighet och manlighet. *Kvinnovetenskaplig tidskrift* 2, 14: 45–56

Kyle, Gunhild. 1979. *Gästarbeterska i manssamhället*. Stockholm: Liber.

Lafferty, William. 1978. Social Development and Political Participation: Class, Organization and Sex. *Scandinavian Political Studies*, 1:233–254

Lafferty, William. 1981. *Participation and Democracy in Norway: The Distant Democracy' Revisited*. Oslo: Universitetsforlaget

Lagförslag om landskapet. Ålands jämställdhetsdelegation. *Lagmt. 3/82*

Lag om jämställdhet mellan kvinnor och män. 1986. *Lag 1986/609* (med senere endringer), Helsingfors

Lagtingets sekretariat, Färöarna: *Kvinnor invalda i Lagtinget på Färöarna 1998*. (Muntliga uppgifter)

Laisi, Tiina. 1994. *Helsingissä opiskelevien nuorten naisten asennoituminen naisten vapaaehtoiseen asepalvelukseen*. Tutkimusselosteita A - G9 -3/1994. Helsinki: Puolustusvoimien Koulutuksen Kehittämiskeskus

Landskapslag 27/89. *Landskapslag om tillämpning i landskapet Åland av lagen om jämställdhet mellan kvinnor och män*. Mariehamn 30 mars 1989

Larsen, Helge O. & Audun Offerdal. 1994. *Demokrati og deltakelse i kommunene. Norsk lokalpolitikk i nordisk lys.* Oslo: Kommuneforlaget

Laxén, Marianne. 1992. Naiset armeijaan vai miehet ulos? *Nainen ja asepalvelus.* Helsinki: Suomen Sadankomitealiitto

Lehto, Marja. 1980. 80 vuotta sosialidemokraattista naistoimintaa. *Naisen työ: sosialidemokraattinen naisliike 80-vuotta. Sosialidemokraattiset naiset.* Joenssuu: Kansan voima Oy.

Leira, Arnlaug. 1993. The 'Woman-Friendly' Welfare State?: The Case of Norway and Sweden. In: Jane Lewis, red. *Women and Social Policies in Europe.* Aldershot: Edward Elgar Publishing

Levi, Margaret & Meredith Edwards. 1990. The Dilemmas of Femocratic Reform. In: Mary F. Katzenstein & Hege Skjeie, red. *Going Public. National Histories of Women's Enfranchisement and Women's Participation within State Institutions.* ISF-Rapport 1990:4

Levnadsförhållanden 1996:40: *Politiska resurser och aktiviteter 1978–1994.* Stockholm: Statistiska Centralbyrån

Ligestillingsrådet. 1990. *Ligestillingsrådet årsberetning 1989.* Viborg

Ligestillingsrådet. 1995. *Kvinder og Mænd.* København: Ligestillingsrådet, Arbejdsmarkedsstyrelsen og Danmarks statistik

Ligestillingsrådet. 1997a. *Årsberetning 1996.* Viborg

Ligestillingsrådet. 1997b. *"Könsgerninger" i kommunen – om kommuner og amters ligestillingsredegørelser 1997.* København

Lindén, Mariella. 1981. Patriarkat och kvinnorörelse i Finland. *Nordisk Forum* 31: Kvinnoidentitet & kvinnorörelse, 16:63–71

Lindström, Ulf. 1989. Politik i Norden 1889–1989; ett socialdemokratiskt århundrade?. *Norden förr och nu. Ett sekel i statistisk belysning.* København: Nordiska Statistiska Sekretariat

Listaug, Ola. 1998. *Confidence in Political Institutions: Norway 1982–1996,* Paper prepared for Nasjonal fagkonferanse i Statskundskab, Geilo.

Listhaug, Ola, Beate Huseby & Richard Matland. 1995. Valgatferd blant kvinner og menn: 1957–1993. In: Nina C. Raaum, red. *Kjønn og politikk.* Oslo: Tano

Lorentzen, Håkon. 1994. *Frivillighetens integrasjon. Staten og de frivillige velferdsprodusentene.* Oslo: Universitetsforlaget

Lotherington, Ann Therese *et al.* 1992. *Foran Fronten? Rapport fra det kvinneretta arbeidet i fylkene.* Forut-rapport Tromsø: FORUT samfunnsforskning

Lov av 9. juni 1978 nr 45 om likestilling mellom kjønnene. Oslo: Likestillingsombudet

Lov av 25. september 1992 nr 107 om kommuner og fylkeskommuner. Oslo

Lovenduski, Joni & Pippa Norris, red. 1993. *Gender and party politics.* London: Sage Publications

Lovenduski, Joni & Pippa Norris. 1995. *Political Recruitment. Gender, Race and Class in the British Parliament.* Cambridge: Cambridge University Press

Lukes, Steven. 1979. *Power – A Radical View.* London: Macmillan Press

Lund, Agga.1992. Ligestilling i Grønland. *Conference on Equality* (upubl.)

Lundström, Tommy. 1995. Staten och det frivilliga sociala arbetet i Sverige. In: Kurt Klaudi Klausen & Per Selle, red. *Frivillig organisering i Norden*. Oslo: Tano

Lundström, Tommy & Filip Wijkström. 1997. *The nonprofit sector in Sweden*. Manchester: Manchester University Press

Lønnå, Elisabeth. 1996. *Stolthet og kvinnekamp. Norsk kvinnesaksforenings historie fra 1913*. Oslo: Gyldendal

McAdam, Doug, John D. McCarthy & Mayer N. Zald. 1996. *Comparative Perspectives on Social Movements. Political Opportunities, Mobilizing Structures and Cultural Frames*. Cambridge: Cambridge University Press.

Mahon, Rianne. 1997. Child Care in Canada and Sweden: Policy and Politics. *Social Politics*, 4

Man är chef. 1992. Statistiska Centralbyrån, Programmet för jämställdhetsstatistik (1992: 5). Örebro: SCB-Förlag

Mathiesen, Thomas. 1982. *Makt och motmakt*. Göteborg: Korpen

Matilainen, Jouko. 1984. Maanpuolustus ja eduskunta. Eduskuntaryhmien kannanotot ja koheesio maanpuolustuskysymyksissä Paasikiven-Kekkosen kaudella 1945–1978. Jyväskylä Studies in Education, *Psychology and Social Research* 55, Jyväskylä: University of Jyväskylä

Matland, Richard. 1998. Women's Representation in National Legislatures: Developed and Developing Countries. *Legislative studies quarterly*, 23 (1): 109–125

Mattila, Kari & Johanna Suorsa. 1994. *Viattomat, vallattomat ja rohkeat*. Helsinki: Naisten kulttuuriyhdistys

Melby, Kari. 1991. Women's Equality Ideology: Difference, Equality or a New Femininity? In: Tayo Andreasen *et al.*, red. *Moving On. New Perspectives on the Women's Movement*. Acta Jutlandica LXVII:1, Humanities Series 66. Aarhus: Aarhus University Press

Menntalamálaráðuneytið 1982. *10 ára áætlun um byggingu dagvistarheimila*. Skýrsla hefnadar

Millaisin toimenpitein turvallisuuspoliittista tietoa voitaisiin nykyistä tehokkaammin lisätä naisten keskuudessa. 1986. Työryhmän muistio. Helsinki: Maanpuolustusopetuksen neuvottelukunta

Ministry for Foreign Affairs. 1995. *Gender Equality in Iceland. National Report to the Fourth United Nations World Conference on Women in Beijing 1995*. Kópavogur: G. Ben. – Edda. Printers Ltd.

Ministry of Foreign Affairs. 1995. *Equality in Denmark. The Danish National Report to the Fourth World Conference on Women 1995*. København

Ministry of Health and Social Affairs. 1994. *Shared Power, Shared Responsibility*. Stockholm

Ministry of Social Affairs and Health. 1989. *Act on Equality Between Women and Men*. Helsinki

Moi, Toril. 1987. *Sexual/Textual Politics. Feminist Literary Theory*. London and New York: Methuen

Morken, Kristin & Per Selle. 1995. An alternative movement in a "state-friendly" society: the women's shelter movement. In: Lauri Karvonen & Per Selle, red. *Women in Nordic Politics: Closing the Gap*. Aldershot: Dartmouth

MTS-tiedote 13/1992. Maanpuolustustiedostuksen suunnittelukunta, Helsinki.

MTS-tiedote 4/1995. Maanpuolustustiedostuksen suunnittelukunta, Helsinki.

Möller, Tommy. 1996. *Brukare och klienter i välfärdsstaten: om missnöje och påverkansmöjligheter inom barn- och äldreomsorg*. Stockholm: Publica

Nagel, Anne-Hilde. 1995. Politiseringen av kjønn: Et historisk perspektiv. In: Nina C. Raaum, red. *Kjønn og politikk*. Oslo: Tano

Nagel, Anne-Hilde, red. 1998. *Kjønn og velferdsstat*. Bergen: Alma Mater

Naisiin kohdistuva väkivalta 1991. Väkivaltajaoston mietintö. Sosiaali- ja terveysministeriö. Tasa-arvojulkaisuja. Sarja B: Tiedotteita 5

Naisten rauhanpamfletti 1981. Rauha on tapa elää. Naisasialiitto Unioni & Naiset Rauhan Puolesta. Helsinki

Nielsen, Ruth & Marit Halvorsen. 1988. *Fagbevægelen og ligestillingsretten i Norden*. Center for samfundsvidenskabelig kvindeforskning. Arbejdsnotat 1. København

NK tema. 1994a. Sverige jämställdhetsombud vill ha flera ilskna kvinnor. Jämställdhet nr. 2

NK tema. 1994b. Anne Grete Holmsgaard: Fra pisk til gulerod – dansk ligestillingsarbeide. Jämställdhet nr. 2

NK Tema. 1994c. Jämställdhetsdelegationen central pådrivare i Finland. Jämställdhet nr. 2

NK Tema. 1994d. Else S. Porkelsdóttir: Islandsk lovgivning og tiltak for likestilling. Jämställdhet nr. 2

NK Tema. 1994e. Den norske likestillingsloven – hovedtrekkene i gjeldende lov. Jämställdhet nr. 2

Nordby, Trond, red. 1985. *Storting og regjering 1945–1985*. Oslo: Kunnskapsforlaget

Nordby, Trond. 1994. *Korporatisme på norsk. 1920–1945*. Oslo: Universitetsforlaget

Norden i tal. Diverse årganger. København: Nordisk Ministerråd

Nordic Statistical Yearbook.

Norris, Pippa, red. 1997a. *Passages to Power. Legislative Recruitment in Advanced Democracies*. Cambridge: Cambridge University Press

Norris, Pippa. 1997b. Equality strategies and political representation. In: Frances Gardiner, red. *Sex Equality Policy in Western Europe*. London: Routledge

Norsk statistisk årbok 1996. Oslo: Statistisk sentralbyrå

NOS (Norges offisielle statistikk, C188). 1995. *Historisk statistikk 1994*. Oslo: Statistisk sentralbyrå

NOSOSKO 1: 1995. *Social tryghed: de nordiske lande 1993*. København: Nordisk Socialstatistisk Komité

NOSOSKO 8: 1998. *Social tryghed: de nordiske lande 1996*. København: Nordisk Socialstatistisk Komité

NOU 1995: 15 *Et apparat for likestilling. En gjennomgang og vurdering av det sentrale likestillingsapparat med forslag til omorganisering av Likestillingsrådet*. Oslo: Barne- og familiedepartementet

Nousiainen, Jaakko. 1992. *Suomen poliittinen järjestelmä*. Juva: WSOY

·*Nytt om likestilling*. 1997. Kvartalsbrev utgitt av likestillingsombudet 1: 97

Oftung, Knud. 1995. Menns bevegelser. *Kvinneforskning* nr. 1:431

Ohlander, Ann-Sofie. 1989. Det usynliga barnet? Kampen om den socialdemokratiska familjepolitiken. In: Klaus Misgeld, Karl Molin & Klas Åmark, red. *Socialdemokratins samhälle. SAP och Sverige under 100 år*. Stockholm: Tidens förlag

Olsen, Johan P. & Harald Sætren. 1980. *Aksjoner og demokrati*. Oslo: Universitetsforlaget

Oskarson, Maria. 1995. Gender gaps in Nordic voting behavior. In: Lauri Karvonen & Per Selle, red. *Women in Nordic Politics. Closing the Gap*. Aldershot: Dartmouth

Oskarson, Maria. 1996. Skeptiska kvinnor – Entusiastiska män. In: Mikael Gilljam & Sören Holmberg, red. *Ett knappt ja till EU. Väljarna och folkomröstningen 1994*. Stockholm: Norstedt Juridik

Oskarson, Maria & Lena Wängnerud. 1995. *Kvinnor som väljare och valda*. Lund: Studentlitteratur

Outshoorn, Joyce. 1996. The Stability of Compromise: Abortion Politics in Western Europe. In: Marianne Githens & Dorothy Stetson, red. *Abortion Politics: Public Policy in Cross-cultural Perspective*. New York & London: Routledge

Paastela, Jukka. 1987. *Finland's New Social Movements in a Frozen Political System*. Paper presented to the ECPR workshop "New social movements and the political system", Amsterdam, April 10–16 1987

Palmunen, Ritva. 1992. "Aitan polulta yhteiskunnalliseksi vaikuttajaksi: keskustalaisen naisliikkeen toimintaa 1906–1985", Suomen Keskustanaiset r.y.

Parvikko, Tuija. 1991. Conceptions of Gender Equality: Similarity and Difference. In: Elizabeth Meehan & Selma Sevenhujsen, red. *Equality Politics and Gender*. London: Sage Publications

Pateman, Carole. 1989. Feminist Critiques of the Public/Private Dichotomy. *The Disorder of Woman*. Cambridge: Polity Press

Petersen, Tove Søvndahl. 1994. Superkvinde og den svage mand. In: Brit Fougner & Mona Larsen-Asp, red. *NORDEN – Kvinners paradis?* København: NORD 1994:14

Peterson, Abby. 1985. The New Women's Movement – Where Have All the Women Gone? Women and the Peace Movement in Sweden. *Women's Studies International Forum*, 8:631–638

Peterson, Abby. 1987. *Women in Political "Movement"*. Monograph, no 37, Department of Sociology: University of Gothenburg

Peterson, Abby & Carolyn Merchant. 1985. Fred med jorden: kvinnor och miljörörelsen i Norden. *Natur och samhälle,* 11:12–18

Petersson, Olof. 1995. *Nordisk politik.* Stockholm: Fritzes

Petersson, Olof. 1996. *Demokrati och lederskap.* Stockholm: SNS förlag

Petersson, Olof, Anders Westholm & Göran Blomberg. 1989. *Medborgarnas makt.* Stockholm: Carlssons

Phillips, Anne. 1991. *Engendering Democracy.* Cambridge: Polity Press

Phillips, Anne. 1995. *The Politics of Presence.* Oxford & New York: Clarendon Press

Pikkala, Sari. 1996. *Kvinnorepresentation i finländska kommuner.* Paper presenterat vid NOPSA '96, Workshop 'Kjønn og Politikk', Helsingfors

Pikkala, Sari. 1997. Kvinnor i kommunfullmäktige. Kvinnerepresentationen och dess variationer i kommunerna. In: Voitto Helander & Siv Sandberg, red. *Festskrift til Krister Ståhlberg.* Åbo: Åbo Akademis Förlag

Pincus, Ingrid. 1992. *Jämställdhetsfrågans plats i tre svenska kommuner.* Arbetsrapport, Kvinnovetenskapligt forum. Örebro: Högskolan i Örebro

Pincus, Ingrid. 1995a. *Män, makt och motstånd. Olika sätt att hindra jämställdhetsreformer i kommunerna.* Utvärderingsrapport, Kvinnovetenskapligt forum. Örebro: Högskolan i Örebro

Pincus, Ingrid. 1995b. *Jämställdhetsfrågans plats och utveckling i tre svenska kommuner.* Opublicerat manuskript, Kvinnovetenskapligt forum. Örebro: Högskolan i Örebro

Pincus, Ingrid. 1996. *Between Insight and Action: Gender Equality, Men and Ambivalence in Municipal Organizations.* Paper presented at conference: Partnerships in Local Government, Gothenburg held by Gothenburg university, Political Science Department and Indiana University, School of Public and Environmental Affairs

Pincus, Ingrid. 1997a. *Manligt motstånd och ambivalens till jämställdhetsreformer,* Kvinnovetenskapligt Forums skriftserie nr. 5, Örebro: Högskolan i Örebro

Pincus, Ingrid. 1997b. Män som hindrar och män som främjar jämställdhetsarbete. In: Anna G. Jónasdóttir *Styrsystem och jämställdhet – Institutioner i förändring och könsmaktens framtid,* SOU 1997: 114. Stockholm: Fritzes

Pincus, Ingrid. 1998. *Den svenska jämställdhetspolitikens utveckling 1972–1997,* Kvinnovetenskapligt forums arbetsrapportserie nr 1, Högskolan i Örebro

Piven, Frances Fox & Richard Cloward. 1977. *Poor People's Movement: Why They Succeed, How They Fail.* New York: Pantheon Books

PLM tiedote 9.3.1987. Helsinki: Puolustusministeriö

Porta, Donatella della & Dieter Rucht. 1995. Left Libertarian Movements in Context: A Comparison of Italy and West Germany, 1965–1990. In: J. Craig Jenkins & Bert Klandermans, red. *The Politics of Social Protest: Comparative Perspectives on States and Social Movements.* London: UCL Press

Proposition 1993/94:147. *Delad makt delat ansvar.* Stockholm

Proposition 1993/94:148. *Vårdnadsbidrag.* Stockholm

Pryser, Tore. 1997. Fra kongemakt til folkemakt. In: Henrik S. Nissen, red. *Nordens Historie 1397–1997*. Nord 1997:11, København: DR Multimedie

Putnam, Robert D. 1993. *Making Democracy Work. Civic Traditions in Modern Italy*. Princeton, N. J.: Princeton University Press

Rafnsdóttir, Guðbjörg Linda. 1995. *Kvinnofack eller integrering som strategi mot underordning. Diskussion kring kvinnliga fackföreningar på Island.* Lund: Lund University Press

Ramstedt-Silén, Viveca. 1998a. Kön och partipolitik under förändrade konjunkturer: En studie av kvinnors intresse och inflytande på centerns och socialdemokraternas partidagar i Finland åren 1986–1996. Paper presenterad vid nordisk demokratisymposium i Sundsvall, Sverige 26.—27.8.1998

Ramstedt-Silén, Viveca. 1998b. Parlamentariskt utskott eller kvinnoförening? Det kvinnliga nätverket i Finlands riksdag. Publiceras i Yhteiskuntatieteen sarjan tutkimuksia 1999. Kuopion Yliopisto

Rantalaiho, Liisa. 1994. Sukupuolisopimus ja Suomen malli. In: Anneli Anttonen, Lea Henriksson & Ritva Nätkin, red. *Naisten hyvinvointivaltio*. Tampere: Vastapaino

Rantanen, Lea. 1980. Naisasialiike ja rauhantyö. *Naisten rauhanpamfletti: Rauha on tapa elää*. Helsinki: Naisasialiitto Unioni & Naiset Rauhan Puolesta

Rauhala, Pirkko-Liisa. 1996. Miten sosiaalipalvelut ovat tulleet osaksi suomalaista sosiaaliturvaa?. Acta Universitatis Tamperensis, ser A vol. 477. Tampere: Tampereen yliopisto

Ravn, Anna-Birte. 1995. Equality versus Difference and Gender versus Class in Danish Women´s History. *NORA. Nordic Journal of Women's Studies*, 3: 45–54

Rokkan, Stein. 1970. *Citizens, Elections, Parties*. Oslo: Universitetsforlaget

Rokkan, Stein. 1981. The growth and structure of mass politics. In: Erik Allardt *et al.*, red. *Nordic democracy*. København: Det Danske Selskab

Rokkan, Stein. 1987. *Stat, nasjon, klasse*. Oslo: Universitetesforlaget

Rokkan, Stein & Seymour Martin Lipset. 1967. *Party systems and voter alignments; cross national prespectives*. New York: Free Press

[Ros, Janneke van der, see Van der Ros, Janneke]

Rothstein, Bo. 1994. *Vad bör staten göra?* Stockholm: SNS förlag

Rubart, Frauke. 1987. *Women in New Social Movements – Women's Lib as a New Social Movement: Reflections on the State of Discussion and the Research Situation in West German Political Science*. Paper presented to the workshop "Women and Citizenship: Rights and Identities", ECPR Joint Sessions of Workshops, Amsterdam, 10–15 April 1987

Rubart, Frauke. 1993. Zwischen Frauenpower und Frauenkultur: Die neue Frauenbewegung in den nordischen Ländern. *UtopieKreativ* 229–30, 54–64

Rubart, Frauke & Abby Peterson. 1985. *New Social Movements and Political Authority in Sweden: Political Protest Between Autonomy and Integration* (upubl.)

Rucht, Dieter. 1996. The impact of national contexts on social movement structures: A cross-movement and cross-nationale comparsion. In: Doug McAdam, John D. McCarthy & Mayer N. Zald, red. *Comparative Perspectives on Social Movements. Political Oppotunities, Mobilizing Structures, and Cultural Framings.* Cambridge: Cambridge University Press

Rule, Wilma & Joseph F. Zimmerman. 1994. *Electoral Systems in Comparative Perspective. Their Impact on Women and Minorities.* London: Greenwood Press

Rupp, Leila & Verta Taylor. 1991. Women's Culture and the Continuity of the Women's Movement. In: Tayo Andreasen *et. al.*, red. *Moving On: New Perspectives on the Women's Movement.* Atla Jutlandica LXVII:1, Humanities series 66. Aarhus: Aarhus University Press

Räsänen, Leila. 1994. *Establishing, Implementing and Making use of National Machinery to Promote Equality.* Strasbourg: Council of Europe

Rönnblom, Malin. 1993. *The Swedish Women's Movement in the 1990s.* Paper presented at the conference "Women and New Perspectives on Democracy in Europe", London, 31 August – 4 September 1993

Rönnblom, Malin. 1997. Local Women's Projects. In: Gunnel Gustafsson, red., Maud Eduards & Malin Rönnblom. *Towards a New Democratic Order? Women's Organizing in Sweden in the 1990s.* Stockholm: Publica

Raaum, Nina C. 1995a. Det politiske medborgerskapet. In: Nina C. Raaum, red. *Kjønn og politikk.* Oslo: Tano

Raaum, Nina C. 1995b. The political representation of women: a bird's eye view. In: Lauri Karvonen & Per Selle, red. *Women in Nordic Politics. Closing the Gap.* Aldershot: Dartmouth

Raaum, Nina C. 1995c. Women in local democracy. In: Lauri Karvonen & Per Selle, red. *Women in Nordic Politics. Closing the Gap.* Aldershot: Dartmouth

Raaum, Nina C., red. 1995. *Kjønn og politikk.* Oslo: Tano

Raaum, Nina C. 1996. *Kvinner og ledelse. Et statistisk utsyn over det private næringsliv.* Oslo: Næringslivets forlag

Saarinen, Terhi. 1990. "Alussa oli kellari": Helsinkiläisen lesboyhteisön historiaa. *Akkaväki* 2/1990

Saarinen, Aino. 1992. *Feminist Research – an Intellectual Adventure?* Research Institute for Social Sciences: The University of Tampere. Centre for Women's Studies and Gender Relations. Publications Series No 4.

Sainsbury, Diane. 1996. *Gender, Equality and Welfare States.* Cambridge: Cambridge University Press

Schneier, Edward. 1992. Icelandic Women on the Brink of Power. *Scandinavian Studies,* 64:417–438

Seip, Anne-Lise. 1991. Velferdskommunen og velferdstrekanten – et tilbakeblikk. In: Anne-Hilde Nagel, red. *Velferdskommunen. Kommunenes rolle i utviklingen av velferdsstaten.* Bergen: Alma Mater

Selle, Per. 1996. Marginalisering eller kvinnemakt? *Frivillige organisasjonar i nye omgjevnader.* Bergen: Alma Mater

Selle, Per & Bjarne Øymyr. 1992. Explaining changes in the population of voluntary organizations: Aggregate or individual level data?. *Nonprofit and Voluntary Quarterly*, 21:147–179

Selle, Per & Bjarne Øymyr. 1995a. *Frivillig organisering og demokrati.* Oslo: Samlaget

Selle, Per & Bjarne Øymyr. 1995b. The changing role within local voluntary organizations: sex segration in the voluntary sector. In: Lauri Karvonen & Per Selle, red. *Women in Nordic Politics. Closing the Gap.* Aldershot: Dartmouth

Selle, Per & Bjarne Øymyr. 1995c. Det frivillige organisasjonssamfunnet i omforming: Vert kjønnsgapet borte? In: Nina C. Raaum, red. *Kjønn og politikk.* Oslo: Tano

Sigurbjarnardóttir, Sigþrúður Helga. 1992. *Kvinnelisten i Island. Underveis fra kvinnepolitikk til feministisk politikk?* Hovedoppgave i sosiologi. Oslo: Institutt for sosiologi, Universitetet i Oslo

Sigurbjarnardóttir, Sigþrúður Helga. 1993. Kvinnelisten i Island. *Nytt om kvinneforskning* 4:3–14

Sigurbjarnardóttir, Sigþrúður Helga. 1998. "On their own premises": the political project of the Icelandic Women's Alliance. In: Drude von der Fehr, Bente Rosenbeck & Anna G. Jónasdóttir, red. *Is there a Nordic feminism? Nordic feminist thought on culture and society.* London & Philadelphia: UCL Press

Siim, Birte. 1988. Towards a Feminist Rethinking of the Welfare State. In: Kathy Jones & Anna Jónasdóttir, red. *The Political Interests of Women. Developing Theory and Research with a Feminist Face.* London: Sage Publiactions

Siim, Birte. 1991. Welfare State, Gender Politics and Equality Policies: Women's Citizenship in the Scandinavian Welfare States. In: Elizabeth Meehan & Selma Sevenhuijsen, red. *Equality Politics and Gender.* London: Sage Publications

Siim, Birte. 1993. The Gendered Scandinavian Welfare States: The Interplay between Women's Roles as Mothers, Workers and Citizens in Denmark. In: Jane Lewis, red. *Women and Social Policies in Europe: Work, Family and the State.* Aldershot: Edward Elgar

Siim, Birte. 1997a. Dilemmas of citizenship in Denmark – lone mothers between work and care. In: Jane Lewis, red. *Lone Mothers in European Welfare Regimes.* London: Jessica Kingsley Publishers

Siim, Birte. 1997b. Politisk medborgerskab og feministiske forståelser. In: Ann-Dorte Christensen, Anna-Birte Ravn & Iris Rittenhofer, red. *Det kønnede samfund: Forståelser af køn og social forandring.* Aalborg: Aalborg Universitetsforlag

Siisiäinen, Martti. 1990. *Suomalainen protesti ja yhdistykset.* Jyväskylä: Gummerus

Siisiäinen, Martti. 1991. *National and International Factors in the Formation of Voluntary Associations in Finland*. Jyväskylä: Department of Sociology, University of Jyväskylä

Siisiäinen, Martti. 1995. Gamla sociala kitt i upplösning – föreningsverksamhetens uppgång och fall? In: Kurt Klaudi Klausen & Per Selle, red. *Frivillig organisering i Norden*. Oslo: Tano

Skjeie, Hege. 1982. *Likestillingsloven som beslutningsprosess eller "De som LO først LO best"*. Oslo: Hovedoppgave i statsvitenskap

Skjeie, Hege. 1992. *Den politiske betydningen av kjønn. En studie av norsk topp-politikk*. Rapport nr. 11, Oslo: Institutt for samfunnsforskning

Skjeie, Hege. 1993. Ending the Male Political Hegemony: the Norwegian Experience. In: Joni Lovenduski & Pippa Norris, red. *Gender and Party Politics*. London: Sage Publications

Skjeie, Hege, Brit Fougner Førde & Marit Lorentzen. 1989. *Forvaltningsansvar: Likestilling*, Rapport 89: 3. Oslo: Institutt for samfunnsforskning

Skjeie, Hege & Helga Hernes. 1997. Fag og feminisme: Kvinneforskning i statsvitenskap. *Norsk Statsvitenskapelig Tidsskrift*, 13:363–381

Skjønsberg, Else, Brita M. Gulli & Eva Munk-Madsen. 1993. *Kvinner og EF*. Oslo: Cappelen

Social- och hälsovårdsministeriet. 1995. *Jämställdhetslagen*. Helsinki

SOU 1972: 34. *Familjestöd*. Stockholm

SOU 1975: 62. *Förkortad arbetstid för föräldrar*. Stockholm

SOU 1987: 19. *Varannan damernas. Slutbetänkande från utredningen om kvinnorepresentation*. Stockholm

SOU 1990: 41. *Tio år med jämställdhetslagen – utvärdering och förslag*. Stockholm

SOU 1990: 44. *Demokrati och makt i Sverige. Maktutredningens huvudrapport*. Stockholm

SOU 1993: 21. *Ökat personval. Betänkande av personvalskommittén*. Stockholm

SOU 1995: 110. *Viljan att veta och viljan att förstå*. Stockholm

SOU 1998: 6. *Ty makten är din ... Myten om det rationella arbetslivet och det jämställda Sverige*. Stockholm

Stabel, Ingse. 1994. Kjønnskvotering – til beste for hvem. *Kvinneforskning 3/94:34–40*

Statistisk årsbok för Finland

Steinby, Ann-Gerd. 1994. Ålands självstyrelse. *Åland*. Stockholm: Utbildningsförlaget Brevskolan

Stetson, Dorothy McBride & Amy Mazur. 1995. Introduction. In: Dorothy Stetson McBride & Amy Mazur, red. *Comparative State Feminism*. Thousand Oaks, Ca.: Sage Publications

Streijffert, Helena. 1983. *Studier i den svenska kvinnorörelsen*. Monograph no. 30 from the Department of Sociology, University of Gothenburg

Strøm, Kaare & Lars Svåsand. 1997. *Challenges to Political Parties. The Case of Norway*. Ann Arbor: University of Michigan Press

Strømsnes, Kristin. 1995. Kjønn og politisk kunnskap. In: Nina C. Raaum, red. *Kjønn og politikk*. Oslo: Tano

Styrkársdóttir, Auður. 1986. From social movement to political party: The new women's movement in Iceland. In: Drude Dahlerup, red. *The New Women's Movement: Feminism and Political Power in Europe and the USA*. London: Sage Publications

'Styrkársdóttir, Auður. 1997. *Konur í stjórnmálum. Nokkrar staðreyndir*. Reykjavík: Félagsvísindadeild Háskóla Íslands, Mimeo

Styrkársdóttir, Auður. 1998. *From Feminism to Class Politics. The Rise and Decline of Women's Politics in Reykjavík, 1908—1922*. Umeå: Department of Political Science, Umeå University

Suhonen, Pertti. 1988. *Suomalaisten arvot ja asenteet*. Juva: WSOY

Sukupuolikiintiöt koulutuksessa. 1986. Tasa-arvoasiain neuvottelukunnan ehdotukset ja asiaa valmistelleen työryhmän muistio. *Tasa-arvoasiain neuvottelukunnan monisteita* 4/1986, Helsinki

Sundberg, Jan. 1995. Women in Scandinavian party organizations. In: Lauri Karvonen & Per Selle, red. *Women in Nordic Politics. Closing the Gap*. Aldershot: Dartmouth

Suonoja, Kyösti. 1992. Kansalaisten parhaaksi – yhteistuntoa ja politiikkaa. Sosiaali- ja terveysministeriö 1939–1992. In: Pekka Haatanen & Kyösti Suonoja *Suurruhtinaskunnasta hyvinvointivaltioon: Sosiaali- ja terveysministeriö 75-vuotta*. Sosiaali- ja terveysministeriö. Helsinki: VAPK-kustannus

Svensson, Hasse. 16.3.1982. Magsurt beslut om jämställdhet, *Tidningen Åland*

Svensson, Palle & Lise Togeby. 1986. *Politisk opbrud: de nye mellemlags græs-rodsdeltagelse: årsager og konsekvenser belyst ved en ungdomsundersø-gelse*. Århus: Politica

Sveriges oficiella statistik: Allmänna val: Kommunala val, div. årgångar. Sveriges statistiska centralbyrå

[Søvndahl Petersen, Tove, see Petersen, Tove Søvndahl]

TANE 15/54/84= Tuominen, Heta: Lausunto Eduskunnan puolustusvaliokun-nalle. 1.3.1984. Tasa-arvoasiain neuvottelukunta, diaarionumero 15/54/84, Helsinki 8.3.1984

TANE 3/43/93= Lausunto Naiset ja sotilaallinen maanpuolustus-toimikunnan mietintöön. Tasa-arvoasiain neuvottelukunta, diaarionumero 3/43/93, Helsinki

Tasa-arvoelinten työnjako. 1995. *Selvitys*. Sosiaali - ja terveysministeriölle Helsinki

Teigen, Mari & Ragnhild Steen Jensen. 1995. *Kjønnskvotering i utdanning og arbeidsliv*, Oslo: Institutt for samfunnsforskning

Tema Nord 1996: 586. *Kvinnor i ledande ställing – kartlägging av de 100 största företagen i de nordiske länderna*. København: Nordisk Ministerråd

Thomsen, Marianne Lykke. 1991. Fra kollektiv manifestation til individuel prestation – kvinder i hjemmestyreprocessen. In: Lise Lennert et al., red. *Kvinder i Grønland – sammen og hver for sig*. Nuuk: Atuakkiorfik

Togeby, Lise. 1984. *Politik – også en kvindesag.* Århus: Politica

Togeby, Lise. 1989. *Ens og forskellig. Græsrodsdeltegelse i Norden.* Århus: Politica

Togeby, Lise. 1992. The Nature of Declining Party Membership in Denmark: Causes and Consequences. *Scandinavian Political Studies,* 15:1–18

Togeby, Lise. 1994a. *Fra tilskuere til deltagere. Den kollektive politiske mobilisering af kvinder i Danmark i 1970'erne og 1980'erne.* Århus: Poltica

Togeby, Lise. 1994b. Political Implications of Increasing Number of Women in the Labour Force. *Comparative Political Studies,* 27:211–240

Togeby, Lise. 1995. A gender gap that vanished: tolerance and liberalism. In: Lauri Karvonen & Per Selle, red. *Women in Nordic Politics. Closing the Gap.* Aldershot: Dartmouth

Tuominen, Harriet. 1984. Åländsk politik. In: Bengt Ahlsén, red. *Åland.* Stockholm: Utbildningsförlaget Brevskolan

Tuominen, Heta. 1984. Naiset miesten töihin. *Iltasanomat,* 16.3.1984

Tyyskä, Vappu. 1993. *The Women's Movement and the Welfare State: Child Care Policy in Canada and Finland, 1960–1990,* a thesis submitted in conformity with the rquirements for the Degree of Doctor of Philosophy. Graduate Department of Sociology in the University of Toronto

Uddhammar, Emil. 1993. *Partierna och den stora staten: en analys av statsteorier och svensk politik under 1900-talet.* Stockholm: City University Press

Van der Ros, Janneke. 1996a. Femokrat, hva slags fugl er nå det? In: Harriet Holter, red. *Hun og han – Kjønn i forskning og politikk.* Oslo: Pax

Van der Ros, Janneke. 1996b. Den staten, den staten. In: Harriet Holter, red. *Hun og han – Kjønn i forskning og politikk.* Oslo: Pax

Van der Ros, Janneke. 1997a. The organisation of equality at the local level: the case of Norway. In: Frances Gardiner, red. *Sex Equality Policy in Western Europe.* London: Routledge

Van der Ros, Janneke. 1997b. *Et femokratisk prosjekt: organisering av likestilling.* Sluttrapport av forskningsprosjektet: "Organisering av kommunal likestilling i 1990-årene". Forskningsrapport nr. 28, Høgskolen i Lillehammer

Verba, Sidney, Nie Norman & Kim Jae-On. 1978. *Participation and Political Equality. A Seven-Nation Comparison.* Cambridge: Cambridge University Press

Verba, Sidney, Kay Lehman Schlozman & Henry E. Brady. 1995. *Voice and Equality. Civic Voluntarism in American Politics.* Cambridge, London: Harvard University press

Vestbro, Dick Urban. 1992. Från liberal rörelse till socialistisk kamp mot patriarkatet. In: Annika Baude *et al.,* red. *Visionen om jämställdhet.* Stockholm: SNS-förlag

Vuosikertomukset. 1990. Kertomus tasa- arvovaltuutetun toimialalta. Tasa-arvoasiain neuvottelukunnan toimintakertomus 1.6.–31.12.1989. *Sosiaala - ja terveysministeriö, tasa-arvojulkaisuja, sarja B, Tiedotteita 3.* Helsinki: Valtion painatuskeskus

Vähäsaari, Maarit: Naisten osuus valtion komiteoissa ja työryhmissa 1991—1995. Sosiaali- ja terveysminiteriö: Tasa-arvon työraportteja 3/1995

Väyrynen, Paavo. 1993. *On totuuden aika. Tosiasioita ja muistikuvia Mauno Koiviston Suomesta.* Porvoo–Helsinki–Juva:WSOY

Vaagland, Jorid og Janneke van der Ros. 1992. *Frivillig aktivitet og offentlig politikk, om fylkes- og kretsleddets rolle i organisasjonslivet i Oppland.* Høgskolen i Lillehammer: ØF-rapport 10

Wikborg, Mette. 1988. Undersøkelse om frivillige organisasjoner. In: *Norges offentlige utredninger, nr. 17: Frivillige organisasjoner*:423–458. Oslo

Winter, Søren. 1994. *Implementering og effektivitet.* Viborg: Systime

Witt-Brattström, Ebba. 1981. Vi är de kvinnor våra män varnade oss för. *Nordisk Forum* 31: Kvinnoidentitet & kvinnorörelse, 16:44–49

Women and Men in Iceland 1997. Hagastofa Íslands

Women and Men in Norway 1995. Oslo: Statistisk sentralbyrå

Women and Men in Sweden 1995. Facts and Figures 1995. Stockholm: Statistiska Centralbyrån

Women and Men in the Nordic Coutries: Facts and Figures 1994. NORD 1994: 3

Wängnerud, Lena. 1998. *Politikens andra sida: om kvinnorepresentation i Sveriges riksdag.* Göteborg: Statsvetenskapliga institutionen, Göteborg universitet

Wängnerud, Lena. 1999. Representing the Interests of Women. In: Peter Esaiasson & Knut Heidar, red. *Beyond Congress and Westminster. Nordic Experiences.* Columbus: Ohio State University Press

Wærness, Kari. 1995. Epilog. In: Ove Bjarnar *Veiviser til velferdsamfunnet.* Bd. 2. Oslo: Norske Kvinners Sanitetsforening

Yeatman, Anna. 1990. *Bureaucrats, Femocrats, Technocrats. Essays on the Contemporary Australian State.* Sydney: Allen & Unwin

Young, Iris. 1990. The Ideal of Community and the Politics of Difference. I Linda J. Nicholson, red. *Feminism/postmodernism.* New York: Routledge

Åland. 7.1.1983. Jämställt val för jämställd delegation.

Ålands landskapsstyrelse. 20.01.1981. *Mötesprotokoll*, ärende nr 9 / B.D. 6964/ 711–79 / 71–73 UA

Ålands landskapsstyrelse. 10.03.1982. *Mötesprotokoll*, ärende nr 35 / B.D. 6964/711–79 / 153 UA

Åländsk center 4.9.1977. *Brev angående jämlikhetskommitté med anledning av skrivelse 21.6.1977*

Aardal, Bernt & Henry Valen. 1994. *Konflikt og opinion.* Oslo: NKS-forlaget

Årsberetning 1995. Javnstøðunevndin/Ligestillingsrådet Färöarna

Ås, Berit. 1975. On Female Culture. *Acta Sociologica,* 18:142–161

Ås, Berit. 1981. *Kvinner i alle land....* Oslo: Aschehoug

ÅSUB nr. 3/1995: Landstings- och kommunalvalet 15.10.1995. Valstatistik med kommentarer. Mariehamn: Ålands statistik- och utredningsbyrå

Additional literature:

Internet 1997a. *Færøerne – Hjemmestyreordningen.* http://www.sleipnir.fo/faroe/HomeRulD.HTM. 12.10.1997.
Internet 1997b. *Finlands riksdag.* http://www.eduskunta.fi/rfakta/.15.6.1997.
Internet 1997c. *Færøerne – Politik.* http://www.sleipnir.fo/faroe/PoliticD.HTM. 12.10.1997.
Internet 1998a. *Självstyrelsen. Ålands lagting – ett parlament.* http://www.aland.fi/virtual/swedish/lt.html. 4.2.1998.
Internet 1998b. *Heading for sovereignity.* http://review.fo/text/election.htm. 22.6.1998.
Internet 1998c. *Valg i Grønland.* http://www.gh.gl/dk/fakta/valg.htm. 5.8.1998.
Internet 1998d. *Folketinget i Danmark.* http//www.folketinget.dk/. 26.2.1998.

Public statistics from the relevant countries.

Parliamentary publications from the relevant countries.

References in Chapter 13:

1984 Diet = 1984 Valtiopäivät. Helsinki..
1. Asiakirjat C2: Valiokuntien mietinnöt ja lausunnot.
2. Pöytäkirjat 1–2, Istunnot 1–89, 1.2.-27.5.1984.
3. Asiakirjat D: Valtiopäiväpäätös, eduskunnan vastaukset ym.
1994 Diet = 1994 Valtiopäivät. Helsinki.
1. Pöytäkirjat, Istunnot 83, 172, 177–179, 185–186, 20.9.1994.–31.1.1995.
2. Puolustusvaliokunnan mietintö n:o 4 hallituksen esityksestä laiksi naisten vapaaehtoisesta asepalveluksesta ja eräiksi siihen liittyviksi laeiksi (+liitteet).